Paul's first letter to the Corinthians i
Christians relate to because it deals wi

though not necessarily easy to resolve. In this commentary, Dr Spurgeon has done a commendable job of exegesis that carefully considers differing views, but is also incisive and illuminating. However, a commentary must not only explain the intended meaning of the text but also make an attempt to interpret the text in terms relevant to the contemporary context. In this case, the Indian context is one that is ancient, pluralistic both culturally and religiously, and very complex. Dr Spurgeon's exposition is not just sensitive, but delves deep to bring out the intricacies of the context, and then relate the biblical text to it. *Twin Cultures Separated by Centuries* is a commentary that will prove to be not just interesting to read, but also helpful in explaining how Paul's teaching is relevant to the contemporary church.

Brian Wintle
Academic Coordinator of Centre for Advanced Theological Studies
SHIATS, Allahabad, India

Anecdotes, snippets of Indian history, newspaper reports, observations on what Indians think or do or say or are – these are the planks Andrew Spurgeon tosses together to build a crisscrossing walkway between ancient Corinth and present day India. One minute the reader is in ancient Greece, taking in just the kind of detail needed to make sense of what Paul was saying then. The next minute the Indian reader is in his home country, making sense of what Paul is saying now. *Twin Cultures Separated by Centuries* is an eminently readable commentary that matches careful exposition with well-researched background, while celebrating the Indian-ness of its author.

Havilah Dharamraj
Academic Dean, Head of Department of Old Testament
South Asia Institute of Advanced Christian Studies, Bangalore, India

An understanding into the cultural context of the Bible is imperative to correct comprehension and right application of the Scriptures. This is especially necessary because the contemporary world is vastly different from the Graeco-Roman one. Dr Andrew Spurgeon bridges biblical culture and Indian culture with his expertise and experience as a scholar who knows both the text and the challenges of teaching in a heterogenous (or, richly diverse) culture.

His work considers the different facets of Indian culture and its parallels in ancient Corinth. In a unique approach, he begins each section with an insight into the Indian setting, explains the biblical text in its historical-cultural setting, and astutely applies the biblical teaching to the Indian context. This commentary is a valuable asset for any Christian (church planter, pastor, seminary student, and Bible reader) in India who desires to "teach the message of truth accurately." I pray that this work is only the beginning of more commentaries like these!

Binoi Abraham Samuel
Elder, Redeemer Church of Dubai, UAE

It is a rarity to find a Bible commentary that seamlessly moves from context to text and vice versa. *Twin Cultures Separated by Centuries* does exactly that, as Andrew Spurgeon draws upon his knowledge of Scripture as well as his experience of the Indian situation to provide us with a thorough contextual and exegetical commentary on Paul's first letter to the Corinthians. Students of the Bible who desire to remain faithful to the text and also relevant to their culture and context, will find his commentary on 1 Corinthians stimulating and, in his own words, "exhilarating!" This commentary is an excellent tool for Bible teachers, pastors, seminary students and laity and must find a place in all theological libraries, especially those in South Asia.

Paul Cornelius
Regional Secretary–India, Asia Theological Association

Understanding the culture of the Bible is key to properly interpreting Scripture. Understanding the culture of today is necessary for expositors to keep the Bible relevant within their contexts. In this unique, one-of-a-kind commentary, Andrew Spurgeon explains both the biblical context and the Indian culture, and often draws parallels between Indian culture and the culture of the Corinthians, making it easier to understand. *Twin Cultures Separated by Centuries* is a must-read for anyone serving in India.

Dave Raj Sangiah
Pastor, Bangalore Bible Church, India

Twin Cultures Separated by Centuries

An Indian Reading of 1 Corinthians

Andrew B. Spurgeon

Langham
GLOBAL LIBRARY

© 2016 by Andrew B. Spurgeon

Published 2016 by Langham Global Library
an imprint of Langham Creative Projects

Langham Partnership
PO Box 296, Carlisle, Cumbria CA3 9WZ, UK
www.langham.org

ISBNs:
978-1-78368-118-1 Print
978-1-78368-140-2 Mobi
978-1-78368-139-6 ePub
978-1-78368-141-9 PDF

British Library Cataloguing in Publication Data
A catalogue record for this book is available from the British Library

ISBN: 978-1-78368-118-1

Cover & Book Design: projectluz.com

To Lori, Ethan, Micah, and Jedidiah

CONTENTS

Foreword

The purpose of this commentary is to help readers understand 1 Corinthians from an Indian cultural perspective. My goal has been to be fair both to the biblical text of 1 Corinthians and to Indian culture. The question that I repeatedly asked myself as I wrote the commentary was, "How would Paul teach the same teachings in India today?" With that thought, I have begun most of the topics with a cultural or religious insight common to Indians, then discussed the passage in 1 Corinthians, and concluded by applying it to the Indian context. The drawback of such a commentary is that I am taking passages out of the literary construct of the original letter. The benefit, however, is that the commentary is contextualized for Indians and those interested in India and Indian culture. My hope and prayer is that the benefit will outweigh the drawback.

In writing this commentary I neither affirm nor deny that Hinduism may lead one to Christ or that it contains divine truths hidden within its practices and beliefs. Likewise, I neither exalt Indian culture above other cultures nor think ill of Indian culture.

I found this study exhilarating. I grew up in India but did not truly know or understand Indian culture or Hinduism. Studying it afresh has given me a great appreciation for Indian-ness. At the same time, it is my passion and prayer that many Indians will come to know God, and that many Indian Christians will learn to interact with other Indians in their own cultural and religious contexts so that the Scriptures might be presented to them in a way they will understand.

All the translations are my own unless indicated otherwise in parentheses. I have tried to be fair to the Greek text and at the same time be reader-friendly. I have taken some liberty in order to make the Scriptures easy to read and understand.

I am not new to Indian culture and Hinduism. Despite my name, I am an Indian. My parents and relatives live in India. I grew up in India until I was seventeen, when I left for higher education. I returned to India aged thirty-one as a married man with children. Since then I have resided in India or nearby. Indian people are culturally as diverse as seashells on the seashore, and Hinduism is ancient and differs vastly between people groups. I have tried my best to authenticate all that I have written. Please forgive the errors and correct me with the facts. I intend no ill towards India or Indians. My prayer is for Indians to know the true Savior of all people, Jesus Christ our Lord.

Acknowledgements

I am indebted to several people for making this cultural commentary possible. I am thankful for my dad and mom (Dr D. S. Spurgeon and Mrs Evangeline Spurgeon) who raised me in a Christian home with Indian cultural practices. They live as Christians and Indians, principles that I value. The same is true of my sisters – Jacqueline Gigi and Caroline Naomi. I am blessed to have them as my sisters.

I am thankful to those who gave me this opportunity to write. Pieter Kwant read a chapter and accepted the proposal. Luke Lewis encouraged me to keep writing every time he saw me. And Vivian Doub kept me updated on the progress of the book and sent periodic notes of encouragement. I am grateful for Langham Partnership for publishing this book.

I am indebted to my teachers and friends who taught me to live a Christian life and to understand cultures. I am especially grateful to Dr Mike Pocock who gave me the opportunity to teach as an adjunct in the World Missions and Intercultural Studies Department at Dallas Theological Seminary where I started writing this commentary.

I am grateful for my wonderful wife, Lori, and amazing sons – Ethan, Micah, and Jedidiah. They are God's gracious gifts to me. They have always uplifted my spirit and trusted me. My wife sacrificed the many hours that I spent hours before books and computer. But without complaining she encouraged me to keep writing.

All glory and honor belong to the Lord of lords and King of kings, the Savior Jesus Christ.

Introduction

Paul was an apostle to the nations. His mission as an apostle was not, however, self-appointed. In fact, in his youth and in his zeal for God, he had opposed any mission to the nations. He was a conservative Jew who had set his mind to stand against Christianity since he thought it was a heretical extension of Judaism. He set out to arrest Christians in order to imprison them and try them for blasphemy. While he was on such a mission, the risen Lord Jesus Christ appeared to him, and that encounter changed his life. Instead of being a persecutor of Christians, he became an apostle to the nations – Jews and Gentiles alike. He traveled far and wide, spreading the gospel from Jerusalem, where it was first proclaimed, to Spain.

On one evangelistic journey he visited Corinth. That journey is commonly known as his "second missionary journey," and it is recorded in Acts 16–18. Paul shared the message of the Lord Jesus Christ with the Corinthians and helped them place their faith in Christ. He taught them basic Christian doctrines as a parent teaches a child. He loved the Corinthians and cared for them. The Corinthians were a mixed group of people – ethnically Greek, politically Roman, and from all strata of life (from slaves to landlords). They sometimes misunderstood Paul's teachings because of their very diverse backgrounds. So he visited them or wrote them letters repeatedly and taught them sound doctrine.

One such letter is 1 Corinthians. In it, Paul first addressed problems within the Corinthian church, as reported to him by people from Chloe's household (chs. 1–6), Then he answered questions that the Corinthians had asked him, possibly through friends who visited Paul or in a letter (chs. 7–16). In answering them, Paul left subsequent Christians a great letter full of doctrine and practical application. These timeless truths must be understood if we are to grow to maturity within our own context and culture.

A Tale of Two Corinths

The culture of a city inevitably affects the people who live within it. I was born in an Indian city called Nagercoil. In my language (Tamil) the name means "cobra temple" (from *naga*, "cobra," and *coil*, "temple"). In line with its name, in the center of the city stands a Hindu temple where worshippers feed milk and eggs to cobras. Allocco writes,

> Snake worship is both old and widespread in India, with roots stretching back to Vedic materials [the Hindu scriptures] . . . It is likely that fear of snakes (*nāgas*) and their poison was an early motivation for their propitiation, or that some snakes' unique characteristics, such as the periodic shedding of their skin, led to their being ascribed magical powers and eventually being deified. Whatever initially catalysed religious and ritual interest in snakes, it is clear that Indic traditions have long regarded them as divinities linked with water, fertility and anthills.[1]

Many statues or depictions of deities show them with snakes around their heads, necks, or hands.

The ancient city of Corinth also had a significant culture. Corinth was located on a small strip of land that connected the lower southwest peninsula of Greece (Peloponnesus) with the rest of Greece in the northeast. It also connected two ports: Lechaeum in the northwest and Cenchreae in the southeast. Thus it was a bridge city between northern and southern cities and between eastern and western ports. Like using the Suez Canal, which saves European and Asian sailors hundreds of kilometers of sea travel around the continent of Africa, passing through Corinth saved sailors 322 kilometers of travel around stormy Cape Malea.[2] Sailors arriving in small ships at Lechaeum or Cenchreae transported those small ships from one port to the other (a distance of 6.5 km)[3] using a system of rollers. Sailors on larger ships transported just the cargo from one port to the other.[4] The passing through of these ships and sailors made Corinth an important city for commerce, culture, art, and religion.

The landscape of Corinth was formed of three natural terraces that sloped away towards the sea. The city itself occupied the highest of the three terraces. Beyond the city was Acrocorinth, a tall rocky hill that rose

---

1. Amy Leigh Allocco, "Fear, Reverence and Ambivalence: Divine Snakes in Contemporary South India," *Religions of South Asia* 7 (2013): 231.

2. Joseph A. Callaway, "Corinth," *Review & Expositor* 57, no. 4 (October 1960): 382.

3. Richard A. Horsley, *1 Corinthians* (Nashville, TN: Abingdon Press, 1998), 24.

4. Emperor Nero, in AD 67, attempted to dig the first waterway between these ports but had to stop after six days because of the hard rock that made the project impossible. The canal was finally constructed between 1881 and 1893, and it has lasted even to this day (Callaway, "Corinth," 382).

457 meters.[5] It housed a temple for the mother–daughter goddesses of Greek religion, Demeter and Kore.[6] Although people had lived in Corinth from as early as 3000 BC, it only became a prominent city from the eighth to the fifth centuries BC, when it became an important leader in the Achaean League.[7] This "Old Corinth" had a reputation for immorality, popularized by one of its enemies, Aristophanes (c. 450–385 BC). He coined the verb *korinthiazō*, which meant "to act like a Corinthian" – that is, to act immorally. Whether Corinth was any more immoral than other port cities is questionable.

The Roman consul Lucius Mummius Achaius destroyed that old Corinth in 146 BC. Thomas writes that he "took the city, slew the men, made slaves of the women and burned the city and razed the ruins."[8] For a century, the land lay desolate. Then in 44 BC Julius Caesar rebuilt Corinth as a Roman colony and named it "Corinth, the praise of Julius."[9] Commerce increased rapidly because of its strategic location. When Caesar Augustus came to power, he made Corinth the capital of the region of Achaia. Old temples were restored and enlarged, new shops and markets were built, old fountains and water supplies were restored and new ones built, and many public buildings were added, including a concert hall that could contain 3,000 people and an amphitheater that seated between 14,000[10] and 18,000[11] spectators. The city's architecture and people were more Roman than Greek. This "New Corinth" was so different from the old city that one could say that "there were in fact two Corinths, one Greek and the other Roman, each with its distinctive institutions and ethos."[12]

Corinth's history continued even after Paul's departure from Corinth in early 50s. During the reign of Emperor Vespasian (AD 77) an earthquake partially destroyed the city. When Emperor Hadrian came to power, he rebuilt Corinth to its former glory, "with baths and aqueducts, so that before 200 AD it was probably the finest and modern city of Greece."[13]

---

5. J. D. Thomas, "Corinth–the City," *Restoration Quarterly* 3, no. 4 (1959): 147.

6. Jerome Murphy-O'Connor, "The Corinth That Saint Paul Saw," *Biblical Archaeologist* 47, no. 3 (1984): 152.

7. J. Brian Tucker, "The Role of Civic Identity on the Pauline Mission in Corinth," *Didaskalia (Otterburne, Man)* 19, no. 1 (Winter 2008): 72.

8. Thomas, "Corinth–the City," 148.

9. Tucker, "The Role of Civic," 72.

10. Ibid., 73.

11. Callaway, "Corinth," 387.

12. Murphy-O'Connor, *St. Paul's Corinth*, 3.

13. Thomas, "Corinth–the City," 148.

The Corinthians: A Mixed Group

Indians: who are they? To many foreigners, all Indians look alike: they are all Hindus, vegetarians, and Hindi speakers. But such a generalization is incorrect. The Indian Genome Variation Consortium reports that the Indian population "comprising of more than a billion people, consists of 4693 communities with several thousand of endogamous groups, 325 functioning languages and 25 scripts."[14] Each one of these groups not only looks and acts differently, but also has its own distinct cultural identity.

The same was true of Corinth. Within its 824 square kilometers lived 80,000 to 100,000 people.[15] They were of diverse backgrounds: Roman freedmen, military veterans, Greeks, Jews, the social elite, and urban poor from Rome, Phoenicia, and Phrygia.[16] Because of such a diverse people group, it had two official languages: Latin and Greek.[17] Paul wrote his letter to them in Greek, implying that at least the leaders in the congregation were literate and knew Greek.

Sport

Cricket is India's most popular national sport. Children and adults alike play cricket. The Indian national cricket team has won several competitions, including the Cricket World Cup in 1983 and 2011. The first definite reference to cricket being played in India goes back to 1721, when English sailors of the

---

14. The Indian Genome Variation Consortium, "The Indian Genome Variation Database (Igvdb): A Project Overview", http://www.imtech.res.in/raghava/reprints/IGVdb.pdf. For the role of these people groups in Indian culture, see Kalpana Rajaram, ed., *Facets of Indian Culture* (New Delhi, India: Spectrum Books, 2013), 4–14. For an argument that there were other people groups in the Indian subcontinent before Hindus arrived, see Arvind Sharma, "Dr. B. R. Ambedkar on the Aryan Invasion and the Emergence of the Caste System in India," *Journal of the American Academy of Religion* 73, no. 3 (September 2005): 843–870.

15. Tucker, "The Role of Civic Identity," 78. Godet suggests a much larger population: 600,000 to 700,000 inhabitants (F. Godet, *Commentary on the First Epistle of St. Paul to the Corinthians*, trans. A. Custin [Grand Rapids: Zondervan, 1957], 5).

16. For Roman freedmen, see Murphy-O'Connor, "The Corinth That Saint Paul Saw," 148. For Jewish settlers, see Leon Morris, *The First Epistle of Paul to the Corinthians: An Introduction and Commentary*, ed. Leon Morris, The Tyndale New Testament Commentaries (Leicester, England: IVP, 1985), 17. For the social elite, see Dirk Jongkind, "Corinth in the First Century Ad: The Search for Another Class," *Tyndale Bulletin* 52, no. 1 (2001): 139. For urban poor from Rome, Phoenicia, and Phrygia, see Tucker, "The Role of Civic Identity," 72.

17. Oscar Broneer, "Corinth: Center of St. Paul's Missionary Work in Greece," *Biblical Archaeologist* 14, no. 4 (December 1951): 82.

East India Company played a game at Cambay, near Baroda. The Calcutta Cricket Club is known to have existed since 1792.

Corinth was also well known for sport: it hosted the Isthmian Games. The Isthmian Games were similar to the Olympics. They were held in Corinth every two years in the months of April–May. These games were "second in rank of the four great Panhellenic festivals."[18] Many from Greece and all the free cities of the east (modern Turkey) came to see the games. Corinth would thus have been a popular city like Olympia, where the Olympics were held. Unlike in today's Olympics, where winners are awarded gold, silver, and bronze medals, in the Isthmian Games winners were crowned with wreaths made of celery or parsley plants.[19] Paul might have attended these Isthmian Games when he visited the Corinthians in AD 51.[20] However, even if he did not actually see the games (being a Jew, he might have been hesitant to see such games where men competed naked), he was aware of their importance in the lives of the Corinthians and made references to runners and boxers to illustrate his message (1 Cor 9:24–27).

Religion

Religion forms an integral part of every culture and India is known for its polytheistic religions. According to the 2011 government census there are 827 million Hindus in India (out of 1 billion 28 million people). In addition, there are 138 million Muslims, 24 million Christians, 19 million Sikhs, 8 million Buddhists, 4 million Jains, and 6 million people of other faiths.[21] Such diversity speaks highly of India's tolerance of different religions.

Corinth also had a variety of religions and worship centers for different religious groups. Besides synagogues for the Jews (Acts 18:4) and house churches for Christians (1 Cor 16:19) there were temples, such as that for Demeter and Kore (mother–daughter goddesses) at Acrocorinth. Old Corinth had a famous temple for Aphrodite, a goddess of love, beauty, and fertility.

---

18. Murphy-O'Connor, "The Corinth That Saint Paul Saw," 148. He also argues that the games were not held in Isthmia until the middle of the first century AD and so would have been played in the vicinity of Corinth when Paul visited Corinth in AD 51 (Murphy-O'Connor, *St. Paul's Corinth*, 13).

19. Callaway, "Corinth," 387. Paul made an allusion to this "perishable" crown when he wrote to the Corinthian believers that they would be awarded an "imperishable" crown (1 Cor 9:25).

20. Murphy-O'Connor, "The Corinth That Saint Paul Saw," 149.

21. http://censusindia.gov.in/

Strabo, a Roman historian, wrote that there were many temple prostitutes in that temple (*Geo.* 8.6.20c). Although the Corinth that Caesar built, with its Roman influence, would not have had such blatant worship of Greek gods and goddesses, it nevertheless would have had a very diverse religious environment that included the Jewish and Christian faiths. Witherington, having expressed doubt as to whether New Corinth would have had such religious overtones and immorality, writes,

> Nevertheless, one should not underestimate the place of sexual expression, not only in some pagan religious festivals (cf. Apuleius *Met.* 10.20–22), but also in some pagan temple precincts. It would be surprising if such activities did not take place in Corinth, especially in connection with the dinner parties (*convivia*) that were often held in the precincts of pagan temples (cf. Livy 23.18.12). There is also evidence from Dio Chrysostom (near the end of the first century AD) that there were in Roman Corinth numerous *hetaerae*, who often served as companions of the well-to-do at meals (8:5–10). 1 Corinthians 10:7 is a meaningful warning only if Paul had good reason to assume that sexual play was a regular part of some meals in one or more of the pagan temples in Corinth.[22]

Broneer narrates the following legend about Old Corinth:

> A well-known Corinthian legend, made famous through the tragedy of Euripides, was the story of Medea, the inhuman sorceress from beyond the Black Sea who murdered her own sons in order to take vengeance on Jason, her faithless husband and father of the children. Less than a hundred yards to the west of the Archaic Temple stands a fountain house, cut out of solid rock, into whose waters the Corinthian princess Glauke, Jason's bride, threw herself when her body was consumed by a poisoned robe, the gift of Medea. Nearby, at the tomb of the slain children, stood a frightful figure of Terror in the guise of woman; and at earlier times annual sacrifices, apparently in the form of human victims, were offered by the Corinthians. By the time of St Paul's arrival these gruesome practices had been discontinued, but the

---

22. Ben Witherington III, *Conflict and Community in Corinth: A Socio-Rhetorical Commentary on 1 and 2 Corinthians* (Grand Rapids: Eerdmans, 1995), 13.

statue existed and images of baked clay were apparently thrown into the fountain in celebration of the event.[23]

Corinth and India

Corinth and India are almost like twins separated at birth. Both are ancient nations, have ancient cultures, and are made up of diverse people groups. Both love sport and have a multitude of religions and religious practices. Katz, in an interesting article, argues that Hindus and Jews have much in common: they both live freely in India, they have the oldest languages (Hebrew and Sanskrit) that have given birth to other languages, both Hinduism and Judaism are "non-proselytizing faiths," and both religions have dietary codes, use ritual bathing, and "our brides circle their husbands seven times."[24] In summary, India still retains an ancient cultural outlook. What was once alive and vibrant in Roman and Greek cultures is still alive and vibrant today in India.[25] That being so, Paul's letter to the Corinthians speaks vividly to Indian Christians today.

---

23. Broneer, "Corinth," 84.

24. Nathan Katz, "Our Hindu-Jewish Romance: A Few of the Reasons Why Jews and Hindus Enjoy a Unique Camaraderie in This Pluralistic World," *Hinduism Today* (April–June 2008): 9.

25. Bennema makes a similar observation, cf. Cornelis Bennema, "Early Christian Identity Formation and Its Relevance for Modern India," in *Indian and Christian: Changing Identities in Modern India: Papers from the First SAIACS Annual Consultation 9–12 November 2010*, ed. Cornelis Bennema and Paul Joshua Bhakiaraj (Bangalore, India: SAIACS Press, 2011), 61.

1

Preliminary Issues

Before proceeding to the commentary on 1 Corinthians, it is necessary to explain a few preliminary issues, such as the nature of Paul's relationship with the Corinthians, who Sosthenes was, and when Paul wrote this letter. This section does not deal with the bridges between Corinthian and Indian culture, yet it is important for an overall understanding of 1 Corinthians.

Paul and the Corinthians

The Acts of the Apostles narrates three missionary journeys that Paul undertook (13:1 – 14:26; 15:36 – 18:22; and 18:23 – 21:17). On his second missionary journey he visited Corinth (Acts 15:40 – 18:22). The following is a brief summary of his trip.

Paul and Silas, his traveling companion, started their journey in Antioch in Syria, and went through Cilicia, Derbe, and Lystra – regions in modern-day Turkey (Acts 15:40 – 16:1a). At Lystra, Paul took Timothy as another traveling companion (16:1b–5). When Paul reached Troas, he received a vision in which a man from Macedonia (modern Europe) invited him to come to Macedonia and share the gospel there (16:9). Paul and his companions soon traveled through Samothrace and Neapolis, and arrived in Philippi, the first European city to hear the gospel (16:10–12). There a jailor, his family, and a purple cloth-dealer (Lydia) accepted Jesus Christ as Lord through Paul's preaching. Paul and his friends then passed through Amphipolis, Apollonia, and Thessalonica, and arrived in Berea (16:13 – 17:13). When opposition arose in Berea, Paul left Timothy and Silas and went to Athens alone (17:14–15). After a brief stay and a key speech in Athens' Areopagus (the high court of appeal), Paul went to Corinth (18:1). He traveled alone because his companions, Timothy and Silas, were still in Berea.

Aquila and Priscilla were in Corinth at that time. This Jewish husband and wife had been living in Rome but were evicted by Emperor Claudius' decree because of their ethnicity and religion.[1] They were leather tentmakers.[2] Jewish people generally did not touch dead animals because doing so defiled them, but in this case necessity obliged them to do this work. Their shop would have been among those that lined the main marketplace, the agora.[3] Nearby was the "meat market" (*macellum*) mentioned by Paul in 1 Corinthians 10:25. Aquila and Priscilla took Paul into their home as a guest, and he worked with them as a tentmaker in order to earn his living. He stayed in their home and preached in the Jewish synagogues every Sabbath (Acts 18:4–5). When the Jews rejected his message, he pronounced a woe upon them (18:6) and moved into the house of Titius Justus, a God-fearer (he was ethnically non-Jewish and believed in the God of the Jews, YHWH). Paul's departure from Aquila and Priscilla's house did not damage their friendship (cf. Rom 16:3–4) but strengthened his ministry among the Gentiles. Titius Justus' house was next door to the synagogue (Acts 18:7). While Paul stayed there, Crispus, the synagogue leader (a lay leader who aided the rabbi in conducting services[4]), his family, and many others believed in the Lord (18:8). Because of the Gentile Christians' zeal to learn more about the Christian faith, Paul stayed in Corinth for eighteen months (18:9–11). Gallio, the proconsul (a chief magistrate who became a governor of a province for a year) of Achaia, the province of Corinth, visited Corinth at that time, probably to attend the Isthmian Games. The Jews who opposed Paul brought charges against Paul to Gallio, but Gallio did not respond to their accusations (18:13–17). As a result, Paul continued his stay in Corinth for many more days before leaving for Jerusalem. This was Paul's first visit to the Corinthians.

After this, Paul made another missionary journey, his third (Acts 18:23 – 21:17). He primarily stayed and ministered in Ephesus for more than two years (19:10). At the end of that time, Paul made plans for another trip to

---

1. The Roman historiographer Suetonius wrote, "[Claudius] expelled the Jews because they were continually rioting at the instigation of Chrestus" (Suetonius, *Claudius* 25.4). Kistemaker comments, "We suspect that he misspelled the name of Christ, which to him was meaningless. He also thought that Christ was personally present in Rome to instigate riots. As a result of repeated conflicts between Jews and Christians, both groups had to leave the imperial city" (Simon J. Kistemaker, *Exposition of the Acts of the Apostles*, ed. William Hendriksen and Simon J. Kistemaker, New Testament Commentary [Grand Rapids: Baker, 1990], 649).

2. Witherington III, *Conflict and Community in Corinth*, 11 n. 24.

3. Callaway, "Corinth," 386.

4. Craig L. Blomberg, *1 Corinthians*, ed. Terry Muck, The NIV Application Commentary Series (Grand Rapids: Zondervan, 1995), 21.

Corinth (19:21; 1 Cor 16:5–9). It was a journey that would start from Ephesus, go through Macedonia (Europe) and Achaia (where Corinth was), and end in Jerusalem (Acts 19:21a). So he sent Timothy and Erastus (the latter was possibly the city treasurer of Corinth[5]) ahead of him to Macedonia, while he himself stayed a little longer in Ephesus (19:22). It is most likely that Paul wrote 1 Corinthians at this time and sent it with Timothy to hand-deliver it to the Corinthians (see below under "Date and Place of Composition"). His stay in Ephesus was not peaceful: Demetrius, a silversmith, started a riot against him (19:23–41). So Paul also left for Macedonia and stayed in Greece for three months (20:2–3). While there, perhaps he visited Corinth one more time, since it was very near and the Corinthians were dear to him. That missionary journey again ended in Paul returning to Jerusalem (Acts 20:7 – 21:17).

In the Scriptures there is only one clear mention of Paul visiting the Corinthians (Acts 18:1–18). Other than this – and the fact that, as just stated above, he might have visited them again while he was in Greece – there is no mention in the book of Acts of any other visit made by Paul to Corinth or of correspondence by letter between him and them. Scholars, however, conclude that Paul visited the Corinthians a few more times and also that he wrote them other letters that are not in the canonical Scriptures (based on 1 Cor 5:9);[6] however, such a conclusion is not inevitable.[7] What is clear, however, is that there was other communication between Paul and the Corinthians. First, "those of the household of Chloe"[8] reported to Paul about matters concerning the Corinthians (1 Cor 1:11). Second, Stephanas, Fortunatus, and Achaicus – men from Corinth – visited Paul and no doubt informed him about the Corinthians' faith (1 Cor 16:17–18).[9] Third, Apollos,

---

5. An inscription found near Corinth's market says, "the pavement was laid to the expense of Erastus" (Callaway, "Corinth," 387). Scholars think it might have been the same Erastus Paul mentioned elsewhere: "Erastus, the city treasurer, greets you" (Rom 16:23), and also the same one who accompanied Timothy to Achaia province, since he came from there.

6. Robertson and Plummer, for example, write, "It is quite certain that our 1 Corinthians is not the first letter which the Apostle wrote to the Church of Corinth; and it is probably probable that the earlier letter (v. 9) is wholly lost" (Alfred Plummer and Archibald T. Robertson, *1 Corinthians*, International Critical Commentary, 46 [Edinburgh: T&T Clark, 1914], xxi). Also, Blomberg, *1 Corinthians*, 22.

7. For a detailed argument, based on the grammar, for 1 Corinthians 5:9 not referring to a lost letter, see Andrew B. Spurgeon, *1 Corinthians: An Exegetical and Contextual Commentary*, ed. Venkataraman B. Immanuel, Brian C. Wintle, and C. Bennema, India Commentary on the New Testament Series (Bangalore, India: Primalogue, 2011), 8.

8. Unless otherwise indicated, all Bible translations are the author's own.

9. Blomberg thinks that these could have been the same people as "those of the household of Chloe" (Blomberg, *1 Corinthians*, 22).

who had visited the Corinthians, was with Paul when he wrote the first letter to the Corinthians and would have told him of the Corinthians' situation (Acts 19:1; 1 Cor 16:12).[10] Fourth, Sosthenes – the co-writer of 1 Corinthians – was a Corinthian believer. It is likely that he came to visit Paul with the questions the Corinthians had. By these four means correspondence could have carried back and forth between Paul and the Corinthians. In addition, the Corinthians might have written Paul a letter asking him to clarify certain doctrines, as 1 Corinthians 7:1 clearly implies: "and concerning what you *wrote*." In short, there was clearly communication between Paul and the Corinthians, and 1 Corinthians was one such "response" letter from Paul to them.

Authors and Addressee

In antiquity, letters began with a reference to the author(s) who wrote the letter, and to the addressee(s) who received the letter, and included a blessing pronounced on the recipient(s) by the author(s).[11] This was true of 1 Corinthians.

There were two authors: Paul and Sosthenes (1 Cor 1:1; 16:21). Paul, the apostle, was the one who first shared the gospel with the Corinthians. He was a Jew by race, Greek by culture, and Roman by citizenship. Possibly his family had served in the Roman military, by means of which he received Roman citizenship.[12] When he encountered the Lord, however, he became a follower of Jesus Christ and an apostle to the nations (Rom 11:13; Gen 22:18). His message became the gospel – the good news that the resurrected Lord Jesus Christ was the Messiah anticipated by the Jews and proclaimed by the Holy Scriptures. For this reason he soon traveled wherever he could and shared the gospel with all, including the Corinthians.

Sosthenes was the second author. It is likely that he had two names – Crispus and Sosthenes.[13] This Sosthenes was also a Jew and the synagogue

---

10. Dunn makes this observation (James D. G. Dunn, *1 Corinthians*, ed. Michael A. Knibb, A. T. Lincoln, and R. N. Whybray, T&T Clark Study Guides (London: T&T Clark International, 1999), 18).

11. For a study of the epistolary structure, see *Dictionary of the Later New Testament & Its Developments*, s.v. "Letters, Letter Form."

12. Witherington III, *Conflict and Community in Corinth*, 3.

13. Fellows makes this argument, for the following reasons. First, both Crispus and Sosthenes were called "the synagogue ruler." Second, it was a common practice to alternate between two different names for the same person in the same story, as in the case of Bar-Jesus and Elymas (Acts 13:6–8). Third, Paul would have changed Crispus (which meant either

ruler in Corinth (Acts 18:17). He came to believe in the Lord Jesus Christ as a result of Paul's ministry (Acts 18:18) and Paul baptized him (1 Cor 1:14). For his defense of Paul and the Christian faith, a mob beat him in front of Gallio, the proconsul of Achaia (Acts 18:17). Later, he visited Paul with news of the Corinthians and co-wrote this letter. He would have been Paul's primary source of information concerning the Corinthians' faith and lifestyle. He might even have been a leader in the Corinthian church.

The acceptance of Paul's authorship of this letter (1 Corinthians) is so widespread, and supported by church fathers such as Polycarp and Clement of Alexandria, that Dunn writes, "1 Corinthians has the kind of attestation of which most students of ancient texts can only dream . . . So firmly is 1 Corinthians linked to Paul that even if we did not have the account of Acts we would have to assume that the Paul of 1 Corinthians was the founder of the church in Corinth."[14] Although Sosthenes was the co-writer, most of the theology no doubt came from the apostle Paul's inspired thoughts. It is therefore considered to be *Paul's* letter to the Corinthians.

Paul wrote this letter to a *church* that was located in the city of Corinth (1 Cor 1:1).[15] The word "church" often brings to mind a picture of a building with a steeple, bell tower, cross, and perhaps a baptistery. In Paul's time, a church was a *group of believers* who gathered in one place, such as a synagogue or a public meeting place, for fellowship, breaking the bread of the Lord's Supper, prayer, and listening to the apostles' teachings (Acts 2:42). More commonly, however, they met in people's homes, especially in the larger houses of wealthy people. Such hosts were "patrons." Patrons often provided "land, jobs, money, and legal protection for the less well-off,"[16] and also

---

"curly headed" or "quivering") to Sosthenes ("salvation strength") after his conversion, just as Saul became Paul, and Simon became Peter/Cephas. Fourth, Sosthenes, as a former synagogue ruler, was an influential character in Corinth. Fifth, both Luke and Paul consistently called him Crispus (Acts 18:8; 1 Cor 1:14) before his baptism and Sosthenes after his baptism (Acts 18:17; 1 Cor 1:1) (Richard G. Fellows, "Renaming in Paul's Churches: The Case of Crispus-Sosthenes Revisited," *Tyndale Bulletin* 56, no. 2 (2005): 112–130).

14. Dunn, *1 Corinthians*, 13.

15. Macchia argues, based on the schism in Corinth, that there were several house churches (Frank D. Macchia, "'I Belong to Christ': A Pentecostal Reflection on Paul's Passion for Unity," *PNEUMA: The Journal of the Society for Pentecostal Studies* 25, no. 1 [Spring 2003]: 1). Even if there were, Paul still saw them as a single church.

16. Blomberg, *1 Corinthians*, 20. For a detailed study of patronage in ancient cultures, see Bruce W. Winter, *Seek the Welfare of the City: Christians as Benefactors and Citizens* (Grand Rapids: Eerdmans, 1994), 107–109. Also, Jerome H. Neyrey, ed. *The Social World of Luke-Acts: Models for Interpretation* (Peabody, MA: Hendrickson, 1999). Also, Dunn, *1 Corinthians*, 50–54.

hosted the church gatherings. This was the case in Ephesus, where the church met in the house of Aquila and Priscilla (1 Cor 16:19). The same was true in Rome, where individual churches met in the houses of Aquila and Priscilla (Rom 16:5), Asyncritus and friends (Rom 16:14), and Philologus and friends (Rom 16:15). The same could have been true in Corinth, where the church might have met in the house of a wealthy person such as Sosthenes or Titius. Some large houses had a dining room (*triclinium*) with a "floor space of 41.25 square meters"[17] and a central court (*atrium*) of 5 x 6 meters – thereby accommodating fifty to sixty seated people.[18] The number could have been larger if they sat on mats and very close to one another, as happens in Indian village churches.

The church in Corinth included both Jews and Gentiles (non-Jews). Some of the prominent Jews were Crispus/Sosthenes (Acts 18:8), and Aquila and Priscilla, whom Paul met for the first time in Corinth (Acts 18:1). In addition, there were many other Jews (Acts 18:10). Paul's casual reference to Pentecost (1 Cor 16:8) and his narration of Old Testament events such as the exodus, the wandering in the wilderness, and death from snake bites (1 Cor 10:1–10) imply that the recipients of his letter were familiar with the history recorded in the Old Testament.[19] Similarly, his reference to the patriarchs as "our fathers" (1 Cor 10:1) and his use of the Aramaic phrase *marana tha* (1 Cor 16:22) imply he was addressing Jews. Of course, there were also prominent Gentiles in the church: Titius Justus (Acts 18:7), Stephanus, Fortunatus, and Achaicus (1 Cor 16:17), and people from many nations who accepted the message that Jesus is Lord (Acts 18:8). In addition, Paul referred to the Corinthians' former lifestyle as idolatrous (1 Cor 12:2), implying that they were formerly worshippers of other gods. The Acts of the Apostles also states that when the Jews rejected his message, Paul turned towards the nations (Acts 18:6). It is best, then, to conclude that the church in Corinth was made up of both Jewish and non-Jewish Christians. Such a mixture could easily give rise to tensions (e.g. the party spirit, 1 Cor 1:12), a clash of cultures (e.g. debate over head-coverings, 1 Cor 11:2–16), and misunderstandings (e.g. lack of proper etiquette during table fellowship, 1 Cor 11:17–34).

---

17. Murphy-O'Connor, "The Corinth That Saint Paul Saw," 157.

18. Witherington III, *Conflict and Community in Corinth*, 30.

19. Of course, one could argue that a Gentile church would have been familiar with these events too, as does Fee (Gordon D. Fee, *The First Epistle to the Corinthians*, First ed., New International Commentary on the New Testament, 46 [Grand Rapids: Eerdmans, 1987], 820).

Date and Place of Composition

When did Paul write this letter, and where was he when he wrote it? The answers to these questions do not affect one's theology but do affirm the historicity of the composition of the letter. Two events stated in the Acts of the Apostles give clues as to when Paul visited the Corinthians the first time. First, Emperor Claudius' decree that expelled the Jews from Rome happened prior to Paul's first contact with the Corinthians, since Aquila and Priscilla were already in Corinth when Paul visited that city. Scholars date this decree to AD 49,[20] so Paul's visit to the Corinthians must have occurred after that date. Second, the proconsul Gallio visited Corinth at the end of Paul's eighteen-month stay there (Acts 18:11–17). Scholars date Gallio's rule roughly from the summer of AD 51 to the summer of AD 52.[21] Gallio probably went there to preside over the Isthmian Games held in AD 51.[22] These two events together suggest that Paul's letter to the Corinthians must have been written after AD 51 or 52, after Paul's second missionary journey was completed.

It is likely that Paul wrote 1 Corinthians in Ephesus, where he stayed for two years as his base of his ministry during the third missionary journey (Acts 18:23 – 21:17). As mentioned at the start of this chapter, at the end of his stay there Paul wanted to visit Macedonia and Achaia one more time, and he sent Timothy and Erastus ahead of him while he stayed in Ephesus until Pentecost (Acts 19:22–40; 1 Cor 16:8–9). It is likely that Timothy carried this letter, 1 Corinthians, to the Corinthians (see 1 Cor 4:16–17; 16:10–11). Therefore, the most likely date for the composition of 1 Corinthians is AD 54–55, a little more than two years after Paul's first visit to the Corinthians. Paul would therefore have written it while he was in Ephesus, a place near enough for him to be able to receive friends from Corinth and hear of the Corinthians' health and spiritual life.

Opponents

Did Paul have opponents in Corinth? The Acts of the Apostles states that when the Jews in Corinth opposed Paul's teachings, he moved to work among the nations (Acts 18:6). But were there opponents of Paul among the Christians

---

20. Dunn, *1 Corinthians*, 14.
21. Blomberg, *1 Corinthians*, 21. Dunn, *1 Corinthians*, 14.
22. Murphy-O'Connor, "The Corinth That Saint Paul Saw," 149.

(or church) in Corinth? Were there opponents of Paul outside the church that were causing the Corinthians unrest and suspicion? Some scholars think that there were and suggest several theories, three of which need discussion.

Some scholars think that the Corinthian church itself had turned against Paul and his teachings. Fee, for example, writes, "The basic stance of the present commentary is that the *historical situation* in Corinth was *one of conflict between the church and its founder.* This is not to deny that the church was experiencing internal strife, but it is to argue that the greater problem of 'division' was between Paul and some in the community who were leading the church as a whole into an anti-Pauline view of things."[23] The emotional tone of the epistle could suggest such a conclusion. But one also wonders, if the Corinthians were in conflict with their founder, would they have written to him and asked for his advice concerning questions they had (e.g. 1 Cor 7:1, 25; 8:1; 12:1; 16:1, 12)? Likewise, would Paul have praised them for remembering all his teaching and maintaining the traditions he had passed on to them (1 Cor 11:2)? In addition, would the Corinthians have sent a "fellowship" offering to him through Stephanus and friends (1 Cor 16:17) if they were in conflict with him?

Other scholars suggest that Apollos was contradicting Paul's teachings and that Paul wanted the Corinthians to have a "critical appraisal of Apollos, particularly when they compare Apollos' contribution to that of Paul himself."[24] Ker draws this conclusion from the fact that "Paul's argument against divisiveness not only devotes considerable attention to Apollos (1:12; 2:4, 5–9; 4:6), but includes a sharp warning about how Apollos had 'built' upon the foundation Paul had laid (3:10–15)."[25] Again, one wonders, if there were such a strong conflict between Paul and Apollos, would Paul have treated him as his equal (1 Cor 3:6–7)? Would Paul have called him "brother" and defended his failure to visit Corinth (1 Cor 16:12)? He explicitly says that he and Apollos agreed in their preaching (1 Cor 4:6). In light of these things, Bruce writes, "There seems to have been no sense of personal rivalry between Paul and Apollos."[26]

---

23. Fee, *First Epistle to the Corinthians*, 6 (emphasis in original).
24. Donald P. Ker, "Paul and Apollos–Colleagues or Rivals," *Journal for the Study of the New Testament* 77 (2000): 97.
25. Horsley, *1 Corinthians*, 34.
26. F. F. Bruce, *1 and 2 Corinthians*, eds. Ronald E. Clements and Matthew Black, New Century Bible Commentary (Grand Rapids: Eerdmans, 1971), 32.

Still others have suggested that the "other apostles," such as Peter and John, were Paul's opponents. Chilton, for example, writes, "Paul goes on to name his opposition: 'the rest of the apostles and the brothers of the Lord and Peter' (1 Cor 9:5). Evidently, from their point of view, Paul was not an apostle. Paul's response is that the appearance of the risen Lord to him with an apostolic commission made him an apostle, just as in the case of Barnabas (9:6)."[27] It is highly unlikely, however, that the other apostles were Paul's opponents, since in Jerusalem they were in total agreement (Acts 15:25–26; also Gal 2:7–9). Likewise, 1 Corinthians gives more evidence of their unity and oneness (1 Cor 4:9; 12:28; 15:4–9) than of their enmity or disunity.

There was strife, unrest, and division within the Corinthian church. Whether a particular person or group caused that unrest is questionable. The man living with his father's wife (1 Cor 5:1–2) certainly would have caused tensions within the congregation and between Paul and the congregation. Members suing each other would no doubt have brought further strain within the church and in its relationship with Paul (1 Cor 6:1–8). Their splitting into groups – "I am of Paul," "I am of Apollos," and "I am of Cephas" – clearly indicated that there were divisions among the members of the Corinthian church. Therefore, instead of seeing a particular opponent of Paul in Corinth, it is better to conclude that several lifestyle choices that the Corinthians made went against Paul's teachings, and that prompted Paul to write a stern letter to them, as a father would address his beloved children (1 Cor 4:15). Ultimately, he wanted them to imitate Christ in their holiness (1 Cor 4:16; 11:1).

Outline of 1 Corinthians

Like other epistles written at this time, Paul's first letter to the Corinthians has three distinct sections: opening greetings (1 Cor 1:1–9), the body of the letter (1 Cor 1:10 – 16:18), and concluding greetings (1 Cor 16:19–24). The opening greetings introduce the author, the addressee, and pronounce a blessing on the Corinthians, while expressing Paul's praise and thanksgiving concerning them. The body of the letter has two distinct sections: Paul's teachings in light of the report he received from Chloe's household (1 Cor 1:10 – 6:20) and his teachings in response to questions that the Corinthians themselves had asked him (1 Cor 7:1 – 16:18). The concluding greetings include greetings from the

---

27. Bruce Chilton, "Churches," *The Living Pulpit* 9, no. 4 (October–December 2000): 18.

Corinthians' friends in Ephesus, Paul's own greetings to the Corinthians, and a benediction.[28]

The body of the letter could be further outlined as follows:

    A. Paul's Responses to Chloe's Report (1 Cor 1:10 – 6:20)
        1. Concerning Spiritual Leaders (1 Cor 1:10 – 4:21)
        2. Concerning Immorality (1 Cor 5:1–13)
        3. Concerning Lawsuits (1 Cor 6:1–8)
        4. Concerning Visits to Prostitutes (1 Cor 6:9–20)

    B. Paul's Answers to the Corinthians' Questions (1 Cor 7:1 – 16:18)
        1. Concerning the Married (1 Cor 7:1–24)
        2. Concerning the Never-Been-Married (1 Cor 7:25–40)
        3. Concerning Freedom and Worship (1 Cor 8:1 – 11:34)
        4. Concerning Spirit-Indwelt People (1 Cor 12:1 – 15:58)
        5. Concerning the Collection for the Saints (1 Cor 16:1–11)
        6. Concerning Apollos and Others (1 Cor 16:12–18)

Structure

This commentary is written to highlight its cultural relevance for India today. One major drawback of such an endeavor is that the beauty of the structure of the letter is thereby lost. Paul was a mastermind in arranging the themes in this letter. I highlight some examples here.

He begins the letter by referring to their conflicts, in which some were saying, "I am of Paul," others, "I am of Apollos," and yet others, "I am of Cephas" (1 Cor 1:12). He then repeatedly refers to Apollos and Cephas in the letter (1 Cor 3:4, 5, 33; 4:6; 9:5; 15:5; 16:12). The message one gets is that all three were co-workers (3:5a) entrusted by the Lord with a specific task (3:5b), who worked for the Corinthians (3:22), and who were united in their faith and practice (4:6). At the same time, each had his own personal preferences (9:5), privileges (15:5), and will (16:12). Just as Paul began the letter by talking about Apollos (1:12), so he concluded it with reference to Apollos. There was

---

28. For a similar outline, see Fee, who divides the book into four sections: Introduction (1:1–9), In Response to Reports (1:10 – 6:21), In Response to Corinthian Letter (7:1 – 16:12), and Concluding Matters (16:13–24) (Fee, *First Epistle to the Corinthians*, 21–23). Also, Barrett, who divides the book into: Introduction (i.1–9), News from Corinth (i.10–vi. 20), A Letter from Corinth (vii.1–xvi.4), and Conclusion (xvi.5–24) (C. K. Barrett, *A Commentary on the First Epistle to the Corinthians*, ed. Henry Chadwick, Harper's New Testament Commentaries [New York: Harper & Row, 1968], 28–29).

no conflict between Paul and Apollos, as the Corinthians had implied there was through their divisions.

In chapter 5 Paul begins the discussion about someone immoral in the congregation: someone sexually cohabiting with his father's wife. After a brief discussion, Paul seems to wander off to the topic of a lawsuit. But he then returns to another incident of immorality: some of the church members visiting prostitutes. In fact, Paul wasn't wandering off; lawsuits are common when family fights occur (such as over a son stealing his stepmother). Not only that, when Paul returned to the topic of immorality in chapter 6, he carried on to talk of "moral" sexual behavior in chapter 7. In other words, if there are un-Christian ways of behaving, such as visiting prostitutes and cohabiting with one's stepmother, there are also Christian ways of behaving, such as loving one's spouse, marrying one's betrothed without causing him or her to "burn," and not divorcing one's spouse. So the immorality discussed in chapters 5 and 6 forms the backdrop to the discussion of faithful Christian marriage in chapter 7.

In chapter 8 Paul discusses eating food offered to idol-gods. One of the reasons why the "mature" Corinthian Christians did so was their self-centeredness: they didn't care if they offended other Christians. So in chapter 9 Paul details how setting aside one's rights for the sake of others is the Christian principle, and he illustrates it from his own life and from other examples (even from the Lord's own teaching). Then in chapter 10 he returns to the topic of eating food offered to an idol-god, food sold in a marketplace, and meat served in a non-Christian's house. Not only that, he further argues that the reason why a Christian must not eat before other gods is because he or she is already committed to one "table," the table of the Lord Jesus Christ, and he expands on the teachings of the Lord's Supper in chapter 11.

In chapter 12, Paul explains who Spirit-indwelt people are and what Spirit-given gifts they have. Paul wants them to use all the gifts in a way that will bring about unity and the good of the church as a whole (12:7). He illustrates how that can be done using the example of body parts in a human body. Just as hands and legs need each other, so the church needs all the different gifts of the Spirit. Just as ligaments hold body parts together, so love holds together all the gifts of the Spirit and makes them functional. If someone can speak a multitude of languages, including angelic languages, but doesn't have love, he or she is just like a noisy gong. After emphasizing the importance of love in chapter 13, Paul returns to, and completes, his discussion of the Spirit's gifts in chapter 14.

In this way, all the topics and all the chapters are beautifully interlocked and intertwined. None of the topics stands in isolation. I hope to bring out some of these beautiful constructions in the commentary.

2

Opening Greetings (1:1–9)

In the opening paragraphs, Paul, as was customary in ancient letter writing style, introduces the authors (1:1) and the addressees (1:2), and gives a personal greeting (1:3). In addition, there is a longer section of thanksgiving for the Corinthians (1:4–9). This last unique section was necessary since some of the teachings within the following sections (the body of the letter) might seem harsh. Paul did not want the Corinthians to think that he did not love them. On the contrary, his love for and appreciation of them led him to rebuke them, as a father would a child (4:14–16, 21).

Two authors co-wrote 1 Corinthians: "Paul and Sosthenes" (1:1). It is likely that the theology came from Paul's pen while Sosthenes represented the Corinthians accurately to Paul so that Paul could write a culturally relevant letter. Sosthenes was thus the Corinthians' representative. Myrou writes, "The choice of Paul to place Sosthenes at the beginning of this Epistle, rather than any other of his capable co-workers, shows that Sosthenes not only was well known to the Corinthian Christians but also enjoyed great respect from all the members of the Church [1 Cor. 16:10–20]."[1] Since he was familiar to the Corinthians, Paul simply introduced him as "a brother," meaning, "a Christian." Together they wrote an epistle that was relevant and appropriate to the needs of the Corinthians.

What's in a Name? (1:1–2)

Many Indian Christians have British or American names. Some Christians borrowed Western names because of Western missionaries who were instrumental in bringing the gospel to India, or because these names were

---

1. Augustine Myrou, "Sosthenes: The Former Crispus (?)," *The Greek Orthodox Theological Review* 44, no. 1–4 (1999): 210.

novel (there are those with the names Martin Luther King or Isaac Newton in India). Mostly, however, they borrowed biblical names because their earlier names had religious connotations they now want to avoid. Someone with the name Ganesh (a god of the Hindus) would prefer people not to call him that after his conversion – he feels as if he is being idolatrous if he is called by another god's name.

Many new converts to Christianity change their names, and such a practice is not new. The church father Eusebius writes about a trial of Christians in Caesarea in Palestine in AD 308. When the governor Firmillianus asked an Egyptian Christian for his name, he stated a prophet's name instead of his birth name. Eusebius continued, "Also the rest of the Egyptians who were with him, instead of those names which their fathers had given them after the name of some idol, had taken for themselves the names of the prophets, such as these – Elias, Jeremiah, Isaiah, Samuel, Daniel."[2] After giving a fascinating account of similar name changes in Egypt, however, Horsley writes, "It is not permissible to claim that name-change is in every case an indication of a shift in religious allegiance; for other factors – cultural, political, and social – may be at work, either singly or in concert."[3] In modern Indian Christianity, the trend is changing and converts are now keeping their birth names in order to fit in among their own people.

Paul also changed his name for a particular reason: evangelism. His preferred name was "Saul" (Acts 7:58; 8:1–3; 9:1–27; 11:25–30; 12:25; 13:1–7). It was a prestigious name for it was the name of the first king of the Israelites, King Saul, who was of the same tribe of Benjamin to which Paul belonged (Phil 3:5). However, it would have alienated him from the people to whom he tried to witness (see Acts 13:9). So when he started on his first missionary journey, he chose a more Roman name in order to diminish his ethnic distinction and to promote his mission to the nations (Rom 11:13; Gal 2:7–8). He went by his *middle* name "Paul," a name registered according to Roman law.[4]

After the mention of his name, the next two nouns refer to his profession: a "called apostle" (1:1). The term "call" referred to a divine invitation to an act of obedience. For example, God called Abraham to leave his father's home and

2. Eusebius, *De Martyribus Palaestinae* 11.8 (Translated by William Cureton).

3. G. H. R. Horsley, "Name Change as an Indication of Religious Conversion in Antiquity," *Numen* 34, no. 1 (June 1987): 12.

4. James D. G. Dunn, *Romans 1–8*, eds. David A. Huggard, Glenn W. Barker, and Ralph P. Martin, Word Biblical Commentary, vol. 38A (Dallas, TX: Word Publishing, 1988), 6.

follow him, and Abraham obeyed (Gen 12:1–3). God called Moses to deliver the Israelites out of Egypt, and Moses obeyed (Exod 3:7–10). God also called Jeremiah (Jer 1:4–5), Amos (Amos 7:15), and Isaiah (Isa 6:8). God called each one to a specific task and each one obeyed. Similarly, God called Saul/Paul to the task of "apostleship." An apostle was a witness to Jesus' life, ministry, death, and resurrection (Acts 1:21–22). It was a special call. Stott wrote,

> Apostle was a distinctively Christian name from the beginning, in that Jesus himself chose it as his designation of the Twelve, and Paul claimed to have been added to their number. The distinctive qualifications of the apostles were that they were directly and personally called and commissioned by Jesus, that they were eye-witnesses of the historical Jesus, at least (and especially) of his resurrection, and that they were sent out by him to preach with his authority. The New Testament apostle thus resembled . . . the Old Testament prophet, who was "called" and "sent" by Yahweh to speak in his name.[5]

Paul was called to be such an apostle. He was mystified that God had given him this call because he had persecuted the church (1 Cor 15:8–9), but he was unswerving in obeying it (Acts 9:1–9; 1 Cor 15:8; Gal 1:16) and considered himself to be equal to the other apostles (2 Cor 11:5; 12:11). He gladly bore the signs of an apostle: the scars inflicted on him through persecution (2 Cor 12:12).

Unlike in Old Testament times, when people received a call from YHWH God, Paul the apostle had been commissioned and sent by "Jesus Christ." The Corinthians, influenced by the Jews among them, would have understood "Christ" as the Greek translation of the Hebrew title "Messiah." Messiah meant "the anointed one" and it referred to how kings were appointed for their role through the pouring of oil ("anointing") upon their heads (1 Sam 15:1; 16:13). This particular Messiah-King's name was "Jesus." In other words, Paul was called and commissioned to be an apostle, a witness, by King Jesus. Further, this commissioning was in accordance with the "will of God." Elsewhere Paul is explicit: "Paul, an apostle – [commissioned] not by men nor by a man, but by Jesus Christ and God the Father who raised him from the dead" (Gal 1:1). Paul's commissioning and sending came from Jesus Christ in accordance with the will of God. It was therefore important that the

---

5. John R. W. Stott, *The Message of Romans: God's Good News for the World*, ed. John R. W. Stott, The Bible Speaks Today (Downers Grove, IL: InterVarsity Press, 1994), 46–47.

Corinthians listen to what he had to say: he was speaking on behalf of God, just as Moses, Isaiah, and Jeremiah had done.

Paul then referred to the recipients of his letter as "the church of God that is in Corinth" (1 Cor 1:2). These days, "church" has become a familiar term, most often referring to a denomination or a local church. But when Paul wrote his letters, it referred to "an assembly duly summoned."[6] Although the believers called themselves the "people belonging to the Way" (Acts 9:2) or "Christians" (Acts 11:26), they called the assembly "church," most likely because of the Lord's promise, "I will build my church" (Matt 16:18). Calling their gathering "church" also distinguished them from the "synagogue" where the Jews gathered. Paul specified that this gathering of believers belonged to God: "church of God." Their identity was found not in their location but in the one to whom they belonged. Paul then mentioned their location: "those who are in Corinth."

Perspective: Sheep or Saints? (1:2–3)

It is often said in India, "If one wants to be a shepherd, one must like the smell of the sheep," implying that sheep smell bad. As picturesque as this illustration is, it is unlike Paul's attitude towards the Corinthians. Although there were problems within the church, Paul saw them as redeemed people, as is shown by the terms he used to describe them: he saw them as purified in Christ Jesus (1 Cor 1:2), a holy people (1:2), those whom God had called (1:2), people who lacked no spiritual gifts (1:7), those whom Christ would present blameless (1:8), the temple of God (3:16; 6:18) in whom God's Spirit lived (3:16; 6:18), wise in Christ (4:10), strong in Christ (4:10), noble in Christ (4:10), people who had been washed by Christ (6:11), sanctified (6:11), justified (6:11), members of Christ's body (6:15), united with the Lord in one Spirit (6:17), bought with a price (6:20), those who faithfully remembered Paul's teachings and maintained the traditions just as he had passed them on (11:2), those who received the gospel and stood firm in it (15:1), those who were saved (15:2).

---

6. Liddle and Scott, s.v. *ekklesia*. Godet writes, "The term [*ekklesia*], Church, formed of the two words, [*ek*] out of, and [*kaleo*] to call, denotes in ordinary Greek language an assembly of citizens called out of their dwellings by an official summons; comp. Acts. xix. 41. Applied to the religious domain in the New Testament, the word preserves essentially the same meaning. Here too there is a summoner: God, who calls sinners to salvation by the preaching of the gospel (Gal 1:6)" (Godet, *Commentary*, 41). Also Witherington III, *Conflict and Community in Corinth*, 90–93.

In 1:2 he sees them as "those purified in Christ Jesus, called holy ones" (1 Cor 1:2a). He referred not to their "stink" (although he would address problems within the church in chs. 5–6), but to their "holiness" or "purification." They were people who were purified in Christ Jesus. As such, they were "called holy ones." The first word, "called," refers to their status – that is, people whom God had called. His specific calling established them as "holy people." But this status of being "holy" and "purified" was not unique to them; it belonged to "all others who call upon the name of our Lord Jesus Christ in all places – theirs and ours" (1 Cor 1:2b).[7] Wherever a church is, the people within it are purified in Christ Jesus, called by God, and declared to be "holy people."

As was customary, Paul concluded his opening greetings with a blessing: "grace to you and also peace from God our Father and the Lord Jesus Christ" (1 Cor 1:3). This greeting is a distinct Pauline signature and is found in all his writings (Rom 1:7; 16:20; 1 Cor 1:3; 2 Cor 1:2; Gal 1:3; Eph 1:2; Phil 1:2; Col 1:2; 1 Thess 1:1; 2 Thess 1:2; 1 Tim 1:2; 2 Tim 1:2; Titus 1:4; and Phlm 1:3). It is a combination of Greek and Hebrew greetings (*charin* "rejoice" and *shalom* "peace" respectively) with a slight modification – *charis* "grace" instead of *charin* "rejoice." Paul seems to have formulated this unique greeting in order to address both his Greek and his Jewish audience. In addition, it has great theological significance: those who have received the *grace* of God have *peace* with him.

The Fatherhood of God and the Son of God (1:3)

For Muslims in India one stumbling block to hearing the gospel is the Father–Son relationship between God and Jesus Christ. The Qur'an explicitly teaches that God cannot have a son. In Arabic, the term "son of" (*ibn*) carries biological overtones. "In fact, the Qur'an (*At-Tawba* 9:30) says God curses anyone who would utter the ridiculous blasphemy that Jesus could be *ibnullâh* ('a son of God')."[8] Pious Muslims may therefore even leave the presence of someone

---

7. The phrase "theirs and ours" could modify either "Lord" or "place" (for defense of it modifying "Lord" see Fee, *First Epistle to the Corinthians*, 34. Godet, *Commentary*, 47). The word order favors the phrase modifying the "place" – "their place and our place." Paul repeatedly appealed to their corporate union with other churches (4:17; 11:16; 14:33, 36), possibly because he did not want the Corinthians to feel isolated in their struggles or have a superiority complex as if they were the only special people. The Lord has many sheep (John 10:16).

8. Collin Hansen, "The Son and the Crescent," *Christianity Today* 55, no. 2 (Fall 2011): 20.

who utters the phrase "Jesus is the Son of God," fearing divine judgment upon them. Some translations, therefore, modify the phrase to say, "the Beloved Son who comes [or originates] from God," in order to remove the difficulty and help Muslims understand the gospel.[9]

The Lord Jesus has been called "son" in different ways: "son of Mary," "son of Joseph," "son of David," "son of man," "son of God," or simply "the son." Although "son of Mary" and "son of David" refer to a biological affinity (one immediate and the other through lineage), "son of Joseph" does not imply any biological affinity since Joseph did not have any physical relationship with Mary until after Jesus was born (Matt 1:25). Similarly, "son of God" does not refer to a biological affinity so much as a religious and political relationship between God and Jesus Christ. In the early history of Israel, YHWH God was their sole ruler (a theocracy). He delivered them from Egypt and led them to the Promised Land. He lived among them and gave them shelter. However, when the nation of Israel wanted a *human* king just as the nations around them had, God gave them Saul and then David. With David, God made an eternal covenant that he would preserve him a descendant who would always sit on the throne of David (2 Sam 7:8–16). In that context, YHWH God declared concerning David's offspring, "I will be to him a Father, and he will be to me a Son" (2 Sam 7:14). In light of that promise, David thought of himself as God's son – "He said to me, 'You are my Son; I have become your Father'" (Ps 2:7; see also 2:12; 72:1; 80:15; 86:16; 144:3). When Jesus came, he too was considered to be the "son" just as David was, but there were more theological nuances to his sonship. In the debate concerning whether it is correct to alter the name Son of God for Muslim audiences, Horrell writes,

> Both terms "Father" and "Son" for God are repugnant to the Muslim. Yet in the Bible and Christian faith these words take on more meaning than mere metaphors or titles; rather they become the divine *names* that most disclose the divine relations. Without the Son there is no Father, and without the Father there is no Son. In the developing theology of the New Testament, the names "Father" and "Son" assume the force of being not merely external (or economic) descriptions but intrinsic to God's own deepest reality.[10]

---

9. For a thorough study of complications related to this new translation see Hansen, "The Son and the Crescent," 18–23.

10. J. Scott Horrell, "Cautions Regarding 'Son of God' in Muslim-Idiom Translations of the Bible: Seeking Sensible Balance," *St Francis Magazine* 6, no. 4 (August 2010): 650.

Paul did not have to quibble over this concept; in his blessing on his readers he presented God as Father and Jesus Christ as Lord: "from God our Father and Lord Jesus Christ" (1 Cor 1:3). By calling God "Father" and modifying it with "our," Paul was affirming God's Fatherhood not only of Christ but also of all Christians. By calling Jesus "Lord," Paul equated him with YHWH and with Caesar Augustus. In the Greek translation of the Old Testament (the Septuagint, or LXX), the translators substituted *kurios* ("Lord") for YHWH; to call Jesus *kurios* was, therefore, to equate him with YHWH God. The citizens of Rome, on the other hand, thought of Caesar Augustus as *kurios* ("Lord");[11] to them also Paul presented Jesus Christ as the new Lord. The implication was obedience to this new Lord. Wright says, "Caesar's messengers didn't go round the world saying 'Caesar is lord, so if you feel you need to have a Roman-empire kind of experience, you might want to submit to him.' The challenge of Paul's gospel is that someone very different to Caesar, exercising a very different kind of power, is the world's true lord."[12]

Thanksgiving for the Corinthians (1:4–9)

As noted above, the opening greetings in most ancient letters contained the author's name, the addressee's name, and a blessing. Paul added another section: thanksgiving to God for his faithfulness to the Corinthians (1:4–9).

He began by saying, "I thank my God always for you because of the grace of God which is given to you in Christ Jesus" (1 Cor 1:4). Paul could always thank God because the Corinthians had received God's grace in Christ Jesus. Their spiritual blessing was the starting point of his thanksgiving. He then explained the nature of the grace: "in all things you have been made rich in him – in all words and in all knowledge" (1 Cor 1:5). The latter phrase, "in all words and in all knowledge," explains the earlier phrase, "in all things," meaning that the Corinthians were rich in "words" and "knowledge." What were these "words" and "knowledge"?[13] Most likely this was a standard phrase

---

11. For a detailed study of the conflict between Caesar as Lord versus and Jesus as Lord, see Joseph D. Fantin, *The Lord of the Entire World: Lord Jesus, a Challenge to Lord Caesar?*, New Testament Monographs (Sheffield, England: Sheffield Phoenix Press, 2011).

12. Tom Wright, *Romans Part 1: Chapters 1–8*, Paul for Everyone (London: SPCK, 2004), 5.

13. Scholars have proposed five views: (a) *word* refers to lower wisdom and *knowledge* refers to higher wisdom; (b) *word* refers to gifts of languages and *knowledge* refers to the gift of prophecy; (c) *word* refers to the gospel and *knowledge* refers to the Corinthians accepting

that meant the Corinthians were given understanding in all spiritual concepts, especially those related to who Christ was and what he had accomplished. Paul explicitly says so in the following section, where he explains that those who have the Spirit of God understand things about God (2:6–16). One example of their *spiritual* understanding was that they understood the testimony (witness) spoken about Christ and were firmly rooted in it (1 Cor 1:6). Others who did not have that *spiritual* understanding about who Christ was crucified him (2:8). Since the Christians in Corinth understood that testimony about Christ (that he was Lord, 1:3, 7), they lacked nothing spiritually[14] as they patiently waited for his revelation.[15] In addition, Christ would sustain them until the end – the day of the Lord – as blameless people (1 Cor 1:8). Kistemaker says, "In the Old Testament, the term *the day of the Lord* is a description of the day of judgment (Joel 3:14; Amos 5:18–20). In the New Testament, the term alludes to the return of Christ (e.g. Phil 1:6, 10; 2:16; 1 Thess 5:2). Christ's return includes judgment in which both God and Christ serve as judge (see Rom 14:10; 2 Cor 5:10)."[16] The Corinthians would be presented "blameless" – that is, as "people against whom there is no accusation" – on the day Christ took the judgment seat. Such a verdict would be possible not because of the Corinthians but because "God is faithful" (1 Cor 1:9). This was a "deeply rooted motif about God found in the OT. The God of Israel was a faithful God, always reliable, always true to himself, who could therefore be counted on to fulfill all his promises (Deut 7:9; Ps 144:13)."[17] It was God's faithfulness that kept the Corinthians blameless. God was so faithful because it was he who had "called them to the fellowship of his son, Jesus Christ, our Lord" (1 Cor 1:9).

The Corinthians were blessed people because God was on their side. He gave grace to them, made them rich by opening their eyes to understand the

---

the gospel; (d) *word* refers to the outward expression of the gospel and *knowledge* refers to the inward expression of the gospel; and (e) *word* refers to "rational" gifts and *knowledge* refers to "ecstatic" gifts (Fee, *First Epistle to the Corinthians*, 40).

14. Although it is possible to take this word (in Greek, *charisma*) as a reference to the spiritual gifts talked about in chs. 12–14, here Paul was most likely speaking in general terms, that is, gifts such as salvation.

15. Perhaps Paul was referring to the "dawning of Christ" in their hearts (as some of my friends at Summer Institute of Linguistics who translated the Bible have understood it), but most likely it referred to the visible return of the Lord Jesus Christ, as the following verse indicates.

16. Simon J. Kistemaker, *Exposition of the First Epistle to the Corinthians*, ed. William Hendricksen, New Testament Commentary Series (Grand Rapids: Baker, 1993), 100.

17. Fee, *The First Epistle to the Corinthians*, 44.

mystery about Christ as Lord, established them firmly as blameless people until Christ's coming, and remained faithful to them and to his invitation to them to fellowship with Christ. Therefore Paul thanked God on their behalf.

Part I

Paul's Responses to Chloe's Report (1:10 – 6:20)

The main teachings of Paul in 1 Corinthians are in 1:10 – 16:18. Here he deals with ten major issues, each with many more sub-issues. The ten major issues fall into two major categories: his *responses* to the report from Chloe's household concerning the Corinthians (1 Cor 1:10 – 6:20) and his *answers* to questions that the Corinthians had asked (1 Cor 7:1 – 16:18). Chloe was most likely from Corinth.[18] Whether she was a Christian is uncertain.[19] She had sent her "household" (a term for either family members or servants/ slaves) to Ephesus, either to see Paul or on her own business. While visiting Paul, these people reported that there were problems in Corinth. Paul first addressed those issues[20] and then answered the questions the Corinthians had asked either by means of a letter (see 7:1) or through someone such as Sosthenes.

Issues dealt with in the first section (1:10 – 6:20) are not clearly marked by Greek constructions, yet the topics are easy to identify. Chloe's report mentioned four abnormalities within the church in Corinth. First, a division had arisen in the church and the members had sided with different leaders,

---

18. Fee, *First Epistle to the Corinthians*, 54.
19. Fee thinks she was a non-Christian (Fee, *First Epistle to the Corinthians*, 54). But would a non-Christian have reported the Corinthians' situation to Paul?
20. For brevity, I use the phrase "Chloe's report" in the commentary, instead of "Chloe's household's report."

such as Paul, Apollos, and Cephas (Peter). Second, someone within the church was living immorally – that is, cohabiting sexually with his father's wife. The church was proud of it and was not taking any actions against it. Third, there were legal disputes among some within the church and they were taking each other to non-believers for judgment. Fourth, there was idolatrous immorality: Christians were visiting temple prostitutes. Hearing of this dysfunction within the congregation in Corinth, Paul immediately penned his rebuke.

3

1 Corinthians 1:10–31

The Church of South India

In the year of India's independence, 1947, another crucial event happened: the Church of South India (CSI) was born. It occurred on 27 September 1947 at St George's Cathedral in Chennai (formerly Madras), India. Three large groups of churches – the South India United Church (which itself was a union of churches from Congregational, Presbyterian, and Reformed traditions), the southern provinces of the Anglican Church of India-Pakistan-Myanmar-Sri Lanka, and the Methodist Church of South India – came together and formed a united congregation. The original vision was a challenge given by Bishop V. S. Azariah (1874–1945) at a conference held in Tanquebar in 1919. He had challenged the twenty-seven Indian Christian leaders and two western Christian leaders who had gathered there to work towards uniting the churches in India. At the end they signed a declaration called "The Tanquebar Manifesto," which stated, "We believe that the challenge of the present hour in the period of reconstruction after the war, in the gathering together of the nations, and the present critical situation in India itself, calls us to mourn our divisions and to turn to our Lord Jesus Christ to seek in him the unity of the body expressed in the visible church."[1] Many years later Bishop Azariah's vision materialized and CSI was born. Oommen expresses CSI's significance: "For the first time in the history of Christianity, the deep division between the episcopal and non-episcopal churches, created during the Reformation,

---

1. Bengt Sundkler, *The Church of South India: The Movement towards Union 1900–1947* (Edinburgh and Madras [Chennai]: United Society for Christian Literature, 1965), 101.

was healed."[2] One attendee at that memorable service recorded, "I am writing these lines while still under the spell of the most impressive church service I have ever attended in any country. The centuries of church history hold no parallel to the drama of Christian reunion which was enacted here yesterday. In this colorful Indian city I saw consummated, after 28 years of patient, prayerful work, the union of three great Protestant churches to form the new Church of South India."[3] CSI's motto was, and is, "That they all may be one," a reflection of the Lord's prayer: "*So that all may be one*, as you, Father, are in me and I in you, so that they also may be in us, so that the world may believe that you sent me" (John 17:21). Today CSI has twenty-two dioceses and more then five million members, and is the second largest denomination in India after the Catholic Church.[4]

Its goal was never to become a denomination. An early interpreter of the self-understanding of CSI, R. D. Paul, writes,

> The Church of South India does not imagine itself to be a Church which has been brought into existence in order that it may be more Church among the various Churches in the world. The CSI, on the other hand, conceives of itself as being the means of bringing together other Churches, and that when the moment comes when other Churches would also unite, it will dissolve itself in its present form, lose its present identity and will agree to take its place in the bigger and larger united Church which would carry out God's will in the world . . . It is willing to give up its identity and its constitution, if by doing it can bring into being something even more in accordance with Christ's will for His Churches in the world.[5]

---

2. George Oommen, "Challenging Identity and Crossing Borders: Unity in the Church of South India," *Word & World* 25, no. 1 (Winter 2005): 61. For details concerning the Church's birth amid opposition, see Paul Hutchinson, "Christianity in a Free India," *The Christian Century* 63, no. 46 (13 November 1946): 1366–1368.

3. F. M. Potter, "Churches Unite in South India," *The Christian Century* 64, no. 43 (22 October 1947): 1263. For a report on Nigeria's desire to follow India and form a united church, see Frieder Ludwig, "Gandhi's India and Nigeria's Christians: Political and Ecumenical Interactions," *Swedish Missiological Themes* 89, no. 1 (2001): 41–54.

4. For a critical evaluation of the stagnation of the CSI and challenges to updating its programs and outreach, see Max L. Stackhouse, "Tensions Beset Church of South India," *The Christian Century* 104, no. 25 (9–16 September 1987): 743–44. Also, Oommen, "Challenging Identity and Crossing Borders," 60–67.

5. Rajaiah D. Paul, *The First Decade: An Account of the Church of South India* (Madras [Chennai], India: Christian Literature Society, 1958), 9.

With such lofty goals and an amazing beginning, CSI thrived for several decades (1947–1971). Since then, it has faced difficulties that Bishop Stanley J. Samartha addressed at the time of its Jubilee celebration (its fiftieth anniversary) in 1997.[6] First, its role in the emergency imposed by Prime Minister Indira Gandhi that threatened democracy (1975–1977) was "not one to be proud of."[7] It had failed to protect against the abuse of power. Second, in its stress on unity, it had failed to form a "distinctively Indian way of Christian life, thought and practice."[8] It still patterned its services on decades-old styles. Third, it had failed in its evangelism and service to the world. A committee appointed by the Synod itself stated the reason for this failure as follows: "Bishops and presbyters are too busy with administration and property development projects to have any time for evangelism. Committees and councils of the parishes, dioceses and synods spend more time on property and other disputes than evangelism."[9] Other problems are outdated approaches to evangelism, irrelevant methods, and greater emphasis on institutions than on evangelism. When CSI takes up the challenge to correct these difficulties, it will once again return to its original vision and goal and will make an impact worldwide.

The Corinthian church was in a similar situation. It had had a lofty beginning. The apostle Paul had established it (Acts 18:1–8). Apollos from Alexandria in Egypt, an eloquent scholar, had taught them (Acts 18:27 – 19:1). The apostles Peter (Cephas) and Barnabas had visited them (1 Cor 1:12; 3:22; 9:5–6; 15:5). Instead of growing in unity, however, the Corinthians had resorted to a party spirit, saying, "I am of Paul's party," "I am of Apollos' party," or "I am of Cephas's party." Some, with even greater pride, said, "I am of Christ's party." Chloe reported this to Paul. He was grieved and began the epistle addressing this very issue (1:10 – 4:21).

The Need for Proper Focus in Order to Dissolve Divisions

The Corinthians' error was an improper focus: instead of focusing on Christ, they were focusing on spiritual leaders. So Paul challenged them to focus on

---

6. Stanley J. Samartha, "Vision and Reality: Personal Reflections on the Church of South India, 1947–1997," *The Ecumenical Review* 49, no. 4 (October 1997): 483–493.

7. Ibid., 484.

8. Ibid., 486.

9. M. Abel, *The Church of South India after Thirty Years* (Madras [Chennai]: Christian Literature Society, 1978), 19. Also cited in Samartha, "Vision and Reality," 487.

what truly mattered: "the cross of Christ" (1:17) and "him crucified" (2:1–2). Refocusing on the cross of Christ would dissolve their party spirit. Since the Corinthians might not have focused on the cross because of the political implications associated with such a death, Paul brought their attention back to the cross through four sub-arguments.

First, the crucifixion alone demonstrated the power and wisdom of God. Therefore Paul would teach no message other than the crucifixion of Christ (1:10–31). Second, only the Spirit of God can make someone understand the importance of the crucifixion. Neither the wisdom of the world nor the eloquence of messengers like Paul and Apollos can affirm or prove the importance of the cross of Christ to a person (2:1–16). Third, the messengers of the crucifixion were of no significance – they were simply day laborers, farmers in God's field, and builders of God's temple. They were co-workers for God. As such, the Corinthians shouldn't focus on them or take glory in them. Instead, they should focus on God's temple: themselves (3:1–23). Fourth, the messengers also had a challenge: to be faithful to their task and imitate Christ. They too were fellow travelers in the imitation of Christ (4:1–21).

Demonstration of God's Power and Wisdom (1:10–25)

The antidote to schism is to focus on the commonalities. When two opposing groups focus only on their differences, there will be no reconciliation. On the other hand, if they begin their dialogue by focusing on what they have in common, unity can arise. Paul applied this principle to the Corinthians' disunity. He said, "Brothers and sisters,[10] I ask you in the name of Jesus Christ: all of you focus on the 'same thing'" (1 Cor 1:10). The "same thing" he wanted them to focus on was the cross of Christ. When they focused on that, there would no longer be division among them; instead, they would be united "in the same mind and purpose."[11] He knew about the schism among them – each one saying, "I am of Paul," "I am of Apollos," "I am of Cephas," or "I am of Christ" (1 Cor 1:11–12). It was so widespread that every one of them was affected by it. The Corinthian church probably met in someone's house

---

10. The Greek text has "brothers," but in Greek letter composition "brothers" stood for both male and female recipients of the letter. Thus, this commentary uses "brothers and sisters," a pattern followed by the New English Translation (NET).

11. Fee points out Paul's play on words. Paul first uses a word for "division" (*schisma*) that could also mean "tearing" of a cloth or a net (Mark 2:21). Then he uses a word for "unite" (*katartizō*) that was used for "mending or restoring" nets (Mark 1:19) (Fee, *First Epistle to the Corinthians*, 54).

and would have had no more than sixty members. If so, each group might have had around fifteen people (roughly two or three families in each side). Imagine a congregation of sixty members with four different groups fighting within it! That was the case at Corinth, and it was because they had lost their focus on the cross of Christ.

Paul drew their focus back to the cross of Christ, not because it had magical powers but because it stressed that what Christ had done for the Corinthians' salvation could not be partitioned off to his workers, such as Paul or Cephas. So Paul asked, "Is Christ subdivided?" Could the work of Christ be credited to Paul so that some could say, "Paul was crucified for us" or "I was baptized in Paul's name" (1 Cor 1:13)? Absolutely not! The cross, the death of Christ, and the salvation that Christ brought couldn't be credited to anyone else. Christ alone accomplished redemption on the cross. No debate or partisan attitude should diminish his role or work.

The importance of the cross in a socio-political context cannot be ignored either. When India sought freedom, Gandhi came onto the scene armed with his three-pronged weapon: *swadeshiwad* (the doctrine of patriotic self-rule), *ahimsa* (the doctrine of non-violence), and *satyagraha* (the doctrine of the pursuit of truth). The Indian theologian Sumithra writes that these principles were "mostly drawn from Christian resources (in fact, primarily from Jesus' Sermon on the Mount!), [and] were opposed to the use of any kind of physical force. 'Blunt-the-blade-by-the-blood' strategy was morally bound to win: for was it not the strategy of the Cross?"[12] In the same way, Paul wanted the Corinthians to focus on the cross in order to fight the factions within the congregation.

Paul then expressed relief that he had not baptized anyone in the Corinthians congregation so that none could in fact boast in him (1 Cor 1:14–15). The words "baptism" or "to baptize" literally mean "washing" and "to wash." In the time of Christ and Paul, ritual cleansing was a significant part of every religion. The Qumran community – a Jewish group in the time of Christ – for example, had manuals on ritual cleansing. Similarly, washing was a sign of acceptance or a lack thereof (see Luke 7:44), as well as of admiration and respect (see John 12:1–8; 13:1–20) and "association." Therefore, when someone became part of a group, he or she was declared "baptized" under that group's leader (e.g. the Israelites were said to have been "baptized" under

---

12. Sunand Sumithra, *Christian Theologies from an Indian Perspective* (Bangalore, India: Theological Book Trust, 1990), 9.

Moses' leadership, 1 Cor 10:2). Such an association was valid even without the presence of water. In Paul's case, however, he was thankful that he had ritually washed ("baptized") no one so that none could claim association with him. Instead, their association was with Christ. Of course, he had actually baptized a few from Corinth: Crispus, Gaius, and the family of Stephanus (1 Cor 1:14, 16).

Crispus was most likely another name for Sosthenes, Paul's co-author (see "Preliminary Issues"). Gaius might have been Titius Justus;[13] if so, he was a native of Derbe (Acts 20:4). He had a house in Corinth where he had hosted Paul (Acts 18:7), and had been persecuted because of it (Acts 19:29). It seems likely that he also had a house in Ephesus, where he hosted Paul and the church of Ephesus (Rom 16:23). Fee postulates that Gaius "belonged to the class of Roman freedmen who had come to Corinth and had 'made it big' in the commercial enterprises of the city."[14] Stephanus was one among the three who had recently visited Paul (1 Cor 16:17). None of them should boast that Paul had baptized them. Who baptized whom was irrelevant; what mattered was that a person was baptized in the name of the Lord Jesus Christ. So Paul trivialized his ministry of baptism by saying, "I don't remember if I baptized anyone else; besides, Christ did not send me to baptize" (1 Cor 1:16b–17a). Paul didn't have a memory lapse; rather, he purposely ignored whom he had baptized because it wasn't important. The act of baptism was important to the Corinthians – as it should be, since the Lord commanded it (Matt 28:18–20); but baptism wasn't to become a divisive element that caused the church to divide into different parties. What really mattered was that Christ had died for them and they were baptized in his name. The cross and the one crucified on the cross were the focal points, and the Corinthians should unite around them.

Paul then talked about his own commissioning, which was to preach the good news. But he abided by a stipulation: not to preach the gospel "in clever speeches so as to nullify the importance of the cross of Christ" (1 Cor 1:17b). Paul wanted the focus to be on the *cross*. Letting a criminal die on a wooden beam (or "cross") was a cruel form of punishment. The practice originated in the Persian Empire and was practiced in India, Assyria, and Scythia a long time before Rome started using it as a punishment for those who committed

---

13. Fellows, "Renaming in Paul's Churches," 129. Also Bruce, *1 and 2 Corinthians*, 34.
14. Fee, *First Epistle to the Corinthians*, 62.

capital offenses such as treason.[15] Lucius Seneca, the teacher of Emperor Nero, wrote concerning death on a cross, "Can anyone be found who would prefer wasting away in pain, dying limb by limb, or letting out his life drop by drop, rather than expiring once for all? Can any man be found willing to be fastened to the accursed tree, long sickly, already deformed, swelling with ugly weals on shoulders and chest, and drawing the breath of life amid long-drawn-out agony? He would have many excuses for dying even before mounting the cross" (*De Ira* 1.2).[16] Without doubt the Greek and Roman world thought of the death of Christ on the cross as a criminal's death and of boasting in a crucified Christ as foolishness (1 Cor 1:18).[17] The Jews indeed would have thought of it as a cursed death because only those who were under the curse of God were hanged on a tree: "Cursed is anyone who hangs on a tree" (Deut 21:23; Gal 3:13). They thought that Jesus, who had been hanged on a cross, a cursed person, couldn't be the Messiah or Lord. Yet the crucifixion of Christ had an amazing secret: it was where God demonstrated his saving power. Paul eloquently wrote, "The message about the cross is indeed foolishness to those who are perishing, but it is indeed a [demonstration] of God's power to those who are being saved" (1 Cor 1:18).[18] The crucifixion of Christ, a concept that is foolishness to unbelievers, was precisely the message of hope for believers. It was on that cross that God's power to save was demonstrated. Therefore Paul was committed to preaching that message alone and not resorting to clever speeches.

The Greeks loved wisdom and philosophy (the word "philosophy" means "love of wisdom"). In Athens, Epicureans and Stoic philosophers listened intently to Paul (Acts 17:16–34). Luke writes that these Greeks had "no leisure except to speak and hear new philosophies" (Acts 17:21). But when Paul spoke about the resurrection of Jesus Christ from the dead, they mocked him and departed (Acts 17:32). To the Greeks, as much as

---

15. Andrew William Lintott and George Ronald Watson, "Crucifixion," in *Oxford Classical Dictionary* (Oxford: University Press, 1996), 411.

16. For an excellent article on the history and the offense of the cross, see Donald E. Green, "The Folly of the Cross," *The Master's Seminary Journal* 15, no. 1 (Spring 2004): 59–69.

17. Tacitus (AD 56–117) wrote, "Christus, the founder of the name [Christians], had undergone the death penalty in the reign of Tiberius, by sentence of the procurator Pontius Pilate" (*Annals* 15.44), thus authenticating the historicity of the Lord's death on a cross.

18. Both the participles – "those who are perishing" and "those who are being saved" – could be either middle voice (where the subject itself does the action) or passive voice (where the subject receives the action). I have taken the first verbal as middle, meaning "they are perishing by their own actions," and the second as passive, meaning "they are being saved by God," based upon the tenor of the epistle as a whole.

they loved philosophy, proclaiming the death of the Messiah on a cross and his resurrection was foolish. Pliny the Younger, a historian from the first century (AD 61–112), referred to belief in the death of Christ on a cross as a "perverse and extravagant superstition" (*Natural History* 10.96.8). But God wasn't concerned with the wisdom of the world. In fact, he had promised to destroy all human wisdom (1 Cor 1:19–20). Paul was referring to an instance recorded in the days of the prophet Isaiah. The Israelites had exchanged the worship of YHWH God in the ways he had prescribed with their own rituals (Isa 29:13). Because of their arrogance God promised, "I will destroy the wisdom of the wise, and I will nullify the understanding of the experts" (Isa 29:14b). Isaiah went on to say that God would destroy their wisdom by bringing deliverance to them through "an amazing act" which the sages among them would neither anticipate nor understand (Isa 29:14a). The wise would thus become fools. Paul cited Isaiah here to tell the Corinthians that God had yet again outwitted the wise of this world through the death of the Messiah on a cross, a completely mystifying event (1 Cor 1:19). Paul's tone is ironic: "Where are the wise people? Where are the interpreters of the law?[19] Where are the clever people?" (1:20). They were nowhere because God had made them fools (1:20b).

It is ironic that their own wisdom had become a trap for them. Paul wrote, "In God's wisdom, the world did not know God through wisdom" (1 Cor 1:21a). In his wise decree God established that those who searched for him through their own wisdom would not find him. Their wisdom would become their trap. Instead, God was pleased to save those who believed the message of the cross, a message that sounded foolish to the wise (1 Cor 1:21b). The wise, the scribes, and the law-interpreters could not understand the cross as God's "amazing act"; they thought of it as foolishness. However, "foolish" people who put their trust in the crucified Messiah found themselves to be truly wise. Because of this upside-down philosophy, Paul was thrilled to proclaim the cross of Christ alone.

Whereas the Greeks loved wisdom, the Jews sought miraculous signs (1 Cor 1:22). When the Lord was ministering in Jerusalem they demanded a sign from heaven so that they might believe him (Matt 16:1). In their history, signs had always been proof that God was at work. Moses saw a burning bush and knew that it meant something special. Jacob saw a ladder to heaven in

---

19. The Greek word *grammateus* refers to those who interpreted the law and gave guidance for proper observance of it. They often held offices as civil leaders and town clerks (Acts 19:35).

his dream and knew that that place was the house of God, Bethel. Gideon repeatedly asked for signs before he would venture to lead God's people. Similarly, the Jews in Corinth sought signs before they would believe in Jesus Christ.

Contrary to what the Greeks and Jews sought, Paul and the other apostles had one message: "we proclaim Christ as one crucified" (1 Cor 1:23).[20] This was, as mentioned above, a scandalous message to the Jews, since they knew the law, and utterly foolish to the Greeks. Yet "to those who are called – both from Jews and Greeks – Christ is God's power and God's wisdom" (1 Cor 1:24). In other words, those whom God had invited to salvation, regardless of their backgrounds (Jews or Greeks), understood the message about the death of the Messiah on a cross as the revelation of God's power and wisdom. It revealed God's power because, just as he gave life to everything that exists, so he also gave the Lord resurrection (life again from death). This was a wisdom that came from God because natural knowledge and wisdom didn't draw anyone to that conclusion; only those whom God invited to partake in salvation understood it. It was like a coded secret, revealed only to those with the code-breaker. In summary, "what appeared as foolishness on God's part is smarter than any wisdom of people; what appeared as God's weakness is actually much stronger than any person's strength" (1 Cor 1:25). The cross was in no way the foolishness or weakness of God; but only those who were called – from both the Jews and the Gentiles – understood it.

For the Church of South India too, the solution for their present difficulties is a refocus on the crucifixion of Christ.[21] The cross is significant. CSI Bishop A. J. Appasamy wrote:

> According to Christian teaching the cross, awful in its pain and suffering, is the central fact of the Christian life. It is at the foot of the cross that age after age millions of devout men and women have obtained a new bliss. The true penitent Christian has approached the Cross overwhelmed with the burden of his sinfulness. But the cross has made a new man of him. The burden of sin has been taken away, the soul is filled with peace

---

20. The perfect tense reflects the state in which something or someone abides (Stantley E. Porter, *Idioms of the Greek New Testament*, Biblical Languages: Greek, vol. 2 [Sheffield: Sheffiled Academic Press, 1999], 21–22). Christ abides as the crucified one.

21. I have only great admiration for CSI. My parents and sisters are members of CSI. The principle taught in this section – focusing on Christ's cross – applies to every church and to every Christian.

rgiveness and the man has come out a different being to
life's struggles. This is the most vital fact of the Christian
experience.[22]

The significance of the cross doesn't end when a person comes to Christ; it continues throughout the rest of the Christian's life and the rest of the churches' lives. When Christians truly live with the cross as the focus and object of their lives, the world will see a new Christianity and will be drawn to the crucified Christ. E. Stanley Jones, a contemporary of Gandhi, said it well:

> If we present Christianity as a rival to other religions, it will fail. Our position should be: There are many religions. There is but one gospel. We are not setting a religion over against other religions, but a gospel over against human need, which is the same everywhere. The greatest service we can give to anyone in East or West is to introduce him to the moral and spiritual power found in Christ. India needs everything. We humbly offer the best we have. The best we have is Christ.[23]

And we present him as one who was crucified for the sins of the world.

Dalits or Brahmins? (1:26–31)

"To whom does the gospel belong – to the poor or to the rich?" This has been a key question as missions and missionaries strategize to spread the gospel in India. Whereas some believe missions should focus on the urban elite, others believe they should focus on the village poor.

India has an economically diverse population. Geyer writes, "India has always had its wealthy elites. But the tens of millions of Indians who live in the humble huts and shabbiest slums, and the millions more who somehow survive homeless in the streets of cities such as Bombay and Calcutta, add up to one of the world's greatest challenges to humanization."[24] Hurley attributes India's economic diversity to the "cottage industry" model promoted by Gandhi – using the spinning wheel and raising goats (basically, "a program of

---

22. A. J. Appasamy, *As Christ in the Indian Church (A. J. Appasamy Speaks to the Indian Church)* (Chennai, India: Christian Literature Society, 1935), 42.

23. E. Stanley Jones, "Report on the New India," *Christian Century* 64 (1947): 556.

24. Alan Geyer, "The NCC's Rediscovery of India," *The Christian Century* 100, no. 14 (4 May 1983): 420.

'thinking small'") – and to the "Soviet model of centralized planning" model promoted by Nehru. He narrates,

> I visited the Gandhi ashram [in Ahmedabad] and was touched by the simplicity of the Mahatma's austerely furnished room, his few belongings and his *chakra* (spinning wheel). Then I visited the facilities of the Indian Space and Research Organization (ISRO) not many miles away. Boasting a superb technical staff and the latest aerospace components, ISRO is promoting the Satellite Instruction and Television Education (SITE) demonstration whereby, with a satellite loaned by NASA, the Indian government would broadcast to 2,400 rural villages for four hours a day. From the Vedic age to the video age: this short trip of mine dramatizes the contrast between the two Indias – as well as the frailty of any meaningful democratic solution.[25]

Hurley calls these two Indias the "westernized progressive India" and a "preindustrial India with archaic rites and sub-cultures."

Social organizations also select either of these groups to work with. Organizations such as the Society of Catholic Medical Mission Sisters (SCMM) primarily work with the poor and the marginalized.[26] The sisters live among the poor in slums and villages and work for their justice, freedom, and equality. On the other hand, young doctors who volunteer to work in villages while in school choose to work in cities soon after their graduation.[27]

The same is true of Christian missions. Some passionately promote work among the poor, like the Dalits; others promote work among the elite Brahmins. Much more significant than the economic difference, however, is an inherent religious difference between these groups. The Dalits worship meat-eating gods whereas the Brahmins do not. Rosario writes, "Being associated with the meat-eating gods, the Dalits who offer animal sacrifices are also considered polluting. In Hinduism, the gods worshipped by the twice-born castes are pure and vegetarian gods, while the gods worshipped by Dalits who accept animal

---

25. Neil P. Hurley, "The Two Faces of India," *Christian Century* 92, no. 33 (15 October 1975): 906.

26. Marie Tobin, "Working with the Poor and Marginalized in India: The Process and Choices," *International Review of Mission* 76, no. 304 (October 1987): 521–522.

27. Sidney Lens, "A Letter from India," *Christian Century* 98, no. 34 (28 October 1981): 1086.

sacrifices are regarded as inferior gods."[28] Because of this inherit impurity "the Dalits are required to maintain, according to Manusmriti [a religious text of the Hindus], a distance of 33 feet from Vaisyas [agriculturalists and cattle-raisers], 66 feet from Kshatriyas [ruling and military elite] and 99 feet from Brahmins. In daily life, Dalits are denied access to public facilities, to wall-schools [schools that were in walled compounds], roads, and also to places of public worship."[29] Because of such caste oppression, the Dalits are quick to accept the gospel that sees no caste segregation. There have been several revivals among them, such that organizations are quick to flock to them.[30] In contrast, however, the Brahmins are slow to accept the gospel, especially since the Dalits are members of the church. Christian organizations are also slow to reach out to them. Richard observes, "Rarely have Christian workers, both missionary and Indian, identified clearly the special need for ministry targeted at high caste Hindus."[31] He attributes such neglect to "the anti-caste egalitarian ideal upheld by most Western missionaries." The outcome is that very few high-caste people come to Christianity.

The gospel sees no such boundaries. It is for everyone who is willing to accept it, whether rich or poor, high caste or low caste, slave or free. The Corinthians were a test case. Paul wrote, "Look at yourselves, who are called by God, brothers and sisters: not many are wise according to human standards, not many are able-bodied, and not many are of noble birth" (1 Cor 1:26). His phrase "not many" implies that some were wise, some were able-bodied, and some were of noble birth. Blomberg writes, "More of the Corinthians might have been tolerably well off than in many of the early churches."[32] But "not many" also implies that the elite and rich were few; most would have been poor and lowly. The gospel belonged to both groups. Status was not the criterion for admission into God's kingdom; God's election was. So Paul wrote, "God chose the fools in order to shame the wise; God chose the weak in order to shame the strong; and God chose the despised and non-nobility of this world – those who have no influence at all in society, to destroy those who have" (1 Cor 1:27–28). Paul wasn't calling the Corinthian

---

28. Jerry Rosario, "Mission from the Perspective of Dalits: Some of Its Concerns and Options," *Mission Studies* 8, no. 1–2 (1996): 282.

29. Ibid.

30. For a history of Dalit Christians, see John C. B. Webster, *The Dalit Christians: A History*, Contextual Theological Education, vol. 4 (Delhi, India: ISPCK, 1992).

31. H. L. Richard, "A Survey of Protestant Evangelistic Efforts among High Caste Hindus in the Twentieth Century," *Missiology: An International Review* 25, no. 4 (October 1997): 419.

32. Blomberg, *1 Corinthians*, 57.

Christians "fools"; he was saying that the world thought of them as fools for believing in a crucified Messiah, but actually they were wise and had become the instruments through whom God would shame the wise of the world (cf. 1 Cor 1:18–25). Also, Paul chose the terms "wise" and "strong" because earlier he had said that the cross of Christ was the demonstration of God's "wisdom" and "power" (1:24).[33] In other words, the world looks at Christians and thinks, "They are stupid and weak for believing in Christ," but God looks at the cross and says, "That's my demonstration of wisdom and power." Those whom God called to salvation look at the cross and say, "There we see God's wisdom and power," and they put their trust in it. In reality, then, it is the unbelieving people who mock the cross who are fools, ignoble, and weak.

God turned the world upside down with the purpose "that no one may boast before God" (1 Cor 1:29). Earlier Paul had said that God, in his wisdom, prevented the wise from understanding his truth through their wisdom (1 Cor 1:21). Now Paul says that God selected the most inappropriate candidates for his kingdom so that they might know it was all of God – "out of him you are in Christ Jesus" (1 Cor 1:30a). God had placed the Corinthian Christians *in* Christ Jesus, and it was that association that made them wise, strong, and noble. That was because Christ Jesus "has become to us the 'wisdom from God,' 'the righteousness,' 'the holiness,' and 'the redemption'" (1:30b). In other words, Christians look at Jesus and say, "He is the manifestation of God's wisdom"; "he is the revelation of God's righteousness"; "he is the exemplification of God's holiness"; "in him is God's redemption."[34] Such acknowledgements from Christians make them wise, strong, and noble in the sight of God.

In addition, such boasting is based on what truly matters: "Just as it is written, 'The one who boasts, let him or her boast in the Lord'" (1 Cor 1:31). Paul was quoting a line from the prophet Jeremiah's writings.[35] In his day, the

---

33. Fee, *First Epistle to the Corinthians*, 80.

34. Scholars debate whether Christians are *made* righteous or only *declared* righteous. Similarly, they also debate if this is talking about the Christians' state or the Lord's state. For discussions, see J. V. Fesko, "N. T. Wright on Imputation," *Reformed Theological Review* 66, no. 1 (April 2007): 2–22. Mark A. Garcia, "Imputation and the Christology of Union with Christ: Calvin, Osiander, and the Contemporary Quest for a Reformed Model," *Westminster Theological Journal* 68, no. 2 (Fall 2006): 219–251. I have interchanged "wisdom" and "to us" in the Greek word order so that the sentence reads something like, "To us, he has become wisdom from God [etc.]," meaning, "we understand him as 'God's wisdom'" (see 1 Cor 1:18–25).

35. For a detailed study of Paul's use of Jeremiah, see Gail R. O'Day, "Jeremiah 9:22–23 and 1 Corinthians 1:26–31: A Study in Intertextuality," *Journal of Biblical Literature* 109, no. 2 (1990): 259–267.

Israelites had wandered away from YHWH God and had started worshipping Baal (Jer 9:14), so YHWH promised judgment: "The dead bodies of these people will lie scattered everywhere like manure scattered on a field" (Jer 9:22). In the midst of destruction, however, there was an escape route: "Let not the wise boast in his or her wisdom, let not the strong boast in his or her strength, and let not the rich boast in his or her wealth. Instead, the one who boasts, let him or her boast in this knowledge and understanding: 'I am the Lord who shows mercy and judgment and righteousness upon the earth'" (Jer 9:22–23, LXX). The response to destruction was humble submission to and exaltation of YHWH, thus finding one's solace, comfort, and strength in YHWH. Similarly, the Corinthians' true boast was to rest in the Lord. Paul has creatively used the title "Lord" (*kurios*) here to refer to Jesus. In the Hebrew text of Jeremiah the speaker is YHWH God. The Septuagint translators used *kurios* ("Lord") for YHWH. By citing the Septuagint version, Paul was equating Jesus the Lord (*kurios*) with YHWH (LORD) God.

So to go back to our question: to whom does the gospel belong – to the poor or the rich, to the Dalits or the Brahmins? The gospel belongs to anyone who is willing to set aside his or her worldly wisdom and seek God's true wisdom, Jesus Christ. It belongs to anyone who is willing to set aside his or her nobility and influence and truly seek God's strength, Jesus Christ. As Fee comments, "The ground is level at the foot of the cross; not a single thing that any of us possesses will advantage him/her before the living God – not brilliance, 'clout,' achievement, money, or prestige."[36]

---

36. Fee, *First Epistle to the Corinthians*, 84.

4

1 Corinthians 2

Paul's Commitment (2:1–5)

Paul was committed to spreading the gospel without any of his own eloquence or wisdom being evident. So in the next few verses (2:1–5) he recollects his first visit to the Corinthians and how he was careful to hide his wisdom so that God's Spirit and power would impact them.

Paul was a Jew and thus naturally spoke Hebrew (Phil 3:5). However, he grew up in a Greek culture and also spoke Greek eloquently (Acts 21:37; 22:2; 26:14). He frequently quoted from the Hebrew Old Testament and from its Greek translation, the Septuagint. He also quoted secular Greek writers such as Epimenides of Crete, Aratus, and Menander (e.g. Acts 17:28a, 28b; 1 Cor 15:33, respectively), implying that he was educated in classical Greek. In addition, he had studied under the prominent Jewish scholar Gamaliel, who would have instilled in him a love for the study of the Hebrew language and the law. Paul's oratory skills amazed Epicurean and Stoic philosophers in Athens (Acts 17:18–20). His letters, such as Romans and Galatians, strictly followed classical guidelines for letter composition and logic.[1] So Paul could easily have impressed the Corinthians when he met them with his eloquence, wisdom, and logic. Yet he chose not to: "Brothers and sisters, when I came to you, I came proclaiming the mystery[2] of God, not in eloquent arguments nor

---

1. Blomberg writes, "Rhetorical criticism is increasingly demonstrating how well-trained in literary artistry Paul was" (Blomberg, *1 Corinthians*, 58).

2. The existing Greek texts have two different words here: whereas some say "testimony" (*marturion*), others say "mystery" (*musterion*). Such a change could have happened accidentally because of their similarity or the use of "testimony" earlier on (1 Cor 1:6). On the other hand, the change could have been purposeful: a scribe who knew that Paul had used "testimony" earlier and saw "mystery" here may have resorted to the familiar "testimony." Apart from this verse, Paul used "testimony" (*marturion*) only once (1 Cor 1:6), but he used

in wise speeches because I had decided to make known to you nothing except Jesus Christ and him as one who is crucified" (1 Cor 2:1–2). The mystery was about Jesus Christ, the crucified one who was truly Lord. This message would have sounded foolish to them at first, yet Paul chose to go to them with only that message.

He reiterated his resolve: "Showing weakness and fear, in great trepidation, I came to you so that my word and my proclamation might not be in persuasive words" (1 Cor 2:3–4a). On the surface, Paul's words suggest that he was physically weak and in a state of alarm when he visited them. There is some truth to this: just before he came to Corinth the first time, he had been violently cast out of Thessalonica and Berea by a Jewish mob and he was alone without traveling companions when he was mocked in Athens. In Corinth he knew no one; two tentmakers (Aquila and Priscilla) sheltered him because he shared in their tentmaking work – not honorable labor for a rabbinic Jew since tentmaking with leather involved touching dead animals. So it is possible that Paul went there in physical weakness, fear, and trepidation.[3] Within the context, however, Paul is not talking about his weakness but his caution. The word "weak" can have a figurative meaning of someone's *moral* (Rom 6:19) or *spiritual* (Rom 8:26) inability or unwillingness. Also, the phrase "fear and trembling" can mean "cautious behavior" (2 Cor 7:15; Eph 6:5; Phil 2:12). Paul thus most likely referred to his own constraint and resolve here: he cautiously made sure that they didn't hear the message and proclamation through his eloquence, wisdom, or persuasive words.[4]

Instead, he wanted them to understand the mystery of God "by the *showing forth* [or *proof*] of the Spirit and power" (1 Cor 2:5). Paul was referring to the Holy Spirit, who alone could convince the Corinthians of the truth of the crucified Messiah, a topic he would speak about next (2:6–16).

"mystery" (*musterion*) five other times: 1 Cor 2:7; 4:1; 13:2; 13:2; 15:51, without any variant. So his frequent usage of "mystery" could also have caused a scribe to change "testimony" here to "mystery." When closely examined, 1 Cor 2:7 clearly speaks of a "mystery" because the next words say "which is revealed." In 1 Cor 13:2 and 1 Cor 14:2 Paul speaks of the special gifts of knowing and speaking mysteries. In 1 Cor 15:51 he speaks of resurrection in a way that the Corinthians hadn't yet understood, as a mystery to them. In 1 Cor 4:1 he refers of himself as a steward of God's mystery. Thus it is difficult to be dogmatic about the original. Some scholars prefer "mystery" (see Bruce M. Metzger, *A Textual Commentary on the Greek New Testament: A Companion Volume to the United Bible Societies' Greek New Testament*, 2nd ed. [Stuttgart: Deutsche Bibelgesellschaft; New York: United Bible Societies, 1994], 480), whereas others prefer "testimony" (English Standard Version). In a way the mystery – that the crucified Jesus is Lord – is also the testimony. So their interchange doesn't make a vast difference in meaning.

3. So argues Fee, *First Epistle to the Corinthians*, 93. Also Blomberg, *1 Corinthians*, 55.

4. For this alternative reading, see Barrett, *A Commentary*, 64.

Paul was cautious to speak to them without eloquence or human wisdom since he didn't want to find himself among the wise whose wisdom God would destroy (1:19–21), and he didn't want their faith to be based on human persuasive words. Instead, he wanted the Corinthians to believe the gospel message through the power of the Holy Spirit (2:5).

Soul-Person versus Spirit-Person (2:6–16)

Hinduism is diverse, and no two groups within Hinduism have either the same texts or the same beliefs.[5] Within Vedanta – a commonly accepted tradition – Hinduism begins by differentiating between body and spirit.[6] The spirit (or the individual self or soul, *atman*) is the reality while the body is temporal and made up of matter (*prakriti*). The eternal self (spirit) enters a material body at conception.[7] The moment an eternal soul unites with a material body, it is entrapped by *maya* (illusion), which in turn urges one to lust, greed, anger, and other vices, resulting in *samsara* – the cycle of repeated birth and death. The law of karma (the universal law of action and reaction), the eternity of time, and three *gunas* (material qualities) further govern one's fate and the cycle of repeated birth and death. A person has no control over karma, time, or *gunas*, resulting in one moving throughout the creation, sometimes going to higher planes, sometimes moving in human society, and sometimes entering a lower species of animals.[8]

The goal of most Hindus, therefore, is to attain *moksha* – liberation from this perpetual cycle of birth, death, and rebirth. (In Buddhism, *moksha* is called *nirvana*.)[9] One attains *moksha* or *nirvana* by "re-identification" with the

---

5. For a detailed study, see Rajaram, ed. *Facets of Indian Culture*, 15–25. To trace its changes through time see R. S. Lemuel, "Salvation According to Hinduism," *Direction* 23, no. 1 (Spring 1994): 22–26. Also see Norman E. Thomas, "Liberation for Life: A Hindu Liberation Philosophy," *Missiology* 16, no. 2 (April 1988): 149–162. For ordinary Hindu's lack of interest in thinking in philosophical terms but rather living Hinduism culturally, see K. Sivaraman, "Meaning of Moksha in Contemporary Hindu Thought and Life," *Ecumenical Review* 25, no. 2 (April 1973): 148–157.

6. For a study of Vedanta philosophy, see Asoke Basu, "Advaita Vedanta and Ethics," *Religion East & West* 4, (June 2004): 91–105.

7. Sri Sankaracharya, for example, says, "Brahman alone is real, the universe is unreal and the individual soul is no other than the Universal Soul" (quoted in Basu, "Advaita Vedanta and Ethics," 91).

8. For a study of the laws of *karma* in Buddhism see Damien Keown, "Karma, Character, and Consequentialism," *Journal of Religious Ethics* 24, no. 2 (Fall 1996): 329–350.

9. Hoyu Ishida, "Nietzhe and Samsāra: Suffering and Joy in the Eternal Recurrence," *Pure Land (Berkeley, CA)* 15, (December 1998): 130.

eternal *Brahman* (the supreme). There are different paths to attain *moksha*, that is, union with the supreme. The best way possible is a strict adherence to universal principles through the practice of one's *dharma* (ordained duty) as revealed through authorized holy books and explained by *gurus* (spiritual mentors). One can understand, then, why it is so important for an untouchable who has been stuck with the job of cleaning up human feces to remain with that task so that he or she might attain *moksha* or *nirvana*.

Christianity is uniquely different from Hinduism in that the body of a person is not considered to be evil, since God created Adam just as a potter creates a piece of pottery with his or her own hands (Gen 2:7; Ps 139:14). The body has inclinations to do evil but in itself it is not evil. The New Testament affirms that even the Lord Jesus had human *flesh* and a *body* while on earth (John 1:14; Rom 5:10; Phil 2:5–11; Col 1:15–20). Even his resurrection was *bodily* and *in the flesh* (Luke 24:36–43; John 20:24–29).[10] Similarly, God created not only the believer's present body (Ps 139:14) but also his or her future resurrected and glorified physical body (1 Cor 15:42–44).

Since all people are created in this way with physical bodies by God, what uniquely differentiates a Christian from a non-Christian is the Christian's oneness with the Spirit of God, the Holy Spirit. Someone who is devoid of the Holy Spirit is a mere "soul-person" (*pseuchikos*, 1 Cor 2:14), and all humanity has existed in this state since creation (Gen 2:7). The one who has the Holy Spirit is a "Spirit-person" (*pneumatikos*, 1 Cor 2:15). Those who have the Spirit (that is, *the pneumatikos*) alone understand the truths taught by the Holy Spirit (1 Cor 2:11–16).

Paul refers to such Spirit (*pneumatikos*)-people as "mature" (*teleios*), meaning that they have attained their completion or maturity in Christ.[11] To them, Paul's teachings were wise, whereas the rest of the world considered them foolishness or scandalous. So Paul writes, "We do indeed speak *wisdom* to the mature, a wisdom not of the rulers of this world which is perishing" (1 Cor 2:6). Who were these rulers? Scholars have proposed three options:

---

10. For a profound and clear understanding of Jesus' bodily resurrection, see N. T. Wright, *The Resurrection and the Son of God*, Christian Origins and the Question of God, vol. 3 (Minneapolis, MN: Fortress Press, 2003).

11. Some scholars have understood Paul's use of the adjective *teleios* mystically. Baird, for example, argues that *teleios* means to have "an esoteric kind of knowledge . . . [they are] an elite inner circle of converts" (William Baird, "Among the Mature: The Idea of Wisdom in 1 Corinthians 2:6," *Interpretation* 13, no. 4 [1959]: 425). But Paul uses the noun *telos* and the adjective *teleios* as contrasts to "part" (1 Cor 13:1), "children" (1 Cor 14:20), and "those who did not comprehend the cross" (1 Cor 2:6). Unlike the rulers of the world, people who understand the significance of the cross are the *completed* ones.

demonic powers (Conzelmann, Bultmann), earthly rulers who were under demonic influence (Cullmann, Bruce, Fee), or a combination of both demonic powers and political rulers (Blomberg).[12] In the historical context, rulers like the priests, Sanhedrin (Jewish court), high priests, and Pharisees did not understand the significance of the death of a Messiah on the cross. In addition, their rule – centered on the temple – ceased when the temple was destroyed in AD 70. Paul's phrase "the rulers of this world *which is perishing*" could be an allusion to the imminent destruction of the temple and the sacrificial system (see Heb 8:13; 1 Cor 2:8) instead of a final destruction.[13] If so, Paul was referring to the Jewish leaders who, without understanding the significance of the cross, handed Jesus over to die on a cross (John 11:49–51).[14]

Paul then affirmed the "hiddenness" of this wisdom: "But we speak the wisdom of God in a mystery which is hidden, which God had foreordained for this world and for our glory" (1 Cor 2:7). The real reason the rulers did not understand it was because God had hidden it until it was explained by him through his apostles such as Peter, John, and Paul. When Paul said it was a "mystery," he didn't mean some form of "higher wisdom" only the elite would understand (Baird) or "secret wisdom" only a few understood (NIV). Instead, Paul meant a wisdom that is incomprehensible until God's Spirit enables one to understand it (e.g. 1 Cor 2:1, 7; 4:1). God had planned this and had revealed the mystery – all for the glory of the Corinthians.

The rulers' lack of knowledge actually promoted God's plan: if they had understood the mystery hidden in the crucified Messiah, they would not have crucified this glorious Lord (1 Cor 2:8).[15] Not understanding the wisdom of a crucified Messiah, they crucified him and thus promoted God's plan. Paul then cited the prophet Isaiah, who looked back at the exodus with awe (Isa 64:3–4). The leaders in Egypt didn't understand that God was at work in the Israelites' exodus. "The eye didn't see and the ear didn't hear; and the heart of man didn't comprehend what the Lord had prepared for those who love him" (1 Cor 2:9). Similarly, the death of the Messiah on a cross was incomprehensible to the rulers of the world; so they crucified him.

---

12. For a comprehensive study, see Gene Miller, "Apcontwn Tou Aiwnou Toutou: A New Look at 1 Corinthians 2:6–8," *Journal of Biblical Literature* 91, no. 4 (1972): 522–528.

13. Cf. Blomberg, *1 Corinthians*, 63.

14. "Given the evidence of v. 8, the 'rulers' here at least include those responsible for the crucifixion" (Fee, *First Epistle to the Corinthians*, 104).

15. The Greek conditional statement (second class) implies that they really didn't understand. Also, the phrase "Lord of glory" is better translated "glorious Lord" (an attributive genitive).

However, to the "Spirit-people" (those who have the Spirit of God living in them) God had revealed this mystery of the importance of the cross (1 Cor 2:10a). God had done it through "the Spirit who searches all things, including the deep things of God" (1 Cor 2:10b). Just as someone's *spirit* alone understands his or her innermost thoughts, so God's Spirit alone truly knows and understands the depth of God's wisdom (1 Cor 2:11).[16] The Holy Spirit of God had revealed this mystery of the importance of the cross to the Corinthian believers. Here again, Paul revealed something new about Christians: "we did not receive the spirit of the world but the Spirit who is from God" (1 Cor 2:12a). Whereas other people were guided by the world, Christians were guided by God's Spirit. That is why the Christians were able to know "the things of God which he graced upon" them (1 Cor 2:12b). The unique aspect of the Christians in Corinth was that they understood God's gracious provisions such as salvation through the crucified Messiah because they were under the guidance of the Holy Spirit. Paul's message, therefore, was not a human wisdom that ordinary people could understand; that was why they thought of it as foolishness and blasphemous. Christians, however, understood it as God's wisdom because the Holy Spirit explained it thus to them. Therefore, Paul concluded, "Whatever we speak, we do not speak in human teachings or wise words but in Spirit-teachings to the spirit-people" (1 Cor 2:13).

Paul then used his term for people who do not have the Spirit of God: "soul-people" (*pseuchikos*). Paul was here drawing from the creation account in Genesis, where God created male and female in the image of God, breathed life into them, and they became *living souls* (Gen 2:7, 21–23). As mentioned above, all human beings are "soul-people" (*living souls*); they have souls, but are devoid of the Spirit of God. They are therefore unable to receive the Spirit of God's teachings because those teachings are for those who have the Spirit, the Spirit-people (1 Cor 2:14). The Spirit-person understands the Spirit's teachings; but those without the Spirit (soul-people) are not able to understand the Spirit-people (1 Cor 2:15).[17]

Paul found the teachings of the Spirit of God so far beyond our understanding and so amazing that he cried out using the prophet Isaiah's words, "Who knows the mind of God? Who comprehends him?" (1 Cor 2:16a; Isa 40:13). Isaiah too saw something incredible – two sides of YHWH

---

16. Paul uses "spirit" and "mind" interchangeably in this passage (see 2:11 and 2:16).

17. It is possible to read this verse slightly differently: those without the Spirit cannot scrutinize the Spirit-people.

God. On the one hand, he was like a shepherd who carefully tended his flock, gathered the lambs within his arms, carried them close to his heart, and led the ewes behind him (Isa 40:11). On the other hand, he measured the waters in the hollow of his hands, marked off the heavens with the span of his hands, and weighed the mountains in a balance and the hills in scales (Isa 40:12). Seeing both these delicate and awesome sides of God, Isaiah cried out, "Who can comprehend the mind [wisdom] of YHWH God, and who can give him counsel?" (Isa 40:13). Similarly, who would have thought of turning the cursed death of a man on a cross into victory? Only God would! And only those who have the Spirit of God understand this mindset and plan of God. Therefore, Paul concluded, "But we have the mind of Christ" (1 Cor 2:16b), meaning that the apostles had the right understanding of who Christ was because they had the Holy Spirit explaining these mysteries to them. This was why Paul didn't rely on his own wisdom or eloquence when he preached the gospel to the Corinthians; instead, he relied on the Spirit and the Spirit's power to prove to the Corinthian Christians the message of the cross.

Thus, unlike Vedantic Hinduism, Christianity teaches that God created the body and made the people soul-people (*living beings*). Although our present bodies are corrupted by sin, God will redeem both, and Christians will be resurrected in glorified bodies of flesh (more on this in 1 Cor 15). What is unique to Christianity is that it separates the soul-people under the world's influence (humanity in general) from the soul-people with the Spirit of God's influence (Christians). Whereas all people are soul-people, only Christians are Spirit-people. They alone can understand God's mystery in Christ: they alone understand a crucified Messiah to be their Lord, because the Spirit of God explains this truth to them.

5

---

1 Corinthians 3

The Stages of a Person's Life (3:1–4)

Shakespeare divided a person's life into seven stages:

> At first the infant,
> Mewling and puking in the nurse's arms.
> And then the whining school-boy, with his satchel
> And shining morning face, creeping like snail
> Unwillingly to school. And then the lover,
> Sighing like furnace, with a woeful ballad
> Made to his mistress' eyebrow. Then a soldier,
> Full of strange oaths and bearded like the pard,
> Jealous in honour, sudden and quick in quarrel,
> Seeking the bubble reputation
> Even in the cannon's mouth. And then the justice,
> In fair round belly with good capon lined,
> With eyes severe and beard of formal cut,
> Full of wise saws and modern instances;
> And so he plays his part. The sixth age shifts
> Into the lean and slipper'd pantaloon,
> With spectacles on nose and pouch on side,
> His youthful hose, well saved, a world too wide
> For his shrunk shank; and his big manly voice,
> Turning again toward childish treble, pipes
> And whistles in his sound. Last scene of all,
> That ends this strange eventful history,

Is second childishness and mere oblivion,

Sans teeth, sans eyes, sans taste, sans everything.[1]

Indian philosophy divides a person's life into four stages. The first is called the student stage (*Brahmacharya*). This is the stage from birth until the age of twenty-five. It is the period of informal and formal education. The second is the married stage (*Grihastha*). This stage begins, as one would imagine, when a person gets married and undertakes the responsibility of raising a family. This is also when he or she starts to earn a living (this explains why Indian young men do not work until they finish college studies and get married). Hinduism encourages a person in this stage to pursue wealth[2] and sexual pleasure. This stage should end around the age of fifty but in reality most Hindus stay in this stage. The third is hermit stage (*Vanaprastha*). A person leaves home, goes to live in seclusion in a forest, and devotes his or her time to prayer. A hermit is allowed to take a spouse but must have no contact with the rest of his or her family. The fourth is the wandering recluse stage (*Sannyasa*). A person in this stage is totally devoted to God. He or she must renounce all desires, fears, hopes, responsibilities, and duties.[3] His or her sole concern is to attain *moksha* – oneness with the divine and release from the birth-death cycle. He or she dies alone.[4] Indians rarely pursue the third and fourth stages of life.

Unlike the Shakespearean and Indian culture life stages, Paul's division of people was into three types: the soul-person, the Spirit-person, and fleshy/fleshly-person. As explained earlier, with the first type – that of the "soul-person" (Greek *pseuchikos*, 1 Cor 2:14) – Paul was drawing from the creation

---

1. *As You Like It*, Act 2, Scene 7, Jaques's Speech. Trudinger skillfully shows how Shakespeare's stages could be used in explaining biblical truths in schools (L. Paul Trudinger, "Shakespeare's 'Ages of Man' and the Development of the Early Church," *Perspectives in Religious Studies* 11, no. 2 [Summer 1984]: 133–138). Similarly, Delasanta shows how Paul influenced Chaucer, Shakespeare, Swift, and Dostoevsky (Rodney Delasanta, "Putting Off the Old Man and Putting on the New: Ephesians 4:22–24 in Chaucer, Shakespeare, Swift, and Dostoevsky," *Christianity and Literature* 51, no. 3 [Spring 2002]: 339–362).

2. Ligela Lugil, "Meaning without Words: The Contrast between *Artha* and *Ruta* in the *Mahayana Sutras*," *Buddhist Studies Review* 27, no. 2 (2010): 139 n. 1.

3. Lise F. Vail, "'Unlike a Fool, He Is Not Defiled': Ascetic Purity and Ethics in the *Samnyasa Upanisads*," *Journal of Religious Ethics* 30, no. 3 (Fall 2002): 375.

4. For a study on women *sannyasa* and the cessation of caste in this stage within the Bengali community, see Jeanne Openshaw, "Home or Ashram? The Caste Vaishnavas of Bengal," *Fieldwork in Religion* 2, no. 1 (April 2006): 65–82. For a study of two female *sannyasa*, see Antoinette DeNapoli, "'Real Sadhus Sing to God': The Religious Capital of Devotion and Domesticity in the Leadership of Female Renouncers in Rajasthan," *Journal of Feminist Studies in Religion* 29, no. 1 (Spring 2013): 117–133.

account when Adam and Eve were created in God's image, God breathed life into them, and they became *living souls* or soul-persons (Gen 2:7). Every human is a living soul or *pseuchikos*. Translations such as "natural man/person" (ESV, HCSB) capture the essence of Paul's usage.

The second type is "a spirit-person influenced by the world" or a "Spirit-person influenced by the Spirit of God" (*pneumatikos*). The soul-person is unable to understand the significance of the cross, but the Spirit-person is able to understand it because the Spirit of God explains this mystery to him or her. Although every human has a spirit, Paul reserved the term Spirit-person, *pneumatikos*, for those influenced or indwelt by the Holy Spirit.

The third (and possibly fourth) type is "fleshy" (*sarkinos*) or "fleshly" (*sarkikos*). Both these words mean that a person is made up of flesh, but this is especially true of *sarkikos*. Paul, for example, wrote to the Romans, "If the nations have shared in the spiritual wealth that belonged to the Israelites, now they are obliged to minister to the Israelites with their fleshly or material blessings" (Rom 15:27). Later in 1 Corinthians Paul writes, "If we sow spiritual blessings among you, are we being demanding when we seek fleshly or material blessings from you?" (1 Cor 9:11). In these examples, *fleshly* (*sarkikos*, that is, material) blessings are contrasted with spiritual blessings. *Sarkinos*, in certain places, has a slightly stronger emphasis on one's thoughts, decisions, and actions being driven by flesh or the needs of the flesh. For example, Paul writes to the Romans, "The law is Spirit-driven but I am flesh-driven, resulting in me being sold to slavery to sin" (Rom 7:14).[5] These nuances are so minute that not only did ancient scribes use these words interchangeably, but also contemporary scholars understand them differently. Fee, for example, takes the opposite view to what is said above: "*Sarkinoi* ["fleshy"] emphasizes especially their humanness and the physical side of their existence as over against the spiritual. The . . . *sarkikoi* ["fleshly"] . . . [is] a word with clear ethical overtones of living from the perspective of the present age, therefore out of one's sinfulness."[6] It is therefore best to treat these words as synonyms. In basic terms both *fleshy* (*sarkikos*) and *fleshly* (*sarkinos*) refer to the material body that consists of skin, bones, blood, and body organs.

---

5. "In Rom 7:14 Paul uses the term to describe his pre-Christian state, *sarkikós*, in Rom 15:27 and 1 Cor 9:11 denotes external things in a neutral sense. It is parallel to *sárkinos* in 1 Cor 3:1ff., and in 2 Cor 10:4 it denotes carnal power as distinct from divine" (*TDNT* [*Abridged*], s.v. "σάρξ σαρκικός σάρκινος," 1006).

6. Fee, *First Epistle to the Corinthians*, 124. Similarly, Toussaint distinguishes between spiritual and carnal Christians (Stanley D. Toussaint, "The Spiritual Man," *Bibliotheca Sacra* 125, no. 498 (April 1968): 139–146).

They are mostly neutral terms, but sometimes these fleshy/fleshly people are easily driven by the desires of the flesh (1 Cor 3:3; Gal 5:24) or influenced by false teachers (2 Cor 3:3). They can yield to sin (1 Pet 2:11) and are prone to death (Heb 7:16). They are not necessarily driven by sexual sins but are simply drawn to the pleasures of the flesh. Barrett writes, "Fleshly men are not those who habitually indulge in sexual sins, but those (cf. the *natural man* of ii.14) whose existence is not determined by God but by consideration internal to themselves, or internal at least to humanity as distinct from God."[7] Essentially, all humanity is included in this category.

The Corinthians were more than mere soul-people because they were under the influence of the Holy Spirit (1 Cor 2:13–15). They should have been Spirit-people, but Paul was unable to speak to them as such because in their strife and jealousy they had resorted to the behavior of fleshy/fleshly-people; they walked as "ordinary people" (1 Cor 3:1, 3). They should have been *extraordinary* people, people under the guidance of the Holy Spirit; instead, they had returned to their infancy. When Paul first saw them they were infants and he fed them milk. Even now he couldn't feed them meat, as he wanted to do, because in their return to infancy they had become unable to digest meat (1 Cor 3:2).

Jewish writers often used this analogy of feeding people milk or meat for "progression in growth of understanding." Philo, an Alexandrian Jew, wrote, "But since milk is the food of infants, but cakes made of wheat are the food of full-grown men, so also the soul must have a milk-like nourishment in its age of childhood, namely, the elementary instruction of encyclical science. But the perfect food which is fit for men consists of explanations dictated by prudence, temperance, and every virtue" (*On Husbandry* 9; also Heb 5:11–13). The Corinthians were still Christians,[8] but they had not moved on to maturity, as evidenced by their fighting. Paul wouldn't have needed to write the first four chapters on spiritual leaders if the Corinthians had not fought over them. Similarly, he wouldn't have written chapters 5 and 6 on sexual immorality within the church if they had moved on to maturity. Therefore, the first six chapters are "milk" for them (basic elementary teachings that needed to be repeated because of their childhood), while the next ten chapters are "meat" – solid teachings on marriage, singleness, spiritual gifts, the Lord's Supper, the resurrection, and so on.

---

7. C. K. Barrett, *The First Epistle to the Corinthians*, ed. Henry Chadwick, Black's New Testament Commentary Series, vol. 47 (Peabody, MA: Hendrickson, 1968), 80.

8. Kistemaker, *Exposition of the First Epistle to the Corinthians*, 100.

Christians are exhorted to live as Spirit-guided people, not as mere fleshy/fleshly- or soul-people. Our actions and characters show whether we have moved on to Spirit-guided life (i.e. adulthood) or we are still in our infancy, our fleshy/fleshly life.

Gurus and God's Workers (3:5–11; 4:1, 15)

A *guru*, from the Sanskrit, refers to "a dispeller of ignorance" (from *gu* for "ignorance" and *ru* for "dispeller").[9] A *guru* is more than a spiritual instructor. Mlecko writes, "If the word 'guru' means many things, it is because the guru is many things. He is an entity which in Western culture has no exact counterpart. For the guru is a teacher, counselor, father-image, mature ideal, hero, source of strength, even divinity integrated into one personality."[10] For this reason, *gurus* are often revered and worshipped.

The Corinthians also fell pray to such a temptation. They were boasting over human spiritual leaders, taking sides with Paul, Peter, or Apollos. But Paul didn't accept such exaltation of leaders; instead, he gave the Corinthians a proper perspective on the leaders: they were servants, farmers, architects, officers, administrators, guardians, and fathers – each a "laborer" in the sight of God (see below for how Paul viewed even earthly fathers as "laborers"). None of these laborers was significant compared with God and the Corinthians (who were God's field, family, and children).

The first term that Paul used for apostles and Christian leaders was "servants" (*diakonoi*). He wrote, "What, then, is Apollos and what, then, is Paul? They are servants through whom you believed" (1 Cor 3:5a).[11] Paul wanted the Corinthians to view both Apollos and himself as mere servants who performed menial tasks. They were not spiritual *gurus*; they were workers under a master. Servants usually followed a master's orders; in the same way, Apollos and Paul followed the Lord's instructions: "Each does his or her work as the Lord has granted" (1 Cor 3:5b).

---

9. Joel D. Mlecko, "The Guru in Hindu Tradition," *Numen* 29, no. 1 (July 1982): 33.

10. Mlecko, "The Guru in Hindu Tradition," 34. For a positive evaluation of gurus see Raymond B. Williams, "The Guru as Pastoral Counselor," *Journal of Pastoral Care* 40, no. 4 (December 1986): 331–340.

11. The question could be "*Who* are Apollos and Paul?" or "*What* are Apollos and Paul?" since the Greek particle (*ti*) could mean either. But since Paul was talking about their metaphorical professions, "what" is to be preferred (along with ASV, HCSB, and NET).

Paul then uses a second image, that of "farmers" – "I planted; Apollos watered" (1 Cor 3:6a).[12] Every rich family had workers in the house (servants) as well as in the field (horticulturalists and farmers). Paul saw Apollos and himself as field workers. Paul was in charge of sowing the seed; Apollos was in charge of watering the seedlings that had taken root. Again, they worked under a master, God, who was in charge of the yield: "But God causes the growth" (1 Cor 3:6b). Even after a farmer's faithful sowing and another's faithful watering, growth or yielding of fruit were not guaranteed – they were God's prerogatives. Therefore, there was no value in the one who sowed and the one who watered; the value or honor belonged to God alone who caused the growth (1 Cor 3:7). In essence, the one who sowed the seeds and the one who watered the sapling were equal; they each received their own reward according to their own assigned task (1 Cor 3:8). Paul here was not talking about the "rewards" in heaven for his or Apollos' work; that would be stretching the imagery beyond its limit. Rather, he was simply emphasizing the unimportance of the workers in the field – the one who sowed and the one who watered received wages accordingly.[13] They received payment since they did not own the crops; the master owned them. Paul and Apollos were day laborers in the field and received a day's wages at the end of their work. The day's wages were not the harvest – that is, the Corinthians; so they could not boast over the Corinthians as their reward (the day's wages were possibly a simple commendation of "good and faithful servant"). Regardless, they were to work faithfully as day workers. In simple terms, Paul and Apollos were co-workers – equal in value – under God (1 Cor 3:9a).[14] This was a humble and accurate self-evaluation in Christian ministry. Even apostles were not *gurus* in the technical sense; they were servants (or *parijana*). God alone was the *guru*.

---

12. Paul used the imperfect for Apollos' work, implying that his work was continuous and enduring. In this way he dispelled any suspicion of competition between himself and Apollos. In addition, he might have been implying that watering was a continuous action compared with sowing seeds (for which he used the aorist), a lesson to emphasize in churches: discipleship is ongoing, while evangelism is episodic.

13. The change of grammar (present *gnomic* aspect) supports this idea that Paul was giving an illustration from daily life where every farm laborer receives wages. Receiving wages implies that he or she is not the owner but a hired hand.

14. To understand this verse to read "we are co-workers of God" is to miss the analogy. A better translation is "we are co-workers under God" or "we are co-workers belonging to God" (as in NET). See also Furnish for a similar view: Victor Paul Furnish, "Fellow Workers in God's Service," *Journal of Biblical Literature* 80, no. 4 (1961): 364–370.

Paul then stated the third image: "a skilled architect" (*architectōn*). They were architects because the Corinthian church was "God's building" (1 Cor 3:9c). Jewish writers often switched between these metaphors of "farming" and "building." Jeremiah, for example, says, "Announce to the nations and kingdoms that they will be *uprooted* and *torn down*, destroyed and demolished, *rebuilt* and *firmly planted*" (Jer 1:10; see also Deut 28:30; Josh 24:13; Philo, *Laws* 2.172; Josephus, *Antiquities* 12.151). In God's building or house of the Corinthians, Paul and other teachers were employed as "architects." Paul took his commission as an architect seriously and so he "laid a foundation as a skilled architect according to the grace of God which was given" to him (1 Cor 3:10a). Paul had received this special calling, a gracious calling. Further, he was a skilled architect not because of his wisdom but because he laid "no other foundation than Jesus Christ" (1 Cor 3:11b). Other skilled architects laid further building work upon that foundation – "each one watching carefully, for no one is able to lay any other foundation than that which has been laid, which is Jesus Christ" (1 Cor 3:10b–11).[15] An architect's skillfulness was seen in how carefully he or she built upon the one true foundation, Jesus Christ, because there was no other foundation that could be laid. Paul would later explain that the reason why no one could lay another foundation was because this building he was talking about was God's temple, and God would destroy anyone who tried to destroy his temple (1 Cor 3:17). So it was important for anyone trying to build to make sure that he or she built properly upon the foundation, without replacing it, and standing firmly upon it. Nothing else qualified him or her; everything else was disqualification. The apostles' works were so firmly established on the true foundation of Jesus Christ and so important that in another epistle Paul referred to them as foundational (Eph 2:20). Blomberg explains that Jesus Christ was the "ultimate foundation" upon which the apostles laid more foundational work.[16] (Paul then continued to talk about how a building lasts and the rewards associated with it in 1 Cor 3:12–17. That will be discussed in the next section, but first we will look at the other imagery Paul used to describe the laborers.)

---

15. Scholars assume that with this phrase Paul was attacking Apollos' work (e.g. Lietzmann, Lightfoot, Weiss), Peter's work (e.g. Barrett, Bruce, Craig, Moffatt), or the Corinthian leaders' work (e.g. Fee). Most likely, Paul was just giving a general principle: every architect must build carefully, without replacing the foundation, in order for his or her work to stand. Paul's use of the present tense, a gnomic present, suggests such a possibility.

16. Blomberg, *1 Corinthians*, 79.

Paul's fourth image is that of "officers" (*uperetes*).[17] This was a political and religious title. In the political realm, an officer was someone below the judge but above the prison guards (Matt 5:25). The officer was responsible for placing people in prison or releasing them (Acts 5:22). In the religious realm, officers guarded the temple (Acts 5:26) and the temple scrolls (Luke 4:20). They knew doctrines (John 7:46) and served the high priests (John 18:22). They had great influence over people (John 19:6) and therefore stood watching the outcome of Jesus' trial (Matt 26:58). Paul, Apollos, and Cephas were "officers of Christ" (1 Cor 4:1a). In other words, again they served the master, Christ, who had commissioned them as officers.

Paul had been slowly moving up the social scale, from deacons to farmers, to architects, then to officers – but with one clear message: they labored for God and the Lord, and they did not own the Corinthian Christians. The fifth image Paul reserved for Apollos and himself: they were "administrators" (*oikonomos*). This term is a compound word from *oikos* "house" and *nomos* "law" (lit. law-keepers of the house). In the Septuagint, the Greek translation of the Old Testament, this term was used for palace stewards like Ahishar (1 Kgs 4:6), Arza (1 Kgs 16:9), Obadiah (1 Kgs 18:3), and Eliakim (2 Kgs 18:18). It was also used for the kings' generals. In the list of leaders in 1 Chronicle *oikonomos* comes in the top category: "The leaders [*archon*] of the families, the leaders [*archon*] of the Israelite tribes, the rulers of units of a thousand [*chiliarchos*] and a hundred [*ekatontarchos*], and the administrators [*oikonomos*] of the king's work contributed willingly" (1 Chr 29:6; see also Esth 1:8; 8:9). In a rich person's house, an administrator (*oikonomos*) was directly under the master and was responsible for all slaves in the household (Luke 12:42). He or she managed the master's property (Luke 16:1) and raised the master's children according to the rules and regulations set by the master (Gal 4:2). Such a person was responsible for carrying out the master's wishes and plans and was second only to the master, in a position similar to that held by Joseph in Potiphar's house (Gen 39:4). Paul considered the apostles and Apollos to be "administrators of God's mystery [i.e. the gospel message concerning Christ]" (1 Cor 4:1b). Interestingly, elsewhere Paul and Peter referred to "elders" (*episkopos*) of the church as administrators (*oikonomos*) of God's work (Titus 1:7; 1 Pet 4:10).

---

17. It is erroneous to understand this word to mean "under-rower," that is, a slave who rowed in the lower tier of a trireme in the Roman army (see Fee, *First Epistle to the Corinthians*, 159 n. 6).

The sixth term reserved for the apostles was "guardians" (*paidagogos*). This word is a combination of *paidion* "a child" and *agō* "to lead." As such, it meant one who *leads a child* to a teacher. A *paidagogos*, usually a family slave, accompanied a child from a wealthy home to the teacher's house. Golden says such a person was a slave who was simply too old for more strenuous work.[18] That slave was responsible for overseeing the child's education and basic discipline. It was the responsibility of the *paidagogos* to ensure that the child was treated well and received the education paid for by his or her master – the child's father. Most of the *paidagogoi* (plural) were literate and could repeat the lessons to the child. Often a *paidagogos* was punished if the child didn't learn what was taught. *Paidagogoi* were highly trusted slaves and occupied a privileged place within the household, for they were responsible for the next master (the child that was growing up). Nevertheless, he or she remained a slave. Paul and Apollos were among many *paidagogoi* that the Corinthians had (1 Cor 4:15a).[19]

The seventh and final term was "father" (*patēr*). Paul alone was the Corinthians' "father" because "I birthed you in Christ Jesus through the gospel" (1 Cor 4:15b). Until now, Paul had been using the imagery of workers in rich person's house, where there were servants, farmers, architects, officers, administrators, and guardians. All of these were "laborers" of various sorts. With this figure of a "father," the tendency is to see him as the "owner" of the children. Such a conclusion is far from the truth and actually in contradiction of what Paul was trying to emphasize here. The roles he assigned a father were to correct children (1 Cor 4:14b), to encourage them (1 Cor 4:16a), to model his life for them so that they could imitate him (1 Cor 4:16b), to teach them (1 Cor 4:17), to send his mature children to remind them of his teachings (1 Cor 4:17), to examine them (1 Cor 4:18–19), and if necessary, to discipline them with a rod or with gentleness (1 Cor 4:21).[20] All of these roles illustrate that he was still one of the laborers of God in serving the children of God, the Corinthians, so that they could attain maturity. Elsewhere, Paul instructed fathers: "Fathers, do not anger your children; instead, nourish them in childhood training and thinking concerning God" (Eph 6:4). Paul became

---

18. Mark Golden, *Children and Childhood in Classical Athens* (Baltimore, MD: Johns Hopkins University Press, 1990), 148.

19. Paul used hyperbole, exaggerated speech, when he said "You have *innumerable* guardians" in order to make the contrast between the large number of guardians and a single father.

20. Perhaps Paul was referring to the "rod of correction" (Exod 21:20) rather than a whip (as in NIV) (Fee, *The First Epistle to the Corinthians*, 193 n. 49).

the Corinthians' father because he had brought them to birth "in Christ Jesus and through the gospel." His sharing the gospel with them brought them to Christ Jesus and into God's family – they were "infants in Christ" (1 Cor 3:1). Now he took the parental role of training them seriously so that they could be "sons" and "daughters" in Christ, just as Timothy was (1 Cor 4:17).[21] The Greeks had different words for the stages of growth of a person: breast-feeding infant (*brephos*), infant (*nēpios*), baby (*paidion*), child (*teknon*), son/daughter (*uios, thugater*), and adult (*teleios* "matured one" or *anēr* "man" and *gunē* "woman").[22] Paul saw the Corinthians as infants (*nēpios*, 1 Cor 3:1), babies (*paidion*, 1 Cor 14:20), children (*teknon*, 1 Cor 4:14, 17), and adults (*teleios*, 1 Cor 14:20). These reflect the various spiritual stages they had reached and also Paul's own responsibilities to reproach, correct, and encourage them as a spiritual father, one who had birthed them into the family of God.

There is a logical progression among the *gurus*: *suchaku guru* being the lowest and *param guru* being the greatest. Similarly, Christians often bestow honor according to a leader's professional degrees: those with doctorates are held in higher esteem than those with minimal education, regardless of their ministry's effectiveness. Fernandes sees a sociological reason behind why Christians in India often honor their leaders: "As a minority, the church leaders feel threatened by what they consider a hostile Hindu majority. Consequently, they seek security by building institutions for their leaders and by finding other ways of pleasing the leaders of the majority. Simultaneously they find it necessary to strengthen their own community."[23] In a way, this is unfortunate since it fails to see all Christian workers as God's servants, fellow workers in God's field. Doctorates are academically required to prove one's expertise in a field of studies, but they don't elevate one's position in Christ. Paul had the right perspective: each laborer had a specific task, but he or she was still just

---

21. Similar to this *inclusio* – a literary structure connecting the beginning and the conclusion with similar thoughts – Fiore sees another *inclusio* in the phrases "I beg you, brothers/sisters to agree" (1 Cor 1:10) and "I beg you, then, be imitators of me" (1 Cor 4:16), connecting all four chapters into a unit (Benjamine Fiore, "'Covert Allusion' in 1 Corinthians 1–4," *The Catholic Biblical Quarterly* 47 [1985]: 85–102).

22. This is similar to the Hebrew Bible having various stages of childhood: newly born infant (*jelled* or *jeldah*, Exod 2:3, 6, 8), breast-feeding baby (*jonek* or a "suckling," Isa 53:2), breast-feeding baby that is also eating some solid food (*olel* or "asking bread," Lam 4:4), weaned baby (*gamul*, Ps 131:2; Isa 11:8), child (*taph*, Esth 3:13; Jer 40:7), young men or young women (*elem* or *almah*, meaning "firm and strong," Isa 7:14), young adult (*naar* meaning "shakes himself/herself free"), and a young warrior (*bachur*, meaning "ripened one," Isa 31:8).

23. Walter Fernandes, "Implications of the Involvement of a Minority Group in People's Struggles: The Case of India," *Mission Studies* 2, no. 1 (1985): 109.

a laborer. Only God and the Corinthians mattered. To the laborers, the Lord gives a particular task, just as day laborers are assigned either to water or to sow. All workers are equal under God and are accountable to God. Therefore, the Corinthians or any other Christians shouldn't boast over their Christian spiritual leaders, and especially should not pit one against another.

Build to Last (3:12–17)

On 4 July 2014 the newspapers and television stations in India reported the tragic collapse of an eleven-story building that was under construction, killing at least sixty-one people. It occurred in Moulivakkam, nearly twenty kilometers away from Chennai, the capital of Tamil Nadu state. A heavy thunderstorm had provoked the building to collapse, but, according to the news media, the investigators believed the most likely cause of the collapse to be improper construction or the use of improper materials.

In contrast, the Taj Mahal is a beautiful monument that Mughal Emperor Shah Jahan built in the seventeenth century in memory of his third wife, Mumtaz Mahal. This white marble mausoleum, located in Agra India, took twenty-one years to build and thousands of artisans and craftsmen worked on it. Over a thousand elephants transported building materials to the site from different places: the translucent white marble was brought from Rajasthan, the jasper from Punjab, the jade and crystal from China, the turquoise stones from Tibet, the lapis lazuli from Afghanistan, the sapphire from Sri Lanka, and the carnelian from Arabia. All these materials properly placed on a solid foundation resulted in an awesome monument that has lasted as one of the world's wonders.

Paul referred to apostles and Christian leaders who worked among the Corinthians as "architects" and builders. Paul was the "skilled architect" because he laid only the true foundation, Jesus Christ. God had given him this grace and wisdom to build only upon Christ Jesus (1 Cor 3:10a). Once he, the skilled architect, had laid the proper foundation, other builders (like Apollos and Peter) built upon it, making sure they were on the proper foundation (1 Cor 3:10b). Some used basic construction materials such as wood for beams and doors and hay and straw for bricks, while others used valuable stones (possibly marble[24]), silver, and gold for aesthetic value (1 Cor 3:12).

---

24. Graeme Fleming, a missionary in the Philippines, suggested this interpretation.

No building was made of pure gold; no building was made of pure hay;[25] but architects and builders fashioned these materials in the appropriate places and in the proper proportions for a building to rise to grandeur. A builder's success or failure was not determined by the material that he or she used (each person builds as God has assigned him or her, so how could one find fault with a bricklayer for not being a goldsmith?). Rather, success or failure was determined by the connection the construction had to the foundation (if a door made of gold leans away from the foundations, it will soon fall). That was why Paul said, "If anyone builds on the foundation . . ." (1 Cor 3:12). Any work that stood firmly on the foundation would last (cf. Matt 7:24–27).

The value of a building is in its longevity, as seen in our earlier comparison of the eleven-story building that collapsed in Moulivakkam with the Taj Mahal that has stood for centuries. So Paul said, "Each one's work will be revealed when the day dawns and the radiance reveals it – that is, it is as if the radiance [of the sun] is examining it" (1 Cor 3:13).[26] Scholars jump to theological application here and assume Paul was talking about the future judgment day, when the quality of work will be tested.[27] Such a conclusion is logical and biblical, but not contextual. Paul hadn't yet introduced to the Corinthians the topic of future judgment, so they would not have understood it as referring to a future judgment day. Fee too objects to "those who would decontextualize it [this passage] in terms of individualistic popular piety (i.e. how I build my own Christian life on Christ)," those who use this passage for Calvinist–Arminian debates, and Catholic scholars who use this passage to defend the doctrine of purgatory; he says, "Paul addresses none of these issues, not even indirectly. His concern is singular, that those currently leading the church take heed because their present work will not stand the

---

25. Interpretations that suggest a contrast between the valuable and non-valuable materials miss the message of the illustration. The absence of a contrasting particle like *de* between the first three and the last three materials suggests that Paul is not making a contrast. Similarly, the presence of present and future tenses in this section indicates that Paul was talking about a general daily occurrence, using a gnomic form.

26. I have understood the "fire" as light or the sun's radiance, in line with the rest of the imagery.

27. Fee, *First Epistle to the Corinthians*, 41–42. Also NCV and NRSV. Evans argues that the apostles themselves will be judged for their work (Craig A. Evans, "How Are the Apostles Judges? A Note on 1 Corinthians 3:10–15," *Journal of the Evangelical Theological Society* 27, no. 2 [June 1984]: 149–150. Also Fee, *First Epistle to the Corinthians*, 145). Blomberg writes, "Paul is not teaching salvation by works but is referring instead to Christ's assessment of the way Christians have lived their lives subsequent to salvation . . . It may be that Paul has in mind also the loss of the reward, that is, diminished praise and increased shame as we stand before Christ's judgment seat" (Blomberg, *1 Corinthians*, 74–75).

fiery test to come, having shifted from the imperishable 'stuff' of Jesus Christ and him crucified."[28]

It is most likely that the Corinthians would have understood Paul as discussing the construction of a house and the evaluation of its stability. Only daylight reveals the quality of a work. When the opening day of a building came and the daylight shone upon that building, its quality would be revealed. The builder would then receive that building as his reward: "If anyone's work remains, whatever he or she has built will be his or her reward" (1 Cor 3:14).[29] The only reason people still know about Mughal Emperor Shah Jahan is because the Taj Mahal he built has been standing for over three hundred and sixty years. On the other hand, "if someone's work falls, that one will suffer loss but he or she will be rescued [or not punished]" (1 Cor 3:15a). This again is a principle from daily life: when terrorists destroyed the Twin Towers (World Trade Center) in New York City, the architect of the building – Minoru Yamasaki – suffered a great loss (he could no longer point to those buildings and say, "Look at my work") but he himself was not fined or punished. This was true of Paul's time as well; the Corinthians understood this. Similarly, builders in God's house must make sure that they build only on the foundation of Jesus Christ for their work to last. Otherwise, it will suffer loss. In other words, there is always a test: "these are the consequences of being exposed to radiance" (1 Cor 3:15b). Scholars again see a connection between this imagery and the final judgment.[30] Blomberg, for example, writes, "Such believers are still saved, but by the skin of their teeth or, to use Paul's metaphor, like escaping from a burning house (v. 15b)."[31] Most likely Paul was still staying with the metaphor of a building being exposed by daybreak and the sun's radiance.[32] Paul could be alluding, however, to the fact that when

---

28. Fee, *First Epistle to the Corinthians*, 137. Unfortunately, later he resorts to the traditional view: Ibid., 144–145.

29. Another translation is: "If whatever one has built remains, he will receive a reward." For such a translation, the middle phrase is combined with the first phrase. Instead, I have treated all three phrases as separate thoughts: "(a) If the work of someone remains, (b) whatever he/she has built (c) will become [his/her] reward" (where "whatever he/she has built" is the subject and "will become reward" is the predicate).

30. For problems that arise from such an interpretation that seems to imply that, while salvation is by grace, there are rewards for works, see Fee, *First Epistle to the Corinthians*, 143.

31. Blomberg, *1 Corinthians*, 75.

32. Hays too stays with the building imagery and sees Paul, through these imageries, to be referring to the "wages paid to workers and fines imposed on builders who do inadequate work" (Richard B. Hays, *First Corinthians*, ed. James Luther Mays, Patrick D. Miller Jr, and Paul J. Achtemeier, Interpretation: A Bible Coommentary for Teaching and Preaching [Louisville, KY: Westminster John Knox Press, 1997], 56).

trials and tribulations come, one's *spiritual* work is tested. Often disciples fall away during times of trial.

The proof that Paul had built to last was the Corinthians themselves: "Do you not know that you are God's temple?" (1 Cor 3:16a).[33] Since Paul had built on the proper foundation of Jesus Christ, the Corinthians became God's temple, a lasting monument. The Corinthian Christians were familiar with temples: in generations past, the temple of Aphrodite (the goddess of love) stood atop the Acrocorinth and in their time the temple for the mother-daughter goddesses, Demeter and Kore, stood at the same location.[34] There was a temple of Poseidon, ruler of the sea and maker of earthquakes, at Isthmia near Corinth. Also, there were temples for Apollo, Hermes, Venus-Fortuna, and Isis, as well as one dedicated to "all the gods" (or Pantheon).[35] Like other Greek cities, there was also a shrine dedicated to Asklepios, the god of healing, and his daughter Hygieia, where petitioners hung clay replicas of body parts – limbs, hands, feet, breasts, and genitals – that were afflicted with illness. The Jewish Corinthians would also have known of their temple back in Jerusalem, which at this time was still standing. Herod the Great enlarged King Solomon's temple and it stood magnificently until Emperor Titus of Rome destroyed it in AD 70.

However, none of these temples was in Paul's mind. He was speaking about the Corinthians as God's temple simply because the Holy Spirit resided (dwelt or was housed) among the Corinthians (1 Cor 3:16b). Fee writes, "Paul is calling their attention to the fact that since there is only one God, he can have only one temple in Corinth, and they are it. They became that new temple by the fact that 'God's Spirit lives in you.'"[36]

Since the Corinthians were the new temple of God, and since God was zealous to protect his residence, anyone who tried to destroy the temple of God would be destroyed by God (1 Cor 3:17a). Just as fire could destroy any building, so someone could try to destroy God's temple, the Corinthians. But that person would be in trouble – God would destroy him or her instead. Darius, king of Persia, understood that principle when he said, "May God, who makes his name to reside there [in the temple], overthrow any king or nation

---

33. Paul uses the literary device "don't you know" here and ten other times in 1 Corinthians (3:16; 5:6; 6:2, 3, 9, 15, 16, 19; 9:13, 24).

34. Murphy-O'Connor, "The Corinth That Saint Paul Saw," 152.

35. For a thorough study of temples in Corinth see John R. Lanci, *A New Temple for Corinth: Rhetorical and Archaeological Approaches to Pauline Imagery*, Studies in Biblical Literature (New York: Lang, 1997).

36. Fee, *First Epistle to the Corinthians*, 147.

who reaches out to destroy this temple of God in Jerusalem" (Ezra 6:12). Paul was probably not referring to other apostles or implying that the Corinthians were in the process of destroying themselves.[37] More likely, he was referring to those who persecuted the churches. The Lord Jesus said elsewhere, "I will build my church, and the gates of Hades will not overpower it" (Matt 16:18). This truth has been repeatedly proven as generation after generation has tried to destroy the church (e.g. the persecutions against the Christians in Odisha, India, in 2008–2009), and yet it has survived for two millennia.

God's temple could not be destroyed because "God's temple is holy, which is who you are" (1 Cor 3:17b). The term "holy" means "set apart" or "sacred." Nothing and no one could approach God's temple with the intention of destroying it, and the same was true of the Corinthians: no one could destroy them (cf. Rom 8:38–39). It is interesting that, regardless of the moral failures of the Corinthians (e.g. chs. 5–6), Paul still saw them as "holy" people, because the Holy Spirit resided in them.

Temple of God (3:16–17; 6:19)

All religions have places of worship, called by different names: temples, cathedrals, churches, mosques, and so on. McDaniel describes the progression of a Hindu temple building: "At the most basic level, the goddess shrine may be a rock, statue, or pot along a roadside or beneath a tree. When the power of the deity is recognized, then a small shrine hut (*than*) is built. There is just enough room inside for the rock or statue, some offerings, and perhaps a person or two. As the deity becomes more popular, a permanent (*pakka*) building with plaster or cement walls may be built, and the local *sevait* will offer food and worship on a schedule."[38] Regardless of its humble beginning, a temple may become large, costly, and monumental. The website TheRichest lists the world's ten most expensive religious temples: Chion-in Temple in Japan ($10 million), Potala Palace in Tibet ($15 million), Temple of Heaven in China ($20 million), Wat Rong Khun in Thailand ($22 million), Srirangam Temple in India ($22 million), Prambanan in Indonesia ($50 million), Angkor

---

37. The second option was suggested by John Proctor, "Fire in God's House: Influence of Malachi 3 in the NT," *Journal of the Evangelical Theological Society* 36, no. 1 (March 1993): 13. Paul's use of the third person singular ("anyone") rather than the second person plural ("you") further argues that Paul wasn't thinking of the Corinthians; instead, he was thinking of an outside force. Also, the present tense offers the possibility of a *gnomic* idea.

38. June McDaniel, "Sacred Space in the Temples of West Bengal: Folk, Bhakti, and Tantric Origins," *Pacific World* 3, no. 8 (Fall 2006): 74.

Wat in Cambodia ($50 million), Borobudur in Indonesia ($70 million), Golden Temple in India ($100 million), and Shwedagon Pagoda in Myanmar ($2.4 billion).[39] Ironically, many of these are in the poorest countries of the world.

Christians are no exception – they too build rich cathedrals and churches. Snyder evaluates modern churches' investments in big buildings thus: "Jesus showed a radical attitude toward the Jerusalem temple. He claimed that he himself fulfilled the temple's meaning and function. Through Jesus true worship can occur any time, any place. Jesus says in Matthew 18:20, 'Where two or three are gathered in my name, I am there among them.' The physical temple is now theologically unnecessary."[40] Snyder's comment reflects Paul's sentiments when he wrote, "You are the temple of God and the Spirit of God dwells [is housed] in you" (1 Cor 3:16). The Corinthians did not need to build large churches or cathedrals; they were the temple of God, which the Spirit of God indwelt.

Paul chose his words carefully. The Greeks, in general, called their temples "holy places" (*heirōn*). Jews gathered in synagogues (*synagōgē*). Christians gathered in various places as groups of individuals called "churches" (*ekklēsia*). Paul said that the Corinthians were a "temple" (*naos*) of God, a word which "clearly carried with it the notion of a dwelling place."[41] Lanci writes, "*Naos* comes from the verb *naiein*, 'to dwell,' and originally referred to the building which ancients understood to be the house of God (the Roman *aedes*) or *cella*, the room within the temple building."[42] The Corinthians themselves were God's temple because the Holy Spirit lived in them, not in their gathering place or in any church building that they might build.

Earlier Paul had separated the ordinary people ("soul-people") from the Spirit-people (1 Cor 2:10–11, 13). The Spirit-people understood the mystery of the crucifixion because the Holy Spirit – he who knows God completely – had explained the mystery to them. Later Paul would say that the Holy Spirit alone had washed them, purified them, and made them right with God (6:11;

---

39. http://www.therichest.com/luxury/most-expensive/riches-and-religion-the-most-expensive-temples-ever-built/ Accessed 8 July 2014.

40. Howard A. Snyder, "God's Housing Crisis," *Christianity Today* 49, no. 5 (May 2005): 54. For an interesting article on one religion's building built on another religion's sacred place (e.g. a cathedral built on a pagan temple's site or a mosque on an old church building), and new trends on building sacred places, see Philip Jenkins, "Whose Holy Ground?," *Christian Century* 129, no. 6 (21 March 2012): 45.

41. Christina M. Fetherolf, "The Body for a Temple, a Temple for a Body: An Examination of Bodily Metaphors in 1 Corinthians," *Proceedings* (Grand Rapids, MI) 30 (2010): 99.

42. Lanci, *A New Temple for Corinth*, 91.

16:18). The Holy Spirit alone had united the Christians with the Lord (6:17) and even enabled them to call Jesus "Lord" (12:3). All the believers partook of the same Holy Spirit (12:13) who distributed gifts to them as he saw fit (12:7–11; 14:12). But, most importantly, he "dwelt" with them, as emphasized in 1 Corinthians 2:12; 3:16; 6:19; 7:40. First Paul said, "we received the Spirit who is from God" (1 Cor 2:12); then he said, "The Spirit of God *was housed* (*oikeō*) in you [plural]" (1 Cor 3:16). These two instances could be collective, meaning that the Holy Spirit indwelt the Christians collectively. In the context of sexual immorality, however, he said, "Your [plural] body [singular] is a temple [singular] of the Holy Spirit whom you [plural] received from God and who is in you [plural]" (1 Cor 6:19), implying that the Holy Spirit indwells each Christian individually.[43] And in the final example, Paul clearly meant individual indwelling: "I think this because I have the Spirit of God" (1 Cor 7:40). In light of these texts, we can conclude that the Holy Spirit dwells among Christians individually and collectively, and that Christians are individually and collectively God's temple(s). That being so, just as Snyder commented, "The physical temple is now theologically unnecessary."[44] The gathering together of Christians is, however, mandatory (Heb 10:25).

Divine or Belonging to the Divine? (3:18–23)

In India, animals (especially cows) are treated with respect and even reverence. One reason for this is because Hindus see people and animals as divine. *Guru* Brahmeshananda of Ramakrishna Mission explains, "When the Hindus say that man is divine, this means that all men and women are divine. When by following the discipline of yoga, one starts realizing that one is divine and not mortal, he also, to that extent, starts seeing that others are also divine and he starts behaving with others similarly."[45] He then cites the example of a mystic, Pavhari Baba, who chased after a thief who had been stealing from his house. The thief ran away when Baba awoke, but Baba chased him, calling him "God," and gave the articles back to him as homage. Through Baba's seeing the divine in the thief, the thief turned his life around and became a saint. Bibek Debroy cites another incident from Baba's life in which, when a dog

---

43. So argues Fetherolf, "The Body for a Temple," 103.
44. Snyder, "God's Housing Crisis," 54.
45. www.hinduism.co.za/natureof.htm.

stole a piece of bread from Baba's hermitage, Baba ran after the dog, praying, "Please wait, my Lord; let me butter the bread for you."[46]

Yahweh God created people, male and female, in his image and breathed life into them (Gen 1:26–27; 2:7). Therefore, humanity represents God over all other created things. But people are not *divine*; instead, they belong to God. They are commanded to worship him alone as God (Deut 6:4). This was why, when Paul and Barnabas were revered as gods (Acts 14:11–14), they immediately resisted it. No human being is divine. Instead, we belong to the divine. Paul explicitly said this in 1 Corinthians: "All things belong to you, you belong to Christ, and Christ belongs to God" (1 Cor 1:22b–23). This statement occurs in the context of the Corinthians boasting that they belonged to Apollos, Paul, or Cephas. Paul instead said, "No, they all belong to you, but you belong to Christ and to God." That was accurate. Thinking that they belonged to a spiritual leader was "deception."

So Paul began, "Let no one deceive him- or herself" (1 Cor 3:18a). The Corinthians were drawn to wisdom and they boasted in their wisdom, even taking sides with "wise" apostles. Paul said, "If anyone thinks he or she is wise among you according to this world's standard, he or she must become a fool so that he or she might be truly wise" (1 Cor 3:18b). The reason for this was because this world's wisdom is foolishness in God's sight (1 Cor 3:19a). Paul had been instructing that the world thought of the death of the Messiah on the cross as foolishness, but God had revealed the excellence of his wisdom in such a death (1 Cor 1:18–25). When the Corinthians sided with God and found themselves "fools" in the world's eyes, they would then be truly wise in God's sight. Paul made two citations from the Old Testament to illustrate how the world's wisdom is foolishness in God's sight. When Job was repeatedly compelled to blaspheme against God, he refused. His reasoning was simple: that kind of worldly wisdom – "curse God and die because he does not care" – was foolishness. In reality, God had made such "wise" people fools: "I beg God . . . who gives rain on the earth, who sends water from the heavens, who raises the humble to heights and destroys the haughty, and *who confuses the wisdom of the crafty* so their hands cannot have success. He overtakes the wise people in their thinking and confuses the council of the exalted ones" (Job 5:10–13, LXX). Similarly, the writer of Psalm 94 says, "Is he who formed the ear unable to hear? Is he who molded the eyes unable to

---

46. Bibek Debroy, *Sarama and Her Children: The Dog in Indian Myth* (New Delhi, India: Penguin Books, 2008), 179.

see and comprehend? Is he who disciplines nations unable to punish? Is he who teaches mankind not able to understand? *The Lord knows the dialogues of mankind, that they are foolishness*" (Ps 94:9–11, LXX). Paul cited portions of these passages to argue that God delights in proving earthly wisdom to be foolishness (1 Cor 3:19b–20).

One such aspect of "earthly wisdom" is boasting in people, especially in spiritual leaders (1 Cor 3:21a). Instead of the Corinthians belonging to their spiritual leaders, "all things belonged" to the Corinthians (1 Cor 3:21b). All things – Paul, Apollos, or Cephas; the world, life, or death; this world or the world to come – belonged to the Corinthians (1 Cor 3:22). In turn, the Corinthians themselves belonged to Christ, and he belonged to God (1 Cor 3:23). Fee writes, "Paul turns their slogans end for end. It is not that the Corinthians belong to Apollos or Paul, but that Paul and Apollos – and everything else – belongs to the Corinthians; indeed, all things are theirs because they are Christ's and Christ is God's. Thus, the main point of 3:5–17 is restated with breathtaking crescendo."[47] The last phrase, "Christ belongs to God," should be understood in terms of his work and not in terms of his being.[48] Just as Apollos and Paul worked for God and his people, even the Messiah Jesus Christ died and rose (his works) for God and his people. The only person to whom the Corinthians belonged was Jesus Christ.

Christians have the Spirit of God living within them and they are increasingly being transformed into the likeness of Jesus Christ every day. But they are not divine. They belong to the Lord Jesus Christ and to God the Father, and to no one else.

Group Identity

A "group identity," a sociological category, is what a people within a group most commonly identify with one another. Persons born between the 1960s and 1980s, for example, are called the Generation-X people and they share particular traits. Persons born after 2000 are called the Generation-Z people. "Hippies" are members of a countercultural group that originated in the UK and USA. People of Generation-X, Generation-Z and Hippies differ greatly from one another in their outlook on life, philosophy, politics, and economics.

---

47. Fee, *First Epistle to the Corinthians*, 151.
48. Fee writes, "This is a soteriological statement, not a Christological one (in terms of his being)" (Fee, *First Epistle to the Corinthians*, 155).

But a person identifies with a group and takes on the traits of that group in order to find acceptance, oneness, and solitude.

In Christianity, however, there is only one group: Christ-followers. There are not to be many sub-group identities, such as "I am of Paul," or "I am of Peter." That was why Paul was grieved and addressed the Corinthians (1:10 – 4:21). His conclusion was to focus on Christ, not be proud of one's wisdom, and to see unity among believers as God's field, building, and people.

6

1 Corinthians 4

The Evaluation of Christian Service (4:2–6)

The word for "hell" in Hinduism is *naraka*. The Hindu scriptures detail twenty-eight different hells, each one dedicated to the punishment of a different crime. The hell called *tamisra* (darkness), for example, is for one who has stolen another's wealth, wife, or children. The guilty person is bound with ropes and denied food and water. The hell called *kumbhipaka* (cooked in a pot) is reserved for the one who cooks animals and birds. The guilty person is cooked alive in boiling oil for as many years as there were hairs on the bodies of the animal victims. The hell called *shwabhojana* (food of dogs) is reserved for a religious student who sleeps in the day and doesn't have the knowledge that even a child has.[1]

The idea of hells with various degrees of punishment comes because in the human mind resides a desire to punish people for crimes that they commit. Such a tendency may often lead one Christian to quickly judge a Christian worker, calling him or her a "heretic," "false teacher," "unorthodox teacher," "blasphemer," or even "lunatic." Paul, although explicitly warning against accepting the doctrines of false teachers, taught that the judgment of a false teacher was the Lord's task and not that of the church.

Having introduced Apollos and himself as "administrators" of God's mystery (1 Cor 4:1), Paul outlined what is expected of such administrators. First, God expected the administrators to be faithful (1 Cor 4:2). Second, it was of no concern how other Christians or any human court evaluated them

---

1. For a complete study see Knut A. Jacobsen, "Three Functions of Hell in the Hindu Traditions," *Numen* 56, no. 2–3 (2009): 385–400.

(1 Cor 4:3a).[2] In other words, Christians shouldn't be engaged in evaluating one another. Third, the administrators were not to evaluate themselves (1 Cor 4:3b). This implies that we are not worthy to evaluate even our own works; that belongs to God. Fourth, even if the administrators did pass the scrutiny of anyone else, it still would not be a reason for them to boast (1 Cor 4:4a). Fifth, the Lord alone would judge the administrators (1 Cor 4:4b). Just as in a house the master (lord) or lady of the house examined his or her workers, so the Lord who appointed the administrator would alone judge him or her. Sixth, since the Lord alone could judge accurately, one must wait until the Lord comes (1 Cor 4:5a). Seventh, when he comes, "he will bring to light all the hidden things of darkness and reveal the motives of hearts" (1 Cor 4:5b). Paul wasn't talking about church discipline (Matt 18:15–17) or judging the sinful believer (1 Cor 5:1–5). These were areas in which the churches were to correct, reprove, teach, and train Christians in light of the Scriptures (cf. 2 Tim 3:16). Rather, Paul was probably talking about judging the faithfulness of administrators like himself and Apollos – that is, evaluating the faithfulness of a Christian's service. That was the task of the Lord. Eighth, when the Lord evaluated the worker, then God himself would bestow praise (1 Cor 4:5c). That was their reward: God calling someone a "faithful worker" (cf. Matt 25:21, 23).[3] Paul saw God as a fair judge who judged appropriately and bestowed honor appropriately. That was why the Christians shouldn't get involved in judging one another or even calling one another names. Unfortunately, we do not take this warning seriously and do get involved in name-calling (and condemning to various "hells" of our own thinking or making).

Paul and Apollos knew these principles that Paul outlined and therefore they transformed themselves into people who did not boast in their own works or merits (1 Cor 4:6a). Paul used the word "transformed" (*metaschematizō*) that was similar to that used to describe the change butterflies go through – *metamorphosis*. In other words, Paul and Apollos transformed themselves for a new role, just as actors take on new roles and live in those particular characters. They transformed themselves so that the Corinthians would learn not to "go beyond the written instruction: 'Do not puff yourselves up over one another'" (1 Cor 4:6b).[4] Paul did not want the Corinthians to boast

---

2. Paul's words are literally "by human *days*," with the figurative meaning of "having one's day in court" (Fee, *First Epistle to the Corinthians*, 161).

3. Also Fee, *First Epistle to the Corinthians*, 164 n. 34.

4. There are different views on the meaning of this phrase "don't go beyond what is written": (1) beyond what was written in the previous three chapters; (2) beyond the

over (or "puff themselves up about") spiritual leaders, for these leaders had transformed themselves so as not to draw attention to themselves. The leaders also knew not to evaluate themselves ahead of time but to wait for the Lord to evaluate them and for God to reward them with praise. The Corinthians were to imitate this principle.

At the End of the Parade (4:7–13)

Thaipusam is a Hindu festival celebrated mostly in Tamil Nadu state on the day of full moon in the Tamil month of *thai*, which is usually in either January or February. Countries that are neighbors with Tamil people, such as Sri Lanka and Singapore, also celebrate this festival. The festival supposedly commemorates the occasion when the goddess Parvati gave the god Murugan a spear (*vel*) so he could kill the evil demon Soorapadman. A unique feature of this festival is carrying *kavadi* or "burdens." The simplest *kavadi* is carrying a pot of milk on one's head. The most difficult and gruesome *kavadi* is piercing the skin, tongues, or cheeks with *vel* (spear or skewers).

Rome also celebrated a festival called the Roman triumph. It was a civil and religious parade that was held to celebrate the return of an army commander who had won a great military victory in a foreign war. On his celebration day, the general wore a crown of laurel and purple triumphal clothing embroidered with gold, called *toga picta* ("painted toga"). He was paraded in a chariot drawn by four horses and a procession of soldiers followed him. It was also a religious parade: two flawless white oxen, covered in garlands, were led to be sacrificed to Jupiter, the god of victory. At the end of the parade came prisoners of war, condemned to die, sometimes along with their families – all walking in chains.[5]

Old Testament; (3) beyond the terms of the rules and regulations (Fee, *First Epistle to the Corinthians*, 167 n. 14; 169.); or (4) beyond a document that Paul had given the Corinthians that subsequent generations did not have access to (James C. Hanges, "1 Corinthians 4:6 and the Possibility of Written Bylaws in the Corinthian Church," *Journal of Biblical Literature* 117, no. 2 [1998]: 298). Tyler has successfully demonstrated that it was a pedagogical tool used in antiquity to call back to remembrance something that the teacher had already taught (Ronald L. Tyler, "The History of the Interpretation of to *Me Uper a Gegraptai* in 1 Corinthians 4:6," *Restoration Quarterly* 43, no. 4 [2001]: 243–252). Similarly, I think that Paul was referring to what he had told them earlier: "Do not puff yourselves up over one another" (1:2929, 31; 3:21). He was bringing that concept to their remembrance.

5. For a detailed study of the Roman triumph, see H. S. Versnel, *Triumphus: An Inquiry into the Origin, Development and Meaning of the Roman Triumph* (Leiden: Brill, 1970). For a critical study of the facts of the Roman triumph, see Mary Beard, *The Roman Triumph* (Cambridge: The Belknap Press of Harvard University Press, 2007).

Paul alluded to this imagery when he wrote to the Corinthians, "God has exhibited us, the apostles, at the end [of the parade] as those condemned for death. We have become a spectacle to the world, angels, and people" (1 Cor 4:9). Paul set this phrase within the context of the Corinthians not understanding their position in Christ. They were siding with apostles and leaders saying, "I am of Paul" or "I am of Apollos." But in reality, Paul, Apollos, the world, life, death, and everything belonged to the Corinthian Christians (1 Cor 3:21–22). They belonged to Christ and Christ belonged to God (1 Cor 3:23). The apostles didn't own the Corinthians; instead, the apostles were administrators of God's mystery whose task it was to be faithful (1 Cor 4:1–5). Paul and Apollos knew these principles and applied them in their lives (1 Cor 4:6).

Now Paul restated the Corinthians' great position in Christ. He began, "What makes you different? Is there anything you have that you have not received? And if you have received, why boast as though you have not received?" (1 Cor 4:7). The Corinthians had received from God many blessings which set them apart from all other people. Since they had received these blessings, they shouldn't act as people who had received nothing and needed the approval of Apollos or Paul. As Paul had told them, everything in this world and the world to come belonged to them; God had graciously given them these as gifts (1 Cor 3:21–22). As such, they shouldn't play the trump card of poverty. In reality, they had everything they had ever wanted; they had become rich (1 Cor 4:8a)! They had become kings, even without the apostles' help.[6] But they had not started to live as kings, so the apostles didn't have the blessing of ruling with them (1 Cor 4:8b). If they had begun to reign as kings, the apostles wouldn't be at the end of the parade as prisoners condemned to die. Paul may have been using this argument sarcastically: that is, they were boasting in their wealth, so Paul said, "If you truly were rich in Christ, you'd act as such – that is, you wouldn't boast in your riches. Instead, you'd boast in your position in Christ and reign with him. Then we'd have

---

6. Some translations place an exclamation mark here, implying that Paul was making an ironic statement (RSV, NAB, NEB, NIV). Others treat it as a rhetorical question in connection with verse 7 (TCNT, GNB, JB). Yet others see it as a false assumption that the Corinthians had about themselves (Fee calls it a "staccato indicative," Fee, *First Epistle to the Corinthians*, 172 n. 36. and my previous commentary, Spurgeon, *1 Corinthians: An Exegetical and Contextual Commentary*, 49). Most likely, however, Paul was stating a real fact about their new position in Christ. Since everything and everyone was serving them, they were kings already (1 Cor 3:21–22). Unfortunately, they were not reigning as kings.

something to boast about you." Since they weren't acting as they should – as those rich in Christ – it jeopardized the apostles' place in the parade.

In other words, because of the Corinthians' current situation, Paul was convinced that God had exhibited the apostles at the end of the parade as men condemned to die – as a spectacle for the world, the angels, and people (1 Cor 4:9).[7] The Corinthians' lack of a victory dance and their strivings and jealousies over spiritual leaders left Paul and the other apostles defeated, as if they had lost the battle. In addition, as Paul had been explaining, his message was also "foolish" on account of the fact that it was about a crucified Messiah, but it nevertheless made the Corinthians "wise," for they understood and accepted God's salvation in the mystery of the crucified Messiah (1 Cor 4:10a). Similarly, the apostles were weak but the Corinthians were strong; the Corinthians had honor but the apostles did not (1 Cor 4:10b). The apostles' lowly state – as those at the end of the parade, condemned to die – was affirmed by the fact even as he was writing he was hungry, thirsty, naked, beaten, and without a home (1 Cor 4:11).[8] Paul was alluding to one of his imprisonments when he would have had little or no food and drink. The guards would have beaten him (cf. 2 Cor 11:23–29). To add insult to injury – for they were Jewish and circumcised – the guards would have left the apostles naked.[9] But Paul wasn't going to give up. He worked hard with his own hands (1 Cor 4:12a; cf. Acts 18:3; 2 Thess 3:8) and followed the Lord's instructions: "we bless those who revile us; we endure those who persecute us; we comfort the slanderers" (1 Cor 4:12b–13a; cf. Matt 5:44). In summary, the apostles had become "the refuse of the world – refuse even now" (1 Cor 4:13b). At the conclusion of the Roman triumph parade, the bodies of the victims were tossed into the refuse heap for their bodies to decay. That was the state of the apostles.

Ministry is not glamorous. The message of crucifixion is foolishness, and its messengers are nothing other than criminals condemned to die in front of the spectators – the world, angels, and people. But the messengers endure such revilings because they know they hold the mystery of God in their teachings. Paul and Apollos were such people – they proclaimed God's mystery and died as condemned prisoners. That is the call on many Christians' lives. Graham

---

7. Paul often spoke of angels as spectators of salvation events: 1 Cor 6:3; 11:10; 13:1; Gal 1:8; 3:19; 4:14; Col 2:18; 1 Thess 4:16; 2 Thess 1:7; 1 Tim 3:16; and 1 Tim 5:21.

8. Fee illustrates how Paul marked off this section with a literary marker called an *inclusio*: "The three verses hold together as a single piece, beginning and ending on the same note: 'To this very hour/up to this moment'" (Fee, *First Epistle to the Corinthians*, 178).

9. The shame of such nakedness was so great that some Jews underwent surgery to reverse circumcision, Josephus, *Antiquities*, 12.241; *Apion* 20.45.

Stains from Australia was a Christian physician who worked among the lepers in the state of Odisha, India. He and his two sons – Philip (ten years old) and Timothy (eight) – were burned alive while they slept in their jeep outside a small church.[10] They were treated as men condemned to die and tossed away as the scum of the earth. That's sadly the cost of discipleship in many leaders' lives. But there is a reward: God himself will bestow praise (1 Cor 4:5c), calling such people "faithful workers" (Matt 25:21, 23).

Honor–Shame and Proper Parenting (4:14–21)

The concept of honor–shame is common to many Asian and Middle Eastern countries. "Honor is defined as the public acknowledgement of one's worth to the group; it is essentially a positive social rating that entitles a person to relate with other group members in socially prescribed ways."[11] Honor is expressed in actions described by synonyms such as prestige, value, significance, respect, worth, status, face, reputation, and dignity. Three major means of acquiring honor are purity (cleanliness), faithfulness (also loyalty), and benefaction (distribution of wealth). For example, a high priest cannot touch a leper because of the leper's uncleanness and the high priest's purity. When this acquired honor (purity, faithfulness, and benefaction) is lost, the person faces "shame."

Honor and shame work daily in the lives of Indians. But here, unlike in other Asian cultures, honor–shame works along with two other factors that control the culture: caste and karma.[12] Rajaram says, "The valuation of individuals and groups and the distribution of societal resources [are] based on status and status was ascriptive, though birth into a group was believed to be based on moral merit gathered during the previous birth as implied in the

---

10. Anton Ankara, "Loving the Lepers: A Murdered Missionary's Widow Carries on Her Husband's Work," *Christianity Today* 44, no. 1 (2000): 32.

11. Jayson Georges, "From Shame to Honor: A Theological Reading of Romans for Honor-Shame Contexts," *Missiology* 38, no. 3 (July 2010): 297. For detailed study see Bruce Malina and Jerome H. Neyrey, "Honor and Shame in Luke-Acts: Pivotal Values of the Mediterranean World," in *The Social World of Luke-Acts: Models for Interpretation*, ed. Jerome H. Neyrey (Peabody, MA: Hendrickson, 1991), 25–66. Also Bruce Malina, *New Testament World: Insights from Cultural Anthropology* (Atlanta, GA: John Knox Press, 1981).

12. "While honor and shame do not play as prominent a role in India as they do in the Far East, many of the dynamics of shame and honor are present throughout Asia, including India" (Timothy Tennent, "Human Identity in Shame-Based Cultures of Asia," *Doon Theological Journal* 4, no. 2 [July 2007]: 188).

theory of karma and rebirth."[13] So although honor and shame are significant, caste strata and karma from the previous life also affect one's social status. An untouchable will never have the same honor that a Brahman automatically acquires, regardless of the untouchable's hard-earned wealth or education.

Paul and the Corinthians were in an honor–shame culture. Finney examines Paul's instructions to the Corinthians concerning head-coverings (1 Cor 11:2–16) against the cultural background of honor–shame and writes, "The semantics of honor would include notions of praise (ἐπαινέω, v. 2) and glory (δόξα vv. 7, 15), whilst shame (αἰσχρόν) occurs at v. 6 and also falls within the categories of 'disgrace' (καταισχύνω, vv. 4, 5) and 'dishonor' (ἀτιμία, v. 14)."[14] Similarly, McRae examines the Corinthians' participation in the Lord's Supper in terms of honor and shame.[15] Tennent writes, "The apostle Paul uses the word *shame* in the broad, common sense of the word when he shames the Corinthians for having people in their midst who are apparently ignorant of the gospel. Paul declares, 'I say this to your shame (ἐντροπή)' (1 Cor 15:34)."[16] Thus there are clear examples indicating that Paul addressed the Corinthians in terms of their commonly accepted social norm of honor and shame.

An exception to this is when Paul was correcting the Corinthians. The Corinthians were Christians who carefully followed Paul's teachings: "I praise you that you remember me always and you keep the traditions just as I handed them to you" (1 Cor 11:2). But they often erred in areas where Paul had not yet instructed them (an example was how to celebrate the Lord's Supper). In chapters 1–4 Paul for the first time was addressing divisions in the Corinthian congregation. Since it was a new issue, Paul concluded his long section by saying, like a good father, "I am writing these things *not* to shame you but to admonish you as my beloved children" (1 Cor 4:14). This is an excellent principle for parenting: when a lesson is taught the very first time, it ought to be taught without humiliating the children.[17] Since this was the first time Paul was addressing this issue, he didn't want the Corinthians to feel shame and not listen to what he had to say. Instead, he wanted them

---

13. Rajaram, *Facets of Indian Culture*, 2.

14. Mark Finney, "Honour, Head-Coverings and Headship: 1 Corinthians 11.2–16 in Its Social Context," *Journal for the Study of the New Testament* 33, no. 1 (September 2010): 32.

15. Rachel M. McRae, "Eating with Honor: The Corinthian Lord's Supper in Light of Voluntary Association Meal Practices," *Journal of Biblical Literature* 130, no. 1 (Spring 2011): 165–181.

16. Tennent, "Human Identity," 156. Also Tucker, "The Role of Civic Identity," 71–91.

17. For a valuable study on how families are often the first place where children learn honor-shame and for a proper utilization of honor-shame in the family see Sara Hines Martin, "Shame-Based Families," *Review & Expositor* 91, no. 1 (Winter 1994): 19–30.

to know that he loved them, so he addressed them as "beloved children." This was an instruction from a loving father to his children (1 Cor 4:15; cf. Col 3:21; Eph 6:4).

Having introduced the imagery of parenting, Paul set out several principles of proper parenting in this section. First, as a good parent he set his life as a model for them so that he could say, "Be my imitators" (1 Cor 4:16). On his first visit Paul had stayed with them for one and a half years (Acts 18:11). They would have seen his way of life alongside his teachings. He wanted them to live according to the model he had set them. Second, in his absence, he sent his "son" Timothy – the Corinthians' "older sibling" ("my beloved child and faithful one in the Lord") – to them to instruct them in everything Paul had been teaching in other churches concerning the Lord's way (1 Cor 4:17).[18] In his absence, Paul didn't just write them a letter; he sent them someone dear to him. Most likely, he sent Timothy bearing this letter (1 Corinthians) so that he could read the letter and explain the contents in detail to them.[19] Timothy had already visited the Corinthians with Paul on the first journey, so they knew him (Acts 16:1 – 18:11). Third, Paul wasn't neglecting his role as a parent and surely would visit them, when the Lord permitted (1 Cor 4:19a). Paul wasn't avoiding visiting them; he wanted to visit them but was waiting for the Lord's permission, the right time, to do so.

Fourth, when he visited them, he would find out about the arrogant people – whether or not they were all speech and no action (whether they were all bark and no bite) (1 Cor 4:19b). No doubt Paul said this to instill fear in those who were causing division.[20] Just as his message to them had come not in mere words but with the power of the Holy Spirit, and as the kingdom of God wasn't in mere words but in power (1 Cor 4:20), so he would check if the new teachers' words had any power behind them. In 1 Corinthians, "kingdom of God" refers to God's ultimate powerful rule (1 Cor 4:20) that was handed to him by Christ (1 Cor 15:24). It is a kingdom where the unredeemed (1 Cor 6:9–10) will not participate and the un-resurrected will have no part (1 Cor 15:50). Paul would examine the troublemakers' power to see if it consisted

---

18. Paul repeatedly referred to the commonness of his teachings in all the churches: 1:2; 7:17; 11:16; 14:33, 36.

19. The aorist verb doesn't mean that he had already reached them (as in RSV, NAB, NEB). Since Timothy was with Paul when he wrote this letter and was getting ready to visit the Corinthians (1 Cor 16:11), most likely Timothy carried the letter with him.

20. Fee understands from this phrase that the trouble in the church came from the community and that a few instigators were causing havoc and confusion in the whole congregation (Fee, *First Epistle to the Corinthians*, 190).

only in words or in words plus action, just as a good parent examines the influence of others on his or her children.

Fifth, as a wise parent, Paul would see if the correction required strict discipline ("rod") or mild rebuke ("in love and the Spirit's gentleness") (1 Cor 4:21). In ancient cultures parents used rods to discipline their children. Even kings' scepters were considered "rods" that emphasized their discipline or power of ruling well. Shepherds carried rods that often comforted the sheep (Ps 23:4). Rods were used more for discipline and comfort than for cruel treatment of children. Some children are so sensitive that they don't require the use of a "rod"; a mild rebuke in love and gentleness is enough. A wise parent will discern which is required and will use the appropriate method of discipline properly. Paul was such a parent to the Corinthians.

Even parenthood is tied up with honor and shame. Malina and Neyrey write,

> As father of a family, [a man's] honor is defined in terms of *gender* (male, father) and *position* (head of the household). When he commands his children and they obey him, his *power* is evident. In this situation of command–obedience, his claim to honor as father and head of the household is acknowledged; his children treat him honorably and onlookers acknowledge that he is an honorable father (see 1 Tim 3:4–5). Were his children to disobey him, he would be dishonored or shamed, for his claim would not be acknowledged, either by family or village. He would suffer shame, that is, loss of honor, reputation, and respect.[21]

Paul was the spiritual father of the Corinthians, for he had birthed them into the family of God. He wasn't as concerned about his personal "honor" so much as about the role of the kingdom of God (1 Cor 4:20). For that, the Christians needed to live in a way that honored God. Leading the children to maturity should be the goal of every Christian leader, if necessary using discipline. Such correction is motivated by love.

---

21. Malina and Neyrey, "Honor and Shame in Luke-Acts," 26.

7

1 Corinthians 5

Incest and Boasting (5:1–2)

Incest is rarely tolerated in any culture, and India is no exception. The Hindu Marriage Act of 1955 prohibits marriage between relatives within five generations on the father's side and three on the mother's side. It does, however, permit the marriage of cross cousins – that is, the marriage of a person with his or her father's sister's child or mother's brother's child.[1] The reasoning is that the father's sister's husband and the mother's brother's wife will have introduced new blood. As such, it is common to see marriages between first and second cousins in South India, and such marriages are not considered incest. In Northeast India, especially in Nagaland, "Taboo against incest is extended to all immediate kins [*sic*] and blood relations and even to the whole clan members."[2]

Cultural practices regarding incest do, however, differ. Western culture does not allow a widow to marry her dead husband's brother. In ancient Israel, however, it was accepted and commanded – called *levirate* marriage (Gen 38:1–10; Deut 25:5–10; Luke 20:27–32; [*levir* being brother-in-law in Latin]).[3] In India, such a marriage of a widow with her husband's brother is

---

1. Niyesh Yadav and Abha Malik, *History of India's Glorious Traditions: Indian Art and Culture* (New Delhi: Arihant Publications (India) Limited, 2013), 128.

2. Joseph S. Thong and Phanenmo Kath, *Glimpses of Naga Legacy and Culture* (Kottayam, Kerala: Society for Naga Students' Welfare, 2011), 132.

3. For the history of levirate marriage see Dale W. Manor, "A Brief History of Levirate Marriage as It Relates to the Bible," *Restoration Quarterly* 27, no. 3 (1984): 129–142. Weisberg argues that the Jewish males found this law discomforting because of its relationship to paternity and property, but Jewish women didn't share the same discomforts (Dvora E. Weisberg, "The Widow of Our Discontent: Levirate Marriage in the Bible and Ancient Israel," *Journal for the Study of the Old Testament* 28, no. 4 [June 2004]: 403–429). For an excellent study of African

called *niyoga*. It has strict regulations: *niyoga* must be carried out only for procreation; sex within the marriage must not be pleasurable; and the man has no parental obligations to any child conceived.[4]

Sometimes individuals stretch the boundaries of incest; for example, Josef Fritzl of Austria imprisoned and raped his daughter Elisabeth for twenty-four years, and a man near Bombay repeatedly raped his handicapped twelve-year-old niece who was unable to speak.[5] Even cultures sometimes go beyond the limits of the law. Kakar, a clinical psychologist, writes of women in India who, in the absence of their husbands, develop a strong liking for their brothers-in-law and wish for the protection of those brothers-in-law (as potential future partners) more than the protection of their husbands.[6]

Similar to these twisted cases of incest, the Christians in Corinth tolerated an incestuous relationship within the church that was not even common in their culture: "a certain man *has* his father's wife" (1 Cor 5:1). The verb "has" is a euphemism for cohabiting sexually (see 1 Cor 7:2). A sexual encounter between a mother and her son was clearly prohibited by Jewish law (Lev 18:7–8) and Paul's phrase "not even practiced among the nations" implies that the national Corinthians would not have had such a practice either.[7] So this person was clearly breaking all common-sense laws when he cohabited with his father's wife (stepmother). What caused him to carry out such an act? It could have been that he was a willful sinner. It could also have been that he was confused. The early Christians called one another "brothers and sisters." Outsiders often misunderstood this term and said that the Christians practiced incest (Eusebius, *Ecclesiastical History*, 5.1.14). Even Paul's statement elsewhere could be construed as promoting incest: "Don't we, Paul and Barnabas, have the right to travel with a *sister* as a *wife*?" (1 Cor 9:5; see also 1 Cor 7:14). Paul clearly meant that he had the right to marry a Christian

---

levirate marriages and the implications for missiology see Gabriel K. Falusi, "African Levirate and Christianity," *AFER* 24, no. 5 (October 1982): 300–308.

4. Concerning the abuse of *niyoga* practice see Sudhir Kakar, *Indian Identity* (New Delhi: Penguin Books, 1996), 15–16. Also Sudhir Kakar and Katharina Kakar, *The Indians: Portrait of People* (New Delhi, India: Viking, 2007), 12–13.

5. Sandhya Nair, "Man Held for Raping Mute Niece," *The Times of India* (27 May 2014).

6. Kakar, *Indian Identity*, 15–16.

7. The ancient Code of Hammurabi said, "If a seignior [an adult male] has lain in the bosom of his mother after (the death of) his father, they shall burn both of them. If a seignior after (the death of) his father has been caught in the bosom of his foster mother who was the bearer of children, that seignior shall be cut off from the parental home" (code 157, 158) (James B. Pritchard, ed., *Ancient near Eastern Texts Relating to the Old Testament* [Princeton, NJ: Princeton University Press, 1969]).

lady and travel with her on his journeys, just as Cephas/Peter did. Because of these unclear statements from Christians, a new convert might have been confused into thinking that it was alright for him to marry his father's wife.[8] Whatever the reason, this man within the Corinthian congregation was living a totally unacceptable lifestyle. Someone (most likely the household of Chloe)[9] reported it to Paul and he expressed surprise ("alas!"[10]).

What particularly upset Paul, however, was the Corinthians' arrogance: "You are boasting, but shouldn't you mourn?" (1 Cor 5:2a). He repeats this a few verses later: "Your boasting is not good" (1 Cor 5:6). In between these two statements (technically called *an inclusio*) Paul explained what they needed to do with such a person – the course of action for the Corinthians to follow (1 Cor 3–5) – as well as the newness of life that separated them from their old ways (1 Cor 5:6–8). He then distinguished the truly bad as "not the people of this world" but "the one who calls him- or herself a Christian but lives immorally" (1 Cor 5:9–10). Such a person has no honor and the Corinthians shouldn't extend hospitality to him or her (1 Cor 5:11). Of course, expulsion from table fellowship will bring about shame.

Since that person "polluted" the congregation, Paul demanded that the church "cast out 'the one who practices' / 'the evil one' from your midst" (1 Cor 5:2b and 1 Cor 5:13). Associating with a socially devious Christian – one who was living with his father's wife, one who was practicing incest – brought shame to the whole congregation, thus leaving no room for boasting. Dissociating the willfully sinning Christian from the congregation would cause that person shame and possibly would bring him to repentance. That is how honor and shame worked in ancient cultures. Malina and Neyrey write,

> Honor means a person's (or group's) feeling of self-worth and the public, social acknowledgement of that worth. Honor in this sense applies to both sexes. It is the basis of one's reputation, of one's social standing, regardless of sex . . . Any human being

---

8. Conzelmann assumes she was an unbeliever and that was why Paul didn't speak about taking an action against her: Hans Conzelmann, *1 Corinthians: A Commentary on the First Epistle to the Corinthians*, Hermeneia: A Critical & Historical Commentary on the Bible (Philadelphia: Fortress Press, 1975), 96 n. 24.

9. Bailey prefers "someone" (i.e. anonymity) to "those of Chloe's household" because "Such a discloser [of a name] would have given the Corinthians a chance to immediately shift the subject from the case of incest to the question, Who ratted on us?" (Kenneth E. Bailey, *Paul through Mediterranean Eyes: Cultural Studies in 1 Corinthians* [Downers Grove, IL: IVP Academic, 2011], 162). It might have been that the Corinthians weren't that secretive.

10. All three uses of this word in Corinthians express Paul's astonishment over the Corinthians' behavior (1 Cor 5:1; 6:7; 15:67).

worthy of the title "human" or any group worthy of belonging to the family of humankind needs to "have shame," that is, to be sensitive to its honor rating and to be perceptive of the opinion of others. A sense of shame makes the context of living possible and dignified, since it implies acceptance of and respect for the rules of human interactions.[11]

Paul, wanting action from the Corinthians, appealed to what would speak to them – honor and shame. Instead of boasting of this man's sinfulness, they needed to grieve; they needed to bring shame on the sinning one so that he would grieve and repent.[12] When they had taken such a strong stance, all of them would be restored to honor.

This principle is applicable even today in Indian churches. Often, churches ignore the sin of someone in the church, especially if that person is in leadership. But ignoring such sin of Christians corrupts the whole church and doesn't lead the sinning person to repent. This is the reason for church discipline – to keep the church pure and to bring about repentance in the willfully sinning Christian.

Intensity of Sin (5:3–5)

In general, there is no excommunication in Hindu religion – that is, no Hindu may be ousted from the Hindu religion for any sin. However, a person may lose his or her caste and be made an untouchable (a *bhangi*) for a wide variety of offenses. Such loss of caste may or may not be reversible. Also, a person or group can be excluded from society. Picking up the dead and human feces are tasks allocated for untouchables or Dalits. Those who refuse to perform these "unclean" activities are given fines, beaten, and are excluded from society.[13]

The early Christian churches practiced excommunication but for the definite purpose of promoting repentance and preserving purity. Excommunication was advocated so that the offender would quickly repent (1 Cor 5:3–5). Should an expelled person repent, he or she would be brought back into the community. Excommunication also preserved the purity of

---

11. Malina and Neyrey, "Honor and Shame in Luke–Acts," 44–45.

12. Their boasting implies either that they had not understood the extent of the problem or that they were rebellious. The immediate (1 Cor 5:9–10) and larger contexts (1 Cor 11:2) imply that they were innocent of rebellion and didn't understand the consequences of their action.

13. N.a., "Imprisoned for Life," *The Hindu*, January 9, 2011.

the community (1 Cor 5:6–8). Just as a little yeast leavened a whole batch of dough, so toleration of a little impurity corrupted the whole congregation.[14]

Within this context, Paul detailed the actions he wanted the Corinthians to take regarding the sinning person. He began by giving his own authority and consent for them to take action: "I – being absent in my body from you but present in my spirit with you – have already made my judgment against the one who worked this deed, as though I am present there" (1 Cor 5:3). There was a genuine reason for Paul to state again his "presence" with them despite his absence: a witness against an accused person had to be present in court in order for his or her witness to be valid and the judgment to be effective. Paul wasn't with the Corinthians, but he would judge as if he were with them because he believed in the accusation and he wholeheartedly believed in the judgment that he proposed. Furthermore, Paul was pronouncing this judgment on the authority of the Lord Jesus: "In the name of our Lord Jesus, when you gather together and my spirit is with you, in the power of our Lord Jesus, hand this man to Satan" (1 Cor 5:4–5a).[15] He repeated the reference to the Lord for emphasis: "in the name of our Lord Jesus" and "in the power of our Lord Jesus." The phrase "when you gather together and my spirit is with you" implies that Paul and the Corinthians were unanimous in this judgment:[16] Paul, the Corinthians, and the Lord Jesus Christ were making this decision together against the sinning brother. The Old Testament law taught, "One witness is not enough to convict a man accused of any crime or offense he may have committed. Accusation and judgment must be established by the testimony of two or three witnesses" (Deut 19:15).

Paul then stated the course of action the Corinthians needed to take: "[I have decided] to hand over this one to Satan for the destruction of flesh so that the spirit may be saved in the day of the Lord" (1 Cor 5:5). This statement

---

14. For a study of excommunication in communities like Qumran, see Adela Yarbro Collins, "The Function of 'Excommunication' in Paul," *Harvard Theological Review* 73, no. 1–2 (January–April 1980): 251–263.

15. The word "spirit" could refer to the Holy Spirit, with Paul calling the Holy Spirit to witness (as Fee interprets it in *The First Epistle to the Corinthians*, 204). On the other hand, the presence of "my" in between the article and the noun ("spirit") seems to favor the idea that Paul was talking about his non-physical presence as in verse 3.

16. There are three different ways in which commentators and translators understand this passage: "(1) 'when you are assembled in the name of the Lord Jesus' (NIV, JB, NEB); (2) 'I have already pronounced judgment in the name of the Lord Jesus' (RSV, GNB, NAB, Moffatt, Montgomery); or (3) '. . . on the one who perpetrated this deed in the name of our Lord Jesus'" (Fee, *First Epistle to the Corinthians*, 204). For the merits and demerits of these views, see Fee, *First Epistle to the Corinthians*, 204; Spurgeon, *1 Corinthians*, 56–57.

is harsher than the previous one: "cast out from your midst the one who practices this act" (1 Cor 5:2b). It is understandable that Paul wanted that sinning person not to be in the church's gathering or fellowship. But what did Paul mean by "hand over this one to Satan"? What did the "destruction of flesh" entail? What did it mean to say, "his spirit may be saved in the day of the Lord"?

The word translated "hand over" (*paradidomi*) could be used when someone was set before a council for trial or flogging (Matt 10:17). Following a trial, if someone was imprisoned, that was considered being "handed over to imprisonment" (Matt 4:12). When someone betrayed a friend to an enemy, that was also called a "handing over" (Matt 10:4). Either of the first two meanings would fit this instance: Paul was handing over the sinner to Satan for trial or flogging; or Paul was handing over the sinner to Satan for imprisonment.

The meaning of the phrase "destruction of the flesh" is a vast topic and scholars take different views. Some understand the phrase to refer to "physical suffering" afflicted by Satan on a person's body (e.g. Lightfoot and Morris). This was true in the lives of Job and Paul – Satan afflicted their bodies with illness (Job 2:1–8; 2 Cor 12:7).[17] Some scholars understand the phrase to mean "physical death" (e.g. Schneider and Käsemann). This was true in the lives of Ananias and Sapphira, who died as soon as they lied to the Holy Spirit (Acts 5:1–10). Likewise, the Corinthians who inappropriately participated in the Lord's Supper faced death (1 Cor 11:30–32). Other scholars understand the phrase to mean the destruction of one's "sinful nature" (Groseheide, Barclay, Fee, and Soards). They understand "flesh" to be in opposition to "Spirit," a doctrine Paul clearly taught (Rom 8:5–9; Gal 5:1–17). Whereas the first two views understand "flesh" as physical, the third understands it metaphorically. One wonders if Paul would really have used Satan as a purifier in the life of a sinning Christian – that is, if Satan could be instrumental in one's sanctification, getting rid of sin's hold on one's life. In addition, all references to "flesh" in 1 Corinthians are physical rather than metaphorical, falling into five categories: "human standard" (1:6), "a person" (1:29; 6:16), "living

---

17. Other instances of demonic destruction of human flesh are the demonic man living among the tombs and cutting himself with stones (Mark 5:5); a demon that possessed a young man, often throwing him into fire or water to destroy him (Mark 9:22); and when the sons of Sceva tried to exorcise demons, the demons jumped on the sons of Sceva, beat them, stripped them naked, and wounded them (Acts 19:16). It seems that Satan and the demons have destructive power over human flesh.

circumstances" (7:28), "human descent" (10:18), and "human flesh versus animal flesh" (15:39, 50). Most likely, then, Paul was referring to the man's physical flesh and its destruction rather than having a metaphorical meaning.

Concerning the phrase "the spirit may be saved in the day of the Lord," there are two prominent views. The first view understands the "spirit" as a reference to "the spirit of the community" or the church.[18] The second view (the traditional view) understands the "spirit" individually – the sinning man's personhood. Although his physical body would be destroyed either by sickness or by death, his soul-spirit (personhood) would be saved in the final resurrection (cf. 1 Cor 1:8). The second view is to be preferred. It argues that Paul was talking about a temporary discipline of the sinning individual for the benefit of his own future – that is, by his present affliction of illness or death he would be prevented from continuing in a lifestyle of sinfulness.

In a way, excommunication meant expulsion from the protection of the church. Kistemaker writes, "Paul's command to hand over a person to Satan is the act of excommunication and is equivalent to purging the evil from the church (cf. v. 13). Believers are safe in the hand of God from which no one, not even Satan, can snatch them (John 10:28–29). But if a sinner is delivered to the prince of this world, he faces destruction. He no longer enjoys the protection that a caring Christian community provides."[19] Paul had already said that God would not let anyone destroy the temple, the church (1 Cor 3:17). As long as the sinning Christian was within the congregation, he was protected. But outside the congregation, he would lose all such protection (at least temporarily, for his life was eternally secured). That was why they needed to cast him out. Of course, the ultimate intention was his repentance. The Corinthians seemed to have understood that, as is evidenced in the second letter Paul wrote them.

---

18. Shillington argues that Paul was alluding to Leviticus 16 and in light of that the "spirit" is a reference to "the Spirit of Christ resident in the new community of faith" (V. George Shillington, "Atonement Texture in 1 Corinthians 5.5," *Journal for the Study of the New Testament* 71 [1998]: 35). See also Barth Lynn Campbell, "Flesh and Spirit in 1 Cor 5:5: An Exercise in Rhetorical Criticism of the NT" *Journal of the Evangelical Theological Society* 36, no. 3 (September 1993): 331–342.

19. Simon J. Kistemaker, "'Deliver This Man to Satan' (1 Cor 5:5): A Case Study in Church Discipline," *Master's Seminary Journal* 3, no. 1 (Spring 1992): 42. Such discipline was necessary since failure to expel him not only could cause impurity within the congregation but also could give an outsider a chance to destroy the temple of God, the church. Rosner makes the original connection between this passage and 1 Corinthians 3:16–17 (Brian S. Rosner, "Temple and Holiness in 1 Corinthians 5," *Tyndale Bulletin* 42, no. 1 [1991]: 137–145). But he might not see the "one who tries to destroy the church" as an outsider as I have understood it.

The Corinthian Christians, upon receiving Paul's instructions, excommunicated the sinning brother (2 Cor 2:9). That act not only grieved the whole church (2 Cor 2:5; contrast with their earlier attitude, 1 Cor 5:2) and grieved Paul (2 Cor 2:5), but it also grieved the sinning Christian to the point of despair (2 Cor 2:7). His repentance was genuine and his pain at their not accepting him into fellowship again was immense. So they interceded and pleaded with Paul to take him back into fellowship (2 Cor 2:10). Hearing of their faithfulness in following his instructions (2 Cor 2:9) and knowing the schemes of Satan (2 Cor 2:11), Paul instructed the Corinthians to forgive the sinner (2 Cor 2:10) and to reaffirm their love for him (2 Cor 2:8).[20] This incident had a happy ending because the Corinthians were serious about purging evil and the guilty from their midst. Temporary separation from the protection of the church and a sensitive heart brought the sinning brother back into fellowship and restored joy to the community. That is the intention behind excommunication and church discipline.

The Purity of the Community (5:6–8)

Yogurt, or "curd," as it is called in India, is a favorite food of Indians. Besides eating it plain (called *dahi*), Indians eat it as *shrikhand* (a sweet dish made with strained curd), as *raita* (a savory sauce with coriander, cumin, onion, mint, and tomato), as *lassi* (a blended drink of curd, water, spices, and fruit), and as *chaas* (buttermilk). Columnist Vir Sanghvi writes, "Just as French cuisine would collapse without butter and the cuisines of Japan and China would be finished without the soya bean, so Indian cuisine would be nothing without dahi [yogurt]."[21] He gives two reasons why Indians love yogurt: in a hot climate, a cooling food like yogurt that needs no heating is preferred; and the bacteria in yogurt act as antibiotics against the bugs in one's stomach. He finishes the essay with an exhortation to keep eating yogurts that are homemade rather than store-bought or pasteurized yogurts that lack the bacteria.

Those minute bacteria within yogurt (commonly called "probiotics") turn plain milk into sour yogurt. Many Indian families are familiar with the process of yogurt-marking: mothers keep a jar in their kitchen with a little

---

20. Kruse also sees the person mentioned in 2 Cor 2:5 and 7:12 as the same man mentioned in 1 Cor 5:1–5. Colin G. Kruse, "The Offender and the Offence in 2 Corinthians 2:5 and 7:12," *The Evangelical Quarterly* 60, no. 2 (April 1988): 129–139.

21. Vir Sanghvi, "Rude Food: The Curious Case of the Indian Curd," *Hindustan Times* (6 October 2012).

curd as a starter, later in the day they add a cup or two of milk to that starter, and the next morning there is a full bottle of fresh yogurt. This process is called curdling (or coagulating).

A similar process happens when bread is made. Yeast, microorganisms in the genus of fungi, turns unleavened bread into leavened bread. Most of these micro-organic yeasts are unicellular. It is a marvel of creation that these tiny microorganisms can turn milk into curd (yogurt), bread into sourdough bread, and can help in a variety of fermentation processes (including making alcohol).

The Corinthians would have been familiar with yeast and the processes of curdling and leavening. The Jews among them would have yearly celebrated the Feast of Unleavened Bread, when they cleansed out all things associated with yeast (leavened bread, moldy clothing, etc.).[22] The people of other nations would have had yogurt, beer, and food or drinks that were leavened or fermented. In his discussion on why the Corinthians needed to expel the sinning Christian from the congregation (1 Cor 5:1–5), Paul thus resorted to imagery with which they were very familiar: "a little yeast leavens the whole batch of dough" (1 Cor 5:6). Paul wasn't implying that sexual sin was "a little" sin; rather, he was saying that if the Corinthians were tolerating one person's sin or one single sin (and especially boasting over it), it would lead to further tolerance and the total corruption of the congregation.

There was, however, a greater reality: their newness in Christ demanded a newness of life. To explain this, Paul referred to two festivals they were familiar with: the festivals of Passover and Unleavened Bread. These festivals were celebrated together. Passover was celebrated to remember the Israelites' departure from Egypt. The final testing/plague upon the Egyptians was the killing of the firstborn children and animals. Anyone who had killed a lamb and spread its blood on the doorposts escaped that horrendous night's massacre. The Israelites celebrated that passing-over yearly. Before they celebrated it, however, they cleaned the whole house of any mold or yeast. Thus the feast of Unleavened Bread preceded the feast of Passover.

Paul argued that Christ was killed as the Passover sacrifice and that the Corinthians were the unleavened bread (1 Cor 5:7b; cf. John 1:29, 36). Both

---

22. For studies on the timing of the Passover and the Unleavened Bread festivals, see Jan A. Wagenaar, "Passover and the First Day of the Festival of Unleavened Bread in the Priestly Festival Calendar," *Vetus Testamentum* 54, no. 2 (2004): 250–268. Also Gershon Hepner, "The Morrow of the Sabbath Is the First Day of the Festival of Unleavened Bread (Lev 23, 15–17)," *Zeitschrift für die alttestamentliche Wissenschaft* 118, no. 3 (2006): 389–404.

these were indicatives or statements of fact – "Christ our Passover [lamb] has been killed" and "you are new dough as you are without yeast." Since these were the realities, they needed to get into festive mode and "cleanse out the old yeast" (1 Cor 5:7a). By "old yeast," Paul was referring to the acts they used to do (cf. 1 Cor 5:11; 6:9–10). Now that they were new dough (unleavened bread) and the Passover lamb had been killed, it was time for them to celebrate the festivals of Passover and Unleavened Bread.[23] They were to celebrate "neither with old yeast nor with bad and evil yeast; instead, without yeast, that is, with honesty and truth" (1 Cor 5:8). One such type of "old yeast" was tolerating or boasting over a fellow believer's immorality. They were to expel the believer from their congregation so that they could remain as unleavened bread and continue their celebrations in Christ. Badness and evil – old yeasts – polluted the festivals; sincerity and truth enhanced them.

Although yogurt and sourdough bread are good to eat, they can also be used symbolically to illustrate allowing something or someone from the old lifestyle to sour the new life in Christ. The newness of Christian living is to be devoid of such old ways of living. Believers are unleavened bread since Christ the Passover lamb has been killed for them. So they are to celebrate the newness of life in sincerity and truth.

Insiders and Outsiders (5:9–13)

Religious communities often use terminologies or have concepts such as "insiders" and "outsiders." "Insiders" refers to those of the same faith, while "outsiders" refers to those outside of that faith. In anthropology and sociology, the equivalent terms are "emic" (studies from within the social group) and "etic" (studies from outside the social group).[24] Sarma explores these concepts with relation to Mādhva Vedānta's teachings and defines the "insiders" as those who claim that the "outsiders" cannot understand them and the "outsiders" as those who are not permitted to enter the community of the "insiders." He then explains how the insiders use rules and regulations to

---

23. Fee thinks this was an allusion to the Lord's Supper celebration (ch. 9), especially in light of v. 11, "not to *eat* with any sinful person" (Fee, *First Epistle to the Corinthians*, 218 n. 18). Most likely Paul was still illustrating the celebration of the Unleavened Bread and Passover.

24. Even in New Testament studies, scholars have used these categories. Marcus Borg, in his debate with Tom Wright, writes, "We both agree that Jesus was a deeply Jewish figure, but we follow different strategies as we seek to describe him; Tom uses emic categories (categories from within the culture), I am using etic (categories from outside the culture)." N. T. Wright and Marcus Borg, *The Meaning of Jesus* (London: SPCK, 1999), 230.

their advantage: "[The 'insiders'] may have doctrines about the ways that root texts are viewed and treated. [They] may also have doctrines about who can and cannot become an insider and why. The first are doctrines about doctrines, while the second are doctrines about the qualifications of the members of the community itself."[25] Some groups argue that only a true insider can fully understand a particular movement. For example, the *Thereavāda* branch of Buddhism argues that if one understands Buddhism, one automatically becomes a Buddhist because one recognizes it as a true religion. If one is not a Buddhist, it is only because one has not understood Buddhism.[26] Others, of course, argue that an outsider can understand a religion but cannot be a member of it until conversion.

Becoming an "insider" is very important to everyone. Sangyl Park writes,

> As a pastor of a Korean-American church, I consider a family-like value to be one of the most important elements my church can offer. People, especially immigrants, are desperate for love and care. In most Korean-American churches, a sense of family is built up through fellowship among the members of the congregation. Eating together is one of the most important rituals every Sunday. Everyone has to sit down and share a meal around a table after worship. While sharing the food, they also share their hardships and joys of (immigrant) lives with one another. Without this ritual, people would say that "I feel like we did not have church today." This way, the community of faith strengthens their spiritual and cultural bond so that they can go on as they are in their lives.[27]

He goes on to argue that this same security becomes a "fence" separating those on the inside from those outside. To those inside it gives security; to those outside it alienates them and even brings distrust. He concludes, "Outsiders can only become insiders when there is a genuine love and care."[28]

---

25. Deepak Sarma, *Epistemologies and the Limitations of Philosophical Inquiry: Doctrine of Mādhva Vedānta* (London and New York: RoutledgeCurzon, 2005), 9.

26. N. Ross Reat, "Insiders and Outsiders in the Study of Relgious Traditions," *Journal of the American Academy of Religion* 51, no. 3 (September 1983): 473.

27. Sangyl Park, "Outsiders Become Insiders," *Living Pulpit* 13, no. 4 (October–December 2004): 18.

28. Ibid., 19. Following an exposition of Galatians 3:28, Bergant says, "[T]he biased categories of the world no longer determine who is an insider and who is an outsider. It is faith in Jesus that makes that determination, and the disciples of Jesus (the insiders) have been

Paul used a similar concept of "outsiders" and "insiders" when he addressed the Corinthians. His instructions were to the "insiders," those he defined as "one who names him- or herself as 'Christian' but behaves sinfully" (1 Cor 5:11). His instructions weren't for the "outsiders," whom he termed "the people of the world" (1 Cor 5:10). He didn't want the Corinthians to misunderstand and think that he was instructing the "outsiders"; his principles of purity were for the "insiders." The lessons in this section are crucial for the churches because often churches are quick to point out the errors and sins of the outsiders (unbelievers) but slow to examine the errors and sins of the insiders. The outcome is impurity among insiders and anger from outsiders.

Before examining Paul's teachings concerning "insiders" and "outsiders," one issue needs to be addressed. This section (1 Cor 5:9–13) is used as an argument that Paul had written a previous letter that the Corinthians had misunderstood and thus he needed to write this letter.[29] Scholars come to this conclusion because of Paul's phrases "I wrote to you" in verse 9 and "now I write to you" in verse 11 (e.g. NIV). That theory is plausible. However, it is also possible that Paul is further clarifying what he has just written. In other words, instead of seeing a time element ("I wrote to you *before* . . . and *now* I write to you"), a better translation might be: "I am writing to you not about the 'outsiders' . . . *now* I am writing to you about the 'insiders.'"[30] Paul's use of the same verb forms (aorist) implies "I wrote to you . . . I wrote to you now." The aorist verb in Greek doesn't imply past tense so much as a comprehensive look at an event. The contrast is therefore not in *time* but in *content*, meaning that he wasn't instructing the Corinthians to shun the outsiders but to shun the insiders who were living inappropriately.

So what was his instruction to the "insiders," the Corinthian Christians? "I write to you in this letter not to intermingle with fornicators" (1 Cor 5:9). The verb "to intermingle" (*sunanamignumi*) gives the picture of turning again and again as in kneading dough. That fits with the earlier imagery of leavened bread, where yeast is intermingled with the flour (also Lev 2:4, 5; 7:10–12;

commissioned to invite everyone in," Dianne Bergant, "The Ousider Becomes an Insider: The New Center Is on the Margin," *Living Pulpit* 13, no. 4 (October–December 2004): 9.

29. Hays, *First Corinthians*, 5, 87. Also, Fee, *First Epistle to the Corinthians*, 6–8. Morris, *The First Epistle of Paul to the Corinthians*, 22–25. Roy Bowen Ward, "Paul and Corinth–His Visits and Letters," *Restoration Quarterly* 3, no. 4 (1959): 158–168.

30. Grammatical support comes from (a) other epistles, where he finishes the letter saying, "I wrote" (aorist), often referring to the letter he has just written (Rom 15:15; Gal 6:11); and (b) 1 Corinthians 9:15, which has the same verb form (aorist) but refers to 1 Corinthians, the present letter. Also the article before "letter" could be a demonstrative article – "this letter."

the Hebrew word is *balal*). Hosea used this concept of "intermingling" with adulterers, saying that was wrong for God's people (Hos 7:4, 8). Paul here instructs the Corinthians not to intermingle with fornicators.

Paul was quick to point out that he wasn't talking about interactions with the "outsiders": "Not at all the fornicators of this world, or the greedy, swindlers, and idolaters" (1 Cor 5:10a). The reason was evident: if they were to avoid the people of the world "they would have to leave the world" (1 Cor 5:10b). Hays writes, "Paul is not calling for the church at Corinth to withdraw from all contact with their pagan neighbors, like the Qumran covenanters withdrawing to live in the wilderness near the Dead Sea to avoid defilement."[31] Paul wanted them to be among the people of the world and to have an impact. At the same time, Paul wanted the Corinthians to avoid Christians who lived in sin: "I am writing now to you not to intermingle with anyone who names him- or herself a Christian and is a fornicator, greedy, idolater, slanderer, drunkard, or a swindler" (1 Cor 5:11a). They were to avoid the one who claimed to be a Christian but lived in non-Christian ways; they were not to intermingle with such a false Christian.

Paul's list of sinners seems random at first, but as Hays writes, "the six items in Paul's list closely correlate with six passages in Deuteronomy that call for the penalty of death, followed by the exact exclusion formula that Paul quotes in 5:13b: 'So you shall drive out the evil person from among you.'"[32] Just as the Jewish community in the Old Testament had to be serious about avoiding such sinful people, so Paul was serious that the Corinthians should avoid them; he said that they weren't even to eat with such people (1 Cor 5:11b). Most certainly Paul was disallowing such a person from participating in the Lord's Supper.[33] In addition, since ancient cultures saw fellowship at a dinning table as a sign of hospitality,[34] he could also be including any association over eating that indicated the tolerance of that person's sin. Paul wasn't asking the Corinthians to depart from the world in favor of seclusion or to avoid the world; he was asking for them to dissociate with Christians

---

31. Hays, *First Corinthians*, 87. Fee points out that "[t]here are associations with the world that Paul will disallow (e.g. 10:14–22)" (Fee, *First Epistle to the Corinthians*, 223).

32. Hays, *First Corinthians*, 87. For a chart, see ibid., 88. See also Brian Rosner, *Paul, Scripture, Ethics: A Study of 1 Corinthians 5–7*, Biblical Studies Library (Grand Rapids: Baker, 1999), 69.

33. Jonathan Schwiebert, "Table Fellowship and the Translation of 1 Corinthians 5:11," *Journal of Biblical Literature* 127, no. 1 (2008): 159–164.

34. For an excellent study on meals and fellowship, see Jerome H. Neyrey, "Ceremonies in Luke–Acts: The Case of Meals and Table-Fellowship," in *The Social World of Luke–Acts: Models for Interpretation*, ed. Jerome H. Neyrey (Peabody, MA: Hedrickson, 1991), 361–387.

who lived in sin. Paul wanted the Corinthians to take swift action against the sinning Christian in order to keep the congregation holy (unleavened).

Paul's reasoning for not judging the "outsiders" is clear: "What benefits me by judging the outsiders?" (1 Cor 5:12a). There was no profit in asking non-Christians to live as Christians. (Here is a great lesson for us as Christians: it is useless trying to change society without changing people's hearts to submit to the Lord first.) In reality, judging the outsiders was God's job all along – "God will judge those outsiders" (1 Cor 5:13a). In Romans he said that the lifestyles of the sinful world were evidence that God's judgment (wrath) had already been revealed (Rom 1:18 – 3:20). In the same way, even in Corinth God would deal with the outsiders.

On the other hand, judging the insiders was the job of the Corinthians. As a matter of fact, it wasn't even Paul's job, and so Paul said, "Aren't you to judge those insiders?" (1 Cor 5:12b). Such self-evaluation and action (a judgment) would bring purity both to the sinning Christian's life and also to the congregation. The sinning Christian, through being excommunicated, would realize his or her errors, repent, and be restored. The congregation, by excommunicating the sinning person, would keep its purity and take a stand for holiness.

So the Corinthian Christians needed to deal with their own believers who were living in sin. Paul concluded, "Cast out the evil one from your midst" (1 Cor 5:13b), citing a principle found in several passages of the Old Testament (e.g. Deut 17:7; 19:19: 22:21, 24; 24:7). In all those passages, the evaluation of the guilty one begins with the inner circle of God's people. The law, for example, said that if a member of the Israelites left them to go and serve another god, the Israelites ought to "expel such an evil person from their midst" after careful investigation and by stoning (Deut 17:2-7). Paul was citing that conclusion to illustrate the importance of the Corinthians dealing with sinning Christians in their midst.

Christianity today also has "outsiders" and "insiders." All outsiders are welcome to come in and join the inner circle of faithful believers. However, insiders are required to live an exemplary lifestyle. When they fail, the church is to deal with them carefully and firmly in order to keep the purity of the church and also to help those who have sinned realize their errors. At the same time, the church's task isn't to judge outsiders; that is God's job.

8

1 Corinthians 6

Lawsuits and Christians (6:1–8)

"The Hindu Law," as it is referred to in contemporary India, refers to a system of personal laws on marriage, adoption, and inheritance applied only to Hindus in India. It originated under the British legal system established in 1772 and became part of the law of India established in the Constitution of India in 1950. The British took the early translation of Sanskrit texts of *Dharmasāstra* or "treaties on religious and legal duties" and applied it for the Hindus.[1] In daily practice, however, there are no religious courts in India. All cases are adjudicated within the state's district courts, presided over by the state's bureaucrats. In addition, there are village tribunals and caste councils that try community members according to customs and local laws. It is normal for a Hindu judge to preside over a Muslim couple's divorce or for a Christian judge to preside over the adoption case of a Hindu family.

Lawsuits are common among all people groups. Therefore there are, unfortunately, lawsuits even among Christians. Stackhouse writes, "One of the symptoms of the church's [Church of South India's] internal strains is the enormous number of cases referred to the secular courts."[2] Churches in India are not alone in this; Nichols tells of a tragic lawsuit between two factions within First Baptist Church, Richmond, Virginia, USA, in 1965 concerning the admission of two sons of Nigerian Baptist ministers into an

---

1. Scholars argue that the British actually misunderstood these laws: Richard W. Lariviere, "Justices and Panditas: Some Ironies in Contemporary Readings of the Hindu Legal Past," *Journal of Asian Studies* 48 (1989): 757–769. Also Ludo Rocher, "Law Books in an Oral Culture: The Indian Dharmasāstras," *Proceedings of the American Philosophical Society* 137 (1993): 254–267.
2. Stackhouse, "Tensions Beset Church of South India," 744.

all-white church.[3] Moll reports that when the pension plan of the publishing arm of the Evangelical Lutheran Church in America (Augsburg Fortress) folded, it left hundreds of workers devastated, and they took the church and the publishing house to the law courts.[4] In June 2005, Ergun Carner (vice president at Arlington Baptist Theological Seminary) sued Jason Smathers (an Arizona Baptist pastor) and Jonathan Autry (a graduate of Liberty Baptist Theological Seminary) for posting a video of him on YouTube.[5] Whether lawsuits are legitimate or not, the churches and Christians worldwide are engaged in them.

The Corinthians were no exception. They too had legal fights. It might have been that the father of the son who had taken his father's wife had sued the son (1 Cor 5:1–5); or the legal fight may have been over livestock or property lines ("life matters," 1 Cor 5:3). Nevertheless, the lawsuit caused trauma in a small congregation of forty to fifty people in Corinth. So Paul dealt with this issue next.

He began expressing his astonishment: "How *dare* any one of you, when you have disputes, go to unredeemed judges instead of going to the holy ones [Christians]?" (1 Cor 6:1). Paul wasn't calling the non-Christian judges "unlawful" or "unjust"; instead he was referring to their status in Christ: they were unredeemed (without God's righteousness) in God's sight. So, even if they were excellent judges regarding state or federal law, they wouldn't understand Christians who had the Spirit of God, and therefore they couldn't be judges over them. Corinth was a Roman colony, a senatorial province. So an appointed proconsul ruled it together with annually elected magistrates and members of the city senate. It is highly unlikely that Christians would have been elected to these posts and would have formed part of this legal system. So when Christians had conflicts they would have gone to these non-Christian lawyers and law courts. Paul didn't want them to do that. Moses' father-in-law had taught Moses how to judge the people in an orderly fashion. Since then, the Old Testament had a clearly defined judging process, involving elders and priests,[6] Paul would have wanted the Corinthian Christians to follow a similar pattern by which they judged their own disputes.

3. Sue Nichols, "Lawsuit in a Richmond Church," *Christian Century* (5 January 1966): 24.

4. Rob Moll, "Pension Tension: Lawsuit Questions 'Church Related' Retirement Plans," *Christianity Today* 54, no. 10 (October 2010): 11–12.

5. Ken Walker, "Youtube's Blocked Testimony: An Ex-Muslim's Lawsuit Has Implications for Law and Church," *Christianity Today* 57, no. 10 (December 2013): 23.

6. For an excellent study of the Old Testament background to 1 Corinthians 6:1–6, see Rosner, *Paul, Scripture, Ethics*, 95–112.

Paul's reasoning for not going to non-Christians as judges was because the Christians would "discern" both the angels and the world (1 Cor 6:2a, 3a). This verb "discern" (*krino* in Greek) can mean "judge." However, in light of Paul's earlier statement – "Who am I to judge the outsiders?" (1 Cor 5:12) – it is best to understand Paul to be saying that Christians with the influence of the Holy Spirit were able to discern the ways of the world and to avoid them, and therefore they shouldn't have worldly judges resolve their disputes. Since the Corinthians were capable of discerning or judging even the angels and the world, they were to deal with their own "small disputes" or "life matters" (1 Cor 6:2b, 3b). These terms "small disputes" and "life matters" imply that the Corinthians might have been fighting over debts or stolen property. Regardless, they were not to seek the help of worldly judges.

Instead, they were to appoint "the despised in the churches" as judges (1 Cor 6:4).[7] This was a command.[8] Paul wasn't promoting class distinction that would go against his earlier teaching; instead, he was promoting a legal system where the least influential people, rather than the most influential, had a say. In most social gatherings it is the influential people who have a say. But Paul wanted the Corinthians to appoint the least influential as judges so that the cases of the oppressed would be heard. A Roman colony like Corinth with multitudes of slaves would have known oppression. Such oppressed people were to judge cases and thus avoid partiality. This would have resembled the contemporary "trial by jury" principle, in which peers determine the outcome of a case.

Ancient cultures operated on the "honor–shame" principle (see the commentary on 4:14–21). In such cultures, exposing shamefulness always drew quick action. Paul wanted swift action from the Corinthians: "I say these things to shame you: Aren't there any wise people among you who could resolve this dispute between these Christians?" (1 Cor 6:5). Of course there were wise people in the congregation, and Paul wanted them to take the case into their hands; so he challenged them. When there are disputes of "one Christian against another Christian," such cases cannot appear before

---

7. For a study of the importance of community in judgment, see Peter Richardson, "Judgment in Sexual Matters in 1 Corinthians 6:1–11," *Novum Testamentum* 25, no. 1 (January 1983): 37–58.

8. Kinman has successfully shown this to be an imperative by taking into account both the cultural and legal situations in Corinth and the Greek grammar (Brent Kinman, "'Appoint the Despised as Judges!' [1 Corinthians 6:4]," *Tyndale Bulletin* 48, no. 2 [1997]: 345–354).

non-Christians (1 Cor 6:6). Christians must settle such disputes among themselves.[9]

Lawsuits between Christians, regardless of the outcome, always result in grief. So Paul said, "Since you have lawsuits between one another, you are already in an adverse situation (or defeat)" (1 Cor 6:7a).[10] They were in an adverse situation (or defeat) because they were involving outsiders in solving their disputes, implying that they didn't have any wise people among themselves to judge those disputes. Further, this showed that they didn't have love for one another to solve the disputes amicably. Lawsuits, in general, were expensive (Matt 5:25; Luke 12:58) and they would have lost money in the process. So lawsuits – regardless of the outcome – always resulted in loss.

A better option was to suffer the loss: "Why couldn't you put up with a little injustice against you?" "Why couldn't you tolerate being cheated a few times?" (1 Cor 6:7b). Paul wasn't promoting injustice or unfairness; rather, he was promoting a little tolerance in place of the hasty filing of lawsuits. The Old Testament is full of examples of people who tolerated injustice against them, such as Joseph, Moses, and David. Even the Lord tolerated injustice: when he was reviled and punished without any cause, he remained quiet as a lamb ready for slaughter. When Peter asked, "How many times should I forgive someone who sins *against me*?" the Lord answered "seventy-seven times" (Luke 18:21–22). So Paul was saying, "Couldn't you tolerate a little injustice against you?" "Couldn't you allow yourself to be defrauded a few times?" The Corinthians were quick to have recourse to the law courts, and that resulted in them being unrighteous: "You are being unjust and you are defrauding, and that against Christians!" (1 Cor 6:8). Failing to forgive one another and failing to seek the help of fellow Christians to resolve tension resulted in defeat, cheating, and defrauding. That was why Paul wanted them to appoint Christians as judges over them and to avoid lawsuits.

In 1951 J. Maurice Trimmer reported an amazing event: "At its 46th annual assembly at the spacious camp-meeting grounds at Scottsville, Ky., the Church of God urged religious groups to 'suffer loss and be defrauded' rather than go to court. In a formal resolution, the assembly challenged churches to steer clear of lawsuits and thereby set a pattern for nations to follow in

---

9. Practically speaking, when there are lawsuits involving corporations and institutions this principle might not apply; one might need to seek the help of the established law system.

10. This noun "defeat" (*hettema*) occurs one other time in Paul's writings where the "disadvantaged" or "adverse" situation of the Jews in rejecting the Lord Jesus as Messiah resulted in the "advantaged" or "favorable" situation for the Gentiles (Rom 11:12).

settling disputes without resort to war."[11] This church was operating on a principle similar to the one Paul was instructing the Corinthians. In a church in Texas, two church members had business dealings. When an unfortunate event happened, instead of quickly suing each other, they sought the help of the church elders, who brought about an amicable solution. Paul was hoping that this was what the Corinthian church would do too: resolve their tensions among themselves and not go to secular courts.

When I had finished teaching this section in a Singapore seminary, a student said to me, "This could never work here, where properties of one mission organization have been confiscated by another mission organization." What Paul speaks of here in 1 Corinthians 6 is about legal disputes between church members, not legal disputes between organizations. In the latter case, a church or a Christian organization must seek the help of the civil government. The application from Paul's teaching in Romans 13 would take precedence. God has set in place governments to punish the wrong and exonerate the right. Organizations involved in disputes may have to resort to using the governmental legal system to set things straight.

Nevertheless, Paul's principle is applicable in most cases involving Christians: they should appoint their own judges (possibly neutral people) to hear the case and resolve it amicably. In this way, they will not be ashamed in the sight of the world.

Property Rights and Inheritance (6:9–11a)

The Hindu Succession Act 1956, an Act of the Parliament of India, enables a Hindu woman to have full rights over her property – to deal with it or to dispose of it according to her own will. It abolished a woman's limited freedom over her property. It was amended in 2005 to allow daughters to have equal property rights with sons. The ancestral property must be divided equally between male and female descendants. An unfortunate addition is that when a descendant converts to another religion, he or she loses the rights to the property until he or she returns to Hinduism.

Property acquisition is significant for every people group. That may have been what drove the Corinthians to draw one another to the civil law court,

---

11. James Maurice Trimmer, "Disciple Laymen Meet at Bethany: Five Thousand Attend Two-Day Even on Historic Campus – Church of God Hits Ecclesiastical Lawsuits," *Christian Century* 68, no. 39 (26 September 1951): 1103.

because they dealt with "life matters," *biō-tikos* (1 Cor 6:1–8). Paul, however, wanted them to focus on a greater inheritance, that is, the inheritance of the kingdom of God. So he wrote, "Do you not know that the unrighteous people will not inherit the kingdom of God?" (1 Cor 6:9a). Paul wasn't saying that the Corinthians were these unrighteous people and would lose their inheritance in the kingdom of God.[12] He would soon list those who were disqualified and remind the Corinthians that this was no longer true of them; instead, it was a reference to their past: "these were some of you" (1 Cor 6:11a). They were no longer among the unrighteous who would not inherit God's kingdom, and therefore they shouldn't fight over earthly inheritance.

Paul then listed the people who characteristically missed God's kingdom: fornicators, idolaters, adulterers, passive homosexual partners,[13] dominant homosexual partners,[14] thieves, greedy people, drunkards, revilers, and swindlers (1 Cor 6:10). People who have these characteristic lifestyles would not inherit the kingdom of God. Paul used "kingdom of God" twice to emphasize that people who live characteristically sinful lives will not have an inheritance in God's kingdom; they will have only an earthly inheritance for which they might fight. The Corinthian Christians were such people who had characteristically sinful lives and who would not have an inheritance in God's kingdom (1 Cor 6:11a). God had redeemed them and therefore they shouldn't quibble over earthly properties but should instead focus on living as inheritors of God's kingdom.

When people have an eternal perspective on life, such as their membership of God's family, they don't get into petty bickering over earthly possessions. The widow with two small coins illustrates this principle: those two coins

---

12. Assuming that Paul was referring to their present state of sinfulness, scholars have proposed various interpretations, which López summarizes: "(a) believers who commit these sins will lose their salvation, (b) people who commit these sins show they were not saved in the first place, (c) believers who commit these sins lose fellowship with the Lord, (d) believers who commit these sins will miss the millennial kingdom, though they will have eternal life, and (e) believers who commit these sins will lose rewards in heaven [López's preference]." René A. López, "Does the Vice List in 1 Corinthians 6:9-10 Describe Believers or Unbelievers," *Bibliotheca Sacra* 164, no. 653 (January-March 2007): 59. However, it is more likely that Paul was stating a general principle rather than describing the Corinthians' state, since he had already called them holy ones (1 Cor 1:2).

13. This word *malakoi* simply meant "soft." But in Classical Greek it referred to "the young, 'passive' partner in a pederastic [homosexual] relationship" (Fee, *First Epistle to the Corinthians*, 243). Paul most likely gave it the same meaning.

14. The word *arsen-o-koites* means "sex with male." But since it is paired up with "passive homosexual partner" (*malakoi*), it most likely meant "dominant homosexual partner." Louw and Nida write, "As in Greek, a number of other languages also have entirely distinct terms for the active [dominant] and passive roles in homosexual intercourse" (22.281).

were all the possessions she had in life, yet she let them go in order to inherit eternal life (Mark 12:41–44).[15] Rarely do we see such "letting go" of material possessions, even among Christians. Our true inheritance is not in earthly possessions; it is in the kingdom of God.

Ritual Washing (6:11b)

Ritual washing or bathing plays a significant role in every religion. In Hinduism, the holiest of acts is to wash oneself in the river Ganges. The Ganges flows from the western Himalayas to the Bay of Bengal, and the river base covers parts of Nepal, China, Bangladesh, and India. Hindus consider the river as the goddess Ganga. In a list of the rivers most at risk from over-extraction, the Ganges is the fifth highest: "Over-extraction of ground water has seriously affected water quality. Inadequate recharging of groundwater impairs the natural cleansing of arsenic which becomes water soluble when exposed to air, and threatens the health of 75 million people who are likely to use water contaminated with up to 2mg/l of arsenic."[16] Yet millions of devotees bathe in this river annually for the cleansing of their spiritual impurity.

The Qumran community, at the time of Jesus and Paul, practiced ritual cleansing every day. Often before a meal, a devotee was to bathe in a *mikveh* (ritual cleansing hole). Some have identified Christian baptism with such a ritual, but Christian baptism is a one-time event.

There is, however, another ritual cleansing that is more significant for Christians. Paul wrote to the Corinthians, "You were cleansed, sanctified, and justified in the name of the Lord Jesus Christ and in the Spirit of our God" (1 Cor 6:11b). This is a spiritual and figurative cleansing that resulted in their being "sanctified," "set apart," as holy people. Such people were also justified, that is, set in the right before God. This cleansing, which is internal, is more important than any outward cleansing or rituals of washing, to the point that Peter said elsewhere, "Can anyone hinder these Gentile Christians from water purification when they have received the Holy Spirit just as we, the Jews, have?" (Acts 10:47). Inward cleansing of the Holy Spirit, in the name of the Lord Jesus Christ, was much more valuable and made someone purer than outward ritual cleansing of any sort. That was what Paul wanted the

---

15. The story is set in the context of the Sadducees debating with the Lord over the resurrection (Mark 12:18–44).

16. C. M. Wong et al., "World's Top 10 Rivers at Risk," ed. WWF International (Gland, Switzerland, March 2007), 22.

Corinthians to focus on, and that is what we, Christians in India, must also focus on – the internal cleansing of the Holy Spirit.

Sanskrit, Greek, and Quotations (6:12)

Sanskrit is the primary language of the Hindu scriptures. The name "Sanskrit" comes from the verbal adjective *samskrta* that means "put together" or "constructed." All the Vedas (the large collection of hymns and incantations) and discussions in them (Brahmanas and Upanishads, Rigveda, and Ramayana) were written in Sanskrit. According to the 2001 census of India, 14,135 people reported Sanskrit to be their mother tongue, making it one of the longest-surviving languages.

Another of the longest-surviving languages is Greek. Concerning the relationship between Greek and Sanskrit Caragounis writes, "The Greek language is one of the three oldest Indo-European (IE) languages with written documentation, the other two being Sanskrit and Hittite . . . Sanskrit, the sacred language of ancient India (belonging to the Anatolian or *satem* branch), the earliest form of which is represented by the Vedic literature (supposed to have been composed in 1200–800 BC though the written form is later) is the language with the latest documentation of the three, whose classical form covers the period 800–400 BC."[17] The New Testament was written in *koine*, the common Greek language, which was in use from 300 BC (when Alexander the Great conquered many lands) until AD 600. This Greek language still survives in a slightly modified form as Modern Greek, spoken by 10 million Greeks today.[18]

Sanskrit and Greek have several commonalities, one of which is lack of punctuation, including quotation marks. As such, quotations are often mistakenly interpreted as statements. But there are patterns that scholars can use to identify where a classical writer of Sanskrit or Greek has cited others. Thus, for example, Okita argues that Baladeva used three distinct patterns when he cited others in his commentary on Brahmasūtras, called *Govindabhāsya*.[19] Similarly, scholars have shown that several statements in

---

17. Chrys C. Caragounis, *The Development of Greek and the New Testament: Morphology, Syntax, Phonology, and Textual Transmission* (Grand Rapids: Baker Academic, 2006), 1.

18. Caragounis and others have strongly defended the position, with sufficient evidence, that Greek is not a dead language (see Caragounis, *Development of Greek and the New Testament*, 17–64).

19. Kiyokazu Okita, "Quotations in Early Modern Vedānta: An Example from Gaudiya Vaisnavism," *Religions of South Asia* 6, no. 2 (December 2012): 209. For a study of quotations

1 Corinthians were the Corinthians' slogans that Paul cited in order to refute them.[20]

The first such slogan was "Everything is permissible for me" (1 Cor 6:12a). Paul cited it four times (twice in 1 Cor 6:12 and twice in 10:23) and modified it each time. The first correction was that, although all things were indeed permissible, "not all things are beneficial or helpful" (1 Cor 6:12b).[21] It is likely that the Corinthians were so thrilled by their new-found freedom in Christ that they assumed they were at liberty to do anything – "Everything is permissible for us," they thought. Paul, instead of directly contradicting their slogan, modified it. The second modification was that "I shall not be mastered by anything" (1 Cor 6:12c). Although all things were permissible, Paul wouldn't allow anything to master him. His only true Master, Lord, was Jesus Christ. No freedom would master him. That was the attitude he wanted the Corinthians to have, since such an attitude would guide them to proper behavior where they had problems, such as in areas like food and sex.

Food and Sex (6:13–14)

Indian culture thinks of food as medical and psychological rather than merely nutritional. Gandhi, for example, saw a close tie between food and his pursuit of celibacy. He wrote,

> Control of the palate is very closely connected with the observance of *brahmacharya* [celibacy]. I have found from experience that the observance of celibacy becomes comparatively easy, if one acquires mastery over the palate . . . Food has to be taken as we take medicine, that is, without thinking whether it is palatable

---

in Job see Edward Ho, "In the Eyes of the Beholder: Unmarked Attributed Quotations in Job," *Journal of Biblical Literature* 128, no. 4 (Winter 2009): 703–715.

20. Denny Burk, "Discerning Corinthian Slogans through Paul's Use of the Diatribe in 1 Corinthians 6:12–20," *Bulletin for Biblical Research* 18, no. 1 (2008): 99–121. J. Murphy-O'Connor, "Corinthian Slogans in 1 Cor 6:12–20," *Catholic Biblical Quarterly* 40, no. 3 (July 1978): 391–396. Jay E. Smith, "The Roots of a 'Libertine' Slogan in 1 Corinthians 6:18," *Journal of Theological Studies* 59, no. 1 (April 2008): 63–95. For well-defined criteria of identifying quotations, see Jay E. Smith, "Slogans in 1 Corinthians," *Bibliotheca Sacra* 167, no. 665 (January–March 2010): 84–86. For a chart explaining the parallel between their slogans and Paul's reply, see Hays, *First Corinthians*, 102.

21. For a study on Leviticus 18 being the background of this passage and how God's moral principles concerning sexuality still apply to the church, see Mark Gravrock, "Why Won't Paul Just Say No? Purity and Sex in 1 Corinthians 6," *Word & World* 16, no. 4 (Fall 1996): 444–455.

or otherwise, and only in quantities limited to the needs of the body . . . And one who thus gives up a multitude of eatables will acquire self-control in the natural course of things.[22]

This concept is not new. For example, the ancient Greek Priscianus Caesariensis suggested avoiding foods that are able to cause flatulence in order to prevent nocturnal emissions, for such foods arouse sexual desire.[23] The Egyptians thought of onion as an aphrodisiac, so priests who had taken the vow of celibacy were forbidden to eat onions. In the contemporary media, chocolate and oysters are considered to be aphrodisiacs.

Somehow, the Corinthians also associated food and sex. Their slogan "all things are permissible" (1 Cor 6:16) eventually led them to sexual acts with prostitutes (1 Cor 6:12–18) and to eating food in the temples (chs. 8–10). So Paul first addressed the topic of visiting prostitutes.[24]

The Corinthians claimed, "Food for the stomach and the stomach for food" (1 Cor 6:13a). Most likely they meant, "Let's eat all foods, since God has made them all." Although there was truth in this claim (and Paul himself would make this claim later, 1 Cor 10:25, 31; also Mark 7:19a), the Corinthians needed to realize that "God will destroy both the food and the stomach," meaning that both food and the stomach were temporal (1 Cor 6:13b). Stomach here represents "appetite" and not the physical stomach (since Paul in the next verse argues that our bodies will be redeemed and will abide). In other words, food and appetites will be destroyed. Therefore, we must not live for food, although we can enjoy food while God provides it.

They must have connected this formula of "food for the body" to that of "the body for sex" (*pornia*, sexual immorality of all kinds). So Paul continued, "The body is not for immorality but it *belongs* to the Lord, and the Lord is *Lord* over the body" (1 Cor 6:13c). The Corinthians may have slipped into a form of pre-Gnosticism that argued that the body was evil and temporal, and that only the soul and spirit were eternal. Paul's teaching elsewhere, as well as the rest of the New Testament, clearly argues that the resurrection will be bodily. Hays writes, "The body is not simply a husk to be cast off in

22. M. K. Gandhi, *From Yeravda Mandir (Ashram Observances)*, trans. Valji Govindji Desai (Ahmedabad, India: Jitendra T. Desai, 1932), 12.

23. John Dugan, "Preventing Ciceronianism: C. Lucinius Calvus' Regimen for Sexual and Oratorical Self-Mastery," *Classical Philology* 96, no. 3 (2001): 403.

24. Deming has an interesting but unsubstantiated hypothesis: the prostitute of 1 Cor 6:12–20 is the stepmother mentioned in 1 Cor 5:1–5. Will Deming, "The Unity of 1 Corinthians 5–6," *Journal of Biblical Literature* 115, no. 2 (Summer 1996): 289–312.

the next life; the gospel of Jesus Christ proclaims that we are to be redeemed body, soul, spirit (cf. 1 Thess 5:23–24; Rom 8:23). Salvation can never be understood as an escape from the physical world or as the flight of the soul to heaven. Rather, the resurrection of the *body* is an integral element of the Christian story. Those who live within that story, then, should understand that what they do with their bodies in the present time is a matter of urgent concern."[25] Paul's statement might have come as a surprise to the Corinthians. They might have thought they were able to enjoy everything, including sex with a prostitute.[26] But they were wrong: their bodies belonged to the Lord; he was Lord over their bodies. These sentences express the ownership of the Lord over Christians' bodies. Thus "God who raised the Lord will also raise them by his power from their death" (1 Cor 6:14). The Corinthians thought in terms of time – that is, that the body was meant for food and sex. But there was an eternal dimension – the body belonged to the Lord, who was its master; it belonged to God, who would raise it from the dead. So they ought to preserve their bodies and keep away from gluttony and immorality.

Often we too slip into a pseudo-Gnostic thinking in which our present bodies are not part of our salvation story. Such an understanding is unbiblical. The bodily resurrection of Christians implies that God cares for our bodies. The Lord Jesus is the Master and Lord of our bodies, and therefore we must preserve them as best we can. Proper diet and exercise should be part of the lifestyle of every Christian, as should be abstaining from immorality of any sort.

Prostitution and Oneness (6:15–20)

Prostitution is exchanging sex for money – that is, "commercialized sex." It is an ancient practice. The eighteenth century BC Mesopotamian law, the Code of Hammurabi, contained stipulations concerning the rights of female prostitutes. In ancient Rome, prostitution was legal. The Ancient Greek

---

25. Hays, *First Corinthians*, 104. The Lord Jesus' resurrection was bodily; he said, "Look at my hands and my feet; it's me! Touch me and see. A ghost does not have flesh and bone. But I have flesh and bone" (Luke 24:39).

26. The Jewish Christians might not have been part of this group, for Judaism had stringent regulations concerning sexuality. Stokes writes, "Judaism placed great importance on companionship in marriage . . . Prostitution, homosexuality, and bestiality – practices that were tied to the other gods, nations, and lands – were not to be allowed among the holy people, or by anyone in the Holy Land" (H. Bruce Stokes, "Religion and Sex: A Cultural History," *Kesher: A Journal of Messianic Judaism* 9, [Summer 1999]: 68).

historian Herodotus records that there were temples and shrines along the rivers Tigris and Euphrates with sacred prostitutes who offered their services to devotees for a fixed price (*The Histories* 1.199).

India today is no different, and its involvement of children in this industry is appalling. Peerman writes, "The commercial sexual exploitation of children is a serious problem throughout the world, but India's record is one of the world's worst. Of the country's more than 2 million sex workers, a conservatively estimated 300,000 are children, according to UNICEF and other sources."[27] Homosexuality is also a part of prostitution. Based on their extensive research at Marina Beach, Chennai, India, K. C. Abraham, a presbyter of the Church of South India, and Ajit K. Abraham, a worker in a community health organization based in Bangalore, narrate the horrible ways in which young men are entrapped into homosexuality: "In India it has been found that many persons have been initiated into homosexuality as children by older, more experienced males who have found children an easy target to satisfy their sexual urges . . . It was found that for some in their late 20s homosexuality was the easiest way to satisfy their sexual drives, as relations with the opposite sex might develop into marital expectations, and many homosexual men who fear and are unable to handle intimacy escape into promiscuous homosexual relations."[28] In short, not only is commercialized sex common in India, but forced child sex and homosexuality using young boys are also prevalent.

Corinth was a commercial port city and would therefore have had as many, or more, prostitutes as sailors. Unfortunately, the Christians in Corinth succumbed to this sin of visiting prostitutes. As Rosner explains, it might have been customary for Corinthians to visit a prostitute after a festival.[29] So, even after becoming Christians, some of them continued their visits to prostitutes, because they thought their bodies were meant for sex (1 Cor 6:13c). Paul was alarmed because their bodies were collectively members of the Lord Jesus Christ: "Don't you know that your body is a body part of Christ?" (1 Cor 6:15a). There was a mystical union between Christ and the Christians. All Christians were members of Christ's body. As such, wherever

---

27. Dean Peerman, "The Flesh Trade in India: Paradise for Pedophilies," *Christian Century* (24 July 2007): 11.

28. K. C. Abraham and Ajit K. Abraham, "Homosexuality: Some Reflections from India," *Ecumenical Review* 50, no. 1 (January 1998): 27.

29. Brian S. Rosner, "Temple Prostitution in 1 Corinthians 6:12–20," *Novum Testamentum* 40, no. 4 (October 1998): 348.

a Christian went, he or she took the whole body of Christ with him or her. Paul, personifying it, said, "Shall I take an organ of Christ's body and make it an organ of a prostitute?" (1 Cor 6:15b). The answer was "absolutely not."[30]

Sexual union with a prostitute was more than a mere physical act: it was also an emotional and spiritual act. Paul asked, "Do you not know that anyone who *glues himself* to a prostitute is one body with her, since it is said, 'the two shall become one flesh'?" (1 Cor 6:16). Paul was quoting Genesis, where Adam said of Eve, "She is one of my own bones; flesh of my own flesh; she shall be called woman, for she was taken from man" (Gen 2:23). The writer concludes, "This is why a man leaves his father and mother, and *glues himself* to his wife, and they become one flesh" (Gen 2:24). These terms "united" and "one flesh" refer to familial oneness.[31] A Corinthian Christian who visited a prostitute was involved in a familial/spiritual relationship with her, much more than he or she expected. Such is the significance of the sexual act with anyone, whether or not the other person is a prostitute. There is an emotional and spiritual bonding, one that should not be formed outside of one's marriage and outside of one's relationship with the Lord.

Paul spoke of the latter first. Intimacy with a prostitute was wrong spiritually because a Christian was already in another intimate relationship: "The one who is *glued* to the Lord [a Christian] is one with the Spirit" (1 Cor 6:17). Given this, if Christians were to visit a prostitute, they would be introducing another person into this intimate relationship, and that would be considered adultery (Rom 7:1–4). The Corinthian Christians who were visiting prostitutes didn't realize the extent of their crime. They were dragging the body of the Lord into an act that was not characteristic of someone who would inherit the kingdom of God (1 Cor 6:9–11). Because of the seriousness of their crime and folly, Paul concluded with the command: "Flee immorality" (1 Cor 6:18a).

Paul then addressed the first of the commitments – one's commitment to one's spouse. He cited another of the Corinthians' slogans: "All sin a person

---

30. Paul often used this "May it never be" (*me genoito*) or "absolutely not" to highlight the absurdity of a belief: Rom 3:4, 6; 3:31; 6:2, 15; 7:7, 13; 9:14; 11:1, 11; 1 Cor 6:15; 7:23.

31. NET footnote on Gen 2:24 says, "To be one's 'bone and flesh' is to be related by blood to someone. For example, the phrase describes the relationship between Laban and Jacob (Gen 29:14); Abimelech and the Shechemites (Judg 9:2; his mother was a Shechemite); David and the Israelites (2 Sam 5:1); David and the elders of Judah (2 Sam 19:12); and David and his nephew Amasa (2 Sam 19:13; see 2 Sam 17:2; 1 Chr 2:16–17)."

commits is outside of one's body" (1 Cor 6:18b).[32] They were implying that sins do not affect one's body. Paul corrected them, saying, "Oh yes, the one who commits fornication does sin against his or her own body" (1 Cor 6:18c).[33] This sin affected the body in three separate ways. First, it affected one's marriage. The Scriptures clearly teach that a husband and wife are one body (Gen 2:24; Matt 19:5). So when a spouse sins by committing adultery or fornication, he or she sins against his or her own body, the spouse. Second, it affects the spiritual body of the church, of which he or she is a member. The church is the body of Christ. This was why Paul wanted the Corinthians to expel sinning Christians, because their sin was not private – it affected the whole body of Christ, the church. Third, it could affect one's own physical body, as in the case of sexually transmitted diseases.

Although sins against one's own physical body and one's spouse are in the background of the concept of sinning against one's own body, Paul's primary concern was sinning against the body of Christ, the collective whole of which each Christian is a part: "Do you not know that your body is the temple of the Holy Spirit – whom you received from God, who is in you? And therefore you are not of yourselves" (1 Cor 6:19). Whereas the Corinthians argued that sin has no effect on one's body, Paul argued that sin did affect one's own body – physically, maritally, and spiritually – and the collective body of Christ, the church (as implied by the plural "you"). They had no right to afflict their bodies with sin because their bodies did not belong to them; they belonged to the Holy Spirit whom God had given them and who indwelt them; and they also belonged to the collective whole, the church (cf. 1 Cor 6:13–14). They no longer had ownership over their bodies since they had been bought at a costly price (1 Cor 6:20a). No doubt Paul was referring to the death of the Lord that purchased their freedom. Since they no longer belonged to themselves, they had only one option: "Glorify God in your bodies" (1 Cor 6:20b).[34] Whereas

---

32. Conybears and Howson first proposed, in 1874, that this verse embedded a quotation from the Corinthians. But this view came to prominence after the writing of Murphy-O'Connor, "Corinthian Slogans in 1 Cor 6:12–20," 391–396. Since then many scholars (including Raymond Collins, Joseph Fitzmyer, Richard Hays, Richard Horsley, Alan F. Johnson, Anthony Thiselton, and Verlyn Verbrugge) have held that 6:18b was a slogan among the Corinthians and 6:18c is Paul's refutation of it.

33. For a study of "body" in this verse, see Brendan Byrne, "Sinning against One's Own Body: Paul's Understanding of the Sexual Relationship in 1 Corinthians 6:18," *Catholic Biblical Quarterly* 45, no. 4 (October 1983): 608–616.

34. There is a hidden reference to the Trinity in these verses. The Spirit was in their bodies, they were bought by Christ's death, and they were to glorify God with their bodies.

the Corinthians claimed that the body was for food and sex, Paul reminded them that the body was to be used to glorify God.

There are two extremes to avoid: some philosophies at the time of Paul (e.g. proto-Gnosticism) taught that the body was evil; but on the other hand, the Corinthians seemed to have thought that God didn't care about their bodies and that they were meant only for food and sex. Both philosophies are wrong. God doesn't think of the body as evil; in fact, the Lord Jesus had a body even after the resurrection (Col 2:9). In this passage, Paul teaches that God cares about our bodies. In addition, our bodies form a collective whole with the body of Christ, the church. A Christian's body is individually and collectively (with those of other Christians) God's temple, and the Holy Spirit lives in it. Therefore, all Christians are commissioned to glorify God in their bodies, both individually and collectively as a church.

We are easily drawn towards an individualized Christianity, but the Christian life is a collective whole. Our actions have consequences not only on our lives but also on the life of the church. That is the message Paul repeatedly brings out in this section. Collectively, we are like dough; a small amount of yeast will leaven the whole lump. So it is important that we not only watch our own actions in light of this truth, but also watch other Christians so that we do not pollute Christ's body, the temple of God where the Holy Spirit lives, the church.

Part II

Paul's Answers to the Corinthians' Questions (7:1 – 16:18)

In the first section of this letter (1:10 – 6:20) Paul dealt with matters that Chloe's household had reported to him concerning the Corinthians. These matters included divisions within the congregation, sexual immorality, lawsuits, and the visiting of prostitutes. Paul addressed each one of these issues but with typical Pauline flair that caused him to expand into many other areas.

In this second section (7:1 – 16:18) Paul answered questions that the Corinthians themselves had asked him. They might have asked these questions through letters and people who visited Paul. Paul took up these six questions and clearly marked his answers by the "and concerning . . ." (*peri-de*) formula (found in 7:1; 7:25; 8:1; 12:1; 16:1; 16:12). The first question related to married people (7:1–24), while the second question focused on unmarried people (7:25–40). The third question dealt with food offered to idols and related issues (8:1 – 11:34). The fourth question dealt with spiritual matters including the Spirit's gifts and the resurrection of the dead (12:1 – 15:58). The fifth topic was about collecting funds for the saints (16:1–11). The sixth and final topic was about Apollos (16:12–20). Although these were clearly the main topics, Paul was expansive in his answers so that he addressed several interrelated issues within each topic.

9

1 Corinthians 7

Marriage and Sex (7:1–5)[1]

In India – a land of 1 billion people – it is, ironically, a cultural taboo to talk about sex. Hindu temples vividly portray erotic statues and Hindu literature such as *Kama Sutra* rivals sex manuals in the West. Devotees worship gods through idols in the shape of *lingams* and *yoni* (male and female genitalia).[2] Yet talking about sex is such a taboo that "many women, especially from the higher castes, do not have a name for their genitals," writes Kakar.[3]

An extension of such modesty extends into family life to the extent that it is wrong for a wife to enjoy sexual pleasures. She "performs" the duty only for her husband's pleasure. Kakar and Kakar write, "With so many traditional women carrying the baggage of shame and guilt in relation to their (sexual) bodies, with all the images of insatiable women and the notion of sex being an act that drains a man of power and vigour running riot in the male cultural imagination, the omens for a joyful sexual life in the average Indian marriage are not promising . . . A Punjabi proverb puts the husband's quandary and its solution in a nutshell: 'A woman who shows more love for you than your mother is a slut.'"[4] Elsewhere they write, "In a fifteen-year-old

---

1. For a comprehensive study of chapter 7 see David E. Garland, "The Christian's Posture toward Marriage and Celibacy: 1 Corinthians 7," *Review & Expositor* 80, no. 3 (Summer 1983): 351–362.
2. For a study of Hindu sexuality see James A. Kirk, "Sport of the Gods: Religion and Sexuality in India," *Iliff Review* 35, no. 2 (Spring 1978): 41–53. Also Padma Kaimal, "Learning to See the Goddess Once Again: Male and Female in Balance at Kailāsanāth Temple in Kāncipuram," *Journal of the American Academy of Religion* 73, no. 1 (March 2005): 45–87.
3. Sudhir Kakar, *Intimate Relations: Exploring Indian Sexuality* (New Delhi, India: Penguin Books, 1989), 20.
4. Kakar and Kakar, *The Indians: Portrait of People*, 93.

study carried out in Bangalore, most wives ranked the traditional purposes of marriage – children, love, and affection, fulfillment of the husband's sexual needs (rather than her own) – very high."[5] Such attitudes are not unknown in the Western world either. Fee writes, "Too many still treat sex as though it were the privilege of the husband and the duty of the wife."[6] Of course, India is changing and Bollywood has been aggressively promoting openness about sexuality.

The Corinthians too seemed to have been confused about marriage and sex. They seemed to have concluded that sex within marriage was wrong and had made a slogan that said, "It is good for a man not to touch a woman" – certainly a euphemism for forbidding a sexual relationship (1 Cor 7:1).[7] In other words, Christians were to be celibates. This teaching resembles some Greek philosophies such as Epicureanism (307 BC) that taught that avoiding sex and food brought both freedom from fear and tranquility in life. Translations such as the King James Version make this verse a simple statement – "It is good for a man not to touch a woman" – implying that Paul was promoting celibacy.[8] Although Paul saw celibacy as a gift from God, he saw marriage also as a gift from God and a union in which a husband and a wife could enjoy themselves (1 Cor 7:5).

The Corinthians coupled the first slogan ("It is good for a man not to touch a woman") with a modifier that said, "But if one is tempted to fornication, then each man should have his own wife, and each woman should have her own husband. Then the husband is obliged to give himself to the wife and likewise the woman to the husband" (1 Cor 7:2–3). In other words, celibacy was best, but if a person could not restrain his or her sexual desire, the second-best option was to marry. Blomberg sees this modifier as Paul's words and thus reasons that "With prostitution and mistresses abundantly

---

5. Ibid., 67.

6. Fee, *First Epistle to the Corinthians*, 285.

7. Moiser sees this chapter as a tension between the "strong" and "weak" Christians in Corinth who wanted to know whose view was correct. Jeremy Moiser, "A Reassessment of Paul's View of Marriage with Reference to 1 Cor 7," *Journal for the Study of the New Testament* 18, (June 1983): 103–122. For a criticism of NIV's translation of the phrase "not to touch a woman" as "not to marry," see Gordon D. Fee, "1 Corinthians 7:1 in the NIV," *Journal of the Evangelical Theological Society* 23, no. 4 (December 1980): 307–314.

8. Thinking that Paul was prohibiting sex, Ciampa suggests that it was "more likely a rejection of recreational or hedonistic sex, sex for pleasure or motivated by passion. The idiom might be best translated as 'it is good for a man not to use a woman for sexual gratification,'" Roy E. Ciampa, "Revisiting the Euphemism in 1 Corinthians 7:1," *Journal for the Study of the New Testament* 31, no. 3 (March 2009): 336.

available (recall 6:12–20), Corinthian men unable to have sex with their wives would often look elsewhere,"[9] and that was why Paul recommended marriage. Unfortunately, such a conclusion devalues the nature of marriage by implying that a person who cannot control his or her sexual urges needs to marry; marriage thus becomes a solution for sexual frustration or lack of self-control.[10] Reichenbach notes the problem: "Indeed, his further contention that marriage is allowable because refraining from it can lead to immorality has raised more than a few eyebrows. The Genesis norm is not based on the possibility of moral weakness, but rather on the ideal of conjugal union."[11] Also, if Paul was promoting this principle, sex becomes an obligation in marriage: "A husband should give to his wife her sexual rights, and likewise a wife to her husband" (1 Cor 7:3 NET). But such a demand goes against Paul's teachings elsewhere in 1 Corinthians about Christians not demanding their rights (e.g. 1 Cor 6:12; ch. 9).

For this reason, it is best to see the first two sayings as the Corinthians' slogans and Paul as giving a correction in verse four. In other words, whereas the Corinthians' slogans are (1) don't touch a woman, and (2) marry if you have no control (1 Cor 7:1–3), Paul's solution is very different: "A wife has no authority over her own body, but her husband does; the husband has no authority over his body, but his wife does" (1 Cor 7:4). In other words, in marriage, the ownership of one's body is passed on to the spouse. Paul repeatedly taught this principle of one's lack of ownership over one's body. Earlier he had said, "The body is not for fornication but for the Lord. The Lord is lord over the body" (1 Cor 6:13). Further he said, "Your body is the temple of the Spirit of God who is in you, whom you received from God. And you are not of yourselves" (1 Cor 6:19). Contrary to the Corinthians' slogan that husbands and wives were obliged to give each other sexual intimacy, Paul highlighted the truth that in marriage, one's spouse had the ownership of one's body. A husband's body no longer belonged to him; it belonged to his wife – just as his body was the Lord's and the Holy Spirit's. A wife's body no longer belonged to her; it belonged to her husband, the Lord, and the Holy Spirit. Bailey writes,

---

9. Blomberg, *1 Corinthians*, 133.

10. Barré, in a different context (i.e. 1 Cor 7:9), calls marriage used as a remedy for sexual fulfillment *remedium concupiscentiae*, Michael L. Barré, "To Marry or to Burn: Pyrousthai in 1 Cor 7:9," *Catholic Biblical Quarterly* 36, no. 2 (April 1974): 193.

11. Bruce R. Reichenbach, "The Gift of Singleness," *Reformed Journal* 32, no. 3 (March 1982): 5.

Equality between the wife and the husband in Christian marriage is here presented in unforgettable terms. Each partner in a marriage has authority over the body of the other. No sexual games are possible in this kind of marriage. There can be no power plays such as, "Give me what I want, and I will sleep with you." No form of abuse is even thinkable. *Each* partner can say to the other, "I have gifts, and I have rights, and I have authority over your body." The granting of these gifts, rights, and powers to each other (on an equal basis) is truly amazing to discover in a first-century document![12]

Since spouses no longer had ownership of their own bodies, Paul could command, "Do not deprive one another" (1 Cor 7:5a).[13] The word "deprive" had the connotation of "withholding something that rightfully belonged to someone else" (just as in the cases of masters withholding the pay of their servants, Jas 5:4). The Corinthians' false notions – sex was wrong; sex was only to prevent immorality; in marriage, spouses were obliged to have sex – prevented them from enjoying sex within marriage (similar to the Indian spouses mentioned by Kakar and Kakar above). So Paul had to command them to stop depriving each other of sexual pleasures. Although spouses might not *demand* sex, they ought to voluntarily *offer it* for each other's fulfillment. Such voluntary offering was in agreement with the earliest commandment: "God blessed them and said, 'Be fruitful and multiply'" (Gen 1:28).

There was one exception to this sexual intimacy: a time devoted to prayer (1 Cor 7:5b).[14] Paul wrote, "Stop depriving one another, except by mutual agreement and for a time, so that you might devote yourselves to prayer" (1 Cor 7:5b). Ezekiel gave a list of the characteristics of a righteous person (Ezek 18:5–9) and one element was that "he does not have sexual relations with his wife during her menstruation" (Ezek 18:6b). Paul might therefore have been euphemistically referring to the wife's time of menstruation, when they were to devote themselves to prayer. On the other hand, this could refer

---

12. Bailey, *Paul through Mediterranean Eyes*, 202.

13. Poirier and Frankovic, based upon the present tense of the verb "deprive," think that the Corinthians had already stopped depriving each other (John C. Poirier and Joseph Frankovic, "Celibacy and Charism in 1 Cor 7:5–7," *Harvard Theological Review* 89, no. 1 [January 1996]: 2). Most likely, however, the present tense refers more to a generalized than to a specific command, meaning Paul was simply stating a command.

14. Some later manuscript add "and fasting," most likely because prayer and fasting are often paired in the Synoptic Gospels. The manuscript and internal evidence favors the shorter reading.

to a normal time set aside for prayer. Regardless, Paul quickly added three caveats: first, such setting aside of time must be by mutual agreement (the Greek word is *symphonos*, "harmoniously");[15] second, it should be for an appointed time; and third, they must come together again soon so that Satan might not tempt them (1 Cor 7:5c). In other words, time devoted to prayer in marriage – that is, time away from sexual intimacy – was to be carefully monitored so that it didn't infringe upon the oneness between husbands and wives. Familial oneness was more significant than personal devotion.

The last condition is similar to Paul's teachings concerning anger, when he states that one must not let anger give an opportunity to Satan (Eph 4:26–27). Satan might tempt the married couple in the Corinthians 7 context on account of their "lack of restriction" (*akrasia*). The word *akrasia* is usually translated as "lack of self-control" (NIV, NET). It does have that connotation; for example, Josephus refers to King Solomon's obsession with sex with many women as a lack of self-control (Josephus, *Antiquities* 8.190). In other words, if the spouses don't come together in sexual union soon after the time set aside for prayer, Satan might tempt them because of their prolonged time away from sexual union; their lack of self-control over their sexuality would then give him an opportunity to lead them to sin.[16] With this understanding, marriage is again seen as a solution for sexual frustration. Another option is to understand Paul to be talking about their "lack of restriction" in prayer time or in their prayer life. In other words, when spouses use prayer as an excuse for not getting together, such undisciplined spiritual life (in prayer) would give Satan an opportunity. The latter view is to be preferred.

In summary, the husband and wife might, by mutual consent, agree to devote themselves to prayer, for a short period of time. Nothing that they do, including prayer, should drive a wedge leading to disharmony between them in their union.

Devotion to Prayer (7:6–7)

As mentioned above in the commentary on 3:1–4, *Sannyasa* is the most glorious of the four age-based stages (*ashrams*) of a person in Hinduism. Men and women who want to enter this stage renounce all worldly and

---

15. This whole chapter is filled with the mutuality of the husband–wife relationship: vv. 3–5, 8–9, 10a/11b, 12–16, and 32–34. See Blomberg, *1 Corinthians*, 136.

16. Fee, *First Epistle to the Corinthians*, 282–83.

materialistic pursuits and dedicate their lives to prayer. They even forsake their spouses and children and go off into seclusion, where they either forsake food altogether or beg for their food. A person following this path is called *sannyasini* (female)[17] or *sannyasin* (male).

Paul, however, did not want the married people in the Corinthian congregation to neglect their marital commitments for the sake of prayer. He granted them permission to set aside time for prayer, but then they needed to get back together so as not to give Satan an opportunity because of their lack of discipline in their prayer life (1 Cor 7:5). However, Paul did not want them to take this statement to set aside time for prayer as a "command"; he wanted them to treat it as a concession (1 Cor 7:6). The spouses' decision to set aside time for prayer must not become a hindrance in marriage.

Not all interpreters take this view. They assume Paul was talking about marriage as a concession, not a command.[18] In light of that, they understand the next verse, "I wish for all people to be as I am" (1 Cor 7:7a), to mean that Paul was advocating celibacy.[19] It is more likely that Paul was talking about a commitment to prayer life as a concession, not as a command. Fee writes, "Even such a good thing as temporary abstinence for prayer will not be raised to the level of command."[20] He would like all people to be diligent and committed to prayer ("pray without ceasing," he said, 1 Thess 5:17; and in Philippi he prayed past midnight, Acts 16:25). At the same time he would not want the married to neglect their marital responsibilities – as do the *sannyasins* – especially concerning sexual union. So, in line with his earlier statement that this was only a concession and not a command, he concluded, "Each one [ought to pray] according to the grace he or she has from God, one regularly and another irregularly" (1 Cor 7:7b). The prayer life is not to be regulated; it is to be carried out according to the grace given to a person. Peter gave similar teaching when he connected married life with the prayer life – a husband's prayers are answered according to how he has treated his

---

17. For a study of female *sannyasini* in Rajasthan, see DeNapoli, "Real Sadhus Sing to God," 117–133.

18. Cf. Blomberg, *1 Corinthians*, 133.

19. Dale C. Jr. Allison, "Divorce, Celibacy and Joseph (Matthew 1:18–25 and 19:1–12)," *Journal for the Study of the New Testament*, no. 49 (March 1993): 6. Poirier and Frankovic, "Celibacy and Charism in 1 Cor 7:5–7," 18.

20. Fee, *First Epistle to the Corinthians*, 284. Earlier on the same page, however, Fee resorts to the traditional view that Paul was advocating the gift of celibacy or not marrying at all.

wife (1 Pet 3:7). Although prayer is important, marital responsibilities trump prayer demands.

People in the state of Nagaland, India, place a high premium on prayer life. Before a person enters ministry after graduating from a Bible college, for example, he or she must spend forty days in fasting and praying for God to give him or her a great ministry. As significant as prayer life is, however, it is important that prayer doesn't become a hindrance to one's family life. God places such a high premium on married life.

Sati and Remarriage (7:8–9)

Sati refers to the practice in India in which a widow kills herself on her husband's funeral pyre. It has religious overtones: "Sati is the name of a goddess, Parvati and/or Durga in a previous life, who immolated herself in protest to her father excluding her husband, Siva, from his sacrifice, an exclusion that amounts to death for an immortal deity. *Sati* is a term for a virtuous married woman who adheres to a life of veneration of and service to her husband. With the British colonial period, *suttee* [the spelling at that time] was used as a term for the immolation of a woman on her husband's funeral pyre."[21]

The burning of widows (or *sati*) lasted from the fourth century BC until the nineteenth century AD in the Indian subcontinent. The British officially outlawed it in 1829. At that time, an estimated 500–600 instances of *sati* occurred per year. The Indian parliament passed the Indian Sati Prevention Act in 1987, officially criminalizing any type of aiding, abetting, and even glorifying *sati* practices. Yet the practice continues, sometimes secretly and other times openly. Lourens P. van den Bosch reports an incident that happened on 4 September 1987 when the eighteen-year-old Roop Kanwar ascended the funeral pyre of her deceased husband Maal Singh (twenty-four years old) in the village of Deorala, about sixty kilometers north of Jaipur, the capital of the Indian state of Rajasthan.[22] Scholars debate whether *sati*

---

21. Paul B. Courtright, "Book Review: Ashes of Immorality: Widow-Burning in India by Catherine Weinberger-Thomas, Translated by Jeffrey Mehlman and David Gordon White (Chicago: University Press, 1999)," *Journal of the American Academy of Religion* 69, no. 2 (June 2001): 516.

22. Lourens P. van den Bosch, "A Burning Question: Sati and Sati Temples as the Focus of Political Interest," *Numen* 37, no. 2 (December 1990): 174.

is voluntary (because of the wife's admiration for her husband or her shame within the society) or whether widows are forced into doing it.[23]

One of the reasons for *sati* is that widows are considered a burden in Indian society. Sen narrates a horrible incident:

> Accosted as she [Kalawati] was entering the local Kali temple for her puja, she was told that "a widow had no right to enter a temple" and [was] beaten up, stripped, disgraced, and paraded naked. They also accused her of causing chicken pox. But her main crime was being a widow and daring to worship in public . . . She is inauspicious, must live in perpetual mourning, cannot take part in celebrations, and must not show her ill-fated face too much, lest she withers the good fortune of others . . . A widow is often called the "husband eater."[24]

In some contexts, widows cannot even wear colorful saris. Singh writes, "Punjabi society maintains a distinction between a widow (*duhagan*, a woman who is unlucky because her husband is dead, and grieves in white or black) and a wife (*suhagan*, who is lucky because her husband is alive, and rejoices in bright colors)."[25] They are so ill-treated and shunned because culturally they are not allowed to remarry. My own aunt was a young widow and a beautiful lady, a Christian, and yet society wouldn't allow her to remarry. Instead of remarrying, such widows reside with a child, thus becoming a burden. But is it necessary that widows and widowers remain unmarried?[26]

Apparently, the Corinthian Christians had similar doubts about the status of widowers and widows. Paul's words are "*unmarried* and widows" – the ambiguity resulting in scholars thinking that Paul was referring to two different groups. But Paul was most likely referring to *widowers* and widows, as evidenced by his pairing of the terms – especially given that New Testament Greek did not have a word for "widower," unlike classical Greek

---

23. Sharada Sugirtharajah, "Courtly Text and Courting Sati," *Journal of Feminist Studies in Religion* 17, no. 1 (Spring 2001): 9. Lata Mani, *Contentious Traditions: The Debate on Sati in Colonial India* (Berkeley, CA: University of California Press, 1998).

24. Antara Dev Sen, "The Living Dead," *The Week* (20 April 2008), 44.

25. Nikky-Guninder Kaur Singh, "Why Did I Not Light the Fire? The Refeminization of Ritual in Sikhism," *Journal for Feminist Studies in Religion* 16, no. 1 (Spring 2000): 63.

26. The biblical answer is that they can remarry (see Rom 7:1–4). Should they remarry, of course, they would no longer be a burden to anyone and they could have an enriched life. For a detailed study of the church's responsibilities to widows, see Andrew B. Spurgeon, "Caring for Widows (and Widowers): 1 Timothy 5:3–16," in *Leitourgia: Christian Sevice, Collected Essays: A Festschrift for Joykutty M. George*, ed. Andrew B. Spurgeon (Bangalore, India: Primalogue, 2015), 287–304.

(where *cheros*, the male form of *chera* [widow] was used for a widower), Paul's specific dealing with the "unmarried" later (1 Cor 7:25–40), and this topic coming in the context of married people (husbands and wives loving each other [7:1–7] and married people not divorcing [7:10–11]).[27] Paul's first thought about *widowers* and widows was that it was best for them to remain "as I am" (1 Cor 7:8). The Corinthians would have known Paul's marital status. He would argue later that he had the right to take a Christian lady as his wife and travel with her, just as Cephas/Peter did (1 Cor 9:5). Paul might have been a widower who chose to continue in his widowhood and wished for other widowers and widows to follow his example.

Paul was also a realist, so he continued, "But if they are not *disciplined* [to remain without being remarried], let them marry" (1 Cor 7:9a). Paul used terminology from the world of sports – "disciplined" (cf. 1 Cor 9:25a). If the widowers and widows weren't disciplined enough to remain single and serve the Lord in their singleness as Paul did, they might marry.[28] In other words, if a widower or a widow couldn't keep his or her emotions intact and remain single, it was better for him or her to marry again (1 Cor 7:9b). Paul's phrase "it is better to marry than to burn" has raised much speculation, such as whether Paul was talking about burning with sexual passion[29] or sinning to the point of burning in hell.[30] A third option is that Paul was referring to one's longing or "love sickness" for another. Ellis compares Paul's writings with Greek works such as *Daphnis and Chloe* by Longus – a writing the Corinthians

---

27. Bailey and Hays also see this as a section dealing with widowers and widows (Bailey, *Paul through Mediterranean Eyes*, 198. Hays, *First Corinthians*, 118).

28. Fee's conclusion – "The implication is that some of these people are doing the same as some of the married in vv. 1–7, practicing 'sexual immorality,' that is, probably also going to the prostitutes. The antidote for such sin is to get married instead" (Fee, *First Epistle to the Corinthians*, 289) – is unwarranted, as he himself gives a corrective: "Paul is not so much offering marriage as the remedy for the sexual desire of 'enflamed youth,' which is the most common way of viewing the text, but as the proper alternative for those who are already consumed by that desire and are sinning" (Ibid).

29. Fee, *First Epistle to the Corinthians*, 286. Also NET Bible footnote says, "a figure of speech referring to unfulfilled sexual passion."

30. Blomberg, *1 Corinthians*, 134. Barré writes, "This is the meaning of παρουσθαι [*parousthai* "burn"] in this text: to be burned in the fires of judgment or Gehenna. Such an interpretation makes perfect sense in light of Paul's argument, in light of the strong eschatological tone of ch. 7, and in light of the uses of παρουσθαι [*parousthai* "burn"] discussed above. In effect, then, Paul is saying to the unmarried Christians of Corinth: 'Don't you see that, even though you are opposed to the idea of marriage, it is more sensible to (re-)marry than to be damned? Face the facts: if you find yourselves continually involved in unchaste conduct you are obviously not called to life-long celibacy but to marriage. So reconsider your options – before it's too late!'" Barré, "To Marry or to Burn," 200.

would have been familiar with – and argues that in such works the "fire" or "sickness" (as in "fever") is a metaphor for "love sickness." Ellis therefore understands Paul's exhortation to be, "If you are love sick [for someone], get married."[31] This option better fits the context since Paul described sex within marriage as God's gift and not as a substitute for uncontrolled sexual passion. In summary, then, it was good for widowers and widows to remain single, just as Paul did. But if they were not disciplined enough to control their love for another, it was good for them to get married.

In the biblical context as a whole, the remarriage of widowers and widows was encouraged (e.g. Rom 7:1–4; 1 Tim 5:14). This is in complete contrast to the practice of *sati* as described earlier. Teays equates the "dowry-burning" in today's India with *sati* of old. When a woman doesn't bring a sufficient dowry ("marriage money") to her husband's family, she may be ill-treated and even killed in a mysterious accident such as a kitchen fire. Teays writes,

> Estimates of dowry death vary, but include a 1984 estimate of twenty-two deaths a day in India from bride burning, with two per day in Bangalore, in South India, and a 1987 estimate of one death every thirty-six hours in Delhi. In 1987, the women's unit of the New Delhi police received thirty-seven hundred dowry-related complaints, ranging from harassment to murder. [Because] they are on the increase – and, from all accounts, this is a rapid increase – dowry deaths are not merely a phenomenon of the 1980s.[32]

Indian Christians were instrumental in abolishing the earlier *sati*; the same should be true of modern-day *sati* or the burning of wives.

Widowers and widows may remain single if they choose. But if they are lovesick for another, let them marry. Either action will glorify God. But killing widows or wives, an abominable action, will never bring glory to God.

---

31. J. Edward Ellis, "Controlled Burn: The Romantic Note in 1 Corinthians 7," *Perspectives in Religious Studies* 29, no. 1 (Spring 2002): 97. This is similar to a fiancé's "love sickness" for his fiancée (Bruce W. Winter, "Puberty or Passion? The Referent of Uperakmos in 1 Corinthians 7:36," *Tyndale Bulletin* 49, no. 1 [1998]: 71–89).

32. Wanda Teays, "The Burning Bride: The Dowry Problem in India," *Journal of Feminist Studies in Religion* 7, no. 2 (Fall 1991): 38.

Divorce (7:10–11)

India once prided itself on a 100 percent success rate in marriages. That was partly true because Hinduism considers marriage (*shaddi*) as the thirteenth among sixteen ceremonies in a Hindu's life. Marriage is a holy and sacred ceremony solemnized in accordance with rituals in the Vedas, the Hindu scriptures. It was also partly true because the culture was secretive about separations and, likewise, disallowed divorces. But India is changing. Ravindra writes, "Recent urbanization and women's growing financial independence are causing the divorce rate to rise. Gender equality is now giving rise to ego clashes between couples, especially where the wife is also well educated and employed."[33] As a result, women initiate nearly 80 percent of the divorces in India.[34] No doubt the fault is not only with the women; men are equally guilty. Unfortunately, divorce is equally on the rise among Christians as among Hindus.

In the Corinthian congregation too some of the married people were seeking divorce.[35] So Paul answered them based on the Lord's teachings – hence the phrase "to the married, I command, not I, but the Lord" (1 Cor 7:10a; cf. Mark 10:5–12).[36] The command was, "the wife must not be separated from the husband" (1 Cor 7:10b). Blomberg envisions a scenario in which a Christian married to a non-Christian contemplated divorce because he or she "feared that sexual relations with an unbeliever would defile them."[37] Whether the scenario was that or someone simply wanted to divorce his wife, the answer was, "no, the wife must not be separated" from her husband. This

---

33. Geetha Ravindra, "Impact of Religion and Culture on Divorce in Indian Marriages," http://www.americanbar.org/content/dam/aba/publications (accessed July 16 2014).

34. Sangeeta Pisharoty, "Marriages Are in Trouble," *The Hindu Newspaper* (15 May 2010).

35. There is little or no difference between "separation" and "divorce" in the New Testament (Fee, *First Epistle to the Corinthians*, 293–294; Blomberg, *1 Corinthians*, 134). This was true of the Corinthian culture as well. After studying various Greco-Roman marriage and divorce papyri, Instone-Brewer concludes, "There is no distinction in the marriage papyri between divorce and separation, and in Graeco-Roman law, separation with intention to end the marriage *was* divorce." David Instone-Brewer, "1 Corinthians 7 in the Light of the Graeco-Roman Marriage and Divorce Papyri," *Tyndale Bulletin* 52, no. 1 (2001): 107.

36. Blomberg writes, "Paul's parenthesis, 'not I, but the Lord' (v. 10), alludes to words of the earthly Jesus widely known in early Christian traditions (cf. Mark 10:11–12)" (Blomberg, *1 Corinthians*, 134–135). Fee writes, "But in saying 'I give this command,' he remembers that Jesus himself spoke to this question, so he appeals to his authority" (Fee, *First Epistle to the Corinthians*, 291).

37. Blomberg, *1 Corinthians*, 135.

wasn't implying that women didn't have the right to divorce,[38] as the context itself shows they could (1 Cor 7:13). Most likely it was a commonly accepted phrase or Paul used the passive voice because those who addressed the question to Paul were men (as implied by the many "brothers" in the epistle) or fathers. Another way of translating the sentence would be, "You men, your wives must not be separated from you," meaning, "you must not separate your wives from you" (or "you fathers, you shouldn't separate your daughters from their husbands"). Regardless, divorce was not the first option. However, there were extenuating circumstances in which divorces were allowed (as the Lord himself mentioned – "except for immorality," Matt 19:9, or "because of the hardening of the heart," Mark 10:5). In such cases the wives had two more options: either to remain unmarried or to be reconciled to their husbands (1 Cor 7:11a).

Paul then commanded the men, "The man must not leave his wife" (1 Cor 7:11b), a simple and direct command. Paul wanted the men to honor marriage by not divorcing their wives.

Basically, Paul wanted the Corinthian Christian women not to be separated or divorced from their husbands. But should such a circumstance arise, the women should either remain unmarried or be reconciled with their husbands. Paul didn't want any Christian men to divorce their wives. Fee concludes, "What is *not* allowed is remarriage, both because for him that presupposes the teaching of Jesus that such is adultery and because in the Christian community reconciliation is the norm."[39]

Such a conclusion raises practical questions, such as whether a woman in an abusive relationship should not seek divorce. Among Christians, the church leaders are to get involved and bring about repentance and reconciliation. If, however, there are extenuating circumstances, then divorce is allowed. Also, should the divorcee never marry again? I believe that each case should be evaluated individually before concluding.[40]

---

38. As suggested by scholars such as Blomberg, who writes, "If there is any difference between the wife 'separating' in verse 10 and the husband 'divorcing' in verse 11, it may be that the man was legally entitled to divorce his wife, whereas the woman often had no recourse but to move out" (Blomberg, *1 Corinthians*, 134).

39. Fee, *First Epistle to the Corinthians*, 296.

40. For excellent help, see David Instone-Brewer, *Divorce and Remarriage in the Church: Biblical Solutions for Pastoral Realities* (Downers Grove, IL: InterVarsity Press, 2006); David Instone-Brewer, *Divorce and Remarriage in the Bible: The Social and Literary Context* (Grand Rapids: Eerdmans, 2002); H. Wayne House, ed. *Divorce and Remarriage: Four Christian Views*, Spectrum Multiview Book (Downers Grove, IL: InterVarsity Press, 1990).

Divorce in Case of Conversion (7:12–16)

The Hindu Marriage Act, 1955, Act 25, section 13, says,

> Any marriage solemnized, whether before or after the commencement of the Act, may, on a petition presented by either the husband or the wife, be dissolved by a decree of divorce on the ground that the other party – (i) has, after the solemnization of the marriage, had voluntary sexual intercourse with any person other than his or her spouse; or (ia) has, after the solemnization of the marriage, treated the petitioner with cruelty; or (ib) has deserted the petitioner for a continuous period of not less than two years immediately preceding the presentation of the petition; or (ii) *has ceased to be a Hindu by conversion to another religion*; or (iii) has been incurably of unsound mind, or has been suffering continuously or intermittently from mental disorder of such a kind and to such an extent that the petitioner cannot reasonably be expected to live with the respondent (italics mine).[41]

Thus divorce is permitted in India for unfaithfulness, apostasy, or mental incompetency. This law has great ramifications for Indian Hindus who convert to Christianity: their spouses could legally divorce them. Along with the spouse, of course, the divorced Christian would lose family, family properties, status, and acceptance.

The Corinthian Christians were faced with similar situations in which conversion to Christianity caused strain in marriages. Some of the spouses who didn't convert wanted to leave, while others wanted to continue in their marriages to the converted Christians.[42] So Paul addressed that issue next.

Since the Lord himself didn't face or address a similar situation, Paul began by saying, "I say, and not the Lord" (1 Cor 7:12a).[43] Then he said, "If any Christian has an unconverted wife and she wishes to stay with him, he must not divorce her" (1 Cor 7:12b). He paired it up with his command to the

---

41. The Hindu Marriage Act, 1955, http://bokakhat.gov.in/pdf/The_hindu_marriage_act.pdf.

42. Fee makes an important observation: what this passage "demonstrates is that not all conversions were household conversions, as in the case of Stephanas (16:15). Illustrations of both phenomena abound in the Greco-Roman world (i.e. where the family took on the religion of the head of the household or where only one, especially in the case of wives, became the devotee of a deity other than that of the spouse)" (Fee, *First Epistle to the Corinthians*, 299).

43. The phrase "to the remaining" or "rest" is better understood as the last class of people or the last question that he is addressing on this topic.

Christian women, saying, "If a Christian lady has an unconverted husband and he wishes to stay with her, she must not divorce him" (1 Cor 7:13). In other words, when a non-Christian spouse chooses to continue to live with the Christian spouse, the Christian must not divorce him or her.

Paul then stated the reason for this decision: "the unconverted husband will be *sanctified* in his wife; the unconverted wife will be *sanctified* in the Christian" (1 Cor 7:14a). Paul's statement is astonishing since in most religions, including Judaism, when a holy person has contact with an unholy person, the holy one is polluted. So when a rabbi touches a leper, the rabbi becomes unclean. The Lord Jesus reversed this status quo: when a woman with an unending flow of blood touched him, he didn't become unclean; instead, she became clean and well (Mark 5:21–43). Similarly, unconverted spouses do not pollute Christian spouses; instead, the Christian spouses cleanse (sanctify) the unconverted spouses. Paul didn't want the Corinthians to misunderstand his earlier statement "not to associate with immoral people" to mean that he was referring to their unconverted spouses. So he said, "it is not the believer who is *defiled* but the unbeliever who is *sanctified* in her or his relationship with the believer."[44]

What does it mean that a Christian spouse sanctifies an unconverted spouse? First, some scholars have proposed that since husband and wife are "one flesh" (1 Cor 6:16), the Christian's faith saves the unbeliever. Orr and Walther write, "The close contact [of marriage] produces a corporal unity between the two so that the unbelieving member actually is made holy by the faith of the believer."[45] If this theory is true, Bailey's observation is noteworthy: "Put bluntly, Paul appears to be saying, 'There are two ways to be saved. One is to believe and be baptized. The other is to marry a Christian!'"[46] A second option is to understand the word "sanctified" as a legal term, meaning that a Christian spouse legitimizes the marriage by staying with the unconverted spouse.[47] However, one would expect Paul to have used *dikaiō* ("righteous") verb cognates if he was concerned about the legitimacy of the marriage.

---

44. Fee, *First Epistle to the Corinthians*, 300. Fee assumes that the Corinthians had already misunderstood Paul because they had received an earlier letter; I, however, think this is the first letter they received and that Paul was therefore anticipating their question and answering it before it had actually been asked.

45. William F. Orr and James A. Walther, *1 Corinthians: A New Translation with Introduction and Commentary*, eds. William Foxwell Albright and David Noel Freedman, Anchor Bible, vol. 32 (New York: Doubleday, 1976), 213.

46. Bailey, *Paul through Mediterranean Eyes*, 208.

47. Michael P. Martens, "First Corinthians 7:14: 'Sanctified' by the Believing Spouse," *Notes on Translation* 10, no. 3 (1996): 35.

Third, some scholars believe that a Christian spouse somehow sets his or her family in a special relationship with God. Fee draws an analogy from Romans 11:16 – "If a root is holy, so are the branches" – and concludes, "From Paul's perspective, as long as the marriage is maintained the potential for them realizing salvation remains."[48] A fourth option is that a non-Christian spouse is drawn to salvation through the believing spouse's lifestyle. Peter told his audience, "Wives, by submitting to your own husbands who are disobedient to God's word, you could win over your husbands not by words but by lifestyle, especially as they see your pure and reverential lifestyle" (1 Pet 3:1–2). Thiselton writes, "The spouse's example, witness, prayer, and living out of the gospel make the spouse and the children *in this sense* holy."[49] In summary, the Christian spouse's conduct – especially in not divorcing a spouse who wishes to stay – could lead the unconverted to faith and salvation.

In addition to the unbelieving spouses being "sanctified" through the lifestyle of the Christian spouses, the children would also be sanctified (1 Cor 7:14b).[50] Similar to the non-believing spouse's salvation through the faithful lifestyle of the believing spouse, the children could be drawn to faith through growing up in an unbroken home and through seeing their parents' faithfulness. Keener explains the cultural situation: "Although husbands' conversions tended to lead to household conversions in the Roman empire, wives' conversions did not always produce the same result. Many converts probably were women, who may have often found themselves in this situation. In ancient Mediterranean divorces, however, the children normally went to the father."[51] He then concludes,

> When Paul talks about children being "holy" in 1 Cor 7:14,
> he is not claiming that the children are saved because they

---

48. Fee, *First Epistle to the Corinthians*, 300. Also, Bailey, *Paul through Mediterranean Eyes*, 209.

49. Anthony C. Thiselton, *The First Epistle to the Corinthians*, eds. I. Howard Marshall and Donald A. Hagner, The New International Greek Testament Commentary (Grand Rapids: Eerdmans, 2000), 530 (italics and bold in original).

50. MacDonald sees Paul's argument in this section as illogical (Margaret Y. MacDonald, "Unclean but Holy Children: Paul's Everyday Quandary in 1 Corinthians 7:14c," *Catholic Biblical Quarterly* 73, no. 3 [July 2011]: 526–546). Such a conclusion is unnecessary and unprofitable. Gillihan, on the other hand, sees Paul as mediating beautifully between Jewish and Gentile cultures in this section (Yonder Moynihan Gillihan, "Jewish Laws on Illicit Marriage, the Defilement of Offspring, and the Holiness of the Temple: A New Halakic Interpretation of 1 Corinthians 7:14," *Journal of the Biblical Literature* 121, no. 4 [2002]: 711–744).

51. Craig S. Keener, "Interethnic Marriages in the New Testament (Matt 1:3–6; Acts 7:29; 16:1–3; Cf. 1 Cor 7:14)," *Criswell Theological Review* 6, no. 2 (Spring 2009): 41.

have Christian parents, nor that infant baptism saves. Their consecration involves the question of status, analogous to mixed households involving Jews (where the question was, to what extent is the child legally Jewish?). Just as the consecrating of the unbelieving partner (7:14) does not automatically save (7:16), neither does that of the children. A believer who remains in the marriage retains an influence on the children, who would otherwise (in first-century marriages) normally remain only with the father, as noted above.[52]

Unlike the Hindu Marriage Act, Paul would not allow the Christians in Corinth to divorce their unbelieving spouses, especially when the unbelieving spouses wanted to remain in the marriage. Paul saw such marriages as an opportunity for the Christians to have an impact on their spouses and their children, so he wanted them to remain in them.

This is very applicable for India, where often a spouse comes to faith and the other wishes to remain with the Christian for love, security, and cultural acceptance. In such a context, the practical Christian advice is to stay with the unbelieving spouse for the sake of being a witness in his or her life and in the lives of the children. A believer's faithful living, coupled with godly behavior, no doubt may draw the spouse and children to Christ. That should be the believing spouse's desire and prayer.

Of course, not all unconverted spouses want to remain with Christians. That would have been the case in Corinth as well. So Paul instructed, "But if the unconverted spouse wishes to leave, let him or her leave. A Christian brother or sister is not *enslaved* in this situation" (1 Cor 7:15a). The verb "enslaved" (*dedoulōtai*) is related to the noun "slave" (*doulos*). Elsewhere Paul said, "Although I am free from all things, I *enslave* myself to all, in order to save more people" (1 Cor 9:19). "Enslave" refers to putting oneself under an obligation. Scholars therefore understand Paul to be referring to remarriage here. Instone-Brewer, for example, writes, "When Paul says they are 'no longer enslaved,' any first century reader would understand him to mean that they can remarry, because they would think of the words on both Jewish and non-Jewish divorce certificates: 'You are free to marry.'"[53] That conclusion might

---

52. Ibid., 43.
53. David Instone-Brewer, "1 Corinthians 7 in the Light of the Jewish Greek and Aramaic Marriage and Divorce Papyri," *Tyndale Bulletin* 52, no. 2 (2001): 241. Also, Gerald L. Borchert, "1 Corinthians 7:15 and the Church's Historic Misunderstanding of Divorce and Remarriage," *Review & Expositor* 96, no. 1 (Winter 1999): 128.

have cultural validity but, within the context here, Paul most likely meant that the Christian spouse was not *enslaved* in that situation, meaning that he or she wasn't required to stay within the entrapment of not knowing whether he or she could allow the divorce of the non-Christian who wanted it. In other words, when a non-Christian spouse wished to free him- or herself from the marriage obligation to the Christian, the Christian spouse could let him or her go (i.e. allow divorce). The Christian spouse was not obliged to keep the marriage; that is, he or she was not "enslaved" to stay married to the non-believing spouse who wanted divorce.

Allowing such divorce to take place was necessary because God had called the Corinthian Christians to live in peace (1 Cor 7:15b). Were they to fight with unbelieving spouses who wanted divorce, and were they to take those people to court, peace and harmony would dissipate. God had, instead, called the Corinthian Christians to live peacefully, even in the midst of a tempest like a divorce. Such peaceful living, in turn, might draw the fleeing unbelieving spouse back to the Christian and to the Lord: "Who knows, woman, if your husband will be saved [in this process]? Who knows, man, if your wife will be saved [in this peaceful separation]?" (1 Cor 7:16). Although the divorce of a Christian from his or her unbelieving spouse was not ideal, a peaceful process in the midst of divorce proceedings could draw the unbeliever to faith. That was to be the aim and prayer of the Christian spouse.

Saṃtoṣa (7:17)

One of the most beautiful Sanskrit words is *saṃtoṣa*. It means "contentment" or "satisfaction." In my language, Tamil, it has come to mean "happiness" (*samthosam*) or "peace" (*samathanam*). A Hindu devotee has ten "observances" to help in his or her spiritual journey, of which contentment is the second: remorse, contentment (*saṃtoṣa*), giving, faith, worship of a god, scriptural listening, developing a spiritual will, sacred vows, recitation, and endurance of the opposites.

Paul likewise taught the Corinthians to be content. This lesson followed Paul's instructions for Christians who were married to non-Christians to choose either divorce when the non-Christian wanted divorce or no divorce when the non-Christian did not want divorce. That concept of flexibility in order to retain peace and an open door for the gospel led Paul to talk about "contentment" regardless of where God had placed a person. He said, "Let each person live the *portion* God has assigned, just as God has called each one" (1 Cor 7:17a).[54] This sentence has both a general and a specific meaning. The specific meaning in the context is that the married should enjoy marriage, the widowed should live in singleness if possible or get married, the married shouldn't divorce, and Christians married to non-Christians should either divorce or remain married according to the non-Christian spouses' desires. Paul would add to these in the passages that follow topics such as circumcision and slavery. The general meaning was that of "contentment." Wherever God has placed a person, or whatever state a person was in when God called him or her to salvation, that person should be content. That was a universal teaching of Paul's: "I give this instruction to all the churches" (1 Cor 7:17b).[55]

Bindi, Tilaka, and Vibhuti (7:18–24)

Hindus wear several different markers on their foreheads or bodies. Three significant ones are bindi, tilaka, and vibhuti.[56] A bindi (from Sanskrit *bindu*, meaning "a drop," "a small particle," or "dot") is a decoration worn on the forehead of women in India. Traditionally it is red in color, representing love and prosperity. Sometimes even jewelry is worn as bindi. It also has religious connotations. In Hinduism the area between the eyebrows, where the bindi is placed, is the sixth *chakra* (energy point), the seat of concealed wisdom. It also represents the "third eye," the abode of the Brahma (cf. Jabala Upanishad).

A tilaka (or *kumkuma*), on the other hand, is purely a religious marker on the forehead or other part of the body (usually the neck, upper arms, forearms, chest, torso, stomach, or shoulder) of a devotee, whether male or female. The marker varies according to one's deity. For example, the worshippers of Vishnu have for a tilaka (or *kumkuma*) a long straight line starting from just below the hairline to the tip of the nose. An elongated U intercepts it in the middle. This particular tilaka is made of sandalwood paste.

Similar to tilaka, vibhuti is also a religious marker.[57] It is a white sacred ash made from a special kind of wood that is burned in a sacred fire in the

---

54. This theme of "do not change your status" runs through the whole chapter (1 Cor 7:2, 8, 10, 12–16, 26–27, 37, 40) (Fee, *First Epistle to the Corinthians*, 268).

55. Paul has four such statements of the universality of his teachings (1 Cor 4:17; 7:17; 11:16; 14:33).

56. For a detailed study, see Arthur Avalon, *Sāradā-Tilaka Tantram* (Delhi, India: Motilal Banarsidass, n.d.).

57. I am indebted to a colleague, Dave Raj Sangiah, for introducing me to the difference between tilaka and vibhuti.

temple. After worship, the priest smears it in the forehead of the worshipper. In certain cases, the eldest member of the family places it on the forehead of the younger members. It is so sacred that it is held on a "throne" (*asanam*) in the temple until it is smeared on the head of the devotee. Interestingly, a tilaka is also worn to represent caste differences. The Brahmans (highest caste) wear white chalk marks signifying purity, for they are priestly in profession. The Kshatriya wear red kumkum marks signifying valor since they belong to warrior races. The Vaishya wear a yellow kesar or turmeric mark signifying prosperity, as they are business people and traders. The Sudra apply a black bhasma made of charcoal signifying service as they are workers in the field.[58]

In this way, these markers (esp. tilaka and vibhuti) can be called "boundary markers" that separate one from the other: a devotee from the rest and one caste from another. Even other religions have such boundary or identity markers. Jewish men, for example, wear a phylactery on their foreheads. A phylactery is a small leather box containing the Hebrew Scriptures and Jewish men wear it on their foreheads at morning prayers to remind themselves to keep the law of God. Muslim men have calloused marks on their foreheads from bowing down and touching their head on the ground, as a sign of their reverence for Allah. These are outward markers that distinguish followers of different religions from one another. There are other markers that are not so visible. Both Muslim and Jewish males undergo circumcision, which becomes a boundary marker that separates them from the rest of the people. Circumcision is the removal of the foreskin in male genitalia.[59]

The law of God required all Jewish males to be circumcised as a sign of God's covenant with Abraham (Gen 17:9–14). When such Jews became Christians, there was sometimes tension in a congregation between those who were circumcised and those who weren't (Christians from non-Jewish backgrounds, Gentile Christians). So Paul, following his theme of contentment (1 Cor 7:17), commanded, "If anyone was called [to salvation] while he was circumcised, he should not try to become uncircumcised; if anyone was called while he was uncircumcised, he shouldn't try to become circumcised" (1 Cor 7:18).

---

58. N.a., "Hindu Rituals and Routines: Why Do We Follow Those?", http://sanskritdocuments.org/articles/Hindu_Rituals.pdf (accessed July 17, 2014).

59. Judaism did not command or practice female circumcision. For Islam's practice of female circumcision see Abdur-Razaq B. Adesina, "Islam and Female Circumcision: A Critical Appraisal," *Hamdard Islamicus* 29, no. 2 (April–June 2006): 59–67.

During the rule of the Maccabees, in order to please the Greek ruler Antiochus, the high priests – Jason and Menelaus – requested permission to build a gymnasium in Jerusalem. In those days, men took part in sport naked in a gymnasium. Josephus says, "When he [Antiochus] had given them permission, they also hid the circumcision of their genitals, that even when they were naked they might appear to be Greeks" (Josephus, *Antiquities* 12.241; also 1 Macc 1:14–15). On the other hand, Paul's letter to the Galatians speaks of non-Jewish Christians circumcising themselves in order to fit in with the Jewish Christians (Gal 5:2; 6:12). Paul's message to both groups in Corinth was to be content in the state (circumcised or uncircumcised) in which God had called them to salvation, since neither circumcision nor uncircumcision mattered; only keeping the commandments of God mattered (1 Cor 7:19; cf. Gal 5:6; 6:15).[60] Instead of trying to change oneself or take pride in something that was valueless (an outward religious marker), it was better to be content in one's state and in one's true inward change brought about by one's obedience to God's commandments. The bottom line was, "Whatever the calling in which one was called, one should remain in it" (1 Cor 7:20).

While circumcision was a religious marker, slavery was a social marker (even a stigma). The Roman Empire had many slaves. Whenever the Romans conquered a land, their prisoners became slaves. Corinth also had many slaves. Witherington says, "Conservative estimates of the growing Roman economy in Roman Corinth strongly suggest that at least one-third of the population there in Paul's day were slaves."[61] He further writes,

> The slave in antiquity was by Aristotle's definition a piece of 'living property.' As such, slaves had no legal rights and so were subject to the will of their owners. In the early empire there were some efforts to mitigate the absolute power of the owners. There is considerable evidence not only for large numbers of slaves buying themselves out of slavery, but also of slaves whose owners allowed them to develop their own businesses and so earn large sums of money.[62]

---

60. This verse doesn't necessarily imply that there were debates between the circumcised and the uncircumcised in Corinth (Fee, *First Epistle to the Corinthians*, 312); it anticipates such problems based on the experience of other churches, such as the churches in Galatia.

61. Witherington III, *Conflict and Community in Corinth*, 183.

62. Ibid., 181.

Unlike in the transatlantic slave trade where slaves were workers in fields, in the Roman Empire they performed various tasks. Some were civil servants and even imperial servants, with prestige and power. There were also temple slaves, agricultural slaves, domestic servants, artisans, pedagogues (those who coached children), and mine workers. The status of a slave was often higher than that of a day laborer because the owner guaranteed a slave food, clothing, and medical expenses. While some slaves sought freedom, some day laborers sought slavery.

Because of this, Paul continued, "If you were called while a slave, do not concern yourself about it" (1 Cor 7:21). The reason was, "The slave who is called in the Lord is truly free in the Lord; likewise, the free person who is called is a slave of Christ" (1 Cor 7:22). The prepositional phrases "*in* the Lord" and "*of* Christ" are significant. A slave could have been in bondage physically, but *in* the Lord he or she was free. The Lord alone was his or her Master. So elsewhere Paul said, "Masters, offer justice and equality to your slaves, knowing that you too have the Lord in heaven" (Col 4:1). Similarly, since Christ purchased them at a great price, they were slaves *of* Christ (1 Cor 7:23a; 7:22b). Paul envisioned salvation in terms of purchasing a slave. People once enslaved to sin had been purchased at a great price – the Lord's death – so they now belonged to him; they were his slaves. Since they were his slaves, they shouldn't become slaves of people (1 Cor 7:23).

Slavery prevails in contemporary India. According to a website, "Slavery experts agree that, by comparison with other countries, India has the largest concentration of slavery in all its forms. Slavery in India, whether in sexual exploitation or other forms of labor, typically uses the mechanism of debt bondage, where slaves are psychologically chained to an illegal debt that they are forced to repay through their labor. If the psychological pressure fails, then slaveholders enforce debt bondage slavery through direct violence."[63] Another website says, "Modern slavery, including human trafficking, is rife in India. The so-called 19th-century abolition of slavery dealt with legal slavery. Illegal and illicit slavery persists and grows at an alarming rate, continuing to evolve in various forms."[64] One report says that in October 1995 in the

---

63. www.freetheslaves.net/india.

64. www.dfn.org.uk/info/slavery. Concerning violence against Dalits, Uprety writes, "During Mayawati's first 10 months in power – from 13 May 2007 to March 2008 – around 540 cases of murder, arson, and rape of Dalits were registered. The comparative figure in 2006–07 was 597. Under the present regime, cases of rape of Dalit women increased to 271, from 252 in 2006–07 . . . On 13 September 2007, two Dalit children from near Kanpur had their eyes gouged out and tongues chopped off before being murdered" (Ajay Uprety, "Butcher's Bill

state of Tamil Nadu alone over 1 million bonded laborers existed.[65] In a most informative article, Tucker states that in India there are "an estimated fifteen million bonded child laborers."[66]

Paul's lesson, in the midst of the exhortation to be content, aptly fits here: "If it is possible to become free, make the best of the opportunity" (1 Cor 7:21b). Some have suggested that the phrase "make the best of the opportunity" implies "stay as a slave but use your freedom for good." Paul did command slaves to serve faithfully. But the phrase "if it is possible to become free" implies he was talking about emancipation and that he wanted the slaves to take the opportunity (he demonstrated it when he pleaded with Philemon on behalf of Onesimus). Were Paul in India today seeing the atrocities of bonded slavery, he would demand that the church works hard to free the slaves. The churches should heed his call.

Where freedom is not possible, contentment (instead of grumbling) is called for: "each Christian is to remain in whatever state in which God called him or her" (1 Cor 7:24). These teachings were not contradictory; instead, they addressed one's state of mind. Seeking freedom, when the opportunity arose, was important; but when there was no freedom, it was no excuse not to be content. Wherever a Christian finds him- or herself, he or she is to be content. Of course, this kind of contentment can come only with the help of God.

Connections

The Corinthians had asked Paul's advice about married people and Paul addressed this question in the first "and concerning . . ." section (1 Cor 7:1–24). Paul instructed that husbands and wives should voluntarily submit themselves to one another. They were to abstain from their sexual relationship only for prayer and only for a limited time. Then Paul talked about widowers and widows, and exhorted them to remain in their singleness, if possible, and serve the Lord. But if they were in love with someone else, they could get married. Then Paul addressed those who contemplated divorce, saying

---

Goes Up: A Dalit CM Doesn't Mean No Dalits Murdered," *The Week* [25 May 2008]: 22). This resembles some of the violence ancient slave-owners inflicted upon their slaves.

65. Krishna Prasad Upadhyaya, "Poverty, Discrimination and Slavery: The Reality of Bonded Labor in India, Nepal and Pakistan," *Anti-Slavery International* (2008): 19.

66. Lee Tucker, "Child Slaves in Modern India: The Bonded Labor Problem," *Human Rights Quarterly* 19, no. 3 (August 1997): 572.

that they shouldn't get divorced. When circumstances demanded that they separate, they should either remain separated or be reconciled to one another. Finally, he addressed Christians married to non-Christians. Should the non-Christian spouse choose to remain with the Christian, the Christian shouldn't divorce the non-Christian. Should the non-Christian seek divorce, the Christian shouldn't resist and cause division. The Christian's good actions might draw the non-Christian spouse and the children to salvation. Paul concluded with his exhortation for Christians to remain content in whatever state they were in when God had called them to salvation.

In the next section (1 Cor 7:25–40) Paul addressed more of the Corinthians' questions with his second "and concerning . . ." formula. Theses questions were related to engaged or betrothed people – whether they could get married or not.

Arranged Marriages Versus Love Marriages (7:25–40)

Most of the marriages in India are "arranged marriages" – that is, the parents of the bride and the bridegroom arrange the marriage instead of the young people choosing their own spouses.[67] In many cases the bride and the groom will not even have met each other before the wedding day. "At most they might meet for a brief conversation, and this meeting would take place only after their parents have decided that the match was suitable."[68] Parents do not force a person to marry someone that either the bride or the groom finds objectionable, but only rarely will young people object to their parents' choice. This practice is common in North and South India. The only exception is Northeast India, in states like Nagaland and Manipur. There the young people select their own partners. But even then, unless the parents agree to their marriage and conduct the engagement discussions, the marriage will not occur. Thong and Kath write, "Traditionally, the system of marriages among the Naga tribes [a tribe in NE India] was through negotiation, when the boy informs his parents about his desire to marry or his acceptance of a marriage proposal, suggesting a girl for partnership. This leads to the start

---

67. For a narrative explanation of the process of arranged marriage, read Nicole A. Wilson, "Confrontation and Compromise: Middle-Class Matchmaking in Twenty-First Century South India," *Asian Ethnology* 72, no. 1 (2013): 33–53.

68. Serena Nanda, "Arranging a Marriage in India," in *Stumbling toward Truth: Anthropologists at Work*, ed. Philip R. Devita (Long Grove, IL: Waveland Press, 2000), 196.

of negotiation in which some elderly persons are made as go-betweens."[69] The "arranged marriage" is so prevalent that the terms "love marriages" or "love match" are used derogatively for Western marriages. In most traditional families, love marriages are frowned upon.

Ancient cultures such as that of ancient Israel and the Greco-Roman culture of Paul's time also practiced "arranged marriages." In such cultures, the engagement period was equivalent to marriage since the wedding contracts (mostly oral) were made and gifts (dowry) were exchanged during the engagement. The marriage was sealed at the time of engagement and any break of engagement caused great offense. When Joseph found that his betrothed, Mary, was going to have a baby, he (being a righteous man) secretly tried to divorce her (Matt 1:18–23; Luke 1:27). If he had been unrighteous or unkind, he would have dragged her to the courts and caused her to be stoned to death, for he would have assumed that she had committed sexual immorality before their wedding. In cultures such as Joseph and Mary's and in Indian cultures today, the time between engagement and marriage is short and as good as a "pre-marriage" marriage.

Sometimes this engagement – the arrangement between parents and a pre-wedding wedding – occurs even when the bride and groom are children. In Rajasthan, my family witnessed the wedding (or engagement) of two children: the boy was eight and the girl was five. They came to a temple and were married before their gods. The priest was quick to point out that the "child bride and groom" would go back to their respective parents' homes until they reached puberty. Then they would have the real wedding ceremony and would cohabit as husband and wife.[70]

In the Corinthian church too there were young people who were engaged or betrothed. They were concerned as to whether they would be sinning if they went ahead and married. So Paul addressed that topic in this section (1 Cor 7:25–40). His basic lesson was that a person could remain in his or her engagement state and not marry, but if a fiancé (betrothed young man) and a fiancée (betrothed young woman) decided to marry, they wouldn't be sinning. Paul referred to the group as "virgins" because that was the cultural term for unmarried young people (1 Cor 7:28, 34, 36–38).

---

69. Thong and Kath, *Glimpses of Naga Legacy*, 172–173.

70. For a detailed study of Hindu weddings, see Arvind Sharma, "Marriage in the Hindu Religious Tradition," *Journal of Ecumenical Studies* 22, no. 1 (Winter 1985): 69–80.

Not all scholars agree that Paul was addressing fiancés and fiancées.[71] Some argue that Paul was addressing the fathers of the fiancées, saying they should marry off their virgin daughters or dedicate them to the Lord's ministry. Such a view is patterned on the Old Testament story of Jephthah, an Israelite judge who made an oath and as a result dedicated his daughter to God and never allowed her to marry (Judg 11:30–40). The proponents of this view receive support from the verb used in 1 Corinthians 7:38 that could mean "to give in marriage" (*gamizō*, as in Matt 22:30; 24:38; Mark 12:25; Luke 17:27; 20:35). Fee points out, "It is fair to say that without v. 38, with its change of verb [*gamizō*], this view would never have arisen, or at least would never have gained popularity."[72] Since the words "fathers" and "daughters" are not in the context and the term "his virgin" (1 Cor 7:36) was never used in the context of a father–daughter relationship, this view is not preferred.

A second view is that Paul was addressing married people who had decided not to consummate their marriage with sex because of their piety for the Lord.[73] In an apocryphal writing, for example, it says, "Blessed are they who have wives as if they had them not, for they shall inherit God" (*Acts of Paul and Thecla*, 5). This was a practice in the church from the second to the fifth century. But such a practice was not common in Paul's time and it would contradict what Paul had been teaching earlier in the section about husbands and wives offering themselves to each other (1 Cor 7:4–5).

Against these two views, then, most contemporary scholars argue that Paul was addressing fiancés and fiancées.[74] That is the view taken in this commentary. Such betrothed couples were wondering if it was sinful to get married.

Paul's basic message in all of chapter 7 has been "remain as you are." He asked widowers and widows to remain as they were (in their singleness) unless they were in love and wanted to marry. He asked slaves to remain where they were unless an opportunity arose for them to receive freedom. He asked believers married to unbelievers to remain in those marriages unless

---

71. For a list of views, see John J. O'Rourke, "Hypotheses Regarding 1 Corinthians 7:36–38," *Catholic Biblical Quarterly* 20, no. 3 (July 1958): 292–298.

72. Fee, *First Epistle to the Corinthians*, 326.

73. R. H. A. Sebolt, "Spiritual Marriage in the Early Church: A Suggested Interpretation of 1 Cor. 7:36-38," *Concordia Theological Monthly* 30 (1959): 176–189.

74. Blomberg, *1 Corinthians*, 153. Fee, *First Epistle to the Corinthians*, 323. Werner G. Kümmel, "Verlobung Und Heirat Bei Paulus (1. Cor 7, 36-38)," in *Neutestamentliche Studien für Rudolf Bultmann Zu Seinem Siebzigsten Gerburtstag Am 20. August 1954.*, ed. Walther Eltester (Berlin: A. Töpelmann, 1957), 275–295.

the unbelievers wanted to leave. In the same way, Paul here recommended that the betrothed remain in their state of singleness, unless they were in love, of marriageable age, and wished to get married. Then they could marry, and they would not be sinning if they did so.

The term "virgin" (*parthenos* in Greek) referred to both males (cf. Rev. 14:4) and females in the Greek world, so some of the teachings in this passage were addressed to both partners (1 Cor 7:25–26), some were addressed to the male virgins (7:27–34a, 37–38), and some were addressed to the female virgins (7:34b–36, 39–40). Just as Paul carefully addressed wives and husbands, widows and widowers, here too he addresses fiancées and fiancés. Paul treated males and females equally. Since the Lord Jesus didn't give specific instructions to the betrothed (although he spoke of eunuchs, Matt 19:12), Paul didn't cite him; instead, Paul gave his own rationale for his teachings, "as one who has been shown mercy by the Lord to be entrusted [with these teachings]" (1 Cor 7:25).[75] In other words, he was instructing them as a commissioned apostle who had been entrusted with these teachings.

Paul first addressed the fiancés (betrothed young men) and said, "it is good for a man to remain as he is" (1 Cor 7:26a, c), meaning, it is good to be in the betrothed state and not marry. Paul then stated the first rationale for this reasoning: "because of the impending calamity" that existed in the world for the Corinthians (1 Cor 7:26b). Scholars think that Paul was referring to the severe famine of AD 51 in Corinth[76] or to childbirth that often involved dangers and expense.[77] Since such calamities (famine and dangers) would affect a marriage negatively, it was better for a man to remain single – that is, "the one betrothed to the woman should not seek release [i.e. freedom from the contract of engagement[78]]; the one un-betrothed should not seek a fiancée" (1 Cor 7:27). But, on the other hand, if he decided to marry his fiancée, he wasn't sinning (1 Cor 7:28a). Paul then addressed the fiancées: "If a fiancée marries, she is not sinning" (1 Cor 7:28b). What he had been saying was true for her as well: "Because of the afflictions of the flesh that they'll

---

75. Paul marked off his "rationale" with clear structural markers: "therefore I think" (1 Cor 7:26), "and this I say" (1 Cor 7:26), "and I wish" (1 Cor 7:32), and "I say this for your benefit" (1 Cor 7:35).

76. Bradley B. Blue, "The House Church at Corinth and the Lord's Supper: Famine, Food Supply, and the Present Distress," *Criswell Theological Review* 5, no. 2 (1991): 236–237.

77. Instone-Brewer, "1 Corinthians 7 in the Light of the Graeco-Roman Marriage," 114. Also Reichenbach, "The Gift of Singleness."

78. Fee explains that the word "loose" (*luō*) was used as a technical term for discharging someone from the obligation of a contract (Fee, *First Epistle to the Corinthians*, 331–332).

face, I am [saying these things] to spare you" (1 Cor 7:28b). Most likely, "the afflictions of the flesh" refers to general forms of trials that all married women face, including complications in childbirth, childrearing difficulties, fear of losing a spouse, financial strains, protection issues, and the like. Fiancés and fiancées might go ahead and get married, but they needed to realize that there would be trials. Marriage was never sinful, but there would be more trials in a married life than in a single life. It would be much harder to see one's spouse hunger and thirst than simply for oneself to hunger and thirst; it would be much more difficult to see one's spouse suffer persecution than simply for oneself to endure persecution. That was why Paul was encouraging the young betrothed to stay in their singleness and not marry.

The second rationale was the imminent end of the present world: "the time is being wrapped up" (7:29b) and "the element of this world is passing away" (7:31b). Paul lived as if the Lord would come in his lifetime. When he wrote 1 Thessalonians, he included himself among those who would be "alive" when the Lord returned (1 Thess 4:15). The same was true when he wrote 1 Corinthians: "*We* will not all fall asleep but we will all be changed" (1 Cor 15:51). He wanted the betrothed in the Corinthian church to live as if the Lord could come at any time. So he wrote, "Those who have fiancées should act and think as though they have none" (1 Cor 7:29). In other words, they shouldn't be thinking of marriage and family; instead, they should live as if they were waiting for the Lord to come, making the most of the opportunity for evangelism. But this principle of living for the Lord until he came applied to all: "Those who are crying as those not crying, and those who are rejoicing as those not rejoicing, and those who are buying as those not possessing, and those who deal with the world as those not utilizing it" (1 Cor 7:30–31).[79] Paul wasn't advocating laziness (cf. 2 Thess 3:10); instead, he was promoting a lifestyle that focused on eternal things. He wanted the Corinthians to be "other-worldly," that is, to think of God's work and not be focused on the present world, since the present world was coming to an end. So the betrothed should not think of marriage either; the time was coming to an end.

The third rationale for remaining unmarried was because of the obligations connected with the married life (1 Cor 7:32–34). Whereas an unmarried man could wholeheartedly devote himself to the Lord and to the works that please the Lord (1 Cor 7:32), a married man has worldly

---

79. It is possible that these are concepts related to a marriage – crying when the bride departs, rejoicing at the wedding, and bargaining over wedding dowry.

responsibilities, such as how to take care of his wife (1 Cor 7:33). His devotion oscillates between God and his wife (1 Cor 7:34a). Likewise, an unmarried woman, a virgin, was devoted to the things of the Lord: how she might be holy both in her body and in her spirit. The married woman was devoted to the things of the world, such as how she might please her husband (1 Cor 7:34b). Paul wished to release his people from such obligations (1 Cor 7:32a). When Paul said that an unmarried woman could keep her body and mind holy, he may have meant that she should abstain from sexual *pollution* – but that would go against everything Paul had been teaching in this section and also against what the Old Testament teaches.[80] Instead, Paul probably meant that she could be wholly devoted to God. Paul was basically instructing that married people had obligations, and rightfully so. Should a person, then, want to be free of those obligations, he or she must remain single. That was why Paul didn't want the unprepared betrothed to get married.

The fourth rationale was a counterpoint to the third: should a person want to be wholly devoted to God, he or she should remain single (1 Cor 7:35). Whereas married people had earthly obligations, as God had intended, celibacy was the solution for those who wanted to wholeheartedly serve God. Historically, Christianity has practiced such celibacy among priests, to the benefit of the church. Having studied the history of priestly celibacy, Igboanyika concludes, "I am convinced that celibacy is a sacrifice which enhances the evangelical witness of priests and religious [sic]. It is not an escape from something that is dirty and unholy as some anti-celibate protagonists suggest. It is the giving up of something really beautiful to collaborate in something more beautiful. You cannot opt for all options and every good thing comes at a price."[81] Such celibates were able to serve the Lord "without distraction" and "notably and constantly," said Paul (1 Cor 7:35). Paul was quick to caution, "I am not saying this to place a limitation on you" (1 Cor 7:35a). This was because a person shouldn't pursue celibacy unless he or she had a specific calling for it. Reichenbach writes, "Singleness is not less than God's best, but is God's best for those called to a distinctive task."[82]

Paul's wish for the betrothed was that they remain single because of the rationales he listed: impending calamity, the end days, the obligations of

---

80. For an explanation of these views, see Fee, *First Epistle to the Corinthians*, 346.

81. Sylbester U. N. Igboanyika, "The History of Priestly Celibacy in the Church," *AFER* 45, no. 2 (June 2003): 104.

82. Reichenbach, "The Gift of Singleness," 5. Reichenbach also speaks of a church's sensitivity to those who are single in the church. This is important for a healthy church.

marriage, and wholehearted service to God. But he didn't want the betrothed to conclude that he objected to them marrying or that marriage was sinful. So he concluded by approving of marriage (7:36–40).

First Paul addressed the betrothed males, the fiancés (7:36–38).[83] Paul's instruction to any fiancé was that if he was acting "insensitively" towards his fiancée, and if he was of marriageable age and full of sexual passion, he should follow his wishes and marry. He was not sinning if they married (1 Cor 7:36).[84] Often the word "insensitively" is translated as "inappropriately," implying there was immorality between the couple.[85] But Paul used that same word elsewhere (1 Cor 13:5) to clearly mean "rude" or "insensitive" ("love is not rude or insensitive"). This is the only other usage in the New Testament, and so it is best to follow that same meaning here as well. Paul was advocating that a fiancé shouldn't make this decision to remain single on his own; he shouldn't be insensitive to his fiancée's desires or approval. Similarly, the phrase "of marriageable age" has an additional meaning in the extra-biblical world: "full of sexual passion" that is characteristic of youth.[86] So Paul was saying that, when a fiancé had the approval of his fiancée, when he was of marriageable age and had sexual passion, and when he was willing to marry, their decision to go ahead and marry would not be sinful. They shouldn't be intimidated by Paul's four rationales given earlier to remain single; instead, they should go ahead with their desires and they would not be sinning.

On the other hand, if the fiancée didn't feel neglected, if she was happy for them to remain unmarried, and if the fiancé himself had established in his heart – without any constraint – that he should keep her a virgin (i.e. in a betrothed state), that was what he should do; that was excellent too (1 Cor 7:37). In this second case, both fiancé and fiancée chose together to remain unmarried and commit themselves to God's work. In such a case, it was good for them to remain single. Fee makes an interesting observation: "What is

---

83. There is no scholarly consensus as to Paul's audience. Some think Paul was addressing fathers and daughters (NASB), some think Paul was addressing partners and celibates (NEB), and others think Paul was addressing the betrothed (fiancés and fiancées) (NIV). Fee's conclusion is appropriate: "The best solution is to see this section as flowing directly out of v. 35 and thus bringing to a specific conclusion the argument that began in v. 25, rather than a special case brought in at the end" (Fee, *First Epistle to the Corinthians*, 350).

84. Paul's phrase "his virgin" is unusual. Fee suggests that perhaps the term came from the Corinthians' letter and that Paul was simply using it consistently throughout the argument. "Here it could mean something close to 'his girl' (Holladay, 105)" (Fee, *First Epistle to the Corinthians*, 351 n. 15).

85. Fee, *First Epistle to the Corinthians*, 351 n. 13.

86. Winter, "Puberty or Passion?," 71–89.

significant here is his description of this man. In no less than four different ways he repeats that such a man must be fully convinced *in his own mind*. First, he 'has settled the matter in his own mind'; second, he 'is under no compulsion'; third, 'he has authority concerning his own will,' meaning no one else is forcing this action on him; and fourth, he 'has made up his own mind.' This verbal tour de force strongly suggests that outside influences might lead him to take such an action, but *against* his own will."[87] That should not be the case; the fiancé and fiancée should make this decision together. So whatever the betrothed male (fiancé) and the betrothed female (fiancée) decided together was perfectly acceptable to Paul. He thus concluded, "the one who marries his fiancée does well; the one who does not marry does well also" (1 Cor 7:38).[88] Basically, whichever choice the fiancé and fiancée made together (to marry or to remain single), it was not sinful. Of course, for some, marriage was more prudent than singleness, and vice versa. The young couple alone could make that decision.

Second, Paul addressed the betrothed females, the fiancées (7:39–40). A fiancée was bound to her fiancé as long as he lived (1 Cor 7:39a). Betrothal was equivalent to marriage (cf. Rom 7:1–4). It was a legal contract. Should the fiancé die prematurely, she was free to marry another, provided that man was a Christian (1 Cor 7:39b). This command was needed because in some ancient cultures betrothed fiancées remained unmarried in the event of the death of the fiancés (as is common in Rajasthan even now). Paul didn't want the Corinthian Christians to suffer such cultural injustice. He wanted a young lady, the fiancée, to have the freedom to marry another Christian if her first fiancé were to die. Just as he concluded the fiancé's note, so he concluded the fiancée's with an exhortation to remain single if possible: "In my thinking, she will be much happier if she remains as she is [in her betrothed state]" (1 Cor 7:40a).

As noted already, this has been Paul's overall theme throughout chapter 7 – "remain where God has placed you." He preferred a single person to remain single to serve the Lord, but that was not a constraint he placed upon anyone. Paul concluded this section with a reference to his apostolic authority: "I

---

87. Fee, *First Epistle to the Corinthians*, 353.
88. Some translations (NET, HCSB, and NIV) have the word "better" (comparative degree). Although the word *kreisson* could imply the *comparative* ("better"), it could also imply the *positive* ("good," as in 1 Cor 11:17) or the *superlative* ("superior," as in Heb 7:7). Since Paul was arguing that the married and the unmarried must live according to the gift God had given, I have translated it as the *positive*.

think [these teachings] *since* I have the Spirit of God" (1 Cor 7:40b).[89] The Corinthians weren't to conclude that these were Paul's own teachings, his own biases; instead, they were to understand that Paul gave these teachings under the guidance of the Holy Spirit. Thus there was great freedom in Christ – to marry or to remain single, as Paul had repeatedly shown.

Paul's instructions to the engaged but not yet married have various implications and applications for Indian culture, where marriage is alone considered appropriate. Paul preferred young men and women to be committed to God first and to remain in their singleness to serve him wholeheartedly, but he also taught that it was not sinful at all to marry. A young engaged couple need to decide whether they would rather devote their lives to God as singles, or marry and honor God with their married lives.

---

89. The grammar of this statement means it could be read as, "And I think [*doko de*] *since* I [*kago*] have the Spirit of God," where the particle *de* functions as "a marker of a summary statement" (Louw & Nida's lexicon, 91.4). But that is not the general interpretation.

10

1 Corinthians 8

Idol Worship (8:1–3)

Idol worship is obviously the worship of an idol. But such a definition is too simple and is fallacious. Gandhi, for example, said, "No Hindu considers an image to be God."[1] Chatterjee explains: "It is a mistake to think that the worship of images, approved by Hinduism, is crude idolatry. For image-worship is really the worship of God as represented by means of images. The images by themselves are neither looked upon as God nor worshipped as such. They are treated only as symbols or concrete representations of God."[2] Idol worship, then, is worshipping a deity *through* an object which is an "idol" or an "image."

The term for images or idols in Hinduism is *murti* (a Sanskrit word). It means a "solid body" or a "material form." Hindus differentiate between iconic and aniconic images. Iconic images are anthropomorphic representations of a god. The deity Shiva is represented in the *murti* of a cosmic dancer (*Nataraja*), who holds a drum in his right hand signifying the sound of creation, a fire in his left hand signifying destruction, and with his second right hand forms a gesture of protection. He dances on a demon called "epilepsy," representing ignorance (Shiva stands on it to signify that he destroys the devotee's ignorance). Aniconic images do not have an exact likeness to the deity, although they represent the deity. A classic example is *linga* (a phallus) that represents the deity Shiva. "While the *linga*, in its early

---

1. Charles F. Andrews, *Mahatma Gandhi: His Life & Ideas* (Delhi: Jaico Publishing House, 2005), 12.
2. Satischandra Chatterjee, *The Fundamentals of Hinduism* (Calcutta, India: The University of Calcutta, 1970), 176–77.

history, might have had phallic associations, it is venerated today only as the mark or sign of Siva."[3]

So when a Hindu stands before an idol or *murti*, he or she is not worshipping that image or idol; instead, he or she is worshipping the god or goddess that particular icon or anicon represents. As such, the location (home or temple) in which a *murti* is placed becomes significant; it is the abode of the deity. A Hindu devotee writes, "Daily taking in the deity's *prasada* [gifts] and performing *kirtana* [songs or chants] for the deity, daily seeing the attractively decorated body of the deity, daily smelling the incense and flowers offered to the deity, daily massaging the body of the deity with fragrant oils and dressing the Lord, making garlands, sewing the clothes, or cooking the food offered to him, the devotee meditates steadily on God."[4] In this way, whether a deity is in a home or in a temple, that deity is revered and respected. The act of showing respect or reverence is called *puja*, the veneration of the deity.

Greco-Roman worship was similar to Hinduism in that the outward manifestations of idols represented their inner meanings. LiDonnici, for example, examines the worship of Artemis in Ephesus and concludes that the many "breasts" may "suggest an extremely nurturant, protective, and sustaining goddess."[5] Thus icons and anicons represent gods.

This is Paul's foundational argument in 1 Corinthians 8. There were "demi-gods" and "demi-lords" behind idols, images, or statues; therefore, eating before an idol was a religious act. The Corinthian Christians, especially the Gentiles, came from backgrounds where they worshipped idol-gods. They would have once gone to the temples of Aphrodite, Apollo, or Demeter/Kore that stood in Corinth and worshipped in front of images or icons. Following the Lord Jesus Christ and the Father God demanded that they cut off all ties with such previous temples and forms of worship, especially since it caused others to stumble and turn back to former worship or religion.

---

3. Anantanand Rambachan, "Seeing the Divine in All Forms: The Culminatio of Hindu Worship," *Dialogue & Alliance* 4, no. 1 (Spring 1990): 6. Many other cultures, ancient and modern, had phallic representations of their deities: Egyptians (for Min), Greeks (for Dionysus), Hamangian, Babylonians, Malians, Mayas, Thai, Korean, Bhutans, etc.

4. William H. Deadwyler, "The Devotee and the Deity: Living a Personlistic Theology," in *Gods of Flesh, Gods of Stone: The Embodiment of Divinity in India*, eds. Joanne Punzo Waghome, Norman Cutler, and Vasudha Narayanan (New York: Columbia University Press, 1985), 84. His Hindu name is Ravindra-Svarupa Dasa.

5. Lynn R. LiDonnici, "The Images of Artemis Ephesia and Greco-Roman Worship: A Reconsideration," *Harvard Theological Review* 85, no. 4 (Ocotber 1992): 408.

Christianity, following Judaism, forbade the worship of the true God through idols. The first commandment in the Old Testament said, "I am the Lord your God who led you out of Egypt, out of the house of slavery. There shall be to you no other gods than me. You shall not make for yourselves idols or images in the likeness of those things in heaven or those in the earth or those upon the waters. You shall not worship them nor serve them because I alone am the Lord your God, a zealous God" (Exod 20:2–5a, LXX). Therefore Jews and Christians made no icons, images, or idols to represent God.

The Corinthian Christians, with such a mix of their background of idol worship and their new understanding of Christianity, made some crucial errors in their theology. So Paul corrected them in this section. Their major error was in their knowledge or understanding (1 Cor 8:4–13), so he addressed that first. But even before he could address their errors of knowledge, he needed to address an even more basic issue: the greatness of love in comparison to knowledge (1 Cor 8:1–3).[6]

The Corinthians prided themselves on the fact that they understood about Christian worship and idol worship. Their slogan was, "We know that we have all knowledge" (1 Cor 8:1a).[7] Paul would later describe their "knowledge" and would correct it, but first he wanted to caution them about the intrinsic danger of knowledge: it exalted one person up above another, a problem that the Corinthians had. So Paul wrote, "Knowledge puffs a person up, but love builds the other" (1 Cor 8:1b). Whereas knowledge exalted the one who had it, love built up the other person. Paul wanted the Corinthian Christians to focus on others. Later he would say, "If I have all knowledge . . . but have no love, I am nothing" (1 Cor 13:2). Thus Paul contrasted knowledge with love: knowledge lifts up oneself, but love builds up the other.

Likewise, a "know it all" attitude actually blinds a person. So Paul wrote, "If anyone thinks he or she knows something, that person automatically fails to understand that same topic as it should be understood" (1 Cor 8:2). If a bus driver were to sit in the cockpit of a plane and boast that he or she could fly a plane based on knowledge of driving a bus, his or her knowledge

---

6. There is a small structural marker (*peri* without *de*) in 1 Cor 8:4 to show that Paul was referring to a different but related topic.

7. Some scholars interpret Paul's phrase *oidamen* ("we know") as *oida men* ("I know indeed"). Although such splitting is possible (since the original Greek writings did not have spaces between words), the context seems to imply that Paul was correcting another slogan of the Corinthians.

would actually be a hindrance and would even be dangerous. Paul wanted the Corinthians to have a learning attitude, not a proud "I know it all" attitude.

The opposite to "the pride of knowledge" and the "know it all" attitude is love for God. Paul wrote, "If anyone loves God, that one will be known by [God]" (1 Cor 8:3). This was a cryptic way of saying that love leads a person to God and what truly matters: "God loving that person." This statement was made in the context of the discussion of idol worship. People's worship before an idol or their knowledge didn't lead them to the true God; instead, when they truly loved God from their heart, God understood them and reciprocated with love. So before people could boast of their knowledge about idols and idol worship, they needed to have love for others and love for God. Love would free them from pride and give true knowledge.

Prasada (8:4–13)

An integral part of Hindu worship is the offering and receiving of *prasada* (singular: *prasad*).[8] Devotees bring fruit and sweets and place them before a deity. The placing of these gifts is called *naivedya*. The deity then "tastes" or "enjoys" the fruit and sweets. This process of the deity enjoying the gifts is called *bhogya*. The deity doesn't consume all the food; instead, he or she leaves it as a gift, *prasada*, for the devotee to enjoy. So the priests take those *prasada* (meaning "a gracious gift") and offer them to the devotees. The devotees then enjoy the fruit and sweets in the presence of the deity. It is one of the most cherished events in a Hindu's life. Often the whole family shares in this precious meal. So one can imagine that when a family member becomes a Christian and refuses to eat the *prasada* with the family, it causes great strain within family relationships.

This was the context in the Corinthian church as well. The Gentiles (non-Jews) within the congregation would once have gone with family members and eaten at the temple any *prasada*-like food offered to gods. Food and meals always played an important role in both Jewish and non-Jewish cultures and religions. Blue writes, "In particular, as in the Jewish communities, food and meals are prominent features in various associations and religious/cultic groups . . . It was not uncommon for a temple to include

---

8. *Prasada* did not always have this *material* meaning. In the ancient Sanskrit Vedic literature, it was metaphysical – a mental state that gods and sages experience (e.g. in Rig Veda). But in later texts (such as Shiva Purana), it attained a material sense – *prasada* became the giving and receiving of gifts between the human devotee and divine gods.

culinary appurtenances and accommodate common meals."[9] Coming to
the Christian faith, however, raised serious question about their continuing
presence in pagan temples and eating of pagan food. So they asked Paul for
God's command.[10]

For entering the temple and eating the food offered to idols, it seems that
the Corinthians had made a slogan: "Concerning food offered to idols, 'we
know there are no idols in this world' and that 'there is no God except one'"
(1 Cor 8:4).[11] The logical conclusion was that they could eat food in front of
other gods or lords, for they were nonexistent.

Part of what they confessed was true, which Paul acknowledged: "For us,
there is one God, the Father" (1 Cor 8:6a). But some of what they confessed
was erroneous. Contrary to their denial of the existence of other gods and
lords, there were "so-called" gods and lords, argued Paul. In other words,
there were nominal gods and lords which, even though not gods at all, were
realities in the minds of the worshippers.[12]

So Paul wrote to them, "Just as there are so-called gods in heaven and
on earth, there are indeed many gods and many lords" (1 Cor 8:5). Barrett
best explains Paul's complex thought: "The word *god* as used by the heathen
certainly does not denote the God of the Old Testament, the God and Father
of the Lord Jesus Christ, but it does not follow from this that it denotes
nothing, and that those beings whom the heathens call *god* have no existence.
The Old Testament itself presupposes their existence, for example in Deut.
x. 17, which, like the present verse, puts *gods* and *lords* together."[13] The Old

---

9. Bradley B. Blue, "The House Church at Corinth and the Lord's Supper: Famine, Food
Supply, and the *Resent Distress*," *Criswell Theological Review* 5, no. 2 (1991): 221–222. Also Fee,
First Epistle to the Corinthians, 361.

10. If chapters 8 and 10 are seen as discussing the same topic, contradictions could arise,
since in chapter 8 Paul totally forbids the eating of food offered to idols but in chapter 10 he
makes an exception (see Horsley, *1 Corinthians*, 116). Fotopoulos has successfully shown that
if these topics are treated as different but interrelated topics, the contradictions disappear (John
Fotopoulos, "The Rhetorical Situation, Arrangement, and Argumentation of 1 Corinthians
8:1–13: Insights into Paul's Instructions on Idol-Food in Greco-Roman Context," *Greek
Orthodox Theological Review* 47, no. 1–4 [2002]: 165–166). That is how this commentary also
treats the topics: 1 Corinthians 8:1–13 deals with entering a temple and eating food offered to
idols; 1 Corinthians 10 deals with food offered in a marketplace or in a non-Christian's house.

11. For a detailed study on chapters 8–10 and Christianity in a polytheistic world, read
Bruce W. Winter, "Theological and Ethical Responses to Religious Pluralism – 1 Corinthians
8–10," *Tyndale Bulletin* 41 (1990): 209–226.

12. Orr and Walther write, "Paul is merely acknowledging the existence of numerous
sacral societies who believe in and worship deities that exist only in the worship and thought
of their believers" (Orr and Walther, *1 Corinthians*, 233).

13. Barrett, *A Commentary*, 192.

Testament, although affirming the presence of demi-gods, clearly states that there are no gods equal to our God, who alone has ultimate and true reality. Matthews writes, "Yahweh was greater than the gods. He was incomparable, singularly unique. There was no other god like him (Exod 9:14; 15:11; Deut 3:23; 33:26). These ascriptions were not philosophical deductions or cultural adaptations. Israel developed them out of her experience with Yahweh."[14] The other gods are either demonic, demi-gods, or are called gods by their respective worshippers. They have no real existence; as Bailey says, "There is no Zeus in heaven, no Athena on the earth and no Poseidon in the sea."[15] They have no true reality, but are imaginary or demonic realities.

Scholars argue that Paul was referring to either emperors or traditional deities as "gods"[16] and other deities of the mystery cults as "lords."[17] Either way, Paul's argument was that there were "so-called" gods and lords whom people worshipped; therefore, there were "realities" behind the idols and images.[18] Dunn writes, "Idols/demons have an all too real *existential* reality – whether merely the human projections of other gods . . . or objectively real demons – and that existential reality can be so crippling and enslaving that it must be given no place."[19] In other words, when a Christian sat in front of an idol, he or she was not sitting before a rock or a statue; he or she was sitting before a projection of a "so-called," or demonic, god or lord (cf. 1 Cor 10:20–22).

Paul elsewhere in his correspondence to the Corinthians referred to Satan as the "god" of this age (2 Cor 4:4). He referred to the Galatians' former lifestyle as one in which they were enslaved to "gods" (Gal 4:8). The golden calf that Aaron built in the wilderness was referred to as a "god" both in the

---

14. Ed Matthews, "Yahweh among the Gods: A Theology of World Religions from the Penteteuch," in *Christianity and the Religions: A Biblical Theology of World Religions*, eds. Edward Rommen and Harold Netland (Pasadena, CA: William Carey Library, 1995), 37.

15. Bailey, *Paul through Mediterranean Eyes*, 235.

16. For emperors as "gods," see Bruce W. Winter, "The Achaean Federal Imperial Cult Ii: The Corinthian Church," *Tyndale Bulletin*, no. 46 (1995): 169–178. Also Derek Newton, "Food Offered to Idols in 1 Corinthians 8–10," *Tyndale Bulletin* 49, no. 1 (1998): 179–182. For traditional deities as "gods," see Fee, *First Epistle to the Corinthians*, 373.

17. Fee, *First Epistle to the Corinthians*, 373. Also, Hays, *First Corinthians*, 139.

18. Hays writes, "Paul's use of the dismissive adjective 'so-called' shows that he does not believe these figures to be real gods" (Hays, *First Corinthians*).

19. James D. G. Dunn, *The Theology of Paul the Apostle* (Grand Rapids: Eerdmans, 1998), 37. Witherington writes, "His view is that though the 'gods' are not gods, there are demons present . . . Thus in a limited sense Paul allows that there are 'many gods and many lords' (8:5) . . . The idols themselves are dumb and nothing, but they are used by the powers of darkness to enslave human minds and hearts. 'Gods' (8:5) refers to the traditional pagan deities, and *kyrioi* ('lords') probably refers to the gods imported into Greece and Italy from the eastern part of the empire" (Witherington III, *Conflict and Community in Corinth*, 188–189).

Old and in the New Testament (Exod 32:1; Acts 7:40). Ironically, the people of Lycaonia thought of Paul as a "god" (Acts 14:11). Paul lived and breathed in polytheistic cultures similar to Indian culture. He was fully aware that each idol was a manifestation or presentation of a god or a lord.

Even unbelievers know this. I cited some of these words of Gandhi above in the commentary on 8:1–3: "I have said I do not disbelieve in idol-worship. An idol does not excite any feeling of veneration in me. But I think that idol-worship is part of human nature. We hunger after symbolism . . . Images are an aid to worship. No Hindu considers an image to be God."[20] In other words, idols represent false deities, a fact the "mature" Corinthians ignored so that they could enter temples and eat food offered to gods and lords. Paul didn't want the Corinthians inadvertently to promote this error. Paul therefore corrected the fallacy in the Corinthians' thinking that there were no other gods or lords in this world – that is, forces that try to take the glory and honor from the true God and the true Lord. However, although there were "forces" behind such idols, in reality there is only one supreme or real God and one supreme or real Lord, and this was Paul's next argument.

"*But for us*, there is one Father God, out of whom all things came to be, and we exist for him; and one Lord Jesus Christ, through whom all things came to be, and we too came to be" (1 Cor 8:6).[21] Christians were not to deny the existence of many "so-called" gods and lords (either demi-gods or demonic forces); at the same time, Christians know that there is only one true God and one true Lord. They were to worship only one God (the Father) and one Lord (Jesus Christ) to the point that they lived as if there were no other gods or lords. Chisholm points out that in God's active involvement in the lives of the Israelites "the pagan gods were revealed to be impotent, unworthy of devotion, and incapable of thwarting Yahweh's purposes."[22] Then he concludes, "Yahweh demanded exclusive worship and tolerated no rivals. He was unwilling to share his glory with any other 'god.' One senses that the word 'pluralism' does not exist in the divine vocabulary; indeed the spirit

---

20. Andrews, *Mahatma Gandhi*, 12.

21. Blomberg's cautionary note is significant: "The contrast between verses 5 and 6 is not between two subjective perceptions of reality, as the 'for us' of verse 6 might suggest, but between one false [unbelievers thinking that there are gods and lords behind idols] and one true perception [the existence of one true God and Lord]" (Blomberg, *1 Corinthians*, 165).

22. Robert B Chisholm Jr, "'To Whom Shall You Compare Me?' Yahweh's Polemic against Baal and the Babylonian Idol-Gods in Prophetic Literature," in *Christianity and the Religions: A Biblical Theology of World Religions*, eds. Edward Rommen and Harold Netland (Pasadena, CA: William Carey Library, 1995), 67.

of religious pluralism was antithetical to Yahwism." Biblical monotheism demands that there are no equals (even if there are in the minds of the worshippers) to God the Father and to the Lord Jesus Christ.[23]

What was unique about this Father God and this Lord Jesus Christ was that all things existed through them, including the wood and stones that were used to make idols. Isaiah narrated an amusing thought that the Lord God had about those who worshipped idols made of the wood and stones he had created:

> A man cuts down cedars . . . uses it to make a fire; he takes some of it and warms himself. Yes, he kindles a fire and bakes bread. With the rest of it he makes a god, his idol; he bows down to it and worships it. He prays to it, saying, "Rescue me, for you are my god!" They do not comprehend or understand, for their eyes are blind and cannot see; their minds do not discern. No one thinks to himself, nor do they comprehend or understand and say to themselves: "I burned half of it in the fire – yes, I baked bread over the coals; I roasted meat and ate it. With the rest of it, should I make a disgusting idol? Should I bow down to dry wood?" (Isa 44:7–19 NET).

Worshipping an idol was thus folly and worshipping "so-called" gods/lords behind the idols was idolatry. Christian faith shuns idolatry. There is only one true God (Deut 6:4) and one true Lord, Jesus Christ, over everything.

Not only did the wood and stones out of which the idols were made belong to God, but so also did the Corinthians: "we are for him" and "we are through him" (1 Cor 8:6). Since they belonged to the Father God and the Lord Jesus Christ, they were to worship and serve them alone. Paul wasn't implying there was only one God who is called "Father" and that Jesus Christ wasn't God. Fee writes, "Although Paul does not here call Christ God, the formula is so constructed that only the most obdurate would deny its Trinitarian implications. In the same breath that he can assert that there is only one God, he equally asserts that the designation 'Lord,' which in the OT belongs to the one God, is the proper designation of the divine Son. One should note especially that Paul feels no tension between the affirmation of

---

23. For a thorough study of the supremacy of the only true God and only true Lord, see Millard J. Erickson, *Making Sense of the Trinity: Three Crucial Questions* (Grand Rapids: Baker, 2000), 18–19. Millard J. Erickson, *Christian Theology*, 2 ed. (Grand Rapids: Baker Academic, 1998), 348–349.

monotheism and the clear distinction between the two persons of Father and Jesus Christ."[24] The Corinthian Christians needed to understand that God the Father and the Lord Jesus Christ had created everything, including the materials that idols are made of and the Corinthians themselves. That was what made God the Father and the Lord Jesus Christ superior to everyone, including emperors, idols, and so-called gods/lords in heaven and on earth.

Not all people shared this knowledge (1 Cor 8:7a), including the new converts to Christian faith. Should such a new (or weak) Christian continue to eat food offered to idols, he or she would be confused and defiled. So Paul wrote, "Those who were accustomed to eating food offered to idols until now, when they eat food offered to idols, won't their conscience (being weak) be defiled?" (1 Cor 8:7b). Paul was presenting a scenario in which a worshipper who used to eat at a deity's temple came to Christian faith. Immediately, he or she stopped eating at that deity's temple. Should he or she then go back to the temple and eat temple food again, that person's conscience (being weak) would be defiled. So no mature Christian should go to another deity's temple to eat food, as this would inadvertently affect younger Christians.

Outside the Mysore Palace in Karnataka (India) are shops and a small Hindu temple. Outside the temple sits a priest in priestly garments with a bowl full of ghee that he dishes out to passers-by. Adults and children stretch out their hands, cup their right palms, receive the ghee, place a bit on top of their heads, and eat the rest. (This event doesn't happen only at the Mysore Palace – it can be seen everywhere.) Should a Christian do the same along with the Hindus, those around would think that he or she also is a Hindu. Worse still, if a newborn Christian sees a mature Christian do it, that young Christian might assume that there is no difference between the God of the Bible and the other so-called gods and lords. If Paul were in India, he would say that Christians passing the Hindu priest outside the Mysore Palace should not stretch out their right hands, cup their palms, and receive the ghee (*prasada*), since such an act not only amounts to idolatry but also may cause a newborn Christian to stumble.

What should a Christian do when a Hindu neighbor or colleague returns from a pilgrimage and gives him or her the *prasada* from the pilgrimage? The best practice is to accept the gift graciously in order to maintain an open channel of communication, and later (and discreetly) toss the food into the trash. But if the non-believer friend stands by you and watches to see

---

24. Fee, *First Epistle to the Corinthians*, 375.

whether you eat it or not, it is better to eat it, since, Paul argued, there is no direct connection between food and spirituality (1 Cor 8:8 – see the following paragraphs). How Christians should behave when non-Christian friends invite them to their houses is addressed in 1 Corinthians 10:27–33.

In Christianity there is no such thing as "kosher" or "halal" food; all food is God's creation and is to be enjoyed (1 Cor 10:30–31). So Paul said, "Food does not present us [as acceptable or unacceptable] before God. If we don't eat we lack nothing; if we eat we don't gain anything" (1 Cor 8:8). Unlike in other religions, where offering food to the gods and eating in their presence were significant, in Christianity it was not so.[25] Further, a Christian's presence in a pagan temple, whether he or she ate there or not, made no difference to his or her spirituality. Paul wasn't saying it was acceptable for a Christian to eat in another god's temple (as the following verse clearly argues against it); he was saying that food and spirituality had no connection in Christianity – a principle the Lord Jesus himself taught (Matt 15:11; Mark 7:18–19).[26] Unlike Judaism, Christianity has no kosher food or food restrictions.

Although food didn't have any moral or spiritual quality, a Christian's presence in a pagan temple had devastating consequences when it was not mixed with love: "Watch that your freedom [to enter and eat at another deity's temple] does not become a stumbling stone to the weak. For if someone sees you partaking of the food placed before an idol, will not his weak conscience be strengthened to eat the food offered to idols? And through your knowledge, the weak brother – for whom Christ died – is on the path to destruction" (1 Cor 8:9–11). It seems that some Christians in the Corinthian church claimed that, as they knew there were no gods in other temples, therefore they could go and eat in other temples. Although the food itself didn't cause any problems for their spirituality, their lack of love for other Christians – weak Christians – did. A weak Christian was one with a "weak conscience." Garland's definition of a "weak conscience" is informative: Conscience refers "to that faculty of moral evaluation that adjudicates whether an individual's actions are right

---

25. The observance of the Lord's Supper needs to be seen in light of this fact, as the commentary will explain.

26. Those who see Paul as promoting eating at temples to other gods find contradictions between Paul and the Jerusalem Council decree of Acts 15 (Herbert Hoefer, "Principles of Cross-Cultural/Ethnic Ministry: The Stories of Barnabas and Paul and the Jerusalem Council," *International Journal of Frontier Missions* 22, no. 1 [Spring 2005]: 21). But Still has eloquently demonstrated that the whole passage (1 Cor 8:1 – 11:1) argues against any eating of temple food (E. Coye Still III, "Paul's Aims Regarding Eidolothuta: A New Proposal for Interpreting 1 Corinthians 8:1–11:1," *Novum Testamentum* 44, no. 4 [2002]: 333–343). Paul was in total agreement with the Jerusalem Council's decree.

or wrong and directs behavior according to recognized norms. It is a moral compass ... The conscience comprises the depository of an individual's moral beliefs and principles that makes judgments about what is right and wrong. A 'weak' conscience is one that is unable to make appropriate moral judgments because of a lack of proper edification."[27] In other words, a person with a weak conscience was a new convert to Christianity. Such a new Christian could see a Christian of longer standing enter a temple to eat food, and he or she too could enter along with him or her and eat the *prasada*, although his or her conscience was weak, and by eating this new Christian could be devastated. He or she – one for whom Christ died – was then on the path to destruction. Paul wasn't saying this Christian was going to lose salvation; Christ had died for that person.[28] But that weak Christian's conscience would be so seared that he or she could face emotional or even physical destruction (1 Cor 5:5). That is what a mature but insensitive Christian's action could do to a weak person. That was not love.

Rather, it was sinful: "Thus you are sinning against your brothers and sisters and wounding their weak conscience. In this way, you are sinning against Christ" (1 Cor 8:12). This was a major crime. By hurting fellow Christians' weak consciences through using their freedom, the strong were sinning against them and against Christ. So although eating food was nothing, hurting the weak Christian's conscience was sinful. Paul here wasn't talking about mere grief; it was a grief associated with a sinful act. The young Christian, who used to eat idol food, went back to eating idol food that grieved him or her, only because other mature Christians were doing so.

So for Paul and the Corinthians the only logical conclusion was: "If food causes my brother or sister to stumble, I will not eat meat for eternity, so that my brother or sister might not stumble" (1 Cor 8:13). Paul moved from the generic "food" to the specific "meat." Some scholars have explained that meat was killed and cooked at temples and that was why the Christians were going to the temples.[29] In other words, when someone really wanted to eat

---

27. David E. Garland, "The Dispute over Food Sacrificed to Idols (1 Cor 8:1–11:1)," *Perspectives in Religious Studies* 30, no. 2 (Summer 2003): 187.

28. Scholars who believe in the security of believers see the term "destroyed" as a synonym for "their conscience being wounded" (1 Cor 8:12, see Bruce, *1 and 2 Corinthians*, 82). Scholars who do not believe in the security of the believers argue that this young Christian would lose his or her salvation (e.g. Fee, *First Epistle to the Corinthians*, 387). The context – "Christ died for him" (1 Cor 8:11), "brother" (1 Cor 8:11), and "my brother" (1 Cor 8:13) – clearly indicates that Paul thought of the weak person as a genuine Christian.

29. Thiselton, *First Epistle to the Corinthians*, 121–145.

meat, temples were the place to go to. Other scholars have pointed out that "Opportunities to eat idol-meat were many – at marriages and funerals of pagan relatives, or at club parties, or when friends sent over meat from the sacrifices, or at banquets in pagan temples to which they were invited, or at public festivals when idol-meat was distributed to all the citizens and resident aliens."[30] It may be that Paul simply used "meat" as a synonym for "food." Regardless, the message was clear: mature Christians going into a temple to get food (or meat) could devastate a new Christian.

A contemporary example to illustrate the severity of the situation would be if a recovering alcoholic came to a church and saw believers drinking alcohol, explaining that drinking alcohol was not sinful. The weak conscience of this recovering alcoholic might thus be "strengthened" to take a drink that would eventually return him or her to alcoholism. Should a Christian's freedom do such damage to another Christian, the mature Christian has sinned against that person and against Christ. Christian freedom shouldn't override love for a fellow Christian. When it does so, it is no longer freedom; it is sinful.

As mentioned in the commentary on 7:18–24, tilaka and vibhuti are purely religious markers. A bindi, on the other hand, could be a religious marker (e.g. of the sixth *chakra* or third eye), but may also have social significance (e.g. red color dot representing love and prosperity) or be a fashion decoration (e.g. jewelry worn on the forehead or a blue dot with a blue sari). Since both tilaka and vibhuti are purely religious markers, the principles Paul instructed concerning food offered to idols applies here too: that is, Christians shouldn't wear tilaka or vibhuti since that would imply that they see no difference between worshipping foreign gods and worshipping the God of the Bible. Similarly, when strong (mature) Christians wear such tilaka and vibhuti, they may inadvertently cause new Christians to stumble and commit idolatry. On the other hand, bindi – when it is purely a sign of fashion – may be worn provided it doesn't cause either a new Christian to stumble or give an impression to non-Christians that Christianity is just one among other religions. Many mature Christian ladies, therefore, do actually avoid wearing bindi because doing so could communicate the wrong message to neighbors and colleagues.

---

30. William G. Thompson, "1 Corinthians 8:1–13," *Interpretation* 44, no. 4 (October 1990): 406.

11

1 Corinthians 9

Brahmin Acharyas (9:1–15)

Acharya is the official title in Hinduism for a religious teacher or *guru*. Most of the *acharyas* are priests from the Brahman (the highest) caste. Their main task is to attain spiritual knowledge from the Hindu scriptures and to impart that to devotees. They are also responsible for religious rituals in temples and homes. They diligently study Vedas (the Hindu scriptures) and learn all the sacred rituals and chants. They are mediators between humans and the gods.

Krishnan narrates the celebration of a person's eightieth birthday that he witnessed in the South Indian city of Coimbatore. A hall was rented for the occasion and eleven priests were invited. At one corner of the hall some priests chanted the Vedas for at least six hours each day. In another corner of the hall the special fire ceremony was constantly being performed by some of these priests. These priests are so much in demand that often they fly to other countries to perform these rituals. In this way the priests become wealthy. Krishnan writes that these "south Indian families are willing to pay the priests whatever they demand."[1] Serving a god can be a lucrative business.

Paul was an apostle (messenger of God) and an *acharya*. As such, he had privileges. However, in order to spread the gospel, he deliberately did not make use of those privileges. He set that principle of "curtailing one's freedom" as an example for the Corinthians to restrain their desire to enter a temple and eat food offered to idols (1 Cor 9:1–27).

---

1. Murali Krishnan, "Hindu Priests Cashing in on Ancient Traditions," *Australia Network News* (16 August 2012).

But why did he insert this long chapter in the middle of his discussion on food offered to idols? Hooker explains the reasoning in terms of Paul's challenge to the "mature":

> The obligation is on those who are wise or strong precisely because they *are* wise or strong. That is what the gospel is about. And that is why Paul spends a whole chapter in the middle of this discussion in 1 Corinthians establishing his rights and privileges as an apostle, in order that he may remind his readers that he has given them all up for the sake of the gospel. He is not wandering off the subject; nor is he being awkward; nor is he boastful. He is simply giving an example of what it means to be weak for the sake of the weak, to be poor, in hope of making others rich.[2]

Paul began by asking, "Am I not free? Am I not an apostle?" (1 Cor 9:1a). He expected them to answer "yes" to both questions. Paul was free and he was an apostle, which meant that he had several privileges – none of which he had taken advantage of (as he would explain). Paul's apostleship was based on two important facts. First, he had seen the Lord (1 Cor 9:1b). The early apostles set that as a criterion for anyone to be an apostle – he or she must have seen the Lord (Acts 1:22b). Second, the Corinthians themselves were proof of his apostleship: "Even if I am not an apostle to others, I am to you; you are the confirmation of my work in the Lord' (1 Cor 9:1c–2). The word "confirmation" is literally "seal" (*sphragis*) in the Greek. Seals were used in legal papers to provide "legal valid attestation."[3] The Corinthians were the legal valid attestation of Paul's apostleship. These were the two proofs that Paul gave anyone who challenged his authority (1 Cor 9:3): "I have seen the Lord," and "the Corinthians are the proof of my apostleship." What a high view Paul had of the Corinthians!

Just as *acharyas* have privileges, so did the apostles. One such privilege was having their food and drink provided by the Christians (1 Cor 9:4). Paul in this verse included Barnabas, implying that the Corinthians were familiar with Barnabas. At the end of the first missionary journey that preceded Paul's journey to Corinth, Barnabas and Paul had a disagreement that separated them (Acts 15:36–41). It must have been a brief separation, though, as this verse indicates (also see Col 4:10; 2 Tim 4:11). Paul and Barnabas had the

---

2. Morna D. Hooker, "Interchange in Christ and Ethics," *Journal for the Study of the New Testament* 25 (1985): 14.

3. Conzelmann, *1 Corinthians*, 152 n. 11.

privilege of "living off" the Christians; yet they didn't take advantage of that privilege. Another privilege that the apostles had was to travel on missionary journeys accompanied by their Christian spouses, a privilege that Peter and James made use of (1 Cor 9:5).[4] When they made these journeys, again it was a privilege of the apostles that the churches paid for their expenses, including those of their accompanying spouses. A final privilege was for the apostles not to have to earn their keep but to have their ministry expenses met (1 Cor 9:6). Paul and Barnabas could have taken advantage of these privileges but they worked anyway (1 Cor 9:12). Thus there were privileges that Paul and other apostles purposefully did not make use of, in order that they might serve people. Paul wanted the Corinthians to learn this principle so that they would not call upon their "rights" to go to temples and eat from food offered to idols.

Paul wanted the Corinthians not to think he was asking for special favors as an apostle. So he cited six examples to prove that apostles had privileges (1 Cor 9:7–15). These examples can be divided into (a) three examples from daily life (1 Cor 9:7), (b) two examples from the law of the Old Testament (1 Cor 9:8–13), and (c) one example from the Lord Jesus' teachings (1 Cor 9:14–15).[5]

The daily-life examples were based on a soldier, a farmer, and a shepherd. A soldier in an army had his expenses paid by the government and the people, not by himself (1 Cor 9:7a).[6] A farmer who grew a vineyard ate grapes from that same vineyard (1 Cor 9:7b). A shepherd who tended flocks drank milk from his own flock (1 Cor 9:7c). These common-sense events (1 Cor 9:8a) illustrated that any of the apostles could have had their living expenses and daily food provided by the Corinthians; those were their privileges.

---

4. Although Paul simply said, "Cephas and *brothers* of the Lord," biblical theology informs us that it would have been the Lord Jesus' brothers mentioned in Mark 6:3 (James, Joses, Jude, and Simon) – two of whom most likely composed the letters James and Jude in the New Testament. Later in 1 Corinthians Paul would refer to James being an eyewitness of the Lord's resurrection and thus an apostle (1 Cor 15:7).

5. Kaiser divides Paul's example into four categories: "(1) the level of illustration from experience: the soldier, vinegrower [*sic*] and herdsman – 1 Cor 9:7; (2) the level of the authority of Scripture: Deut 25:4 (cf. 1 Tim 5:18 in subsequent usage) – vv 8–11; (3) the level of illustration from current practice in the Church and in pagan religions – vv 12–13; and (4) the authoritative teachings of Jesus – v 14" (Walter C. Kaiser Jr., "The Current Crisis in Exegesis and the Apostolic Use of Deuteronomy 25:4 in 1 Corinthians 9:8-10," *Journal of the Evangelical Theological Society* 21, no. 1 [March 1978]: 15–16).

6. Caragounis explains that "wages" here refers to "paid expenses" (see Chrys C. Caragounis, "Opsonion: A Reconsideration of Its Meaning," *Novum Testamentum* 16, no. 1 [1974]: 51–52).

The law also attested to this principle (1 Cor 9:8b). The law said, "Do not muzzle an ox while it is treading out the grain" (Deut 25:4; 1 Cor 9:9a). Fee explains the scene: "The text reflects the ancient agricultural practice of driving an ox drawing a threshing-sledge over the grain to release the kernels from the stalk. Out of mercy for the laboring animal the Israelites were forbidden to muzzle the ox, so that he might have some 'material benefit' from his labor."[7] This method is still used in India, where the ox is usually replaced by water buffaloes; but the principle is the same. Paul's next phrases – "God was not concerned about the oxen, was he? Is he not speaking for our benefit?" (1 Cor 9:9b–10a) – are puzzling at first. A careful look at the context of the law in the Old Testament reveals that the law about the oxen was sandwiched between two sets of commands to the Israelites: judges inflicting forty lashes on those who committed wrong (Deut 25:1–3), and levirate marriage – in which a man was obliged to give a child to his dead brother through marriage and sexual intercourse with his sister-in-law (Deut 25:5–10). Why did the law include the note about the oxen? The answer is that these three sets of laws emphasize the principle of "just" and "unjust." It was *just* to inflict forty lashes on a criminal, but *unjust* to inflict more than forty; it was *just* to use an ox to tread grain, but *unjust* to muzzle it so as not to allow it to eat; and it was *just* for a man to give a child to his sister-in-law when his brother died prematurely, but *unjust* to cohabit with her without providing her with a child.

The law about the ox actually promoted the principle of justice, so Paul could say, "God wasn't concerned about oxen, was he?"[8] He was concerned about the people and the principle of justice, which included the apostles rejoicing in the benefits they received from the Corinthians: "The one who plows and the one who threshes works in the hope of enjoying the harvest" (1 Cor 9:10b). Paul had earlier used the imagery of sowing and watering with regard to himself and Apollos (1 Cor 3:5). Now he uses the imagery of sowing and threshing for himself and Barnabas. He had the right to "enjoy the harvest," so he wrote, "If we sowed spiritual things among you, can we not reap earthly blessings from you?" (1 Cor 9:11). Paul and Barnabas had

---

7. Fee, *First Epistle to the Corinthians*, 406–407.

8. Kaiser summarizes various approaches to Paul's use of this Old Testament text: allegorical, rabbinical, Hellenistic, and literal (Kaiser Jr., "The Current Crisis in Exegesis," 3–18). The view expressed in this commentary is "literal," and Godet has a similar position – he sees these and other commands in Deut 24 as "duties of *moral beings* to one another" (Godet, *Commentary on the First Epistle of St. Paul to the Corinthians*, 45).

enriched the Corinthians spiritually; in turn, the Corinthians could provide for all their needs, especially given how much the Corinthians cared for other apostles. Paul wasn't in competition with other apostles; he was simply explaining the principle of how the Corinthians were obliged to them – Paul and Barnabas – so he could show that they had declined the use of those privileges for the sake of the gospel, the same lesson he wanted the Corinthians to learn. So he concluded, "We did not make use of that right; instead, we endured everything so that we might not give anyone an obstacle to accepting the gospel of Christ" (1 Cor 9:12).[9] That was the lesson Paul wanted them to learn: place no obstacle before anyone that might hinder him or her from accepting the gospel of Christ.

Paul hadn't finished with his illustrations. The fifth illustration was again taken from the law: Leviticus instructed that those who served in the temple of God in Jerusalem had the right to eat food from the temple (Lev 6:26), and also that those who served at the altar of the temple received part of the offering, especially the meat (Lev 2:10; 1 Cor 9:13). Paul cited this particular example for two reasons. First, earlier he had written that the Corinthians were the temple of God because the Holy Spirit was in them (1 Cor 3:16; 6:19). Therefore, when Paul was serving the Corinthians, he was serving in the temple of God and was entitled to the food in the temple. Second, the Corinthians were exercising their "authority" to enter pagan temples to eat food (especially meat), while Paul was illustrating that he had abstained from exercising his rightful "authority" to eat from them (the true temple of God); similarly, they too needed to limit their freedom for the sake of others. Interestingly, Paul used a word for "serve at the altar" (*paredreuō*) that does not occur anywhere else in the New Testament or in the Septuagint (the Greek translation of the Old Testament). Scholars therefore think that Paul was referring to a pagan temple altar.[10] If that were so, Paul was using their own word to illustrate to them that he had the right to take food from them because the Corinthians were the true altar of God's temple; yet he didn't take advantage of that right.

Paul's sixth and final illustration came from the Lord's own teachings recorded in the Gospels (1 Cor 9:14). Hays writes, "And finally, dropped

---

9. Fee points out that this was Paul's concern, one which appears elsewhere in Paul's writings (Rom 15:19; Gal 1:7; 2 Cor 2:12; 9:13; 10:14; Phil 1:27; 1 Thess 3:2) and always in the context of taking the gospel to non-Christians, especially Gentiles (Fee, *First Epistle to the Corinthians*, 411 n. 80).

10. Fee, *First Epistle to the Corinthians*, 412 n. 87.

in almost as though it were an afterthought, is the trump card of the whole argument: Jesus himself commanded that proclaimers of the gospel should get their living by the gospel. Here we see what a skilled rhetorician Paul was: He has saved his knockdown argument for last, yet he introduced it without fanfare or elaboration, allowing the point to carry its own considerable weight."[11] The Lord Jesus had instructed the disciples, "Take nothing for your journey – no staff, no bag, no bread, no money, and do not take an extra tunic . . . proclaim the good news" (Luke 9:3–6). Without citing this or any other quotation, Paul simply said that this was what the Lord had instructed.

Yet Paul never took advantage of those rights (1 Cor 9:15a). By saying this, he wasn't expecting them to rethink their giving and start supporting him (1 Cor 9:15b). In fact, Paul would rather die of starvation than hear someone say, "Paul lived off of us; that was the motivation behind his work" (1 Cor 9:15c). Paul was using hyperbole, exaggerated speech, to illustrate the importance of putting off anything that might hinder the spread of the gospel. Paul would rather die of starvation than hinder gospel proclamation. That was the lesson Paul wanted the Corinthians to learn: do nothing to hinder the gospel.

The Gospel (9:16–18)

The gospel (in Greek, *euangelion*) is Paul's code word for his message about Jesus Christ. The word "gospel" means "news" or "good news." It occurs sixty times in Paul's writings. In the epistle to the Romans he defined it three times (1:1–5; 1:16–17; 10:2–13). In 1 Corinthians he defined it once (1 Cor 15:3–6).

In antiquity, "gospel" or "good news" was associated with a king announcing the birth of his firstborn or declaring his victory over an enemy. The birth of Emperor Augustus[12] and the victory of Emperor Vespasian over Vitellius[13] were considered "good news" or "gospels." Similarly, Paul considered the birth of Jesus Christ and his victory as Messiah to be the core elements of the gospel. So he wrote to the Romans that he was "set apart for the gospel . . . concerning his son who was born out of the lineage of David according to humanity and appointed as the Son of God by the power of the

---

11. Hays, *First Corinthians*, 152. Paul had earlier cited the Gospel teachings (7:10, 12), giving evidence that he was familiar with them.

12. Adolf Deissmann, *Light from the Ancient East*, trans. Lionel R. M. Strachan (New York: George H. Doran, 1927), 366.

13. Josephus, *Jewish Wars* 4.655–56.

Spirit of Holiness by the resurrection, Jesus Christ our Lord" (Rom 1:1). To his protégé Timothy he wrote, "Remember Jesus Christ raised from the dead and out of the lineage of David; this is my gospel" (2 Tim 2:8). Basically, Paul proclaimed the message ("good news") of a King born in the lineage of David and of the Messiah resurrected from the dead by the power of the Holy Spirit. This King and Messiah was Jesus Christ, the Lord.

Of course, Jesus' birth, death, and resurrection had consequences. Paul summarized them in 1 Corinthians: "Christ died for our sins according to the Scriptures, he was buried, he rose [from the dead] on the third day according to the Scriptures, and he was seen by Cephas and the Twelve [apostles]" (1 Cor 15:3–6). Along with this he stated that all who confessed with their mouths that Jesus is Lord and believed in their hearts that God had raised him from the dead were saved (Rom 10:9). These various elements became the core teachings, the "gospel" or the "good news," that Paul proclaimed. Dodd calls it the *kerygma*, "that which is proclaimed." He adds the following:

> It is true that the *kerygma* as we have recovered it from the Pauline epistles is fragmentary. No complete statement of it is in the nature of the case available. But we may restore it in outline somewhat after this fashion:
>
> The prophecies are fulfilled, and the new Age is inaugurated by the coming of Christ.
>
> He was born of the seed of David.
>
> He died according to the Scriptures, to deliver us out of the present evil age.
>
> He was buried.
>
> He rose on the third day according to the Scriptures.
>
> He is exalted at the right hand of God, as Son of God and Lord of quick and dead.
>
> He will come again as Judge and Saviour of men.[14]

Paul had just told the Corinthians that he would rather die of starvation than receive any gifts from anyone, in order that the gospel proclamation might not be hindered. He was saying that in the context of his discussion

---

14. C. H. Dodd, *The Apostolic Preaching and Its Developments: Three Lectures with an Appendix on Eschatology and History* (London: Hodder & Stroughton Limited, 1936), 17.

concerning some "mature" Christians entering temples to eat food offered to idol-gods, which was driving new Christians back to idolatry. He wanted the mature to learn to limit the use of their freedom for the sake of the salvation of others. So he illustrated this by describing the constraints on his own life in order to further the gospel.

In this section (1 Cor 9:16–18) Paul explained to the Corinthians his relationship to the gospel. First, he was under compulsion to proclaim the gospel and therefore he could not boast (1 Cor 9:16a). Most likely Paul was referring to his apostolic calling, which originated with his conception. Elsewhere Paul says, "God who set me apart in my mother's womb called me, by his grace, and revealed to me his Son so that I might preach the gospel of him in all the nations" (Gal 1:15–16; also Acts 26:16–18). Since God had commissioned and appointed him to that task, he could not boast or take any credit. Rather, he was under compulsion to proclaim the gospel; and he pronounced a woe upon himself if he didn't do so (1 Cor 9:16b).

Second, he was happy and willing to proclaim the gospel, since a reward awaited him (1 Cor 9:17a). Paul was quick to explain that reward: "What is my payment? I may present the gospel without charge and not make use of the authority that comes from sharing the gospel" (1 Cor 9:18). The payment was the joy of sharing the gospel without receiving any payment or privileges. No one could say, "Paul drew money from us to share the gospel with us," or "Paul took advantage of us while he shared the gospel." The joy of having no obligations was his reward. Elsewhere Paul said, "Owe nothing to anyone, except love" (Rom 13:8). Paul lived by that principle. He owed no one anything; none could say Paul had benefited from them. That was his reward for sharing the gospel freely; that peace of mind was his payment.

Third, even if he hadn't been happy or willing to proclaim the gospel, he had no option but to do so: he was entrusted with the responsibility (1 Cor 9:17b). This was similar to what he said earlier about being under compulsion to proclaim the gospel. Paul couldn't stop proclaiming the gospel free of charge.

A reading of Paul's life and ministry in Acts clearly indicates that he cherished sharing the gospel whether he was in jail (Acts 16:25–34) or in front of a governor (Acts 24:1–21), whether he was with a lady by a river (Acts 16:13–15) or at Mars Hill in Athens (Acts 17:16–34). He was eager to share the gospel with Jew and Gentile, slave and free, male and female.

Caste and Gospel (9:13–23)

The discrimination between high caste and low caste is what many think of when they hear about the caste system in India.[15] Only rarely does someone point out that within a caste there are layers of segregations and prejudices. Gupta writes, "Interestingly, a Brahman who performs priestly functions in a temple is considered lower than a domestic priest, and together they are seen as being lower than Brahmans who are landlords and do not perform any priestly functions. A landed Brahman would never give his daughter in marriage to a priest. The first thing Brahmans do when they come into wealth is give up priestly activities. Only then can they legitimately claim to be on top of the heap. The name of the game in caste ordering is power and wealth."[16]

In the world of Paul there were also clear segregations between people groups. There were Jews who worshipped YHWH God and abstained from non-kosher food. They thought of themselves as separate from the rest of the world because they were God's people and they had stringent lifestyles. Among the Jews were law-keepers like the Pharisees and scribes. They thought of themselves as elite because they were not only Jewish but also "law-abiders." Of course, some swung to the other extreme and didn't keep any of the law. They thought of themselves as "liberated" or "truly free people" because they didn't place themselves under the constraints of the law. Then there were weak people who wanted to live a law-abiding life but couldn't. Paul ministered to all four groups because he was free and he was driven by the passion to save people from all groups.

Paul wrote, "Being a free person, I enslave myself to all things, so that I may gain more" (1 Cor 9:19). Paul's cryptic words were basically saying that he was free to do all things – a claim the Corinthians had made (1 Cor 6:12; 10:23) – but he enslaved his freedom for a purpose: he wanted to draw more people to the gospel by not being a hindrance to anyone. This was Paul's overall message: curtail your freedom for the benefit of others.

---

15. Although the last caste census (where each person was to declare his or her caste) was taken in 1931 under British rule, since 1990 all census forms require a person to state his or her caste. If India has truly abolished the caste system, why is it still included in the census? Engineer writes, "India is going to live with increasing stratification for a long time to come. We can hide our head like ostrich in the sand [sic] of unrealistic ideas and ideals we violate on every step. Our very culture is caste culture and it is being reinforced by our ethos, our status symbols and above all our politics" (Asgharali Engineer, "Politics of Identity, Caste and Religion in India," *Hamdard Islamicus* 33, no. 3–4 [July–December 2010]: 187).

16. Dipankar Gupta, "Killing Caste by Conversion," *The Hindu* (13 November 2001).

Paul then listed the various groups. First, Paul served Jews: "to the Jews, I became a Jew so that I might gain Jews" (1 Cor 9:20a). We might wonder why Paul, a Jew, said that he was a Jew for the Jews. He had become an apostle to the nations and as such he lost his uniqueness among the Jews. On one occasion the apostle James said to Paul, "You see, brother, there are many thousands of Jews who have believed [in Jesus Christ] and are zealously keeping the law. They have been told about you, that you teach all the Jews living among the nations to forsake Moses' teachings, that is, not to circumcise or to walk according to our customs" (Acts 20:20–21). James then suggested a course of action: for Paul to take four other men with him, purify himself, and to pay for them to have their hair cut according to the custom. Paul did just that. Paul kept the customs of the Jews while he was with the Jews in order to gain some of them. Fee writes,

> How can a Jew determine to "become *like* a Jew"? The obvious answer is, in matters that have to do with Jewish religious peculiarities that Paul as a Christian had long ago given up as essential to a right relationship with God. These would include circumcision (7:19; Gal. 6:15), food laws (8:8; Gal 2:10–13; Rom 14:17; Col 2:16), and special observances (Col 2:16) . . . On the other hand, he had no problem with Jews continuing such practices, as long as they were not considered to give people right standing with God. Nor did he exhibit unwillingness to yield to Jewish customs for the sake of the Jews (cf. Acts 16:1–3; 21:23–26).[17]

Second, Paul served those living under the law as one under the law himself – while he didn't place himself under the law – in order to save some (1 Cor 9:20b) Such a principle was demonstrated when Paul circumcised Timothy. Timothy was a son of a Jewish mother but his father was a Gentile. As such, other Jews wouldn't have accepted him as a legitimate child. So although Paul vehemently spoke against Gentiles circumcising themselves (e.g. the letter to the Galatians), he circumcised Timothy so as not to hinder his ministry among the "law-keepers" (Acts 26:3). Paul wasn't being hypocritical; a man didn't need to be circumcised and keep the law of Moses in order to be saved (Acts 15), but he could be circumcised for the sake of ministry among the law-keepers.

---

17. Fee, *First Epistle to the Corinthians*, 428.

Third, Paul served the nations (the Gentiles). Paul referred to them as "a-lawful ones," but not meaning that they were lawless people; he meant that they didn't have the Mosaic laws. He served them as if he had no law, although he was under the law of Christ, so that he might save them (1 Cor 9:21). For example, he wouldn't circumcise Titus, a Greek (Gal 2:3), or demand that the Gentiles in Galatia keep the kosher laws (Gal 2:11–14). At the same time, he was under the law of Christ, as he told the Galatians: "Bear the burdens of one another and thus you will fulfill the law of Christ" (Gal 6:2).

Fourth, Paul served the weak people, a group he had already mentioned (1 Cor 8:7–12). He said, "To the weak people, I became weak, so that I might gain the weak people" (1 Cor 9:22a). He would abstain from any freedom he had in order to gain the weak people. This was the lesson he wanted the "strong" to learn, and therefore he didn't mention the strong explicitly in this context. But earlier he had mentioned that he was speaking spiritual words to the mature or strong (1 Cor 2:6) and they formed the subjects in this discussion too.

In this way Paul became "all things to all people so that he might save some of them" (1 Cor 9:22b). One can envision Paul eating kosher food in a Jewish home, non-kosher food in a Gentile's home, vegetables in a new Christian's home (see Rom 14), and meat in a strong Christian's home. The sole purpose of such a chameleon lifestyle was the progress of the gospel: "I do all things for the sake of the gospel so that I might partake in [the gospel]" (1 Cor 9:23).[18] Paul considered it a privilege to share the gospel and lead people to Christ. He would do everything necessary in order to have the privilege of spreading the gospel. Blomberg writes, "There is inherent blessing in fulfilling his commission and seeing the result – people saved from their sins."[19] Paul wanted the Corinthians too to put their desire to save others above their desire to take advantage of their freedom and have a carefree lifestyle.

There is a very practical lesson for Christians in India. In a culture that abhors eating meat, especially that of cows, it is acceptable for a Christian to abstain from eating beef (at least in public) for the sake of drawing a non-Christian to Christian faith. Cows are sacred for Hindus, as instructed in

---

18. Paul's words were "I might partake in *it*," and Fee reads it as "sharing . . . its *benefits* ('blessings, promises')" (Fee, *First Epistle to the Corinthians*, 432). The closest antecedent is the gospel, so I have interpreted it as Paul's association with the gospel.

19. Blomberg, *1 Corinthians*, 184.

the Vedas.[20] Margul argues that, although many animals are worshipped in India (like the zebu, elephant, tiger, and serpent), "the supreme position, a 'Brahmanic' one, is held, without saying, by the cow."[21] Part of the reason for the cow's supremacy is that cows give people milk, yogurt, and cheese – foods that play an important role in Hindu worship. To many Hindus it is a sacrilege for Christians to eat beef in front of them. A Christian should therefore not make use of any freedom he or she has (even to eat beef) for the sake of a neighbor's salvation.

Disqualification (9:24–27)

Shiny Abraham Wilson, from the state of Kerala, is an outstanding Indian female athlete.[22] She is a fast runner who represented India in over seventy-five events in international competitions. She became the first Indian woman to carry the national flag in the 1992 Olympics in Barcelona. She won seven gold, five silver, and two bronze medals in Asian competitions. In addition, she won eighteen gold and two silver medals in the South Asian Games.[23] This outstanding athlete was once disqualified: in the 1986 Asian Games in Seoul, South Korea, while far ahead of the runners she cut into the inner lane. Even the very best athletes can be disqualified from a competition if they are undisciplined or careless.

The Corinthians were very familiar with sports and sports imagery because the Isthmian Games were held in the vicinity of Corinth. These were second only to the Olympics and were held every two years. The games would have been held in AD 51, the year Paul visited Corinth for the first time. Paul might have watched those games. And he used imagery from those games to illustrate the Corinthians' need to have zeal in sharing the gospel.

Paul said, "Do you not know that among all the runners who run in a stadium, only one receives the medal? Run like that one, so that you may receive the medal" (1 Cor 9:24). Paul wanted the Corinthians to be victorious in their running – their Christian discipleship – so that they would win the award. Paul wasn't talking about salvation, implying that only one out of

20. Frank J. Korom, "Holy Cow! The Apotheosis of Zebu, or Why the Cow Is Sacred in Hinduism," *Asian Folklore Studies* 59, no. 2 (2000): 185.

21. Tadeusz Margul, "Present-Day Worship of the Cow in India," *Numen* 15, no. 1 (Fall 1968): 63.

22. Another outstanding Indian female athlete is P. T. Usha, who won four gold medals in the 1986 Asian Games in Seoul, Korea.

23. Chitra Garg, *Indian Champions* (New Delhi: Rajpal & Sons, 2010), 52–54.

many would win; instead, he was talking about evangelism, with the imagery of success emphasizing the importance of living the Christian life with a purpose (winning souls). Paul then said, "All athletes stay disciplined so that they might win a withering crown. We receive a non-perishable [crown]" (1 Cor 9:25). At the Isthmian Games, the winners were crowned with a coronet made up of celery or parsley plants.[24] Contrasted with that, Paul and the Corinthians would receive a non-perishable crown (1 Cor 9:25; cf. 2 Tim 4:8). Therefore, they needed to be disciplined. The word Paul used was *enkrateuō*, meaning "empowered" or "disciplined." Fee writes, "Any athlete entered in the games was required to go into ten months of strict training and was subject to disqualification if he failed to do so."[25] Just as an athlete needed to stay focused and disciplined in order to gain the medal, so the Corinthians needed to be disciplined and focused in order to win souls.

Paul himself practiced these disciplines in his life and ministry. He ran with a purpose and he boxed at the opponent (instead of boxing vainly in the air) (1 Cor 9:26).[26] He wanted to receive that crown and he wanted to defeat his opponents. Such goals required stringent discipline, so he said, "I subdue my body and enslave myself" (1 Cor 9:27a). He, for example, worked hard with his hands so that he would not be accused of living off his converts. He endured hardship such as imprisonment and hunger so as to spread the gospel without being indebted to anyone. Such strenuous discipline was for the sake of the gospel, especially to avoid disqualification after proclaiming the gospel to others (1 Cor 9:27b). Paul wasn't talking about him risking losing his salvation or some form of future reward;[27] he was talking about the privilege of sharing the gospel – "I do all these for the sake of the gospel so that I might become a partaker of the gospel" (1 Cor 9:23). He didn't want to be disqualified by the Lord and lose his ministry opportunity. He wanted to have the continuous joy of sharing the gospel and reaping the reward of souls. For that, he would curtail the use of all his freedoms and minister to all people so that he might save some.

Paul had repeatedly said that the Corinthian Christians needed to limit the use of their freedom for the sake of the salvation of others. This was an important lesson, not only for the Corinthians then, but also for us today.

---

24. Callaway, "Corinth," 387.
25. Fee, *First Epistle to the Corinthians*, 436.
26. Paul states this negatively: "I run as not without aim" and "I box not as if hitting just air."
27. The term "reward" (as stated in NIV) is not in the verse.

Often we demand our "rights"; but the Christian life should be characterized by love, which looks to see others' rights satisfied first. The Christian life is to be exemplified by sacrifice and humility, just as were the Lord's life and also Paul's practices. "The Son of Man did not come to be served, but to serve and lay down his life for others" (Mark 10:45). That should be the motto of every Christian for the sake of saving the lost.

12

1 Corinthians 10

History as Example (10:1–14)

In a thought-provoking article, Dharamraj and Rotokha illustrate how "in times of crisis, group identity can be mobilized by appeal to that group's history."[1] They first illustrate this concept by the way in which the writer of Chronicles wrote Israelite history as cultic-centered in order to emphasize the importance of the community's faith. They then describe how two communal groups in India (Hindu and Muslim) were also utilizing history to mobilize group identity. They concluded the essay asking how Indian Christians will read their history in order to form their own identity.

Although some may have reread or rewritten history with a specific purpose, Paul was not rewriting or rereading the Old Testament stories in this section; instead, he was appealing to the stories of the Old Testament to illustrate the need for the Corinthians to be careful in their dealings with idols. One of the repeated themes in the Old Testament is the people's constant flirting with idolatry. Since the Corinthians were also flirting with idolatry, Paul brought out lessons from the Old Testament to illustrate the danger of idolatry (1 Cor 10:1–13).[2]

---

1. Havilah Dharamraj and Angukali V. Rotokha, "History, History Books and the Blue Jackal," in *Indian and Christian: Changing Identities in Modern India (Papers from the First SAIACS Annual Consultation 9–12 November 2010)*, eds. Cornelis Bennema and Paul Joshua Bhakiaraj (Bangalore, India: SAIACS Press, 2011), 14.

2. Smit uses rhetorical analysis to argue "that 1 Cor. 10:1–22 forms a distinct and coherent round of argument within Paul's exposition on idol offerings, which comprises 1 Cor. 8:1 – 11:1" (J. Smit, "'Do Not Be Idolaters': Paul's Rhetoric in First Corinthians 10:1–22," *Novum Testamentum* 39, no. 1 [January 1997]: 42). Similarly, Sumney explains the connection between this section and the previous chapter: Jerry L. Sumney, "The Place of 1 Corinthians 9:24–27 in Paul's Argument," *Journal of Biblical Literature* 119, no. 2 (Summer 2000): 329–333.

Paul began with a classic rhetorical statement: "I do not want you to be ignorant, brothers and sisters,"[3] and then narrated events from the Israelites' history: "Our fathers all were under the cloud and all went through the sea and all were baptized into Moses under the cloud and the sea" (1 Cor 10:1–2).[4] When the Israelites left Egypt and were trekking towards the Promised Land, they were under the protection of a cloud (Exod 13:21; Ps 105:39). When they reached the Red Sea and their enemies pursued them from behind, the sea opened and they passed through it unharmed (Exod 14:21). The key word in these two stories is "all," since Paul would later use it to make a contrast. *All* the Israelites were under the cloud's protection, and *all* the Israelites passed safely through the Red Sea. In a way, they were grouped together under the leadership of Moses. Paul used the word "baptized" to emphasize their oneness within this particular group. In addition, "*All* ate the same food given by the Spirit and *all* drank the same water given by the Spirit, for the rock that accompanied them was by the Spirit's doing and the rock was Christ" (1 Cor 10:3–4). Paul's statement "the rock was Christ" has prompted various theories: Paul was quoting an extra-biblical source;[5] Paul was allegorizing;[6] or Paul was using rabbinic hermeneutics.[7] Paul may have been arguing that the pre-incarnated Christ accompanied the Israelites on their journey, and when they needed water it was he who caused the ordinary rocks to give water. Such teaching agreed with what the LORD God said: "*I will be standing before you there on the rock* in Horeb, and you will strike the rock, and water will come out of it so that the people may drink" (Exod 17:6).[8] Just as *all* marched under the same cloud and *all* passed through the same Red Sea, *all* also drank and ate the same Spirit-given water and bread. So there was no difference in the

---

3. This rhetorical formula was often used "to introduce important instruction (Rom 1:13; 11:25; 1 Cor 12:1; 2 Cor 1:8)" (William Baird, "1 Corinthians 10:1–13," *Interpretation* 44, no. 3 [July 1990]: 286).

4. Since Paul was a Jew, and some in the Corinthian church were Jews, he used the phrase "*our* fathers."

5. For the description of this view without endorsing it, see Larry Kreitzer, "1 Corinthians 10:4 and Philo's Flinty Rock," *Communio Viatorum* 35, no. 2 (1993): 109–126.

6. Baird, "1 Corinthians 10:1–13," 287. Fee, *First Epistle to the Corinthians*, 449.

7. According to the rabbinic teachings, Miriam's well, shaped like a rock, was following the Israelites. For a discussion see E. Earle Ellis, "Note on 1 Corinthians 10:4," *Journal of Biblical Literature* 76, no. 1 (March 1957): 53–56.

8. Hays makes another key observation: "One more factor that may have influenced Paul's identification of Christ with the rock is that the Hebrew text of Deuteronomy 32, a passage central to Paul's thinking in this chapter . . . repeatedly ascribes to God the title 'the rock' (Deut 32:4, 15, 18, 30, 31); perhaps Paul, rereading this text through Christian lenses, saw here a hidden christological reference" (Hays, *First Corinthians*, 161).

source of blessings. However, the Israelites' actions were different, with the result that "God was not pleased with many of them and they were scattered in the wilderness" (1 Cor 10:5). They all received the same blessings (safety, food, and drink), but God wasn't pleased with their behavior (which Paul would explain as idolatry), and therefore they didn't all reach the Promised Land; instead, their dead bodies were scattered over the wilderness – a tragic end to a wonderful beginning.

Paul then said, "These people have become examples for us so that we might not crave evil as they craved it" (1 Cor 10:6).[9] He then described four cravings they had, along with the destruction that these cravings brought upon them.

First, they craved idolatry: "Do not become idolaters as some of them were. Just as it is written, 'The people sat down to eat and to drink; they rose up for idolatrous orgies'" (1 Cor 10:7; cf. Exod 32:6). When Moses went up Mount Sinai to talk with God, the people and Aaron made a golden calf. Before that idol they ate, drank, and took part in idolatrous orgies (Exod 32:1–6). Although Paul didn't describe the destruction, "the judgment in the case of Israel was the slaying of three thousand by the Levites ([Exod 32] v. 28) and a subsequent plague (v. 35)."[10] Food and sex were often united in ancient cultures. Kakar, for example, writes, "Again, we must remember that in the Indian consciousness, the symbolism of food is more closely or manifestly connected to sexuality than it is in the West. The words for eating and sexual enjoyment . . . have the same root, *bhuj*, in Sanskrit, and sexual intercourse is often spoken about as the mutual feeding of male and female."[11] Such thinking often led people of all other religions to combine eating with sex in worship. The God of the Israelites, of course, hated such immorality and forbade the people from participating in it. The same was true of the Father God and the Lord Jesus Christ of the Corinthians, and so Paul commanded, "Do not become idolaters, as some of them were" (1 Cor 10:7a).

Second, they craved immorality: "Let us not fornicate just as some of them fornicated and twenty-three thousand fell on a single day" (1 Cor 10:8). While the Israelites were in a place called Shittim, they started to commit

---

9. Collier argues that this whole pericope (10:1–13) was written as a "homily" (a sermon) on Num 11 on the word *epithumia* ("crave"), prior to Paul's composition of 1 Corinthians. Gary D. Collier, "'That We Might Not Crave Evil': The Structure and Argument of 1 Corinthians 10.1-13," *Journal for the Study of the New Testament* 55 (1994): 55–75.

10. Fee, *First Epistle to the Corinthians*, 454.

11. Kakar, *Intimate Relations*, 91.

sexual immorality with the daughters of Moab. The women, in turn, were inviting the people to sacrifice to their gods and the Israelites followed these other gods (Num 25:1–2). One Israelite even openly caroused and as a result God sent a plague that killed 23,000 to 24,000 people in a single day (Num 25:9; 1 Cor 10:8).[12] Paul cited that incident as his second example to say, "Let us not commit adultery" as the forefathers did.

Third, they craved testing God: "Let us not test Christ[13] just as some of them tested [God] and were killed by serpents" (1 Cor 10:9). Paul was referring to a time when the Israelites were wandering in the wilderness, saying, "Why did you bring us from Egypt here to die? We have no bread or water and we detest this worthless food [called manna, lit. 'What is this?']" (Num 21:5). God heard their "testing" – dissatisfaction with what the Lord had provided – and sent into their camps poisonous snakes that killed many Israelites. Their testing – questioning God's faithfulness – led to their deaths. Paul pointed the Corinthians to that event to exhort them: "Let us not test Christ" by unbelief in his faithfulness.

Fourth, they craved complaining: "Do not murmur, just as some of them murmured and were destroyed by a destroyer" (1 Cor 10:10). Paul was referring to an incident recorded in Numbers 16 (vv. 1–40). Korah and 250 Levites rebelled against Moses and his brother Aaron. God detested their rebellion against the spiritual leaders he had placed over them. So he caused an earthquake to swallow up Korah and his family, and he sent fire from his presence to kill the 250 Levites. The Israelites, instead of being reverent, had complained or "murmured" against Moses and Aaron saying, "You have killed the Lord's people" (Num 16:41). Their complaint brought further destruction: a destroyer (plague), sent by God, killed 14,700 people in a single

---

12. Concerning the discrepancy in number between that given in the Old Testament (24,000 people died) and that in the New Testament (23,000), scholars think Paul was either confused or had a slip in his memory (e.g. Baird, "1 Corinthians 10:1–13," 288; Fee, *First Epistle to the Corinthians*, 456; Hays, *First Corinthians*, 164). However, it is possible that the numbers are "rounded off" numbers, or that the Numbers account refers to *all* who died, including the Moabites, whereas the 1 Corinthians account refers just to the *Israelites* who died that day. Morris argues similarly: "Both are obviously round numbers, and in addition Paul may be making some allowance for those slain by the judges (Num 25:5)" (Morris, *The First Epistle of Paul to the Corinthians*, 141).

13. Whereas the earliest manuscripts have "Christ," others have "Lord" or "God." The presence of "Christ" is the difficult reading, since not many scribes would have liked seeing "Christ" in the Old Testament; therefore that is to be preferred. In addition, Paul has already introduced the presence of "Christ" (pre-incarnate Christ) in the exodus journey (1 Cor 10:4).

day (Num 16:49; 1 Cor 10:10). Paul referred to that incident to say, "Do not murmur" against God.

These four examples[14] from the history of the Israelites – idolatry, adultery, testing God, and murmuring against God – became examples or warnings for the Corinthians to heed. So Paul wrote, "These happened to them as lessons and have been written down as instructions for us, upon whom the end of the ages has begun" (1 Cor 10:11). Paul saw Christians as people in the "end days" – that is, people "upon whom the end of the ages has come."[15] Given this, they were to be careful not to succumb to the same errors that the forefathers had committed.

Paul concluded, "The one who thinks to be standing, watch out that you don't fall" (1 Cor 10:12). The context was the Corinthians' entering temples of foreign gods and eating food offered to those gods. Paul was saying that if they were that bold, they should listen to the stories in the Old Testament of how Israel, who played around with idolatry and adultery, were punished. The Israelites were punished for each event of idolatry and rebellion. The Corinthians should realize that they could also become arrogant and that their simple eating could turn into idolatry, adultery, or rebellion against God. Should that happen, they would be in danger of punishment, including death (1 Cor 5:5). Therefore, they needed to make sure that they stood firm in their faith. Of course, their desire to enter temples and eat food was not a unique temptation. So Paul wrote, "No temptation has overtaken you that is uncommon to humans" (1 Cor 10:13a): such a desire was common to all people in Corinth. In the midst of their temptation, however, God remained faithful to make sure that they weren't tempted beyond their capacity and to provide them with the ability to endure (1 Cor 10:13b).[16]

In conclusion, the bottom line was, "Flee from idolatry, brothers and sisters" (1 Cor 10:14). The Corinthians were playing with danger without realizing it. They were entering temples of other gods and eating food offered to those gods. They were thinking, "Oh, it's nothing. We know there are no other gods. So we can eat food offered to idols in these temples." But in reality, there were other so-called gods and lords (also *daimonia*, cf. 1 Cor 10:19–20).

---

14. The Greek word used is *tupikōs*, which is seeing "a correspondence between earlier biblical events and the present situation" (Fee, *First Epistle to the Corinthians*, 443 n. 10).

15. Baird, "1 Corinthians 10:1–13," 289.

16. The last phrase – "to provide them the ability to endure" – could mean that God would provide them with an escape route or way out of temptation (as many translations have understood it). But since Paul's concluding phrase is "to endure it," a translation that suggests "the ability to endure" is a better option.

By playing around with other gods, the Corinthians were playing with danger (idolatry), just as the Israelites had done. The Israelites' careless playing with idolatry, adultery, testing, and complaining had brought them great distress – the loss of many lives. The same could happen to the Corinthians if they weren't careful. Paul wasn't talking about them losing their salvation; he was talking about them facing physical destruction. It was a natural desire to enter the temples and eat food – especially meat, if it was only available there. But such an act could cause them insurmountable pain. God remained faithful to give them restraining power from falling to such natural desires and temptations. So they should, with his strength, flee from all forms of idolatry.

Pongal (1 Corinthians 10:15–22)

Pongal (or Pongala) is a very popular festival in southern India that is celebrated in January every year. It marks the beginning of the sun's journey northward. Since it also marks the beginning of the Tamil month of *thai*, it is called "Thai Pongal." The word *pongal* means "boil over" or "spill over." For this reason, rice is allowed to cook until it boils over the pots. As it boils over, people shout, "*Pongalo pongal!*"

It is more than a harvest festival; it is a religious festival dedicated to the goddess Amma ("mother"). Devotees sometimes substitute the names Devi (goddess) or Bhagavati (powerful or supreme) for Amma. Jenett writes, "Pongala is an offering of rice, boiled until thick white foam spills over the top of the pot, which represents an overabundance, 'more than enough,' and it is offered to fulfill a woman's vow to the Goddess. The ingredients are simple, and almost any woman can afford to do it. Rice, after being boiled out in the open in a new red clay pot over a coconut fire, is sweetened with jaggery, a dark brown, unrefined sugar from the palm tree."[17]

One of the key elements of this festival is sharing the pongal with families, neighbors, and even strangers. Jenett writes,

> The women cooking are required by the Goddess to share with strangers all resources necessary to perform Pongala, and the Goddess is paying attention. According to Chandramadi, the matriarch of the rural matrilineal family, "when you go to the Pongala, you try to share everything there. There is nothing

---

17. Dianne Jenett, "A Million *Shaktis* rising: Pongala, a Women's Festival in Kerala, India," *Journal of Feminist Studies in Religion* 21, no. 1 (Spring 2005): 40.

that belongs to you exclusively. So you don't try to exclusively appropriate whatever you have taken; not to give it to another person. If you did that, then you would be immediately given a [disapproving] sign of it before you reach home. You would have to share." According to this principle, the transformed and blessed food, Pongala, is shared not only with families and neighbors but also with strangers. The women on their way home often give it to people on the street.[18]

The Corinthians lived in a similar culture where food was cooked in the temples and shared with the devotees. Some of the Corinthians were partaking in such festivals and eating this food; others were not. So Paul called the mature within the congregation to think with him about this matter: "I am speaking to you who think [you are wise]; consider what I am saying" (1 Cor 10:15). In other words, if they really thought along with him, they would come to the same conclusions he had come to.

The Corinthians were now part of a new festival meal: "The cup of blessing which we bless, is it not a fellowship with Christ? The bread which we eat, is it not a fellowship with the body of Christ?" (1 Cor 10:16).[19] Paul attributed this cultic imagery to the Lord's Supper *not* to imply that somehow the wine and bread were mystical, divine foods; instead, he was emphasizing the *oneness* of the participants. All the Corinthians were eating *one* bread and thus they were sharing in *one* bread, although they were many in number (1 Cor 10:17; see 11:17–34). Paul then supported his argument of the oneness of the participants in the Lord's Supper with reference to the Old Testament festival meal: "You observe the traditional Israelites: those who eat the sacrifices – do they not share the same food from the altar?" (1 Cor 10:18). In other words, the priests and people became one with each other as they ate the same meal (sacrifice). This was one reason why all the Israelites gathered together to celebrate Passover – it was a fellowship meal, a fellowship offering (Lev 7 – 9). That oneness was a two-edged sword: on the one hand, it emphasized the oneness of the believers with one another; on the other hand, it meant that if the same Corinthian Christians partook of the food of other gods, they would become one with worshippers of those gods. Since they had partaken of the Lord's bread and wine together with fellow Christians, when they went to the

---

18. Ibid., 48.
19. This passage illustrates that there is no strict sequence such as that the bread should precede the cup.

temple of an idol and participated in their food, such as pongala, they were uniting themselves with followers of another "so-called" god.

Pongala is not merely a festival of eating some boiled food; it is participation with followers of another god, the goddess Amma. Likewise, neither was the Corinthians' involvement in other "so-called" gods' meals a simple participation in a meal in a temple. Paul had earlier stated that there were other "so-called" gods and lords, which are false gods and false lords (1 Cor 8:5). He repeated it again here: "What am I saying? That idol food is nothing or idolatry is nothing? Instead what I am saying is this: whatever is sacrificed, it is sacrificed to *daimonia* and not to God" (1 Cor 10:19–20a). *Daimonia* is often translated as "demons," conjuring up evil imagery in Christians' minds. For the Corinthians, however, *daimonia* was the normal vocabulary for their gods (similar to Hinduism, where a ghost like Vetalas and the flesh-eating demon Pishchas are called "demons" who help other major deities like Shiva). Marcus writes, "The Corinthians with whom Paul is corresponding, however, may have seen *daimonia* in a more positive sense, as intermediate members of the divine hierarchy [cf. Acts 17:18] and in fact the *daimonia* terminology in 1 Cor 10:20–22 may have originated with them"[20] Paul's point was that, when someone offered a meal to a god or goddess in a pagan temple, that devotee was making an offering to a foreign *daimonia*, not to the true and real God of Christians. Therefore, to fellowship in that meal was to engage in idolatry. So he concluded, "I do not wish for you to become partakers with *daimonia*" (1 Cor 10:20b).

In fact, it was impossible to be at both tables: "It is absolutely impossible for you to drink the cup of the Lord and drink the cup of the *daimonia*. It is absolutely impossible for you to partake of the Lord's Table and also of the table of *daimonia*" (1 Cor 10:21). Paul wasn't saying that a person wasn't physically able to do so; he was talking about spiritual health. One couldn't be a participant in the Lord's Supper and afterwards join in a pagan festival. There was no such synchronism. Indeed, when someone tried it, Paul asked, "Are you not provoking the Lord? Are we stronger than him [to resist his anger]?" (1 Cor 10:22). God is a jealous God; the Lord is easily provoked to anger when his followers play with idolatry. All the stories in the Old Testament of terrible deaths resulting from God's judgment illustrate that point clearly. So the Corinthians shouldn't be "prostituting themselves" – eating at the

---

20. Joel Marcus, "Idolatry in the New Testament," *Interpretation* 60, no. 2 (April 2006): 159–160.

Lord's Supper and then entering a pagan temple to eat pagan festival food. Rosner, who sees Deuteronomy 32 as the background to this verse, says, "all the Pentateuchal references to God's jealousy have to do with idol-worship . . . 1 Corinthians 10:22b turns out to be a frightening threat of judgment upon those Corinthian Christians who provoke God to jealousy, if not upon the church in Corinth as a group on account of the behaviour of some of its members . . . Paul is convinced that the God of the Jewish Scriptures is unchanged in his attitude to idolatry."[21] It was no innocent behavior to enter a pagan temple to participate in a pagan dinner; it was idolatry, and dangerous.

One Body without Caste Discrimination (10:17)

As stated in the introduction, the Corinthians were a mixed group of Jews and Gentiles, freed people and slaves, males and females, Romans and Greeks. Paul repeatedly taught them that they were "one body" (1 Cor 10:17; 12:12–14, 18–20, 27). This is likewise a significant teaching for the Indian church. India is plagued by caste discrimination. One of the most oppressed communities is the Dalit, who are actually without a caste, or "outcaste." They make up 16 percent of the Indian population[22] and the majority of India's Christians.[23] Christians have characteristically fought for their acceptance and inclusion in their communities. But sometimes the ugly head of discrimination shows up even in churches. The important lesson to remember is that all Christians – regardless of their race or caste, as society categorizes people – are one body, the body of Christ.

Jhatka and Kutha (10:23–26)

"Kosher" refers to the way the Jews ceremonially prepare their meat.[24] Its equivalent in Islam is halal meat. In Hinduism, there are two distinct terms for killing animals: *kutha* (or *kutta*) and *jhatka* (or *chatka*). The first kind,

---

21. Brian S. Rosner, "'Stronger Than He?' The Strength of 1 Corinthians 10:22b," *Tyndale Bulletin* 43, no. 1 (1992): 178–179.

22. Sathianathan Clarke, "Dalits Overcoming Violation and Violence: A Contest between Overpowering and Empowering Identities in Changing India," *The Ecumenical Review* 54, no. 3 (July 2002): 279.

23. John C. B. Webster, "The Dalit Situation in India Today," *International Journal of Frontier Missions* 18, no. 1 (Spring 2001): 17.

24. Fee explains that the Mishnaic tractate *Hullin* was devoted to regulations concerning the killing of animals for food (Fee, *First Epistle to the Corinthians*, 481 n. 25).

kutha, is killing an animal slowly and with an accompanying prayer. Such killing is done as a sacrifice to gods and in the temple precinct. *Jhatka*, on the other hand, is killing an animal with a single stroke to severe the head from the body. Hindus prefer *jhatka* since it is less painful for the animals. In India, marketplaces are segregated, with a separate section for vegetables and a separate place for meat. Meat shops are further segregated into chicken stalls, fish stalls, goat stalls, beef stalls, and pork stalls. By law, the shops are required to make it clear whether *jhatka* meat is sold in them.

Similarly, in Corinth, meat that was killed ritualistically or as part of religious practice was sold in the marketplace. The meat market was called the *macellum*. Paul explicitly referred to such a *macellum* in this section (*en makellō*, 1 Cor 10:25). Gill says that archeological excavations at Corinth have not found with certainty such a *macellum*. However, a similar building in the ruins of Pompeii, another Greco-Roman city, gives us an idea of how these stalls would have been located. What was striking was that "in addition to stalls, there were a range of other rooms in the building, including shrines of the emperor. The walls were decorated with lavish paintings, such as that showing Argos and Io [goddesses in Greek mythology]."[25] Religion was intricately associated with marketplaces. It is similar in India, where every shop has an idol, with incense burning in front of the idol. Since meat sold in the marketplace could have been sacrificially killed (*kutha*) and shops have idols, should a Christian eat such meat? Paul had so far been addressing the situation of a Christian entering a temple to eat meat, and his instruction was "flee idolatry." But would Paul object to eating meat bought in the marketplace?

Not all Corinthians were waiting to hear Paul's reply. They had already started eating meat sold in the marketplace, with their favorite slogan being "All things are lawful" (1 Cor 10:23; cf. 6:12). Paul again repeated his basic lessons: "But not all things are beneficial" (1 Cor 10:23a); "Not all things build up a person" (1 Cor 10:23b); and "Do not seek your own good but the good of the other" (1 Cor 10:24). These have been his basic guiding principles throughout the discussion on eating food in connection with idols. Having mentioned these principles, Paul addressed the issue of meat offered in the meat market (*macellum*) specifically.

He instructed, "You may eat all food sold in a meat market without questioning, for the sake of conscience" (1 Cor 10:25). The reason for not

---

25. David W. J. Gill, "The Meat-Market at Corinth (1 Corinthians 10:25)," *Tyndale Bulletin* 43, no. 2 (1992): 393.

asking questions and not having a guilty conscience for eating such food was because "the earth and its abundance belong to the Lord" (1 Cor 10:26). Paul was citing a familiar psalm that the Israelites sang as they climbed the hills of Jerusalem when on a pilgrimage to the Holy City. As they ascended, they acknowledged that every blessing they received came from the Lord. In the same way, Corinthian Christians who went to the market were to think of the meat offered at the stalls as God's provision for their sustenance. Such thinking would keep them from questioning whether they could eat such meat or from having a bad conscience about doing so.

Likewise in India, Christians should not ask shopkeepers any questions about where the meat has come from; instead, they are to purchase the meat remembering that God is the ultimate provider of all food, and eat it in gratitude to God for the provision. This is true of restaurants ("hotels," as they are called in India), where *pujas* (worship) are done for other deities; Christians are to ignore that and remember that God is the ultimate creator of all food, thank him, and eat with a clear conscience.

Dana and Food (10:27–33)

There are ten "observances" or "practices" (*niyamas*) to abide by in order to be a good Hindu. The third of these observances is *dana*, or "giving." Basically, it is giving liberally without thinking of any return or reward. Hindus give a tenth of their gross income (*dasamamsa*) to their deity but, in addition, they are required to give *dana* generously. They express this *dana* in giving gifts to the priests, feeding the poor, giving to those in need, investing their talents without seeking praise, and showing hospitality (treating guests as they would treat gods or goddesses).

Hospitality, therefore, is prominent in Indian culture. One cannot visit a neighbor's house without drinking a drink offered (tea, juice, or water). One cannot attend a wedding reception without eating sweets (sometimes confectionaries and other times desserts). Weddings cannot take place without the whole neighborhood being invited for the feast.

The ancient culture in Corinth was similar. Friends invited each other round for meals. So what should Christians do if unbelieving friends gave them some meat to eat and it was unclear whether the meat had been killed in a temple? Paul addressed that question next.

Paul's answer was, "If any non-Christian invites you [to his or her house] and you wish to go, eat everything placed in front of you without questioning [where it came from] for the sake of conscience" (1 Cor 10:27). Baird succinctly summarizes the contrast between this passage and what Paul had said earlier: "In a pagan culture where some of the meat of the market place has been sacrificed to idols and where believers may be served this meat at an unbeliever's dinner party, Christians need not be preoccupied with details about the source of the food. Yet a Christian cannot go into a pagan temple and actually participate in a cultic meal."[26] Since this situation of eating food in a friend's house was different from willfully entering a temple and eating food offered to other gods, Paul permitted such eating. Paul's answer was similar to his advice concerning eating food offered in a marketplace: eat everything placed in front of you, without asking questions (1 Cor 10:24). Again, the thought should be that everything in this world belongs to the Lord (1 Cor 10:26), so the Christian should eat with a clear conscience.

The situation changed, however, when "someone says, 'this is sacrificial food'" (1 Cor 10:28a). So far Paul had been dealing with food offered within a temple (*eidolothyton*), but now he addressed the *sacrificial food* itself (*hierothyton*). If someone at the meal were to say, "This is sacrificial food," the situation would change. Fee suggests three options for who this "someone" might be: "(1) the host; (2) a pagan fellow guest; (3) a fellow believer."[27] Regardless of who said it, the response was to be the same: "Do not eat it, on account of that one who revealed this fact and for his or her conscience' sake" (1 Cor 10:28b). In other words, although eating this food was acceptable, once it had been declared aloud that it was sacrificial food, it was no longer acceptable for a Christian to eat it.

So far Paul had been saying that a Christian could always have a clear conscience since God was the source of the food, but now Paul said that, for the sake of the one who had brought to everyone's attention that it was sacrificial food, the Christian should abstain from eating that sacrificial food (1 Cor 10:29a). A Christian was free from another questioning his or her conscience (1 Cor 10:29b), but a non-Christian or a new Christian wouldn't have that privilege, which was why the Christian needed to abstain from eating such food in a neighbor's house. That weak neighbor's or weaker Christian's conscience – and not the mature Christian's own conscience – was the reason for abstaining. So Paul rephrased it: "If I partake of food thankfully, why am I blasphemed for that for which I give thanks?" (1 Cor 10:30). This

---

26. Baird, "1 Corinthians 10:1–13," 286.
27. Fee, *First Epistle to the Corinthians*, 483. He prefers the second option.

was a rhetorical way of affirming a truth in that culture.[28] The conscience of a mature Christian shouldn't be troubled by any food offered outside a temple. He or she should eat it without asking where it came from, knowing that God was the source of all food. The situation only changed when someone other than the Christian said, "This is sacrificial food"; then, for the sake of the one who had made that revelation, the mature Christian should abstain from eating.

This passage answers a question that (mostly young) converts from Hinduism to Christianity face: can they eat *prasada* (gifts given to gods and shared with family members) when they go to their parents' or relatives' houses and are offered them? Paul would say: yes, they may eat it without asking any questions or raising any doubts in their hearts. Instead, they can say to themselves, "All that is in the earth belongs to the Lord," and can eat whatever is given to them. But if the family members invite them to enter a temple and eat before the gods, they should refrain (if possible).

Paul then stated the correct attitude the Corinthians should have: "Whether you eat or drink or whatever you do, all these you do for the glory of God" (1 Cor 10:31). That should be the ultimate driving force behind every action of a Christian. The Corinthians' slogan was, "All things are permissible." Paul wanted them to say, "All things are for the glory of God." That principle would guide them into truth in their selection of what to eat and what not to eat.

One way God would not receive glory was when the Corinthians offended others. So Paul said, "Do not become an offense to the Jews or Greeks or to the church of God" (1 Cor 10:32). Paul didn't want the mature Christians in the Corinthian church to be an offense to the Jewish people who had not yet believed in the Lordship of Jesus Christ, the Greeks who were still following other gods, or the new Christians (both Jews and Gentiles) within the congregation who had weak faith. Paul wanted the mature Christians to be sensitive in their behavior towards all these people so that their actions would bring glory to God.

The opposite of "being an offense" was "being a witness" who drew people to Christ. So Paul said, "So I try to please all people; I seek to please all people, without seeking to please myself, so that I may save others" (1 Cor 10:33). That was Paul's motivation behind all the restraints he endured: the

---

28. For Paul's rhetorical skill in this section (10:23 – 11:1) see Duane F. Watson, "1 Corinthians 10:23–11:1 in Light of Greco-Roman Rhetoric: The Role of Rhetorical Questions," *Journal of Biblical Literature* 108, no. 2 (1989): 301–318.

salvation of others. Whereas the Corinthians emphasized their own freedom and were quick to eat in temples and other places, Paul constrained every freedom for the sake of the salvation of others. That was to be the goal of the Corinthians too.

Food plays an important role in India. First, food is associated with health and is classified into various sub-categories. For example, food is classified according to taste: sweet, sour, and salty. It is also classified according to "post-digestive" taste. Thus, for example, banana and milk are not eaten together: although both are sweet on the tongue, banana is sour inside the stomach while milk is sweet inside the stomach; therefore they shouldn't be mixed. Food is then classified as either "heating" or "cooling": pork is a cooling food and chicken is a heating food. And it is classified according to the "personality" of the food – "whether a food has a purgative or a binding quality" (e.g. eating melon with milk is prohibited).[29]

Second, food is associated with the gods. Hindus, for example, do not cook meat or fish in a house where someone is afflicted with smallpox because they believe that the goddess *Sitala* (also known as "Mother"), who is responsible for bringing smallpox to families, loves meat and she would linger in that house.[30]

Third, food is associated with religion itself. Pure Hindus do not eat any meat. Others eat some forms of meat. But most Indians hesitate to eat beef because of its sacredness and out of respect for Gandhi. As for its sacredness, the *Mahabharata* (a Hindu scripture) says, "He who kills a cow lives as many years in hell as there are hairs on the cow's body."[31] Regarding respect for Gandhi, he vehemently opposed the killing of cows. He said,

> The central fact of Hinduism, however, is "Cow Protection." "Cow Protection" to me is one of the most wonderful phenomena in all human evolution; for it takes the human being beyond his species ... Man through the cow is enjoined to realize his identity with all that lives. Why the cow was selected for apotheosis is obvious to me. The cow was in India the best companion. She was the giver of plenty. Not only did she give milk, but she also made agriculture possible . . . She is the "mother" to millions of Indian mankind . . . "Cow Protection" is the gift of Hinduism to

---

29. Kakar and Kakar, *The Indians*, 121–125.
30. Babagrahi Misra, "*Sitala*: The Small-Pox Goddess of India," *Asian Folklore Studies* 28, no. 2 (1969): 136.
31. Korom, "Holy Cow!," 188.

the world; and Hinduism will live so long as there are Hindus to protect the cow.[32]

Because of these strong ties between food and religious and social life, Christians in India need to be careful not to give offense to Hindus. Christians shouldn't live for food; instead, they should thank God for food and glorify God through the food. One way to glorify God is to limit the enjoyment of their freedom for the sake of weak Christians and non-Christians.

---

32. Cited in Margul, "Present-Day Worship of the Cow in India," 64.

13

1 Corinthians 11

Mimesis (11:1–2)

Mimesis (from Greek *mimesis*, "imitate") is the representation of the real world in art or literature. It has a key role in religion. Geetz writes, "Religious narrative promulgates, extrapolates, and investigates the significance of virtual worlds in real time contexts, while at the same time refining them in all their majestic virtuality. Religious narrative provides paradigms for human identity, thereby providing narrative governance of human cognition and emotion . . . One of the primary subject matters of mimesis is to communicate states of mind and emotion (feigned or otherwise) to others."[1]

Barata Natyam is a classic Indian dance that originated in the temples of Tamil Nadu in southern India. *Devadasis* (young girls dedicated to the worship and service of a deity in a temple) performed it as a solo dance.[2] They imitated the dances portrayed in the temple statues for the amusement of devotees. The statues themselves were thought to be of celestial dancers (*apsaras*) performing dances for the pleasure of gods. The dance is known for its grace, sculpture-like poses, and difficulty. The dancers tell the divine stories through their expressions of emotion, body movements, reciting of poetry, and costume. In contemporary India it has become an art form, performed for people's entertainment on stages and at functions.

The concept of mimesis was expressed even in the time of Plato. Paul used it often in his letter to the Corinthians. In 1 Corinthians 4:16 he explicitly said, "Become imitators [*mimetai*] of me." In other places he expressed the

---

1. Armin W. Geetz, "Religious Narrative: An Introduction," *Bulletin for the Study of Religion* 42, no. 4 (November 2013): 3.
2. Rajaram, *Facets of Indian Culture*, 109.

concept indirectly: "I am sending to you Timothy . . . he will remind you of my way of life in Christ Jesus" (1 Cor 4:17), implying that they needed to copy it. Now in chapter 11 Paul explicitly challenged them to imitate him (1 Cor 11:1) and commended them for having done that so far (1 Cor 11:2).

Paul had been setting himself as an example to the Corinthians in constraining their desires or rights for the sake of others (ch. 9). He continued that thought into two difficult topics: head-coverings and the careful participation in the Lord's Supper (ch. 11). He therefore used these two verses as a link between these sections.

Paul wanted the Corinthians to imitate him just as he imitated Christ (1 Cor 11:1). Of course, "the apostle and his church understand themselves to be called to imitate not the day to day conduct of the historical Jesus, but rather the act of self-effacement which the Cross represents, the fact of the divine self-emptying (2 Cor. 8:9)."[3] The Lord Jesus left every privilege for the sake of others and deliberately went to the cross and gave his life (Phil 2:5–11). Paul was imitating him, and the Corinthians were to imitate Paul.

When Paul wrote 1 Corinthians, he didn't use verse or chapter divisions. Robertus Stephanus (also known as Robert Estienne) introduced verse division in his fourth edition of the Greek text in 1551. For this reason, scholars disagree in certain cases about where a verse or chapter division should go. Such a case is 1 Corinthians 11:1: some translations see it as continuing the thought of chapter 10 (e.g. NIV), whereas others see it as part of chapter 11.[4] I think it is a bridging verse connected to chapter 10, where Paul challenges the Corinthians to follow his example of setting aside personal rights for the sake of others, but also fitting with chapter 11, where he commends the Corinthians for their faithful following of his teachings (11:2) and exhorts them to continue to follow his example in faithfully worshipping and observing the Lord's Supper.

So far, the Corinthians had been exemplary in following Paul's teachings, so Paul praised them first: "I praise you that you remember me in all things and you have kept the traditions, just as I have handed them to you" (1 Cor 11:2).[5] However, there were traditions he hadn't handed to them which they

---

3. Robert G. Hamerton-Kelly, "A Girardian Interpretation of Paul: Rivalry, Mimesis and Victimage in the Corinthian Correspondence," *Semeia* 33 (1985): 72.

4. Wilson argues that the δε ("now") introduces a new section. Kenneth T Wilson, "Should Women Wear Headcoverings," *Bibliotheca Sacra* 148, no. 592 (October–December 1991): 443.

5. Some scholars think Paul was being sarcastic here (e.g. Robertson and Plummer, and Fee) but most likely Paul was genuinely praising them "in view of the literary device

were mishandling (e.g. the Lord's Supper). Therefore, he would proceed to instructed them in these traditions. The first was the uncovering and covering of the head. The second was proper behavior at the Lord's Supper.

Karva Chauth (11:3)

Hindu women in North India observe a one-day festival called *karva chauth*. On that day, the married women observe fasting from sunrise to sunset for the safety and longevity of their husbands. Unmarried women observe the fast for their fiancés or desired husbands.[6] In Hinduism, wives greatly respect their husbands. One of the Hindu scriptures, *Matsya Purana*, describes the creation of people. Brahma, by his magical powers, created the goddess Shatrupa. From their union came Manu, the first man. By his penance he received his wife, Ananthi. Indian women therefore respect their husbands because they came into being because of their husbands' reverence.

The same was true of Paul's tradition, Judaism. Genesis 1 taught that God created mankind in his image, as his viceroys on earth. He created mankind as male and female (Gen 1:26). They were to populate and rule the earth. Genesis 2 then outlines how man and woman were interdependent. Man didn't see a suitable mate for him among all creation and therefore God created for him his wife from his "side." Man and woman were thus one body and one flesh. But since man was created first, he was held accountable for the fall and sin (Rom 5:12). His priority in creation also implied his priority in honoring God.

These historical stories formed Paul's anthropology. He wrote, "I want you to know that Christ is the *head* of every man, the husband is the *head* of a wife, and God is the *head* of Christ" (1 Cor 11:3).[7] The terms "husband" and "wife" here are the generic Greek terms for "man" and "woman," but it is most likely that Paul was talking about married men and women, given the subject

---

whereby Paul introduced a section with praise when possible and then gave a needed rebuke or correction [e.g. 1 Cor 1:4–9]" (Wilson, "Should Women Wear Headcoverings," 443).

6. Sohindar Singh Wanajara Bedi, *Folklore of the Punjab* (Bombay: India Book Trust, 1971), 53.

7. Wilson's observation is pertinent: "The order in which the examples of hierarchical relationship appear – Christ–man; man–woman; God–Christ – places the relationship under discussion in the middle for emphasis. They may also have been an intentional ordering to avoid placing woman at the bottom of the list (as also in vv. 12–13)" (Wilson, "Should Women Wear Headcoverings," 445).

matter; therefore I have changed it to "husband and wife."[8] In other words, Paul wasn't talking about all men's headship over all women[9] but a husband's headship over his own wife.[10]

Paul was referring to a *figurative* head or headship.[11] But what does *head* or *headship* mean in this context?[12] Three popular views are listed here. First, some scholars argue that "head" means "ruler" or "authority over": just as God is the ruler or authority over Christ, and Christ is the ruler or authority over men, so husbands are the rulers or authorities over their wives.[13] However, while the Scriptures do affirm that Christ has authority over the church and Christians (Eph 5:23; Col 1:18), they never claim that God has authority over Christ. Christ submitted himself voluntarily to God, even at his death (John 10:17). So "ruler" or "authority over" might not be the best meaning for *head* in this context. Second, some scholars argue that "head" means "source": just as God is the source of Christ, and Christ is the source of all people, so man (Adam) is the source of woman (Eve).[14] This theory has validity since Eve was created from the "side" of Adam; and also the place where a river starts is called the "head" of the river, meaning the source of the river. But the Scriptures again do not claim that God was the source of

---

8. Collins argues that it is a reference to the creation account of Adam and Eve (Raymond F. Collins, *First Corinthians*, ed. Daniel J. Harrington, Sacra Pagina Series, vol. 7 [Collegeville, MN: Liturgical Press, 1999] 406). Orr and Walther write, "The whole passage, however, could be referring to conduct of a man and his wife; and 'woman' would be 'wife' in the critical occurrences and possibly in all instances" (Orr and Walther, *1 Corinthians*, 259).

9. For example, Charles Hodge, *1 Corinthians*, eds. Alister McGrath and J. I. Packer, Crossway Classic Commentaries (Wheaton, IL: Crossway Books, 1995) 188–189.

10. Wenham writes, "It is hard to avoid the conclusion that Paul believed the husbands to have a position of God-given leadership in the family" (David Wenham, *Paul: Follower of Jesus or Founder of Christianity* [Grand Rapids: Eerdmans, 1995] 238 n. 54).

11. Besides the concrete meaning of a "physical head" (as in "head of an animal" or "head of a person") or a "brim" (of a vessel), this word has a range of figurative meanings: (a) "superior rank," "lord," "chief," "prominent," "preeminent," "master"; (b) "uppermost part," "extremity," "end," "point"; (c) "source" (as in *source* of a river); (d) "authority"; or (e) "life" (UBS Lexicon; *Thayer's Greek-English Lexicon*; Louw & Nida's *Greek-English Lexicon*; Liddell & Scott's *Greek-English Lexicon*).

12. For a comprehensive list of views and analysis, see Harold W. Hoehner, *Ephesians: An Exegetical Commentary* (Grand Rapids: Baker Academic, 2002), 285–287.

13. Plummer and Robertson, *1 Corinthians*, 229; Wayne Grudem, "The Meaning of *Kephale* ('Head'): A Response to Recent Studies," in *Recovering Biblical Manhood and Womanhood*, eds. John Piper and Wayne Grudem (Wheaton, IL: Crossway, 1991), 425–468; Wayne Grudem, "Does *Kephale* ('Head') Mean 'Source' or 'Authority over' in Greek Literature? A Survey of 2,336 Examples," *Trinity Journal* 6, no. 1 (Spring 1985): 38–59.

14. Fee, *First Epistle to the Corinthians*, 503–505. Stephen Bedale, "The Meaning of *Kephale* in the Pauline Epistles," *Journal of Theological Studies* 5, (1984): 211–215. John P Meier, "On the Veiling of Hermeneutics (1 Cor 11:2–16)," *Catholic Biblical Quarterly* 40, no. 2 (April 1978): 217–218.

Christ; God and Christ are co-equal and co-eternal. So "source" might not be the best option in this context either. Third, some scholars have suggested "preeminence" as the meaning for head: just as in the God–Christ relationship God is preeminent, and in the Christ–man relationship Christ is preeminent, so in the husband–wife relationship the husband is preeminent.[15] Paul had already stated that God and Christ have preeminence over all things created (1 Cor 8:6); however the Scriptures in general teach ontological co-equality of husbands and wives (Gen 1:26; Gal 3:28) and the husbands' loving attitude of service towards their wives (Eph 5:25–33). Therefore, "preeminence" might not be a good meaning for head in this context.

Two contextual clues guide our conclusion. First, Paul had earlier said, "You are of Christ and Christ is of God" (1 Cor 3:23). The context there was that everything and everyone (like the apostles) was serving the Corinthians; in turn, the Corinthians were serving Christ, and Christ was serving God. As Fee points out, "This is a soteriological statement, not a Christological one (in terms of his being)."[16] Similarly, here too Paul might not be talking about ontological headship so much as functional headship. Second, in the immediate context, Paul said, "Imitate me as I imitate Christ" (1 Cor 11:1). Mimesis implies copying or following the lead of another. In the Old Testament, often the term "head" was used to express the concept of following a leader. Moses taught that if the Israelites disobeyed the law, foreigners among them would become richer than them and would *lead* them (i.e. be their "head") and the Israelites would *follow* them (Deut 28:44). Also, the elders of Gilead went to Jephthah and asked him to "be their head" and *lead* them into battle (Judg 11:6–11). Queen Esther lamented her *leadership* over the people: "O my Lord, you alone are our King, help me . . . You know my humility, how I abhor the sign of authority over my *head* as I abhor a menstrual rag" (Esth 14:1–19, LXX). In light of these examples, most likely Paul was being culturally sensitive in a context where wives followed the lead of their husbands. So he was saying that just as Christ followed God ("Whatever the Son sees the Father do, the Son does likewise," John 5:19), so the apostles followed Christ, the Christian men followed the example of Christ, and the wives followed the example of their husbands. "Head" thus referred to the *example* or *model* to follow. Paul elsewhere exhorted wives to *imitate* their husbands: just as Christian men in church ought to submit

---

15. Richard S. Cervin, "Does *Kaphale* Mean 'Source' or 'Authority over' in Greek Literature?," *Trinity Journal* 10, (1989): 85–112.

16. Fee, *First Epistle to the Corinthians*, 155.

to one another (Eph 5:21), so wives ought to submit to their husbands (Eph 5:22). Unlike in the creation account, where a man failed to follow the lead of the Lord and guide his wife to follow God's commandments, in the Christian family a husband is to diligently follow the leader (Jesus Christ) so that others, especially his wife, will follow his lead in imitating Christ.

The Scriptures do not teach an ontological denigration of women; instead, they teach ontological oneness of husbands and wives: God created male and female together, in his image, and commissioned them to work together in managing the world. The husband's primary task is to follow God's commandments faithfully so that he can lead his wife and family. In the fall account, he failed to do that. But in Christian living, a husband who faithfully follows Christ also leads his wife (who follows him faithfully) in the path of the Lord Jesus Christ. That is the model Paul proposed in his "head" imagery in this passage – not some ontological superiority of husbands or of men in general. When Christian husbands take on the responsibility to follow Christ faithfully, their Christian wives will faithfully follow them (as they follow Christ) and will respect them with far greater respect than that shown on the one-day festival *karva chauth*.

Ghoonghat (11:4–16)

Ghoonghat (also *ghunghat* or *jhund*) is the Hindi word used for a veil or a scarf that a woman in northern India wears to cover her head or face (in states such as Gujarat, Rajasthan, Haryana, Bihar, Uttar Pradesh, and Assam). Sometimes the end of a sari or *dupatta* (a long scarf) is pulled over the head or face to function as a *ghoonghat*. A woman wears a *ghoonghat* as a veil to hide her face from all men to whom she is related by marriage and who are senior to her husband. The purpose is to limit her interaction with older men as well as to show respect to elder males in the extended family.[17] (In certain contexts, however, women cover their faces from all men.)

In ancient Corinth, headwear was an important part of the lives of men and women. Finney writes, "The wearing of suitable apparel by men and women within Greco-Roman first-century CE culture was wholly immersed within considerations of honour and status, and so was of prime import to most. Indeed, one's attire often gave the clearest and most highly visible indication

---

17. Pran Nevile, *Lahore: A Sentimental Journey* (New Delhi, India: Penguin Books, 2006), 77.

of social rank."[18] Similarly, Thompson and Gill have shown that religious leaders wore headwear (toga, wreaths, or crowns) while they performed priestly duties.[19] Thompson describes one of the statues of Augustus as follows: "The statue is reconstructed from four pieces and is preserved as a standing figure extending from the head to ankle level of the left leg. His toga, the draped outer garment of the Roman citizen, is worn over the head, as it was characteristically in a Roman religious sacrifice, which would have been performed with the two arms that are missing."[20] Even Aaron and his sons wore head-coverings when they served in the temple (Exod 28:4, 40).[21] Because of the cultural significance of headwear, Paul instructed the Corinthians about their own head-coverings at church gatherings so as to foster reverence. His instructions were similar to Peter's: "Focus not on the external – braiding of hair, wearing of jewelry, or elaborate clothing – but on the internal and hiddenness of the heart of a person, such as imperishable gentleness and a quiet spirit – that are honorable before God" (1 Pet 3:3–4). Similarly, Paul addressed both men and women in this section equally: 1 Corinthians 11:3–4 (man) versus 11:5 (woman); 1 Corinthians 11:6 (woman) versus 11:7 (man); 1 Corinthians 11:8–10 (man) versus 11:11–12 (woman), and 1 Corinthians 11:14 (man) versus 11:15 (woman). Both genders were to be careful how they behaved in church.[22]

Paul addressed the men first: "Any man who has *something* on his physical head, while praying or prophesying, humiliates his leader-head, Christ" (1 Cor 11:4). Paul was referring to men having a wreath crown or a toga on their heads while they prayed or prophesied.[23] When men did have such a head-covering, in that culture, it implied that they were priests (cf.

18. Finney, "Honour, Head-Coverings and Headship," 35.

19. Cynthia L. Thompson, "Hairstyles, Head-Coverings, and St Paul: Portraits from Roman Corinth," *Biblical Archaeologist* 51, no. 2 (June 1988): 99–115. David W. J. Gill, "The Importance of Roman Portraiture for Head-Coverings in 1 Corinthians 11:2–16," *Tyndale Bulletin* 41, no. 2 (1990): 245–260.

20. Thompson, "Hairstyles, Head-Coverings, and St Paul," 101.

21. Samuel Krauss, "The Jewish Rite of Covering the Head," *Hebrew Union College Annual* 19, (1945–1946): 130. Krauss concurs with Lauterbach, saying that for the Jews, praying bareheaded or with a covered head was not a question of the law but instead a matter of decorum or social propriety (Ibid., 168).

22. Mount sees this whole passage (vv. 3–16) as an interpolation, meaning Paul didn't originally write it. Christopher Mount, "1 Corinthians 11:3-16: Spirit Possession and Authority in a Non-Pauline Interpolation," *Journal of Biblical Literature* 124, no. 2 (2005): 313–40. There is no solid manuscript or contextual evidence for such a conclusion.

23. Some have suggested Paul was talking about men having long hair because of the phrase "hanging down from the head." For arguments against that view, see Wilson, "Should Women Wear Headcoverings," 446.

Exod 8:4, 40). If they sent that message to those around them they would be dishonoring their leader-head, Christ, the true high priest. Paul elsewhere said, "There is one God; there is one mediator between God and mankind – the man Christ Jesus" (1 Tim 2:5). The Corinthian Christian men were therefore not to cover their heads.

The situation was different for women, so Paul wrote, "Any wife, while praying or prophesying, who does not cover her head shames her leader-head [the husband]" (1 Cor 11:5a).[24] For a woman, hair was her glory (1 Cor 11:15). In Corinth, as in other cultures, women took extra care of their hair on special occasions "such as mourning, some Greek wedding ceremonies, or religious rites."[25] Peter acknowledged this (1 Pet 3:3), but when it came to church gatherings, women were to be modest (1 Pet 3:4).[26] Just as men couldn't imply that they were priests while they prayed and prophesied, so wives shouldn't shame their husbands while they prayed and prophesied. Just as a married woman in North India who refuses to wear a *ghoonghat* over her face and head in front of her husband's male relatives shames her husband, so a married woman in the Corinthian congregation who refused to wear a head-covering while praying or prophesying in the congregation shamed her husband. But were she to cover her glorious hair at the time of praying and prophesying, her actions would signify humility, the "same as if she had shaved her hair" (1 Cor 11:5b).[27] Covering one's hair while praying and prophesying was equal to having it shaved off; that is, it implied the humility of the women.

In fact, there were two other options for those with long hair who did not want to cover it: short hair and a shaven head: "If a wife wishes not to cover her hair, let her cut it; and if it is a shame for her to cut it or shave it, let her cover it" (1 Cor 11:6). For a woman, long free-flowing hair was her beauty (1 Cor 11:15). She could restrict the expression of her beauty at the time of

---

24. Fee suggests that long free-flowing hair (or "loose hair") was a sign of prophetesses in the pagan temple to show their authority and that was what Paul wanted to avoid (Fee, *First Epistle to the Corinthians*, 496–497). If that were Paul's reasoning, it was not explicitly stated in the text.

25. Thompson, "Hairstyles, Head-Coverings, and St Paul," 112.

26. Holmyard sees this passage as addressing a non-church context (Harold R. III Holmyard, "Does 1 Corinthians 11:2-16 Refer to Women Praying and Prophesying in Church?," *Bibliotheca Sacra* 154 [October-December 1997]: 472). But if a woman was required to have a head-covering in a non-church setting, would she not be expected to do the same in a church setting?

27. Some have suggested wrongly that hair is the covering (based on 1 Cor 11:15). As the commentary will show, the "covering" in verse 15 is a different concept.

praying and prophesying by covering her hair, or she could keep it short if she preferred not to cover it. But if keeping it short or shaving it off was shameful to her, she should keep it long but cover it at the time of praying and prophesying. The decision was up to the wives.[28] Regardless, their motivation was *not to shame their husbands by their actions*.

So Paul's first teaching was that a man was not to cover his hair in order to honor his head or leader, Christ, and a wife was to cover her hair in order to honor her leader-head, her husband. The key for contextualization of this passage is finding out what "honors" a leader-head in a particular culture. In the southern states of India, men wear a loose outfit called a dhoti or lungi, a sheet-like length of cloth that is wrapped around the body. Since it is hot and inconvenient, however, men often fold it in half and wear it like shorts. But there are particular stipulations within the culture: should a teacher, elder, or woman approach a man wearing a dhoti or lungi folded in half, the man must immediately untie it and wear it full length in order to give honor to the teacher, elder, or lady. Similarly, in rural Rajasthan, a bride/wife must cover her face when she addresses her husband or father-in-law; but she is not required to cover her face when addressing her brother-in-law, sons, grandfathers, or uncles. Cultures determine what "honors" a person and what "dishonors" a person. (In schools in India, for example, when a teacher enters a class, the students stand in respect.) Thus it is the principle of following what honors or shames that should be applied in our culture; not a mere senseless copying of the practice of head covering.[29]

There was a second reason why a man was not to cover his head and a wife was to cover her hair at the time of praying and prophesying: authority. Paul writes, "A man ought not to cover his head since he is the image and glory of God" (1 Cor 11:7a). Paul was referring to Genesis, where God said, "Let us create man in our *image* . . . and God created *man* in his own *image*"

---

28. Both the presence of the middle voice (where the subject acts on its own behalf or interest) and the first class condition ("let's assume – for the sake of argument – that a woman does not want to cover her hair") imply that the choice was up to the wives.

29. For an excellent article on how mimesis is not mere cloning but a creative articulation of the principle behind a practice, illustrated by Jesus washing the disciples' feet, see Cornelis Bennema, "Mimesis in John 13: Cloning or Creative Articulation?," *Novum Testamentum* 56 (2014): 261–274. Similarly, contemporary churches must not blindly imitate the practice of head-covering without understanding the principle behind it. Once the principle is found, it must be applied culturally. Asking the unmarried and even children to cover their heads is nothing but a blind imitation of a tradition, just as is requiring feet-washing as an ordinance without applying the principle of serving one another contextually.

(Gen 1:26–27). Man's being the image of God gave him authority.[30] Of course, those same verses stated that the mankind he created was both male and female (Gen 1:26), and that was why Paul didn't say that "woman was in the image of man."[31] She too was the image of God. What is different, however, is that man was the glory of God, meaning that a man brought glory to God by being his representative on earth.[32] (Of course, both men and women were to bring glory to God, 1 Cor 10:31; but in this context, Paul illustrated two diverse ways in which men and women were to do so.) Since he was the image and glory of God, man shouldn't cover his head.

Similarly, a godly woman brought glory to her husband (1 Cor 11:7b; "A noble wife is the crown of her husband," Prov 12:4), which in turn brought glory to God.[33] One of the ways she did this was by her not bringing shame on her husband; and in the Corinthian culture she would bring shame on her husband by refusing to cover her long free-flowing hair when she prayed or prophesied. Another way she brought glory to God was by her claiming her rightful and honorable place in creation. To illustrate that, Paul went back to the Genesis account. He first stated the process of creation: "The man is not out of the woman but the woman is out of man" (1 Cor 11:8). Genesis said, "So the LORD God caused the man to fall into a deep sleep, and while he was asleep, he took part of the man's side and closed up the place with flesh. Then the LORD God made a woman from the part he had taken out of the man, and he brought her to the man" (Gen 2:21–22, NET). Paul then stated the purpose of woman's creation: "The man was not created for the woman but the woman was for the man" (1 Cor 11:9).[34] The Genesis account stated that in all creation only one event was considered "not good," and that was for

---

30. Although the word "authority" is not in the verse (Fee, *First Epistle to the Corinthians*, 501 n. 39), the concept of "image of God" implies authority (Gen 1:28 says, "*Rule* over the fish of the sea, the birds of the air, and every living creature that moves on the ground").

31. Fee makes a similar observation (Fee, *First Epistle to the Corinthians*, 515), which is contrary to Meier, who writes, "Since woman is created later, from man, she is not the direct image of God. In fact, the image-terminology cannot be used of her at all" (Meier, "On the Veiling of Hermeneutics (1 Cor 11:2–16)," 219).

32. A term such as "glory of God" could mean "God's own glory" (a Greek construction called subjective genitive) or "glory to God" (objective genitive). I have taken it here as the objective genitive: man brings glory to God.

33. Blomberg shows an interesting parallel between the "glory" stated here and the "dishonor" or "shame" mentioned in vv. 4 and 5 (Blomberg, *1 Corinthians*, 211).

34. Since the preposition in this verse, *dia*, could mean either "for" or "through," some scholars argue Paul was referring to Eve coming *through* Adam here. But for that meaning, the construction required was *dia* plus genitive noun. Paul instead used *dia* plus accusative, which meant "for."

Adam to remain single (Gen 2:18). So the Lord God created Eve as a fitting counterpart for him. Seeing her, Adam said, "This is now bone of my bone, flesh of my flesh; she shall be called 'woman,' for out of man this she is taken out" (Gen 2:23, LXX). Man's state of "not good" was changed to "good" when Eve was made for him. That was why Paul said, "The man was not created for the woman but the woman was created for man" (1 Cor 11:9). He needed her.

This creation order – her formation from him and for him – and her oneness with her husband, as expressed in her putting on a head-covering, gave her the *right* to pray and prophesy in front of the congregation, and even before angels (1 Cor 11:10). Some scholars have understood the "authority" (which I have translated as "right") negatively, as if a covering kept her under the husband's authority: "So a woman should wear a covering on her head as a sign that she is under man's authority" (The Living Bible).[35] Others understand it positively. For example, Blomberg writes, "A wife should exercise control over her head, i.e. keep the appropriate covering on it."[36] In the New Testament, however, often the phrase "has authority" refers to *someone's power to speak or do something with certainty*. When Jesus taught, the people said, "He teaches like one who *has authority*, not like the experts in the law" (Matt 7:29). Jesus said, "You need to know that the Son of Man *has authority* to forgive sin on earth" (Matt 9:6). Jesus also said, "Fear the one who *has authority* to throw you into hell" (Luke 12:5). Likewise, the meaning in 1 Corinthians 11:10 was that a woman with her head covered while praying and prophesying was exercising her right in that she belonged to her husband (1 Cor 11:9) and she was not dishonoring him (1 Cor 11:5). So the head-covering became a woman's authority to boldly pray and prophesy.[37]

Why did Paul refer to angels in this context? Winter suggests that Paul was referring to Roman messengers (another meaning of "angel") who were spying on the church.[38] Padgett suggests that they were Paul's co-workers,

---

35. Plummer and Robertson say, "the woman has the symbol of *subjection*, a veil on her head" (Plummer and Robertson, *1 Corinthians*, 232). Translations reflect this tendency by inserting phrases like *symbol* (NET, HCSB, NRSV) and *sign* (ASV, NIV).

36. Blomberg, *1 Corinthians*, 212. Murphy-O'Connor, "The Corinth That Saint Paul Saw," 271.

37. Ekem refers to this as one of the two best options. Cf. John David K. Ekem, "Does 1 Cor 11:2-16 Legislate for 'Head Covering'?," *Neotestamentica* 35, no. 1–2 (2001): 174.

38. Bruce W. Winter, *Roman Wives, Roman Widows: The Appearance of New Women and the Pauline Communities* (Cambridge; Grand Rapids: Eerdmans, 2003), 95–97. Weber-Han connects the reference of angels to Gen 6:1–4 and says, "The woman is capable of seducing the man or having power over the man like the angels in Genesis 6:1–4" and that was why Paul wanted the women's hair to be covered (Cindy Weber-Han, "Sexual Equality According to

such as Phoebe and Priscilla.[39] But since the other references to "angels" in 1 Corinthians all refer to angelic beings (1 Cor 4:9; 6:3; 13:1), it might be best to understand Paul to be still talking about angelic beings who were curious about church orderliness (cf. 1 Pet 1:12). Whatever the meaning, the message was that when a wife covered her hair while she prayed or prophesied, she exercised her rightful authority, in front of any spectators – human or angelic. A man received authority because he was the image of God and the glory of God. A wife received authority since she was the rightful wife of her husband and, because she had covered her hair, she didn't bring dishonor upon him. Whereas man's authority came from his role as God's representative on earth, a wife's authority came from her role as partner to her husband. When a wife covered her head, then, she claimed her authority to pray and prophesy – even in front of angels.

In the Lord, however, neither was independent of the other, just as in birth neither man nor woman is independent of the other: "Nevertheless, in the Lord, a woman is not apart from man, neither a man apart from a woman – just as [in birth] a woman is from a man and a man is through a woman. And all are from God" (1 Cor 11:11–12; cf. 1 Cor 6:16–17; 7:4–5). In Christ, a man or his wife had equal status and interdependency (Gal 3:28). Similarly, in birth men and women were dependent: a female child comes from a father, and a male child comes from a mother. Ultimately, all people were from God. So Paul wasn't talking about a person's ontological worth or role in these verses; he was talking about how culturally both men and women glorify God by their orderly worship. When men did not pretend to be priests by covering their heads, and when wives did not show disrespect towards their husbands by not covering their heads in front of other men (that is, while they prayed and prophesied), they both brought glory to God.

Paul, in the next four verses (1 Cor 11:13–15), explained that this was a cultural practice that had universal application. Paul asked, "Judge for yourselves: is it fitting for a woman to pray to God uncovered?" (1 Cor 11:13). A women's long hair is a sign of beauty in any culture, ancient or modern. King Solomon described his love's hair in this way: "Your hair is like a flock of female goats descending from Mount Gilead" – probably a reference to the fullness and length of her hair (Song 4:1; 6:5); and "The locks of your hair

---

Paul: An Exegetical Study of 1 Corinthians 11:1–16 and Ephesians 5:21–33," *Brethren Life and Thought* 22, no. 3 [Summer 1977]: 169). Such an interpretation is speculative.

39. Alan Padgett, "Paul on Woman in the Church: The Contradictions of Coiffure in 1 Cor 11:2–16," *Journal for the Study of the New Testament* 20 (1984): 81–82.

are like royal tapestries; the king is held captive in its tresses" – probably a reference to its abundance and captivating attraction (Song 7:5). Likewise, tied hair or loose hair also had various connotations. Cosgrove gives the following extensive and versatile meanings of women's hair being covered or uncovered:

> When a woman wears her hair unbound/unbinds her hair, this can be a sexually suggestive act, an expression of religious devotion, a hairstyle for unmarried girls, a sign of mourning, a symbolic expression of distress or proleptic grief in the face of impending danger (and a way of pleading with or currying the favor of those in power, whether gods or men), a hairstyle associated with conjury, a means of presenting oneself in a natural state in religious initiations, and a precaution against carrying demons or foreign objects into the waters of baptism . . . In certain social situations it is right for an ancient Mediterranean woman to unbind her hair in public, to do 'the opposite' . . . of what is conventionally decorous, often (but not always) to express a state of extremity or liminality.[40]

Similarly, the Corinthians had cultural nuances that explained why, if a married woman were to pray or prophesy without her hair properly covered, she would be shaming her husband. On the other hand, if she was covering her hair, she had the authority, the right, to speak.

Paul stated a particular reason for such an emphasis on hair: ornamentation. He said, "Does not nature itself teach you that if a man has long hair it is dishonorable and if a woman has long hair it is to her glory since hair is given to her as an ornament? (1 Cor 11:14–15). Paul was not saying that nature taught that men should not have long hair. In fact, the priests and the Nazarites (people who had taken a special vow of not cutting the hair) would have had long hair. What he was saying was that long hair was not an *ornament* for men; it was a sign of disgrace or self-denial.[41] That

---

40. Charles H. Cosgrove, "A Woman's Unbound Hair in the Greco-Roman World, with Special Reference to the Story of the 'Sinful Woman' in Luke 7:36–50," *Journal of Biblical Literature* 124, no. 4 (Winter 2005): 691.

41. Murphy-O'Connor argues that the hair issue was about homosexual men (who had long hair) and lesbian women (who had short hair) (Jerome Murphy-O'Connor, "1 Corinthians 11:2–16 Once Again," *Catholic Biblical Quarterly* 50 [1988]: 269). But Thompson points out that others, such as philosophers, priests, peasants, and barbarians, also often had long hair in the Greco-Roman world (Thompson, "Hairstyles, Head-Coverings, and St Paul," 104).

was why priests and Nazarites had long hair instead of short hair: they were denying themselves for the sake of God. That being so, Jesus instructed that those who were fasting should not let their hair look unkempt so as to draw attention to themselves: "When you fast, put oil on your head and wash your face" (Matt 6:17), a teaching based on the law of Moses: "The high priest must neither dishevel the hair of his head nor tear his garments; instead [he] must have his head anointed with oil and wear the priestly garments" (Lev 21:10). In general, unkempt long hair was a sign of disgrace for men in Paul's time in Corinth.

On the other hand, for women, long hair was an ornament, a sign of beauty. Paul's words were "the hair is given to a woman *as an ornament [anti peribolaiou]*" (1 Cor 11:15). *Peribolaion* is different from the "covering" he talked about earlier (*katakaluptos*, 1 Cor 11:5, 6, 7, 13). So it is wrong to conclude that hair was a covering given to women (scholars draw such a conclusion because there were cases where *peribolaion* was used for "clothing" or "awning," e.g. Ezek 27:7).[42] Instead, it is best to translate *peribolaion* as "ornamental headwear," similar to the *keter* mentioned in Esther (1:11; 2:17; 6:8)[43] or to the purple ornamental headwear [*peribolaion*] worn by the Midianite kings (Judg 8:26), the Messiah's ornamental headwear (*peribolaion*) of deliverance (Isa 59:17), and Israel's ornamental headwear (*peribolaion*) made up of multi-colored hair and linen – possibly a hat (Ezek 16:13).[44] Paul was saying that for women, hair was an ornament, a sign of beauty (1 Cor 11:15b), and that was why women needed to cover their glory and beauty while they prayed and prophesied. Peter agreed: "Focus not on external beauty – braiding of hair, wearing of jewelry, or elaborate clothing – but on the internal and hiddenness of the heart of a person, such as imperishable gentleness and a quiet spirit – that are honorable before God" (1 Pet 3:3–4).

Although these teachings were culturally conditioned, the principle of men not dishonoring their leader-head (Christ) and the wives not dishonoring their leader-heads (their husbands) was universal, so Paul

---

Paul most likely reflected the general consensus that for men, in general, long hair was not an ornament, but for women it was.

42. To understand hair as a "covering" leads to the conclusion "cover the covering [hair]." E.g. "Just as 'nature' teaches that women should wear long hair as a head covering, so it is appropriate for women to further cover their heads according to the established custom of the day" (Blomberg, *1 Corinthians*, 213).

43. Alison Salvesen, "Keter (Esther 1:11; 2:17; 6:8): 'Something to Do with a Camel?," *Journal of Semitic Studies* 44, no. 1 (Spring 1999): 35–46.

44. Sometimes translations substitute "silk" for "wool" (goat's hair) in this verse (see NET).

concluded, "If anyone thinks to be quarrelsome on this matter, neither we nor the churches of God have any other practice" (1 Cor 11:16). In other words, orderly worship was the standard rule for every church. Sometimes cultures dictate what is acceptable and what is not. In North India, in contexts where a married woman who uncovers her face in front of her in-laws, especially her father-in-law, would shame her husband and so must wear a *ghoonghat*, she should probably therefore wear a *ghoonghat* in church at the time of praying and prophesying.

This passage does not address how unmarried women should have their hair when praying and prophesying. Since they wouldn't be shaming their husbands, for they had none, presumably they didn't have to cover their hair. They were ultimately living for God alone, as Paul had instructed earlier (1 Cor 7:25–40).

Langar (11:17–22)

Sikhism is an important religion in India. Singh writes, "The origins of the Sikh faith are traced to Guru Nānak (1469–1539) who lived historically and geographically between the Hindu and Islamic traditions . . . The Gurus who succeeded him added their own contributions and the Guru Granth reached its final form on October 6, 1708. Guru Gobind Singh, the tenth and the last Guru, apotheosized the Granth and passed the succession of guruship to the Holy Book itself in perpetuity. It thus became the sole visual and aural icon of the Sikh religion. From that time on, the Guru Granth has provided the Sikhs with guidance and solace."[45] Sikhism is the fifth-largest organized religion in the world, with nearly thirty million followers.

The Sikhs gather in gurdwara to worship. "Gurdwara" literally means "the gateway to the *guru*." One unique feature of Sikhism, celebrated in every gurdwara, is *langar*. *Langar* is a term used for the common kitchen or canteen where food is served to all visitors for free. The meal is distributed without discrimination of race, gender, caste, or religion. It is usually a pure vegetarian meal to ensure that all people can eat as equals, without dietary or religious restrictions. There are variations of *langar* in which meat is served (e.g. Hazur Sahib).

---

45. Nikky-Guninder Kaur Singh, "The Sikh Bridal Symbol: An Epiphany of Interconnections," *Journal of Feminist Studies in Religion* 8, no. 2 (Fall 1992): 43–44.

The Corinthian Christians also had a special meal, called the Lord's Supper. It was open to all who gathered in the church. It usually consisted of bread and wine. It was to remember the Lord Jesus Christ, who instituted it on the night he was betrayed. He transformed the commonly practiced Passover meal of the Jews into a specific supper at which his death was to be remembered until his return (Matt 26:26–29; Mark 14:22–25; Luke 22:15–20). Therefore, when the disciples ate the bread, they remembered Christ's torn body on the cross. When they drank the wine, they remembered his shed blood. It became a tradition from the earliest formation of the church in Jerusalem and continued even in Corinth.

The Corinthians, however, misunderstood the supper's significance and celebrated it simply as a pagan festival, where some got drunk and overfed while others were left hungry and thirsty. Paul addressed this issue next. Unlike earlier, where he commended them for having remembered his teachings and faithfully kept them (1 Cor 11:1), he couldn't commend them on this particular practice (1 Cor 11:17a). In fact, their time of gathering to participate in the Lord's Supper had become a disaster (1 Cor 11:17b). That was why Paul addressed it here.

One reason for the abuse of the Lord's Supper was divisions within the church (1 Cor 11:18). This "division" was different from the one Chloe had reported (chs. 1–4) since it didn't include "quarrels" and "jealousy." Most likely, this division was based on the poverty and wealth line at mealtime. Schottroff explains a possible scenario:

> In keeping with Hellenistic-Roman custom, people bring their own food for the meal. However, there exist wide social distinctions in the community (cf. 1 Cor. 1.26), and those who are well off have better food and other customs at table than the hired workers and slaves. The rich do indeed understand themselves as part of the community, and they come to its assembly, but on the whole they separate themselves from the others and eat what they have brought as a private meal (11:21, 23). They show no consideration for those who are worse off, who cannot bring much, and whose food is also of poorer quality. This results in inequality: some go hungry, while others are drunk (11:21, 22).[46]

---

46. Luise Schottroff, "Holiness and Justice: Exegetical Comments on 1 Corinthians 11.17–34," *Journal for the Study of the New Testament* 79 (2000): 55. See also Fee, *First Epistle to the Corinthians*, 537.

The famine that occurred in Corinth at this time could have contributed to this division of rich and poor.[47] Paul objected to such division and misbehavior at the Lord's Supper.

Before he continued, Paul answered a key cultural question: were Christians to be uniform? Could there not be differences in their wealth status? Paul's answer was that certain divisions were acceptable. He called this good division a "discerning" division (Greek *aireseis*). This good division was opposite to divisions based on leaders, castes, or people groups (for such bad divisions Paul had used another Greek term in chs. 1–4, *schismata*). So Paul wrote, "It is necessary to have *discerning* [*aireseis*] among yourselves so that those who are of repute might be honored" (1 Cor 11:19). In other words, improper divisions (*schismata*) were wrong, but good divisions – discernments (*aireseis*) that separated honorable people from dishonorable people – were necessary. This honor wasn't based on their birth but on their behavior in church gatherings. The Corinthians lacked such good discernment and tolerated, for example, a man living with his father's wife (ch. 5) or visiting of prostitutes (ch. 6). The Corinthians therefore needed *discerning division* (*aireseis*) so that they could deal with sin. However, dividing over who ate the Lord's Supper according to the wealth–poverty line was not appropriate or acceptable.

When such an inappropriate division occurred in the church, especially at the Lord's Supper, it was shameful: "Your gathering at the same location was not for eating the Lord's meal" (1 Cor 11:20). It appeared as if they were fellowshipping, but in reality they were gathering to flaunt their wealth or disgrace the poor: "Each one eats his or her own meal; as a result, some are hungry and others are drunk" (1 Cor 11:21). The wealthy and their friends ate and drank plenty and as a result got drunk; the poor and their friends ate nothing and remained hungry – all in the same room and within the same house church. This was disgraceful! They could have done this in their own homes; why come to the church to behave in this way? So Paul asked, "Do you not have your own houses in which to eat and drink? Do you despise the church of God? And do you wish to shame those who have nothing to eat? [Were these the reasons why you come and flaunt your wealth?]" (1 Cor 11:22a). If rich people wanted to eat plenty of food and drink plenty of wine, couldn't they do it in their own homes? Why were they doing it in the congregation, shaming those who had nothing to eat? This was not

47. Blue, "The House Church at Corinth," 239.

like the *langar* meal, where everyone eats the same food, or the behavior of the early Christians in Jerusalem, who were one in heart and mind and had all their possession in common (Acts 4:32). The Corinthians' behavior was not gracious or driven by love, so Paul could not be proud of them. He said, "What can I say to you – that I praise you for such acts? I have no praise for such a demonstration" (1 Cor 11:22b). Their flaunting of wealth or suffering from lack of food at the Lord's Supper was a disgrace, and Paul would not praise them for their appalling behavior.

In rich cultures, there is an abundance of food, material goods, and wealth, and those in such cultures are not expected to share their wealth with those around them. In simple agricultural cultures, however, the sharing of *limited* goods is valued and the rich are expected to share their wealth with the poor. In Nagaland, India, among tribal cultures, such customs are still practiced today: the rich in the village buy many pigs for the Christmas dinner, and the whole village benefits from such hospitality. The Jewish world had such a culture; thus the poor man, Lazarus, at the gates of the wealthy man longed for the food left over from the rich man's banquets, and the rich man was judged for not sharing his wealth with Lazarus (Luke 16:19–31). Corinth was also such an agricultural world, where the rich were expected to share their wealth with the poor. Yet the rich Christians were eating and drinking at the Lord's Supper without sharing with the poor, who were going hungry and thirsty. Such a gathering was nothing to be proud of; instead, it was shameful that they even gathered together. After pointing out their error, Paul set out to explain the true meaning of the Lord's Supper.

Often we too forget to care for the poor as we celebrate the Lord's Supper. Our celebrations are not feasts; they are mere representations. Yet the principle remains the same: do we have divisions over caste, creed, race, color, and gender at the Lord's Supper? If so, we haven't understood the basic meaning of celebrating the Lord's Supper, and the Lord himself would be ashamed of our gatherings.

The Lord's Supper (11:23–26)

Celebrating the Lord's Supper, which was eating the bread and drinking the wine in remembrance of the Lord, was a key event in the early church. The Lord Jesus established this tradition in the midst of his twelve disciples on the night he was betrayed. His disciples passed on that tradition to other Christians. The Corinthians seemed to have understood the significance of this supper and celebrated it – but wrongly. So Paul wanted to pass on the tradition to them again. Paul received this tradition either by a special revelation or from the writings that recorded the words of the Lord.[48] Regardless, he wanted to pass on the essentials to the Corinthians: "What I received from the Lord, I hand over to you" (1 Cor 11:23a).

"The Lord Jesus, on that night when he was betrayed, took bread, and having blessed it he broke it, and said, 'This is my body for you. Do this in remembrance of me.' Likewise also, [he took] the cup along with the meal, saying, 'This cup is the new covenant in my blood. Drink this often in remembrance of me'" (1 Cor 11:23b–25). This event was narrated in the three Synoptic Gospels, Matthew, Mark, and Luke (Matt 26:26–28; Mark 14:22–24; Luke 22:19–20). Although each Gospel writer differed slightly, they all included these basic elements: the bread was eaten in remembrance of the Lord's body that was crucified, and the wine was drunk in remembrance of the Lord's shed blood. The key concept was remembrance: it was for the disciples to remember the Lord's action of laying down his life for them.[49] That was why they were often to repeat it – so as not to forget. That was the instruction that the Lord God gave the Israelites about the Passover meal: they were to repeat it every year so as not to forget God's provision in the past. The Corinthians weren't to forget the Lord Jesus' body that was torn and the blood that was shed for their benefit.

That cup established the new covenant between God and his people (Luke 22:20; 1 Cor 11:25). The prophets Jeremiah and Ezekiel had talked about God establishing a new covenant with his people in which he would forgive their sins and live with them forever, and it was the Lord Jesus' blood that established that new covenant. Therefore, the Lord's Supper was more than a mere remembrance of his death; it was a remembrance of the establishment of the new covenant.

In addition to remembrance, it was also a time of anticipation. The Lord Jesus' death was temporary. He was resurrected on the third day, ministered among his disciples for forty more days, and then ascended to the right hand of God with the assurance that he would come back again. Therefore,

---

48. Evanson argues for a special revelation, whereas Fee argues for Paul having learned it from written documents (George O. Evenson, "Force of *Apo* in 1 Corinthians 11:23," *Lutheran Quarterly* 11, no. 3 [1959]: 244–246; Fee, *First Epistle to the Corinthians*, 548).

49. A missionary in North India pointed out that the structure in the Greek could also imply that this meal was done as a reminder to the LORD God of the sacrifice made, just as the Passover lamb's blood on the doorposts was a reminder to the LORD not to destroy those within the house.

every time the disciples or the Corinthians celebrated the Lord's Supper, they demonstrated that they were patiently awaiting his return. So Paul wrote, "As often as you eat this bread and drink this cup you proclaim the death of the Lord until he comes" (1 Cor 11:26).

Therefore, because of its theological significance, the Lord's Supper was a sacred time of remembrance and anticipation. That was to be its focus, as Gaventa explains:

> The community's celebration of the Lord's Supper is not a time for rejoicing in one's salvation. Instead, the celebration of the Lord's Supper proclaims the death of Jesus and waits his return . . . We often go with our own contemporary concerns and questions . . . What constitutes the right observance of the Lord's Supper? Who should be included at the table and who excluded from it? Is the Lord's Supper to be understood as a sacrifice or as a memorial meal? As significant as these questions are, our own preoccupation with them may prevent us from hearing Paul . . . His question is whether the celebration actually proclaims the death of the Lord or whether it proclaims simply the standards and values of the larger society.[50]

The focus must be on the Lord's death (the body broken on the cross and the shed blood), his resurrection, and his imminent return.

Yama and Judgment (11:27–34)

Yama is the god of death and judgment in Hinduism. Nichols writes,

> Initially, Yama was a very minor figure in the Vedic pantheon, serving as a once mortal figure who became king of the dead and overseer of the realm of the patriarchal ancestors . . . With the development of epic and *purānic* thought and literature, the myths of Yama absorbed other figures such as Mrtyu and Kāla, becoming a more frightful representation of death. Indeed even in the Brāhmana text onward, Yama is said to employ snares and a host of terrifying servants (called *yamadutas*) to capture and carry the dead to his realm. By the time of the *Parānas*, this

---

50. Beverly Roberts Gaventa, "'You Proclaim the Lord's Death': 1 Corinthians 11:26 and Paul's Understanding of Worship," *Review & Expositor* 80, no. 3 (Summer 1983): 385.

trope is well-established and one finds . . . lengthy descriptions of how these awful beings bind . . . and carry them away to the realm of Yama, where the god himself appears, "with very red eyes, looking like a mass of ground collyrium," bearing a "gaping mouth full of frightful fangs" . . . [He] bears the staff of judgment (*danda*), and constantly observes the behavior of all humans, duly administering rewards or punishments . . . At heart, the mythical figure of Yama in Hinduism eventually becomes an ambiguous signifier of death: fearsome and remorseless, but conquerable through proper behavior and religious practice.[51]

Yama judges a person based upon whether or not he or she has closely observed caste duties and performed good deeds. Those who perform their duties properly in this life and do good deeds will be incarnated into a higher caste, spending a short period of time between incarnations in bliss and in heaven. Those who don't perform their caste duties properly and don't do good deeds will incarnate into lower castes or lower life forms (such as animals). Some will even go to *naraka*, the equivalent of a hell. They will also endure various tortures between incarnations.

Christianity also has concepts of hell and judgment. But in 1 Corinthians Paul referred to physical judgments believers would endure because of their sins. He had already condemned the man who was cohabiting with his father's wife and called for him to be handed over to Satan for the destruction of his physical body (1 Cor 5:5). In this passage, he explained that a similar fate had come upon those who misused the Lord's Supper (1 Cor 11:29–30).

As stated above, the celebration of the Lord's Supper was a reverential and sacred occasion to remember the Lord's death and resurrection, and to anticipate his return. The Corinthians, however, were treating it irreverently – exalting wealth divisions between the rich and the poor (1 Cor 11:17–22). So Paul outlined the core elements of celebrating the Lord's Supper (1 Cor 11:23–25). Because of its reverence, Paul continued, "Anyone who eats the bread and drinks the cup of the Lord unworthily is guilty of the body and the blood of the Lord" (1 Cor 11:27). What was this unworthiness? Hays writes, "Paul's words must be understood in the context of the specific situation that he is addressing: The more affluent Christians were consuming their own

---

51. Michael David Nichols, "Dialogues with Death: Māra, Yama, and Coming to Terms with Mortality in Classical Hindu and Indian Buddhist Traditions," *Religions of South Asia* 6, no. 1 (June 2012): 14–15. See also Lynn Thomas, "The Identity of the Destroyer in the Mahābhārata," *Numen* 41, no. 3 (September 1994): 255–272.

food and shaming the poorer members (vv. 20–22). In this context, to eat the meal unworthily means to eat it in a way that provokes division (v. 18), with contemptuous disregard for the needs of others in the community."[52] When a Christian, then, provoked division and had contemptuous disregard for other Christians, especially at the Lord's Supper, Paul saw that Christian as "guilty of the body and blood of the Lord." In other words, he or she was guilty of crucifying the Lord, just as the Roman soldiers and religious leaders – who actually killed the Lord – were guilty. That was the seriousness of their misbehavior at the Lord's Supper. So they needed to examine themselves as they participated in the Lord's Supper (1 Cor 11:28). This self-examination either meant asking oneself whether one was eating or drinking the Lord's Supper without "thought of the body [of Christ, the church]" (1 Cor 11:29) or was, as Hays says, "a straightforward call to consider how their actions at the supper [were] affecting brothers and sisters in the church, the body of Christ."[53]

Their participation without careful examination caused them harm. Paul wrote, "On account of this, many became liable to weakness, sickness, and death" (1 Cor 11:30). The majority of scholars understand some of the Corinthian Christians to have been physically weak, sick, and even to have died because of their unworthy participation in the Lord's Supper.[54] Thiselton argues that, since Paul "earlier actually mentions *drunkenness* (11:21), it is just conceivable that a serious decline in health could result causally from excess in gluttony and drink."[55] Others, especially Ramelli and Schneider, have argued that the weakness, sickness, and death that Paul referred to were *spiritual* in nature.[56] (One should not thus conclude that all sicknesses are divine punishment, as the Lord himself warned, John 11:4.) Thiselton's view is to be preferred: they had self-inflicted heath problems from their over-eating and over-drinking. However, regardless of whether they many among them were physically or spiritually sick, weak, and dead, they needed to act

---

52. Hays, *First Corinthians*, 200.

53. Ibid.

54. Blomberg, *1 Corinthians*, 231; Fee, *First Epistle to the Corinthians*, 565; Witherington III, *Conflict and Community in Corinth*, 252.

55. Thiselton, *First Epistle to the Corinthians*, 256.

56. Ilaria L. E. Ramelli, "Spiritual Weakness, Illness, and Death in 1 Corinthians 11:30," *Journal of Biblical Literature* 130, no. 1 (Spring 2011): 145–163. Schneider points out that if "some are dead" referred to the physically dead, the phrase "among you" would be awkward, and so argues for a spiritual death (Sebastian Schneider, "Glaubensmängel in Korinth. Eine Neue Deutung Der 'Schwachen, Kranken, Schlafenden' in 1 Kor 11:30," *Filología Neotestamentaria* 9 [1996]: 3–20).

quickly. Paul wrote, "If we examine ourselves, we will not be judged" (1 Cor 11:31). Likewise, the intention of the punishment was disciplinary: "When we are judged by the Lord, it is disciplinary so that we may not be judged along with the world" (1 Cor 11:32). Orr and Walther write, "The judgment is of the nature of *discipline*, not of final condemnation. Condemnation has been removed by the death of Christ, but selfish and sinful perversion of the supper produces damaging results that may serve as corrective influence toward repentance."[57] It was better for the Corinthians to avoid any judgment from the Lord. However, if they endured judgment, even that was meant for their betterment; it was discipline from the Lord because he loved them.

Paul then urged them towards avoiding the judgment altogether and proposed specific guidelines: "My brothers and sisters, when you come to eat together [to celebrate the Lord's Supper], wait for one another" (1 Cor 11:33).[58] In other words, they shouldn't hastily unpack their meals and eat before the rest of the congregation arrived. They should wait for one another. In addition, "If someone was hungry" and couldn't wait until all had arrived, "let him [or her] eat at home. And this way one will not bring judgment on oneself" (1 Cor 11:34a). In the first half of these verses, Paul addressed the rich: when they came with their food, they needed to wait for everyone to arrive; they shouldn't be selfish and feed themselves alone. In the second half, he addressed the poor: they shouldn't come to the Lord's Supper expecting someone to feed them good food. Instead, they should eat what little they had at home before coming to the Lord's Supper so that they wouldn't expect the rich to feed them and wouldn't get upset if the rich didn't provide for them. In this way, divisions caused by their self-centered desires would be avoided. Each group should be concerned about the other. That was the purpose of participating in the Lord's Supper: it was a time to remember the Lord and to love one another.

Paul concluded this section with a note that he would continue further discussion on this matter when he visited them (1 Cor 11:34b). Paul knew that the Corinthians would have more questions and that he would visit them, so at that time, he would give them further clarifications.

---

57. Orr and Walther, *1 Corinthians*, 274.

58. For an excellent article on the *communal* nature of the Lord's Supper, pictured in the African tribal meals, see J. Ayodeji Adewuya, "Revisited 1 Corinthians 11.27-34: Paul's Discussion of the Lord's Supper and African Meals," *Journal for the Study of the New Testament* 30, no. 1 (2007): 95–112.

Typically in India (as in many other places), the Lord's Supper is treated as a miniature remembrance act (with small pieces of broken bread and drops of grape juice), reserved for the "inner" circle, true believers. But if Christians practiced it as did the early churches, and had a big feast to which even non-Christian are invited, it would give an opportunity for those non-Christians to hear about the death, burial, resurrection, judgment, and the coming again of the Lord Jesus Christ. Through this they might even be drawn to salvation.[59] The message of salvation would be magnified if the non-Christians also saw oneness and unity among Christians as they gather to celebrate the Lord's Supper. The Lord's Supper, properly practiced, could then become a point of attraction for non-Christians.[60]

---

59. Some argue that non-Christians should not participate in the Lord's Supper (Blomberg, *1 Corinthians*, 218). If so, still, they could be invited to a fellowship meal where they mingle with Christians and then witness the special celebration of the Lord's Supper in an orderly fashion, so that they are drawn to the gospel. Tartanic argues for a similar practice (Martha Smith Tatarnic, "Whoever Comes to Me: Open Table, Missional Church, and the Body of Christ," *Anglican Theological Review* 96, no. 2 [Spring 2014]: 287–304).

60. Athyal points out that the message of unity in Christ can be easily spread when Christian communities learn to unite at the Lord's Supper (Leelamma Athyal, "India: The Joint Council of the Church of North India [CNI], Church of South India [CSI], and the Malankara Mar Thoma Syrian Church [MTC]," *The Ecumenical Review* 52, no. 1 [January 2000]: 19).

14

1 Corinthians 12

Connections

In the last four chapters (chs. 8–11) Paul has addressed issues related to purity and reverence under the overall topic of "food offered to idols." The Corinthian Christians could not enter a pagan temple to participate in their festival suppers, but they could eat meat sold in the marketplace or given to them by non-Christian friends (ch. 8). They needed to learn to restrict the enjoyment of their freedom for the sake of others so as not to reap punishment, as the Israelites of old did, but should instead spread the gospel to everyone (chs. 9–10). They shouldn't give the impression of priesthood or be culturally insensitive at the time of prayer and prophesying. Above all, they were to properly observe the Lord's Supper, with unity and oneness of mind as they remembered the Lord's death, burial, resurrection, ascension to the Father, and return (ch. 11). That was the third "and concerning . . ." topic.

In this section (1 Cor 12 – 15) Paul explained spiritual matters such as the gifts that they had received from the Spirit for the common benefit of the church, the proper use of those gifts, the role of love in using those spiritual gifts, and the ultimate gift of resurrection.[1] This is the fourth "and concerning . . ." topic.

---

1. For an excellent article on the unity of chapters 12–14, see James Patrick, "Insights from Cicero on Paul's Reasoning in 1 Corinthians 12-14: Love Sandwich or Five Course Meal?," *Tyndale Bulletin* 55, no. 1 (2004): 43–64.

Curses (12:1–3)

Curses are common in every culture. They are common in Indian mythology too.[2] Some say that fifty-one curses are recorded in the Hindu scriptures (such as the curse of Rama [a god] by Tara [a goddess], and the curse of Hanuman [a god] by the sages).[3] Curses are uttered by opponents, and usually in anger and rejection. The Corinthians too had a curse: "Cursed be Jesus" (1 Cor 12:3). Those with the Spirit of God couldn't utter that curse, so Paul talked about it first before addressing other spiritual matters (1 Cor 12:1).

That curse ("Cursed be Jesus") was part of the Corinthians' earlier lifestyle of worshipping other speech-less gods: "You know that when you were mere people of the nations you were leading yourselves to speech-less idols as followers" (1 Cor 12:2). Paul's audience included both Jews and Gentiles,[4] yet he addressed both groups as "people of the nations" (ethnos). In the Old Testament, when the Israelites didn't worship God properly they were addressed as "nations" (Jer 10:5; Hab 2:18–19). Whether they were Gentiles worshipping idol-gods or Jews who didn't worship the Lord Jesus, they were asserting the same belief: "Jesus is cursed." Then he mentioned that they were, by their own actions, following idols that couldn't speak – the Gentiles through nature and the Jews through ignorance (as Paul himself had done).[5] Such people couldn't possibly say, "Jesus is Lord"; all they could utter was, "Jesus is cursed." Scholars have proposed three prominent theories as to "who" would have uttered such a curse: (a) a Christian in the Corinthian church might have said this curse (an unlikely possibility because Paul would have vehemently opposed such a person); (b) a person under demonic influence would have uttered this curse (but nothing in the context says anything about demons or Satan); or (c) it is a hypothetical utterance,

---

2. For curses and magic in biblical times, see Edwin M. Yamauchi, "Magic in the Biblical World," *Tyndale Bulletin* 34 (1983): 169–200.

3. Shiva Purana, a scripture dedicated to Shiva, records another interesting curse that might explain why Brahma is not worshipped in temples in India; see Madhuri Guin, "Brahma the Creator Amongst the Hindu Trinity," *DollsofIndia* (2004): 6.

4. For an excellent article that argues that the early church was a combination of Jews and Gentiles, see David Seccombe, "The New People of God," in *Witness to the Gospel: The Theology of Acts*, eds. I. Howard Marshall and David Peterson (Grand Rapids: Eerdmans, 1998), 349–372.

5. Paul used the middle voice (where the action is done by the subject upon itself) to illustrate that the Corinthians themselves were leading themselves to idolatry.

reflective of the Corinthians' past, when they thought of Jesus as a cursed name.[6] The last option is to be preferred.

In other words, merely by their non-Christian living they were expressing the belief "Jesus is cursed." The Gentiles would have thought that Jesus was a criminal who was hanged on a tree for his punishment. To worship him as divine was foolish if in fact he was a cursed man, a traitor. The Jews also would have considered him to be under the curse of God because Jesus was hanged on a tree – a cursed death according to the law of Moses (Gal 3:13; Deut 21:23). So to both groups, before salvation, Jesus was a cursed man, and consciously or unconsciously they would have expressed that view. In contrast, only those who were indwelt by the Holy Spirit of God could say, "Jesus is Lord" (1 Cor 12:3). This confession meant *allegiance*. To the Jews, there was only one God: LORD God was his name. To the Gentiles, there were many gods and lords, including Caesar. To confess "Jesus *is the* Lord" was therefore a significant statement of allegiance both for the Jews and for the Gentiles.[7] A person could utter that confession only by the indwelling of the Holy Spirit. And it was only such Spirit-indwelt people who could understand the rest of Paul's teachings on Spirit matters.

In a way, every non-Christian is living a lifestyle that reflects the basic belief that Jesus was a cursed person. He was under the Roman government's wrath or God's wrath, so he couldn't be the Savior, they think. Only when the Holy Spirit opens their spiritual eyes do they realize that he is Lord and they confess, "Jesus is Lord."

Dana or Gifts (12:4–11)

Although hospitality is highly valued in India, giving gifts to people is not that high a priority, even though giving gifts to gods and taking care of beggars is. Even on birthdays, it is those with the birthdays who give sweets to others. They themselves do not receive gifts. This hesitancy in giving gifts might have

---

6. Bruce, *1 and 2 Corinthians*, 118; Fee, *First Epistle to the Corinthians*, 579–581.

7. Paul required a similar confession of the Christians in Rome (Rom 10:9). In that context, Wright says, "First, in Paul's world 'Lord' was a title for Caesar. Saying Jesus was 'Lord' meant, ultimately, that Caesar wasn't. Secondly, when Paul quotes from the prophet Joel in verse 13, 'Lord' in that passage refers of course to the 'Lord' of the Old Testament, YHWH, Israel's God. As in several other places . . . Paul is quite clear that Jesus the Messiah, who died and rose again, was the personal embodiment of Israel's God, coming at last to do what he had always promised" (Tom Wright, *Romans Part 2: Chapters 9–16*, Paul for Everyone [London: SPCK, 2004], 33).

arisen from Hinduism that has strict codes for giving and receiving gifts. The manual on man (*Manusmrti*) sets out these guidelines, which include the following. A Brahman shouldn't get accustomed to receiving gifts because it might diminish and eventually extinguish his or her Vedic energy (spiritual power) (4.186–94). Only the Brahmans (the learned in the Vedas, the Hindu scriptures) are able to guide ordinary people on proper giving and receiving. If an unlearned person gives or receives gifs improperly, the gifts will turn to ashes, like a piece of burned wood. It is important that there is mutual respect between the giver and the receiver for a gift to last and for them to receive reward (4.235). Before a person accepts a gift, he or she must tirelessly give sacrifices and offerings to deities (4.226–28). Because of all these guidelines engrained in the culture, gifts are not often exchanged. The influence of other cultures is changing contemporary India, such that people are beginning to give and receive gifts on birthdays, Valentine's Day, and even Christmas.

The Corinthians received special gifts that became a hindrance to them because of their culture. They received gifts from the Holy Spirit that gave some of them "special" abilities (such as performing miracles or speaking in other languages), whereas others received "ordinary" abilities (such as helping or serving others). Those who received special abilities boasted about the gifts and undermined others with ordinary abilities. So Paul instructed them about the gifts from the Holy Spirit – their nature, purpose, and proper use.

God had ordained that special gifts, ministries, and empowerments would be part of Christian living: "There are diversities of gifts but by the same Spirit, and there are diversities of ministries but by the same Lord, and there are diversities of empowerments but by the same God who works all things in everyone" (1 Cor 12:4–6). In these three short verses Paul explained that God, the Lord, and the Spirit – the three persons of the Godhead, the Holy Trinity – were instrumental in equipping the Christians with gifts, ministries, and empowerments.[8] Paul's primary topic in chapters 12 and 14 is the "gifts" (*charismata*) of the Holy Spirit. "Gifts" referred to the special abilities given by the Holy Spirit to prophesy or speak in another language, for example. There were also "ministries" or "services" (*diakonos*) and the Lord

---

8. The doctrine of the Trinity basically affirms that there is only one God (Deut 6:4), but, in an unexplainable manner, God exists in three distinct but co-equal and co-eternal persons: the Father, the Son, and the Holy Spirit. This doctrine is implicit throughout the New Testament and this verse is one such example. Some of the other passages are: Luke 10:21; John 14:26; 15:26; 16:15; Rom 1:9; 8:15; 15:30; 1 Cor 12:3; 2 Cor 13:13; 2 Thess 2:13; Gal 4:6; Eph 1:3–14; Heb 10:29; and 1 Pet 1:2, 22.

Jesus was in charge of appointing people to such tasks. Stephen and Philip, for example, were appointed to *diakonos* or to servant tasks: they made sure that widows in the church were fed (Acts 6:1–6). Then there were people with special "empowerments" (*energema*), possibly the apostles, whom God enabled and appointed. The core message, however, was that, although there was a diversity of gifts, ministries, and empowerments, there was absolute oneness in the giver – *one* Spirit, *one* Lord, *one* God.

Further, every Christian was endowed with at least one gift: "The manifestation of the Spirit is given to each one for bringing all together as one" (1 Cor 12:7). Therefore, no Christian could say that he or she was without a gift of the Holy Spirit and therefore couldn't perform his or her rightful role in the church.

Paul then described the different gifts that Christians could have: "To one indeed through the same Spirit is given a word of knowledge, to another, a word of understanding by the same Spirit, to another, faith by the same Spirit, to another, gifts of healings by one and the same Spirit, to another, powerful workings, to another, prophesying, to another, differentiating the spirits, to another, genuses of languages, and to another, interpretation of languages" (1 Cor 12:8–10). The key elements are the *diversity* of the gifts, the *diversity* in who receives which gift, yet the *oneness* of the Spirit who gifts them these different gifts. The gift of the "word of wisdom" most likely meant "the gift to understand the gospel message of the crucified Christ" (cf. 1 Cor 2:6–9). When he mentioned the gift of the "word of knowledge" earlier (1 Cor 1:5) he sandwiched it between "the grace of God has been given to you" and "testimony of Christ has been confirmed among you," so it most likely meant "a proper understanding of God's grace shown in Christ."

The gift of "faith" was more than faith to believe the gospel message, but similar to a faith that can move mountains (Matt 17:20; 1 Cor 13:2).[9] The gift of "healings," plural, meant "the ability to heal various illnesses" (such as giving sight to the blind, enabling the deaf to hear, etc.). The gift of "powerful workings" referred to wondrous signs in the heavens and on earth, such as the Lord calming the storm.

The gift of "prophesying" referred to the ability to predict the future by the power of the Holy Spirit (e.g. Agabus predicting famine, Acts 11:28). There were several prophets in New Testament times: Agabus (Acts 11:28; 21:10),

---

9. Faith is elsewhere also listed as a gift (Rom 12:3, 6; 1 Cor 13:2; Eph 2:8; 6:23; 1 Tim 4:12; 6:11) or a fruit of the Spirit (Gal 5:22).

Barnabas, Simeon, Lucius, Manaen, and Paul (Acts 13:1 [some of them might have been "teachers," as the verse says "prophets and teachers"]), Philip's four daughters (Acts 21:9), Timothy (1 Tim. 4:14), and unnamed prophets from Jerusalem (Acts 11:27). God inspired true prophets (2 Pet 1:20–21).[10] The gifts of "differentiating the spirits" referred to both authenticating the prophecies proclaimed and authenticating the prophets themselves.[11]

The gift of "genuses of languages" has been highly debated. At the very least it referred to speaking in a foreign language (known as *xenoglossy*).[12] At most it referred to speaking a divine communication or in a divine language (known as *glossolalia*). Phillips describes how one practices *glossolalia*: "Glossolalia begins simply through opening one's mouth and uttering verbal worship toward God, typically in an upward stance and gaze, as if facing God. As energy increases one's hands are raised, and the utterances of praise, once intelligible to the speaker and listener, become unintelligible. In this moment, the divine language arrives – a moment when, the believer reports, God both speaks through the speaker and to the speaker."[13] Regardless of whether scholars think that *xenoglossy* or *glossolalia* was meant, they consider it to be speaking in a language (whether intelligible to others or intelligible only to God). As such, this gift referred to different kinds (genuses) of languages. Paul would later instruct that if the language didn't communicate meaning to those around, the speaker should be quiet in church and speak to him- or herself only and to God (1 Cor 14:28), implying that it was a language that was foreign to the hearers (whether earthly or heavenly). The gift of

---

10. Later Paul would outline the validity and function of prophets (1 Cor 14).

11. Walvoord argues for authenticating the prophets (John F. Walvoord, "The Holy Spirit and Spiritual Gifts," *Bibliotheca Sacra* 143, no. 570 [April–June 1986]: 121). Fee argues for authenticating the prophecies (Fee, *First Epistle to the Corinthians*, 597). Most likely both are included, since there are explicit passages that argue for examining the prophecies (1 Cor 14:29; 1 Thess 5:20–21) and explicit passages that argue for examining the prophets (1 Cor 14:29; 2 Pet 2:1).

12. Edward A. Engelbrecht, "'To Speak in a Tongue': The Old Testament and Early Rabbinic Background of a Pauline Expression," *Concordia Journal* 22, no. 3 (July 1996): 302.

13. Holly Phillips, "Glossolalia in the United Pentecostal Church International: Language as a Relationship," *Council of Societies for the Study of Religion Bulletin* 37, no. 3 (Spring 2008): 65. Goodman compares four different people groups that speak in *glossolalia* and concludes that "glossolalia is an artifact of the trance" and it is genuine (Felicitas D. Goodman, "Phonetic Analysis of Glossolalia in Four Cultural Settings," *Journal for the Scientific Study of Religion* 8, no. 2 [Fall 1969]: 227–239). Ferguson examines the linguistic and neurological studies on glossolalia and concludes: "while it was not a normal human language, it does have language-like features. It functions in the brain in a different way to normal human languages and so appears to be a unique event" (Neil Ferguson, "Separating Speaking in Tongues from Glossolalia Using a Sacramental View," *Colloquium* 43, no. 1 [May 2011]: 56).

"interpretation of languages" was the ability to interpret teachings spoken in another language (intelligible or unintelligible); this gift was needed because the gift of genuses of languages was present in the church.

Although these gifts were diverse and distributed widely among the church members, one person – the Holy Spirit – orchestrated it all: "All these gifts work according to the one and the same Spirit who distributes them to each one just as he wishes" (1 Cor 12:11). That was the key lesson: the divine distributor and conductor distributed these gifts to every individual Christian within a congregation and conducted (orchestrated) their cooperative working according to his wishes. Thus these were not gifts to possess or to take pride in; instead, these were the Holy Spirit's gifts to individual Christians, as he wished, to be used for the common benefit of the whole church (cf. 1 Cor 12:7).

Ayurveda and Health (12:12–31)

Ayurveda, which is native to India, is more than a system of medicine. Kakar and Kakar write, "Ayurveda comprises the Indian notions of the constituents of the person and the nature of the body's connection with the psyche, the polis, the natural environment and the cosmos. These ideas constitute a cultural prism through which men and women in India have traditionally viewed the person and his or her state of well-being."[14] A person's health is based on his or her connection to the body, the soul, and the environment – the *tridosha* principle of Ayurveda.[15] Kakar and Kakar describe a situation involving Ramnath, a fifty-one-year-old shopkeeper in Delhi who suffered a mysterious illness including weight loss. Having tried different medications he approached the Kakars for psychotherapy. After hearing his story, the Kakars concluded,

> At first glance, Ramnath's cognitive space in matters of illness and well-being seems incredibly cluttered. Gods and spirits, community and family, food and drink, personal habits and character, all seem to be involved in the maintenance of health. Yet these and other factors such as biological infection, social pollution and cosmic displeasure, all of which Indians would also

---

14. Kakar and Kakar, *The Indians*, 109.
15. Michel Danino, *Indian Culture and India's Future* (New Delhi, India: D. K. Printworld Limited, 2011), 66.

acknowledge as curses of ill health, only point to the recognition of a person's simultaneous existence in many different orders of being. To use Western categories, from the first birth cry to the last breath, an individual exists equally in a *soma*, a *psyche*, and a *polis*; in other words, a person is simultaneously a body, the self, and a social being.[16]

This is why in India, as soon as a person says "I have a cold," the response is, "It's because of the change in the weather." A Westerner may be puzzled because he or she attributes the cold to microorganisms such as a bacteria or virus; the Indian attributes it to meteorological changes. Fundamentally, though, the message is the same: the body is easily affected by external changes (microorganisms or the weather).

Paul used the imagery of a body to illustrate how the Spirit's gifts affect the health of a congregation. The purpose of the Spirit's gifts was to promote the health of the body of Christ (1 Cor 12:7). In Corinth, however, that purpose was not achieved; instead, enmity between body parts occurred because there was misuse of the Spirit's gifts.

So Paul talked of the plurality of body parts that form a single unit, the body. Paul said, "Just as a body is a single unit but has many body parts, and the many parts of the body are not considered 'the body,' so also [is] Christ" (1 Cor 12:12). A body has many parts (ears, eyes, nose, hands, feet, etc.); but the individual body parts are not considered to be the whole body; only together do the body parts form the single unit, the body. The same was true of Christ's physical body and also of Christ's metaphorical body, the church (1 Cor 12:27). Paul expanded: "All of us are baptized [i.e. grouped together] into one body by one Spirit – whether we are Jews or Gentiles, slaves or free – all are made to drink [commune in] one Spirit" (1 Cor 12:13). Paul used two images: "baptized," meaning "grouped into" (in the same way that all the Israelites were *grouped* into one group under Moses, 1 Cor 10:2); and "made to drink," meaning "commune in" (in the same way that the Lord offered the drink of flowing water, the Holy Spirit, to the woman in Samaria, John 4:7–15; 7:38–39; cf. also Ezek 36; Jer 34; Joel 2). Regardless of one's background – Jew or Gentile, slave or free – God, who drew them all to salvation, grouped them all together into one body, the body of Christ, by the Spirit.[17] Each individual

---

16. Kakar and Kakar, *The Indians*, 109.

17. Both verbs in this verse – "were baptized" and "were made to drink" – are in the passive voice, implying that God was the agent of these events. These are commonly called "divine passives" (Daniel B. Wallace, *Greek Grammar Beyond the Basics: An Exegetical Syntax*

Christian in Corinth, by the work of the Holy Spirit, was a body part of Christ. Individual Christians were not "bodies" themselves; they collectively formed *the* body. The body was not a single part; it was a single unit composed of multiple parts such as hands and feet (1 Cor 12:14).

Since a healthy body was composed of many diverse and significant parts, there could be no self-devaluation among body parts: "If the foot says, 'I am not a hand and therefore I am not part of the body,' by its statement would it be considered not part of the body? Similarly, if an ear says, 'I am not an eye and therefore I am not part of the body,' would it be dismissed from the body by its statement?" (1 Cor 12:15–16). How absurd for a body part to consider itself not part of the body because it was not another body part! Diversity of body parts is what makes a body functional.[18] Therefore, one body part was not to underestimate its importance in the body and dismiss itself from the body. Such a notion was absurd.

Similarly, if a body was a single organ, that too would be absurd: "If the whole body were an eye, how would it hear? If the body were an ear, how smell [when it has no nose]?" (1 Cor 12:17). For a human body to be perfectly functional, it requires all the body parts and organs. That was why "God placed the body organs, each one of them, in the body as he planned" (1 Cor 12:18). God placed the feet at the base of our bodies so that they can carry us and walk us from place to place. God placed the nose at the front of our bodies so that we can smell food and also detect poison and so avoid it. God placed the ears on each side of our heads so that we can hear from both sides. God placed the right number of body parts in the right locations so that our bodies can be fully functional.

So, if a body consisted of a single organ, it would not be a body (1 Cor 12:19). Equally, if there was no unity between all the different body parts, there would be no "body" then either – they would be like body parts laid out on the floor. Instead, according to God's wise planning "now there are many body organs but a single body" (1 Cor 12:20).

Since a body needs all the organs in order to function properly, there can be no discrimination against particular body parts. "An eye cannot say to the hand, 'I have no need of you.' Or the head cannot say to the feet, 'I have

---

of the New Testament with Scripture, Subject, and Greek Indexes [Grand Rapids: Zondervan, 1996], 437–438).

18. Fee writes, "A careful reading of the whole indicates that *diversity*, not unity, is Paul's concern; the fact of the body's unity is the *presupposition* of the argument" (Fee, *First Epistle to the Corinthians*, 572 n. 12).

no need of you'" (1 Cor 12:21). Such a thought would be absurd. In reality, the body knows that "the thinking members of the body, although they are weaker, are essential" (1 Cor 12:22). Paul was referring to the heart, liver, or brain (ancient cultures had different views from today as to where thinking occurred). The body knows that even a fragile organ like the heart is essential and will not reject it. Not only does the body know this, but we also know it. As a result, "We place greater honor on what we think to be dishonorable body parts, and we cover the shameful organs for modesty" (1 Cor 12:23). By "dishonorable body parts," Paul was most likely talking about organs such as the brain or heart that are not pleasant to look at when seen outside the body, yet which people value and look after. By "shameful organs," he was probably referring to private organs that people cover in order not to shame themselves.[19] Both the human body and we ourselves know how to take care of weak and dishonorable body parts: we protect them from danger or cover them to avoid shame. Of course, the honorable body parts have no such need (1 Cor 12:24a). For example, men often like to flex their muscles to show their strength. The body knows how to cover what is dishonorable and show off what is honorable. Nevertheless, each individual body part is important.

God had combined the honorable organs with the dishonorable, the weak organs with the strong, so that there would be mutual honor ("the honorable one shares with the less honorable"), unity ("there may be no division"), and mutual concern for one another (1 Cor 12:24b–25). The result is that "when one member suffers, all the organs suffer together" (1 Cor 12:26a). This is greatly evident when we get a cold: our noses run, our heads ache, our bodies hurt, and our brains cannot think. All the parts of the body suffer together. Similarly "when one member is honored, all the members rejoice together" (1 Cor 12:26b). This is evident when the skillful fingers of a pianist playing on stage bring great honor to that musician as a whole person; or when the work of the brain seen in a chess player's brilliant tactics brings honor to that player as a whole person. The whole body, although made up of many diverse parts, functions as a single unit. It suffers together or rejoices together. This was God's design in the human body.

Paul said that the same was true of Christ's body: "You are Christ's body and individual body parts" (1 Cor 12:27). The Corinthians were a *single* body, the body of Christ. Each one of the Corinthian believers was an individual member, a body part, of this body. In this way Paul emphasized the oneness

---

19. Fee, *First Epistle to the Corinthians*, 613–614.

and yet the diversity among the Corinthians. All the members, with their diverse gifts, worked together for the benefit of *the* single body, the church in Corinth.

Just as there is diversity among body parts (ears, eyes, nose, etc.), so there was diversity in the Spirit's gifting among Christians. God was the agent in placing these gifts or gifted people (the body parts) within the congregation. Paul wrote, "So God placed them in the church, that is, first apostles, second prophets, third teachers, then powers, then gifts of healings, helps, guidance, and genuses of languages" (1 Cor 12:28). "Apostles" literally meant "those who were sent." The apostle Peter defined who was qualified to be an apostle: someone who had seen the earthly Jesus and had witnessed the resurrected Lord (Acts 1:21–22). Many in Corinth also fitted into that category (1 Cor 15:6). These men and women would have been instrumental in starting churches in various locations. "Prophets" were those who predicted the future (e.g. Agabus, Acts 11:28; also 1 Cor 14:32). "Teachers" were people who explained the written Scriptures or oral traditions to people in the church (e.g. Simeon, Lucius, and Manaen, Acts 13:1). Paul mentioned these by referring to the people (apostles, prophets, and teachers) rather than the gifts.

The remainder he referred to only by the gifts: "powers . . . gifts of healings, helps, guidance, and genuses of languages." "Powers" (the ability to perform powerful acts), "gifts of healings," and "genuses of languages" he had already referred to. "Helps" and "guidance" were new to the list. "Helps" referred to someone aiding or assisting another in need (Pss 22:19; 89:18). Fee writes, "Perhaps it is similar to the final three items in the list in Rom 12:8 (service, giving to the needs of others, doing acts of mercy)."[20] "Guidance," the translation of a word that otherwise occurs only in the Old Testament Greek translation and not elsewhere in the New Testament, referred to what counselors gave people in times of crisis. For example, "Without guidance people perish, but with many counselors there is deliverance" (Prov 11:14, LXX).[21]

God placed all these people and gifts in the congregation, just as he carefully placed the different body parts in the right places for them to do their

---

20. Ibid., 621.
21. Fee writes, "Since the word 'administration' in contemporary English conjures up the idea of 'administrative skills,' which is a far cry from what Paul had in mind, the better translation here might be 'acts of guidance,' although it is likely that it refers to giving wise counsel to the community as a whole, not simply to other individuals" (Fee, *First Epistle to the Corinthians*, 622).

particular tasks in order for the body to function properly. Paul's numbering "first, second, third" must not be construed to mean that he was promoting the superiority of certain gifts; rather, he was either narrating the historical order (apostles preceded prophets, who preceded teachers) or contrasting "calling" with "gifting." He might alternatively have been emphasizing the relative significance of gifts, just as in the human body certain parts are more fragile than others: for example, should a heart puncture, one's life comes to an end; but should the skin be punctured, it eventually heals. In the same way, the task of an apostle was much more critical (he or she could lead someone astray if careless, e.g. Peter at Antioch, Gal 2:10–14) than that of a help. The basic message, however, was that all the body parts worked together for the common good of the body. God was the agent in dispersing these diverse gifts.

Because God placed various gifts in the church as he willed, "All are not apostles, all are not prophets, all are not teachers, all do not perform powerful acts, all do not have gifts of healing, all do not speak in [various] languages, and all do not interpret [languages]" (1 Cor 12:31).[22] Paul's intention was to show that God, in his wisdom, had placed a variety of gifts in the congregation; therefore, they should not seek *one* gift alone but should seek a plurality of gifts. He explicitly said so in the next statement: "Be zealous for larger amounts of gifts" (1 Cor 12:31a).[23] The verb could mean "devote oneself to something," "zealously do something," or "zealously practice something."[24] Some have understood the phrase "larger amounts of gifts" as "greater gifts," implying that some of the gifts were greater than others (e.g. apostleship was greater than helps).[25] But such an understanding would undermine the lesson of the whole chapter, where Paul had been saying that a hand shouldn't seek to be an eye, an eye shouldn't seek to be feet, and so on. In addition, the

---

22. Paul could have made the above statements as questions (as some translations understand them). When Paul wrote, there were no punctuation marks such as question marks, so the context determines whether they were statements or questions. If they were in fact questions, Paul expected the Corinthians to answer by agreeing with him.

23. This sentence could have been a quote from the Corinthians, with the second part of the verse ("I'll show you a better way") being Paul's reply; or it could have been Paul's summary of what the Corinthians were doing; or it could have been what Paul commanded them. For a discussion of the pros and cons of these views, see Gordon D. Fee, "Tongues–Least of the Gifts? Some Exegetical Observations on 1 Corinthians 12-14," *PNEUMA: The Journal of the Society for Pentecostal Studies* (1980): 11–13. The last option is preferable since later Paul again commands the Corinthians to be zealous for spiritual gifts (1 Cor 14:1).

24. Willem C. van Unnik, "The Meaning of 1 Corinthians 12:31," *Novum Testamentum* 35, no. 2 (1993): 152.

25. Translations such as NET, NIV, HCSB, and ASV have "seek the greater gifts." KJV has "seek the best gifts."

Spirit was responsible for distributing the gifts as he wished; so how could a believer seek another gift? Further, the word *megas* could mean "greater," but it could also mean "more," as in "If we sowed spiritual seed among you, shouldn't we reap *much more* [*megas*] material sustenance from you?" (1 Cor 9:11). In light of this, we should understand Paul to be saying that he wanted the Corinthians to seek as many gifts as possible. A body with all body parts was much healthier and functioned much better than a body with only one kidney or with only one lung, or with one eye that couldn't see, or one ear that couldn't hear. Similarly, a church with a greater number and more diverse kinds of gifts of the Spirit was healthier than one with few or the same gifts.

While they sought a larger amount of gifts, Paul didn't want them to forget the concept of oneness. Just as all body parts work for the betterment, health, or better functioning of the one body, so in the body of Christ all gifts must work together for the benefit of the one body. Therefore Paul talked about this unifying factor: love (ch. 13). He called it "the far exceeding path" which he would show them (1 Cor 12:31b) before proceeding to describe it.

Just as a physical body is healthy when all the body parts work properly and fulfill their tasks, so it is with the body of Christ, the church. The Spirit's gifts enable the body of Christ to function properly. Believers must be willing for the Spirit to enable them to benefit the church. That was the intention of the gifts all along – the health and maturity of the body of Christ, the church. Often, however, gifts become a point of contention because of their abuse or because people have used their gifts to lord it over others. These were not the reasons why the Lord gave these gifts. Churches in India, therefore, are not to fear the gifts of the Holy Spirit or abuse them; instead, they need to learn to properly use their God-given gifts for the health of the church.

15

1 Corinthians 13

Love (13:1–3)

In Hinduism there are several kinds of love. *Kāma* is selfish love, usually associated with pleasurable or sexual love. *Karuna* is compassion or mercy shown to someone who is suffering. *Bhakti* is devotion to God. *Prema* is selfless and sacrificial, the love for another that doesn't expect anything in return. When a devotee exercises such love towards a god, it is called *prema-bhakti*.

Similarly, scholars have differentiated the words used for "love" in the New Testament: *eros*, *philē*, and *agapē*. *Eros* is erotic love, *philē* is brotherly love, and *agapē* is sacrificial love. Caution, however, must be exercised, since New Testament writers sometimes use *philē* and *agapē* interchangeably: The Father *agapē*-loves the Son (John 3:35) and the Father *philē*-loves the Son (John 5:20); the Father *agapē*-loves the people (John 3:16) and the Father *philē*-loves the people (John 16:27); the believers *agapē*-love the Lord (Eph 6:24) and the believers *philē*-love the Lord (1 Cor 16:22); Jesus *agapē*-loved John son of Zebedee (John 21:7) and Jesus *philē*-loved John son of Zebedee (John 20:2); and the Lord asked Peter if he loved him using both *agapē*-love and *philē*-love words (John 21:15–17).

Paul talked about the importance of *agapē* love. Having discussed the diversity of gifts that were given by the Holy Spirit in the Corinthian church, all for the benefit of the church, Paul explained how love (*agapē*) played a crucial role.[1] Paul told the Corinthians that *agapē* love was the glue that

---

1. Walker, against the majority of the commentators, argues that this section, 1 Cor 12:31b – 13:13, is a "non-Pauline interpolation," meaning that Paul didn't write this but someone else added it later (William O. Walker Jr., "Is First Corinthians 13 a Non-Pauline Interpolation?,"

brought together the gifts of the Spirit and enabled the proper functioning of the gifts; as Fee says, "Love [is set forth] as the necessary ingredient for the expression of all spiritual gifts."[2] Paul began by stating the absurdity of gifts without love: "If I speak in the languages of people and of angels but I do not have love, I have become a noisy gong or clanging cymbal" (1 Cor 13:1).[3] Some have wondered whether Paul did actually speak the angels' language ("ecstatic utterances"[4]). Most likely Paul was using hyperbole, exaggerated speech, to make his point: any utterance from him without love would be nothing more than noise! Similarly he said, "Even if I have prophetic utterances, I know all mysteries, I have all understanding, and I have all kinds of faith so that I can move mountains, but I still have no love, I am nothing" (1 Cor 13:2). Paul listed several gifts here – gifts of prophesying, knowing mysteries, understanding, insurmountable faith – only to show that all these gifts without love made him a zero, a "nothing." In sum, having love was more important than having any variety of gift. He continued, "Even if I give away all my belongings and I give away my body so that I might boast, but yet I have no love, I gain nothing" (1 Cor 13:3).[5] Even if Paul was the model of a sacrificial Christian by giving away all his wealth (cf. Mark 10:21; Acts 4:32–35) and even his own body, gaining the right to boast, but he didn't have love, he would gain nothing in anyone's sight. Love was supreme compared with

---

Catholic Biblical Quarterly 60, no. 3 [July 1998]: 484–499). Corley examines the passage in light of possible allusions to the Septuagint (Old Testament in Greek), potential influences from the developing Jesus tradition, and the impact of the cultural context. He concludes, "In accordance with the opinion of the majority of commentators, we have in 1 Cor 12:31b – 13:13 a characteristic piece of Paul's writing" (Jeremy Corley, "The Pauline Authorship of 1 Corinthians 13," *Catholic Biblical Quarterly* 66, no. 2 [April 2004]: 274). Smith outlines the rhetorical nature of this section (J. Smith, "The Genre of 1 Corinthians 13 in the Light of Classical Rhetoric," *Novum Testamentum* 33, no. 3 [1991]).

2. Fee, *First Epistle to the Corinthians*, 572.

3. The phrase "noisy gong" is literally "echoing bronze." Klein argues that bronze was never used as a musical instrument and questions Paul's usage here (W. W. Klein, "Noisy Gong or Acoustic Vase? A Note on 1 Corinthians 13:1," *New Testament Studies* 32 [1986]: 286–289). Even if bronze was never used as a musical instrument, it would still communicate Paul's point: "meaningless noise."

4. Dale B. Martin, "Tongues of Angels and Other Status Indicators," *Journal of the American Academy of Religion* 59, no. 3 (Fall 1991): 547–589.

5. There is a variant (difference between manuscripts) on how this verse is read: "I might give up my body that *I might boast*" (*kauchesomai*) versus "I might give up my body *to be burned*" (*kauthesomai*). Ancient and reliable manuscripts have "I might boast." Had Paul written "to be burned" (an allusion to Dan 3:28), no scribe would have been tempted to rewrite it. But if Paul had written "that I might boast," scribes might have been tempted to change it to the imagery of burning. For this reason, "that I might boast" is considered the harder but authentic reading. See NET Footnote, Metzger, *A Textual Commentary*, 497–498. Fee, *First Epistle to the Corinthians*, 634–635. Orr and Walther, *1 Corinthians*, 291.

every spiritual gift or every Christian attribute. Interestingly, when the Lord was asked to summarize the greatest commandment, he said, "First: Hear O Israel, the Lord is our God, the Lord is unique. Love the Lord your God with your whole heart, and with your whole soul, and with your whole mind, and with your whole strength. Second: Love your neighbor as yourself. There are no commandments greater than these" (Mark 12:29–31). Paul echoes this sentiment in this passage. Love was supreme.

Characteristics of Love (13:4–7)

Paul then defined the various attributes of love. "Love waited a long time before showing forth anger. Love was kind to those around a person. Love did not long for what others had, especially with jealousy.[6] Love did not brag about oneself. And love did not puff up one person over another" (1 Cor 13:4). Earlier Paul had talked about the Corinthians being puffed up, ignoring the sin of a member in the congregation (1 Cor 5:1). Love, on the other hand, did not puff anyone up in arrogance. Further, "love was not rude, that is, insensitive to someone's feelings [e.g. 1 Cor 7:36]; love did not seek one's own exaltation or advantage; love did not provoke easily; and, love did not wish evil upon someone else" (1 Cor 13:5).[7] In addition, "love did not rejoice in unrighteous acts – whether they were done to oneself or others. Instead, love rejoiced with those who lived truthfully" (1 Cor 13:6). In reality, "love endured all things, including trials and persecutions [just as the apostles endured trials and hardship, 1 Cor 9:12]; love believed everyone and gave all the benefit of doubt; love had hope in all circumstances, and, above all, love endured when everything else failed" (1 Cor 13:7). What an awesome list of the characteristics of love! When these characteristics were present, all spiritual gifts would function properly.

---

6. The word "zealous" has two different meanings in Greek, one noble and one ignoble. "When noble, it 'earnestly desires' something nobler for oneself; when base, it 'jealously longs' for the betterment of oneself to the detriment of another" (Fee, *First Epistle to the Corinthians*, 637, n. 10).

7. Translations prefer "it keeps no record of wrongs" (NIV), "not resentful" (NET, NRSV), "thinketh not evil" (KJV), or "is not conceited" (HCSB). KJV is more literal than other translations.

Whole versus Parts (13:8–13)

An Indian fable commonly taught in schools goes as follows. One day, two hungry cats found a round Indian bread called *chappati*. They divided it into two but couldn't agree as to which piece was bigger. Since they couldn't resolve the problem, they approached a monkey for help. The money bit each half of the *chappati* bit by bit, as if to equal the sizes, only to eat all of it. The cats went away hungry and disappointed. The moral of the story is that, when fights occur, both sides lose. Unfortunately, adults don't remember this lesson in daily living.

The Corinthians also missed this lesson. Instead of properly exercising their gifts for the benefit of the whole community they were fighting over their gifts, especially gifts that they thought were "better" or "good" gifts (e.g. prophesying, speaking in foreign languages, and knowledge). Paul's argument was that each of those spiritual gifts was useless without love. Love was supreme. Love glued those spiritual gifts together into a functional unit, just as ligaments unite body parts into a functional body. So in this section he set out to contrast love with spiritual gifts.

He began, "Love never terminates," meaning "love never stops functioning" (1 Cor 13:8a).[8] On the other hand, the spiritual gifts have a termination point or time. Prophesying, for example, would be set aside or destroyed, most probably by God.[9] Similarly, languages would come to an end on their own.[10] Also, the gift of knowledge (cf. 1 Cor 12:8) would be set aside or destroyed, again, most likely by God ("divine passive") (1 Cor 13:8b).

Unlike Asians or Eastern Europeans, most Americans are monolinguists (they speak one language) because there is no need for them to interact with people of other languages – most of their neighbors are English-speakers. In a country like the USA, other languages may cease to be used. Similarly, when Alexander the Great marched through Asia Minor, Syria, Palestine, Israel, and Egypt, he changed their languages. Hebrew speakers forgot their religious languages, to the extent that the Old Testament had to be translated into Greek (the Septuagint). Languages, by nature, cease when there are no more speakers. Prophecies come to an end when God no longer speaks.

---

8. Translations usually say, "Love never fails [*piptō*]." Paul elsewhere used this verb *piptō* to refer to people dying or coming to an end of their lives (1 Cor 10:8), and probably intended that meaning here as well.

9. Paul used the passive voice, implying that God was the agent (it is called the "divine passive").

10. Paul used the middle voice – action done on the subject by the subject.

Knowledge also comes to an end when one approaches old age or mental incapacity. In contrast, love will never terminate or cease to function; love abides forever (cf. 1 Cor 13:13).

Paul was still speaking of spiritual gifts within the congregation. So he said, "We know *partly*, we prophesy *partly*; when the *fullness* comes, the 'partly-things' will cease" (1 Cor 13:9–10). The word "fullness" is *teleion*, which is often translated as "perfect." Standard English translations say things like, "when the perfect comes" all the parts will disappear – leading one to guess what the "perfect" is. Some suggest that the "perfect" refers to "love," and that when love comes, spiritual gifts will cease.[11] Love is referred to in 1 John 4:18 as the "perfect love," adding credibility to this view. If that were Paul's thought, however, he would not have repeatedly asked the Corinthians to seek spiritual gifts (1 Cor 12:31; 14:1). Some suggest that the "perfect" refers to the full revelation of the New Testament – that is, when the canon was completed, gifts would cease.[12] However, Paul would not have thought in terms of the "canon" at the time of writing; also, those who hold this view do not consider gifts of "knowledge" or "teaching" to have ceased. They make sub-categories of gifts that will cease (e.g. languages and prophesying) and of gifts that do not cease (e.g. teaching and pastoring). Others hold that the "perfect" refers to the concluding work of Paul's ministry to the Gentiles: that is, when the Jews and Gentiles became one body, the gifts would cease.[13] However, Paul said elsewhere that the Jews and Gentiles had already been made one in Christ Jesus on the cross (Eph 2:16), a fact that the Jerusalem Council acknowledged (Acts 15); therefore, "perfect" couldn't have meant the oneness of Jews and Gentiles in Paul's ministry. Some conclude that "perfect" refers to the second coming of Christ: when Christ returns, all spiritual gifts will cease.[14] Although in practice that will be true, Paul wasn't talking about end times in the context.

All these views have merit but they ignore the fact that Paul had been talking about "parts" in the context. He said, "You are all the body of Christ and members [*parts* or organs]" (1 Cor 12:27). In light of that, Paul was most

---

11. Bruce, *1 and 2 Corinthians*, 128.

12. Myron J. Houghton, "A Reexamination of 1 Corinthians 13:8-13," *Bibliotheca Sacra* 153, no. 611 (July-September 1996): 344–356.

13. John R. McRay, "To Teleion in 1 Corinthians 13:10," *Restoration Quarterly* 14, no. 3–4 (1971): 168–183.

14. Steven L. Cox, "1 Corinthians 13 – an Antidote to Violence: Love," *Review & Expositor* 93 (1996): 529–536. Kenneth A. McElhanon, "1 Corinthians 13:8–12: Neglected Meanings of *Ek Merous* and *to Telion*," *Notes on Translation* 11, no. 1 (1997): 43–53.

likely saying that when the fullness (the body) came together, the specialness of individual body parts would diminish.[15] Gifts were like body parts in the way that, when one part hurt, all hurt; when one rejoiced, all rejoiced (1 Cor 12:26). However, all individuality of gifts would diminish when the church gathered together; all gifts worked together for the betterment or glory of the body. When the *wholeness* of the body came, the significance of the *individual body parts* would cease. When an eye, a hand, a foot, a mouth, and so on, came together, it was no longer the individual body part that mattered; it was the *whole* body, the *whole* person that mattered. Therefore, when the church gathered together, every Christian should think of the health of the church as a whole, not of the exaltation of his or her own gifts.

Paul's examples support and illustrate this principle. The first example was: "When I was a baby [*nepion*] I thought as a baby and I reasoned as a baby. When I became a man, I set aside the childish ways" (1 Cor 13:11). Paul had used this concept earlier: he called the Corinthians babies (*nepioi*) for exalting spiritual leaders and siding with them (1 Cor 3:1); when they understood the gospel of the crucified Messiah, they would be mature, *teleioi* (1 Cor 2:6). In that culture, it was thought that children characteristically lacked understanding, while adults had understanding. Jewish writers often associated a lack of understanding, and also individuality and selfishness, with children. Philo, for example, wrote, "To boast about one's own mind or to think one is lord over his or her own mind, and to be pleased with one's own senses or to think senses are his or her own property . . . is wholly *childish* and rejected by the sacred congregation."[16] When Paul was ignorant of the truth of the Messiah (before his encounter with the risen Lord), he exalted himself over the church and was a child in understanding (1 Cor 13:11a). Now he too had become a man. Adults set aside selfishness (Paul said earlier that he and Barnabas had set aside all their rights for the sake of the gospel, ch. 9). The Corinthians must also act as adults and focus on the wellness of the *whole* body and not on the glory of the *individual* and the individual's gifts.

The second illustration was: "Now we see obscurely through a mirror; but then we will see face to face; now I am known in part; then I will be known as I should be known" (1 Cor 13:12). The word translated "obscurely" occurs only here but it has the sense of a riddle or dimness. This illustration explains that all Christians have an obscured understanding of eternity. It is like seeing

---

15. Josephus also expressed the concept of wholeness or completeness with the expression "*to telion*" (*Antiquities* 3.230 and *Wars* 7.268).

16. Philo, *Cherubim* 73 (my translation; emphasis added).

a glorious parade through a dirty, mud-covered window. In such a s
one thinks of oneself alone. The Corinthians were guilty of that. Their
understanding of the future marred their present living. Instead of living for
the community, they were exalting individuality and the individual's gifts. Yet
gifts were given for the common good. An understanding of that principle
would remove the dirt on the mirror and give a clear picture of the church
now and in eternity to come. When they saw the church for what it was –
God's work and not their own – they would get a clearer vision of why they
had their gifts. The gifts were for the benefit of the church and not for self-
exaltation.

What were the Corinthians to focus on, then? Paul answered: "Now faith,
hope, and love – these three remain. The greatest of all these is love" (1 Cor
13:13). They needed to focus on faith, hope, and love, the eternal things, the
things that united the church. When they focused on those the wholeness of
the body would be enriched and the individuality of spiritual gifts would be
diminished. Love was the greatest because it helped them achieve that goal.

16

1 Corinthians 14

Languages (14:1a)

The Republic of India does not have a national language, according to the Gujarat High Court.[1] However, Hindi serves as the official language of the union government. Oomman writes, "The controversial question of a common language for the Union of India was settled recently [1949] when the Constituent Assembly adopted an article to be included in the constitution providing that Hindi in the Devanagari (Sanskrit) script shall be the official language."[2] Hindi is most commonly spoken in North India. In addition, English is spoken nationwide. English serves as the language that unites the North and the South. Besides these two, many other languages are spoken: according to the 2011 census, there are 1,635 languages in India,[3] and according to the 2001 census, over thirty languages have a million native speakers. Anyone who lives in a tri-state area in India easily speaks two or three languages. In fact, the majority of Indians are multilingual – able to speak in many languages.

The city of Corinth didn't have as many languages as India, yet Romans, Greeks, Jews, Phoenicians, and Phrygians all lived there.[4] The official languages were Latin and Greek,[5] but others in the Corinthian church would

---

1. Saeed Khan, "There's No National Language in India: Gujarat High Court," *The Times of India* (25 January 2010).
2. Philip P. Oomman, "Adopt Hindi as Indian Language: Constituent Assembly Authorizes Use in Official Matters: Study of English to Be Retained," *Christian Century* 66, no. 43 (26 October 1949): 1271.
3. www.languageinindia.com/feb2011/vanishreemastersfinal.pdf
4. For Roman freedmen, see Murphy-O'Connor, "The Corinth That Saint Paul Saw," 148. For Jewish settlers, see Morris, *First Epistle of Paul to the Corinthians*, 17.
5. Broneer, "Corinth," 82.

have spoken Phoenician or Phrygian languages. The Jewish converts would have spoken Hebrew or Aramaic in addition to Greek. So we can imagine that Corinth would have been a polylinguistic culture like India, and that the Corinthian church would have included people of diverse cultures and languages. In such a context, multilinguists and translators would have been highly valued, especially when, by the power of the Holy Spirit, they were enabled to speak languages previously unknown to them. Setting such a high value on the multilinguists and translators may have aroused jealousy and strife between them and the monolinguists. Similarly, if a multilinguist was to speak in a foreign language and there were no interpreters, or no one who could understand that language, it would increase the multilinguist's pride and not edify the congregation. These were some of the issues the Corinthians faced and which Paul now addressed.

Paul was concerned that his discussion of the importance of love in order for the Spirit's gifts to operate successfully in a church shouldn't deter the people from seeking the work of the Holy Spirit in their lives and congregation. So he began with an exhortation: "Pursue love and be zealous for the Spirit's gifts" (1 Cor 14:1a). Both love and the Spirit's gifts were vital for the church's health. When pursuing gifts, however, there was a criterion to use: which gift would bring greater good to the whole congregation?

In order to demonstrate this principle, Paul first contrasted the gifts of languages and prophesying (1 Cor 14:1b–5). Then he contrasted the gift of languages with the gifts of revelation, knowledge, prophesying, and teaching (1 Cor 14:6–12). However, he didn't want the Corinthians to conclude that the gift of speaking foreign languages was useless, so he explained the importance of speaking various languages accompanied by a translator who could make the congregation understand the message (1 Cor 14:13–19). Of course, any communicator was only as effective as his or her understanding of the intended audience, which Paul emphasized next (1 Cor 14:20–25). In the concluding section, he stated his theme: "Let all these be done for the building up of the church" (1 Cor 14:26b), and listed a variety of gifts. That should always be the motivation in using the Spirit's gifts in the church.

Prophecy (14:1b–5)

All religions have prophecies that they cherish. Hinduism has a significant prophecy concerning the coming of the Golden Age (the *Kalki Avatar*). The present age is called the Dark or Iron Age (*Kalki Yuga*). It will last five thousand years. Then there will be a "steady decline" that ends in a "chaotic, pre-apocalyptic *kaliyuga*."[6] After that, the Golden Age will start and last ten thousand years. When the Golden Age comes, Krishna will manifest himself to humanity, as promised in the *Bhagavad Gita*. Their scripture says, "Whenever there is decay of righteousness . . . and there is exaltation of unrighteousness, then I myself [Krishna] come forth . . . for the destruction of evil-doers, for the sake of firmly establishing righteousness. I am born for this age to come" (*Bhagavad Gita*, fourth discourse).

The Bible has similar *prophetic* statements about the end times. However, the term "prophecy" was also used in at least four other ways. First, prophecy referred to the composition of the Scriptures themselves. Peter said, "First of all, you must understand that no *prophesying* of the Scriptures came to be by one's own interpretation, since it did not originate with the will of people. Instead, people moved by the Holy Spirit spoke from God" (2 Pet 1:20–21). Second, it was a prediction of an event in the immediate future. Agabus, for example, prophesied that there would be a severe famine throughout the entire Roman world (Acts 11:28), and the famine came to pass soon thereafter. Third, prophesying was a proclamation that brought about conviction and repentance. Paul wrote, "Imagine that all believers prophesy and an unbeliever or an illiterate person comes to the church, would he or she not be called into conviction by all and held accountable by all? Also, the secrets of the heart will be revealed so that he or she will fall down upon his or her face and will worship God, declaring, 'Truly God is in your midst'" (1 Cor 14:24–25). Fourth, it was a lesson taught with a word of encouragement. Paul again wrote, "[When prophets take turns] then you are all able to prophesy so that all might learn and all might be encouraged" (1 Cor 14:31). In this section Paul was referring to the last two types: proclamation that brings about conviction, and lessons taught to bring encouragement.

Paul's overall theme in this section was to explain that the Corinthians should seek those gifts that edified the congregation. So he first contrasted the gift of speaking unknown languages (multilinguists) with the gift of prophesying (14:1b–5). He started by saying, "Be zealous . . . that you might prophesy" (1 Cor 14:1b). Then he explained why they should be zealous to prophesy, contrasting prophesying with those who speak in foreign languages: "The one who speaks in foreign languages speaks not to people

---

6. Lynn M. Thomas, "Does the Age Make the King or the King Make the Age? Exploring the Relationship between the King and the Yugas in the Mahābhārata," *Religions of South Asia* 1, no. 2 (December 2007): 183.

but to God because no one understands and he or she speaks in mysterious words to the Spirit" (1 Cor 14:2). A truly enabled multilinguist (one who spoke another language without having learned it, by the help of the Holy Spirit) was unable to understand what he or she was saying, for it was a language unknown to him or her; likewise the audience did not understand it either, without a translator. God the Holy Spirit, however, understood every language and, while it was a mystery to others, it was not to the Holy Spirit. (Paul's assertion is true even if one holds to the view that this "language" is *glossolalia* or heavenly language – even then the speaker or the hearer doesn't understand the language, but the Holy Spirit does.) In contrast, "the one who prophesies speaks to the people with uplifting, encouraging, and consoling words" (1 Cor 14:3). When prophecies were spoken in the common language, everyone understood them and would be benefited by them – encouraged, uplifted, and consoled. So the gift of prophecy was more beneficial for the congregation than the gift of speaking foreign languages. In summary, "the one who speaks in languages builds him- or herself up; on the contrary, the one who prophesies builds up the church" (1 Cor 14:4).

In a Hindi-speaking congregation, if a Marathi-speaking guest speaker came and spoke in Marathi, would the congregation be edified? Absolutely not! But the guest speaker (who knows Marathi) and the Holy Spirit would understand the content of the speech. On the other hand, if the guest speaker could speak in Hindi (with or without a translator), the whole congregation would be edified, encouraged, and consoled. So Paul concluded, "I wish for all of you to be multilinguists, but I desire all the more that you prophesy. That is because the one who prophesies benefits a greater number of people than the one who speaks foreign language, unless there is interpretation so that the church receives instruction" (1 Cor 14:5). Although Paul desired that all of them might be multilinguists and able to talk with every visitor to the church or city, he wanted them to focus on what was more beneficial – talking to the people in languages that they understood so that there would be greater benefit for the church. Speaking in foreign languages, though, was also equally valuable when there was an interpreter to interpret the message to the congregation.

In other words, the gifts of speaking foreign languages and prophesying were equally good when they both communicated with and edified the congregation. Fee writes, "It needs to be emphasized once more that Paul does not say that tongues is inferior to prophecy. What he says is that in church intelligibility is preferred to non-intelligibility, because the former seeks to edify the whole community while the latter is only for one's own edification."[7] Whereas prophecies automatically communicated to the people and edified them (since they were in the people's language), foreign-language speakers needed a translator to achieve such a goal. The value of the gifts was in communication and the way they benefited the church.

Foreign Language Etiquette (14:6–13)

In India, on formal occasions people will greet a guest with the word *Namaste*. Foreigners often learn that word and say *"Namaste"* to ordinary Indians. Although it communicates friendliness, it has no more in-depth meaning, for ordinary people don't use *Namaste* to greet one another. Also, if the Indian assumes that the foreign visitor knows Hindi (because he or she said *Namaste*) and converses further in Hindi, the foreigner's ignorance quickly becomes evident. In a way, then, learning a mere greeting in another culture is "useless" (unless the person intends to learn more). Similarly, Paul, in this section (1 Cor 14:6–13), argued that a mere citation of foreign words, especially without any in-depth meaning, was useless. He said, "Now, brothers and sisters, if I come to you and utter foreign words, which of you would be benefited unless I also say something useful, revealing something, making something known, prophesying, or teaching?" (1 Cor 14:6).[8] For example, if Paul were to say a short phrase to the Corinthian Christians in the Phoenician language (since there were some Phoenician Christians in the Corinthian congregation), he would communicate nothing spiritual except friendliness. On the other hand, were he to speak to them spiritual truths, reveal spiritual matters, explain to them God's truth, prophesy, or teach them about the gospel in the Greek language (which all the Corinthians spoke, even the Phoenician Christians), then they all would be blessed by his words. Paul illustrated his thought using two illustrations: musical instruments and pronunciation of foreign words.

A meaningless recitation of foreign words is "like inanimate sound objects, a flute or a harp; unless they give distinct sounds, how can one interpret what

---

7. Fee, "Tongues–Least of the Gifts?," 13.

8. The phrase "reveal something" is actually "revelation" and refers to a gift of the Spirit (Eph 1:17; 1 Cor 14:26, 30). It refers to revealing a hidden truth, such as a message about the second coming of Christ (1 Cor 1:7) or a person's sin (Acts 5).

is being communicated by a flute or a harp?" (1 Cor 14:7).[9] In the ancient
world, musical instruments were used to sound the alarm, such as in time of
war or at the approach of enemies (based on the tune, pitch, notes, etc.). In a
psalm, Asaph instructed, "Blow the trumpet in an understanding way in our
festival of New Moon" (Ps 81:3). So if a trumpeter took the "trumpet and made
an unclear sound, who would get ready for war?" (1 Cor 4:8). No one would.
Similarly, random foreign words communicate no clear message. Paul wrote,
"If you speak in foreign languages but do not give understandable thoughts,
how will anyone know what you have said?" (1 Cor 4:9a).[10] When there was no
communication of spiritual truth, their words were vain – "speaking into the
air" (1 Cor 4:9b), just as working without purpose was "boxing aimlessly into
the air" (1 Cor 9:26). Therefore, if someone ventured to speak to a foreigner
in that person's language, the speaker was to say meaningful words, not just
clichés or greetings (such as mere "*Namaste*").

A meaningless recitation of foreign words was also like a foreigner
mispronouncing words. Paul gave a linguistic lesson: "Doubtless, there
are different genuses of 'sounds' in this world, and none without meaning"
(1 Cor 4:10). Paul used the word "sound" (*phonē*) instead of "languages." In
linguistics, phonetics refers to how sounds are produced in human speech.[11]
People groups often have difficulty pronouncing words used by other people
groups. Some Indians, for example, have difficulty pronouncing "w." Instead of
saying, "Show me the way," they'll say, "Show me the *vay*" (Professor Higgins
refers to this in the musical *My Fair Lady*). The Old Testament narrates a story
of the fight between the Gileadites and the Ephraimites (Judg 12:1–6). When
the fugitives of Ephraim tried to pass through the region of the Gileadites,
the Gileadites would ask them, "Are you an Ephraimite?" If the fugitives said,
"No," the Gileadites would ask them to say, "Shibboleth." The Ephraimites had
difficulty making the "sh" sound (*phonē*) and inadvertently said, "Sibboleth."
That way, the Gileadites were able to recognize them and slaughtered a total of
42,000 Ephraimites.[12] Paul continued, "If I do not know the distinction of these
sounds (*phonē*), I will speak as a *barbarian* and my words will be *barbarous*"

9. The words for "inanimate sound objects" in Greek is "soul-less sound-givers," implying
that the musical instruments themselves do not make the music – the musicians do.

10. In Ps 81:3 (LXX) and 1 Cor 4:9 the same word "understandable" (*eusemeion*) is used.

11. Peter Avery and Susan Ehrlich, *Teaching American English Pronounciation* (Oxford:
Oxford University Press, 1992), 11.

12. This difference might shed light on what happened at Babel: "Let us go down and
confuse their *glossa* ('language') so that they will not understand each other's *phonē* ('sound')"
(Gen 11:7; cf. Jer 5:15).

(1 Cor 4:11).[13] Paul was aware that proper intonation and pronunciation were needed for proper communication. Just as musical instruments without proper notes or pitches do not communicate, neither does speaking foreign languages without proper intonation and pronunciation.

So were the Corinthians to avoid speaking in foreign languages altogether? No; rather they were to seek additional help: "Since you are zealous for the spiritual gifts, seek what builds up the church so that you might excel; that is, the one who speaks in foreign languages must pray so that he or she might also interpret" (1 Cor 4:12–13). The Corinthians were zealous for the Spirit's gifts, and Paul exhorted them to seek those gifts. But they should seek gifts with the goal of building up, edifying, the church. A multilinguist could edify the church if he or she also had the gift of interpretation. That way, the multilinguist could convey messages that built up the church.

Silent Speech (14:14–33)

Monastic silence is when a monk takes a vow not to speak to any human beings but to dedicate himself wholly to a deity and commune with the deity alone in his spirit. One such silent monk was Sri Ramana Maharshi (1879–1950). He was born in Tiruchuli, Tamil Nadu, in South India. His birth name was Venkataraman Iyer. At the age of sixteen he left his home, isolated himself, and became a monk. He then remained silent for many years. According to his followers he still taught in his silence. Godman writes,

> At this stage of his life Sri Ramana was speaking very little and so his teachings were transmitted in an unusual fashion. Instead of giving out verbal instructions he constantly emanated a silent force or power which stilled the minds of those who were attuned to it and occasionally even gave them a direct experience of the state that he himself was perpetually immersed in. In later years he became more willing to give out verbal teachings, but even then, the silent teachings were always available to those who were able to make good use of them. Throughout his life Sri Ramana insisted that this silent flow of power represented his teachings in their most direct and concentrated form. The importance he

---

13. Fee writes, "The word *barbaros* originally was onomatopoeic, meaning something like speaking gibberish" (Fee, *First Epistle to the Corinthians*, 665 n. 41). Scholars like Josephus thought of languages other than Latin, Greek, and Hebrew as "barbarian" languages (*War* 1.3).

attached to this is indicated by his frequent statements to the effect that his verbal teachings were only given out to those who were unable to understand his silence.[14]

It seems that the Corinthians had a similar belief whereby a prayer made in a foreign language, because it ministered to one's spirit, was better than a prayer made in one's own language. Paul here argued that it was just the opposite: a prayer made with understanding and communication was more beneficial than a silent prayer or prayer in a foreign language that none understood (1 Cor 14:14–19). Paul first acknowledged the validity of a prayer in a foreign or unknown language, saying, "If I pray in a foreign language, my spirit prays but my mind is unproductive" (1 Cor 14:14).[15] This was true of anyone who claimed he or she was speaking angelic language, ecstatic language, or a foreign language. Regardless, when a prayer was made in a language unknown to the person praying, his or her own mind was unproductive. If a native Greek-speaking believer, through the enabling of the Holy Spirit, spoke in Phoenician, that speaker wouldn't understand what was said, although a Phoenician might. So "what can be said?" asked Paul, and he concluded, "I would rather pray both with my spirit and with my mind. I would rather sing both with my spirit and with my mind" (1 Cor 14:15). Meaningful prayer and singing were much more profitable than non-meaningful prayer, even if the Holy Spirit completely understood.

In addition, if people couldn't understand a prayer because it was prayed in a language known only to the Spirit, how could they agree with the prayer's content and say "Amen" (1 Cor 14:16)? Silent prayers were good in private life, but in congregations such prayers weren't meaningful. Although the speaker was giving thanks to God, the hearers were unaware of the content and were not edified by such prayers (1 Cor 14:17). In summary, a person's ecstatic, angelic, or multilingual prayers were not edifying either to the speaker or to the hearers. God and the Spirit understood, and therefore those prayers could be prayed, but they were to be kept private. Paul expressed it from his own life: "I praise God that I speak in more languages than all of you, but I would rather speak five words in the church intelligently than thousands of words

---

14. David Godman, ed., *Be as You Are: The Teachings of Sri Ramana Maharshi* (St. Ives, England: Clays Ltd, 1985), 4.

15. For the Southern Baptist Convention's stance on forbidding missionaries in their denominations to practice "private prayer language," see Deann Alford, "Tongues Tied: Southern Baptists Bar New Missions Candidates from Glossolalia," *Christianity Today* 50, no. 2 (February 2006): 21.

in foreign languages. This way others would be instructed" (1 Cor 14:18–19). Paul without doubt spoke Hebrew, Aramaic, Greek, and Latin. He might also have learned a few more languages, and the Spirit might have enabled him to speak even more. Nevertheless, he would rather speak in Greek, so that his audience understood, than in any other language. So also the one with the gift of speaking in many languages, like Paul, shouldn't use the church as a platform to show off his or her intelligence in speaking many languages. The purpose of speaking in church was edification. Such edification was better done with known languages than with foreign languages (including angelic and ecstatic languages).

Paul realized that the Corinthians were motivated to show off their abilities to speak in other languages, and said, "Brothers and sisters, don't be children in your thinking (except towards evil things), but be adults in your thinking" (1 Cor 14:20). The children (*paidia*) mentioned here are slightly more grown up than the children mentioned earlier (*nēpioi*, 3:1; 13:11); nevertheless, this is not adulthood. The only area in which the Corinthians could be childlike was towards evil; that is, they shouldn't have an abundance of knowledge of evil, especially not through experience. Towards spiritual things, however, they needed to be adults.

Adults had a proper understanding of the *target audience* of the gifts of both speaking in languages and prophesying. The Old Testament gave instructions concerning this. Isaiah the prophet, for example, spoke of a time when Ephraim (Israel) would be so sinful that God would have to judge them (Isa 28). The judgment was that they would become drunk and covered with their own vomit, and in the midst of their drunkenness they would try to teach the people. But their instruction would sound like that of infants and babies – meaningless babbling (Isa 28:7–9). At that time, God would speak to them words of rebuke through foreigners in foreign languages, and Israel would not understand (Isa 28:11–12). Paul quoted that last line: "'Through foreign languages and through foreign lips I will speak to my people. Even then, they will not listen to me' says the Lord" (1 Cor 14:21). In that context, God spoke to *sinning people* through foreign languages; instructions in foreign languages were thus a sign of God's judgment. So Paul said, "Speaking in languages is a sign to unbelievers and not to the believers" (1 Cor 14:22a). In other words, instructions in foreign or unintelligible language were a sign that God's judgment rested on the people. This was true even at Babel: the divine punishment was evident in the coming of diverse languages and sounds (Gen 11:9). On the other hand, "Prophecy is a sign to believers and not unbelievers"

(1 Cor 14:22b). Thus God used "strange languages" or "foreign languages" to address his people who were sinning, but he spoke in prophecies to his people who were following him.

The same was true in the Corinthian church. Paul wrote, "When the church gathers and everyone speaks in various languages, if an uneducated person or an unbeliever comes in [and hears all the languages], would he or she not say, 'You have become insane'?" (1 Cor 14:23). Early churches kept the doors open for anyone to come in and fellowship with them. Witherington writes, "Strangers, including unbelievers, could drift into the Christian meeting. Perhaps some even showed up to get a free meal."[16] Should an illiterate person or an unbeliever come in and hear the commotion – people speaking in various languages simultaneously – would he or she not think that the people had gone crazy or that God had confused their minds? Instead of communicating God's favor resting upon the church, such an occurrence would cause that stranger to walk away thinking they were under God's judgment or simply insane. Grudem writes, "Uninterpreted tongues are a sign to unbelievers of God's displeasure and impending judgment (vv. 21-22a), and Paul, not wanting the Corinthians to give unbelievers this sign, discourages the childish (v. 20) use of uninterpreted tongues in the Corinthian church meetings (v. 23)."[17]

On the other hand, should the church speak prophecies, the response would be very different: "If all of you prophesy, and an unbeliever or an unlearned person comes in, would he or she not be convicted by you all as he or she is examined by you all? Then the hiddenness of that person's heart will be manifested so that he or she will fall upon his or her face before God declaring, 'Truly God is in your midst'" (1 Cor 14:24–25; cf. Isa 45:14; Ezek 8:23). The verbs Paul used – "convicted" and "examined" – together "imply the deep probing work of the Holy Spirit in people's lives, exposing their sins and thus calling them to account before the living God."[18] Whereas a visitor hearing languages would conclude that the congregation was insane, that same visitor, hearing prophecies, would be convicted of his or her sins, would acknowledge God's presence in the congregation, and would even repent. As such, it was far better to speak in prophecies among the congregation than to speak in languages. "Uninterpreted tongues only isolate and alienate

---

16. Witherington III, *Conflict and Community in Corinth*, 32.

17. Wayne Grudem, "1 Corinthians 14.20-25: Prophecy and Tongues as Signs of God's Attitude," *Westminster Theological Journal* 41, no. 2 (Spring 1979): 395.

18. Fee, *First Epistle to the Corinthians*, 686.

unbelievers while edifying the individual believer, but prophecy both edifies the people of God and convicts unbelievers."[19] That was why Paul wanted them to speak in prophecies rather than in foreign (or angelic or ecstatic) languages.

Paul had taught that the Spirit's gifts were meant for the edification of the church (1 Cor 12:7). Whatever gift one had, it should be used for "building up" the church: "Brothers and sisters, when you come together and one has a psalm, one has a teaching, one has a revelation, one has a language, one has interpretation – all these should be used for edification" (1 Cor 14:26). Paul added one more gift to the list: having a psalm. This variety of gifts in Paul's writings implies that there were diversities of gifts. The following is a partial list of the Spirit's gifts: apostleship, prophesying, teaching, speaking words of wisdom, speaking words of knowledge, being empowered, receiving revelation, healing, performing miracles, discerning spirits, speaking languages, interpreting languages, evangelizing, shepherding, helping, serving, having faith that moves mountains, exhorting (or encouraging), giving, having a psalm (or songs), guiding, and showing mercy (1 Cor 12:8–10, 28–30; 13:1–3, 8; 14:6, 26; Rom 12:6–8; Gal 3:5; Eph 1:17; 4:11; 1 Tim 1:18; 4:14). All these gifts were to be used for edification.

How could a gift like speaking in languages or prophesying be used to edify the whole congregation? The answer was: through orderliness. "If anyone speaks in languages, two, at the most three, should speak, each in his or her turn, while one translates" (1 Cor 14:27). Their taking turns would prevent any confusion that might arise if all spoke at the same time, and the interpreter would make the message understood and instructional. On the other hand, "if there is no interpreter, speakers of foreign languages should be quiet or speak to themselves and God" (1 Cor 14:28).

People with the gift of prophesying also had guidelines: "Let two or three prophets speak, and others examine" (1 Cor 14:29). This command supports the view that Paul wasn't talking about direct divine revelation (which needed no evaluation) so much as other kinds of prophecies: proclamation that brings about conviction, and lessons taught to bring encouragement. When such prophecies were made, other prophets were to examine them for authenticity and orthodoxy. In addition, if someone sitting in the congregation were to receive a special revelation from God, the prophets must conclude their prophesying and listen to the revelation (1 Cor 14:30).

---

19. David E. Lanier, "With Stammering Lips and Another Tongue: 1 Cor 14:20–22 and Isa 28:11–12," *Criswell Theological Review* 5, (Spring 1991): 282.

Prophets and prophecies were subordinate to God's revelation and God's revealed message. When prophets and people with gifts of revelation took turns, "all are able to learn and all are encouraged" (1 Cor 14:31). Similarly, when prophets submitted to one another's examination, again there was edification (1 Cor 14:32).

In conclusion, there should be no confusion when exercising the Spirit's gifts, since God doesn't like disorder or confusion; instead, "he desires peace within the congregation, in every location" (1 Cor 14:33).

Hindu Priestess (14:34–36)

Most of the priests in Hinduism have been men. There have, however, been exceptions. Gargi Vachaknavi was a woman from the Vedic period (when the scriptures were composed). She was mentioned in *Brihadaranyaka Upanishad* (the Hindu scriptures). Bhairavi Brahmani was a *guru* (teacher) of Sri Ramakrishna (famous mystic of the nineteenth century). She led Sri Ramakrishna into the sixty-four major trantric sadhanas (mystic rituals) that he completed in 1863. Ramakrishna Sarada Mission, established in 1960, is the newest monastic order for Hindu woman. Nowadays, female priests are in demand. Phalnikar reported that in Pune, India, Pradnya Patil had invited a female priest to come and perform rituals because women priests perform rituals faster than men priests. She continued, "They're very sincere and committed. Now, my relative and even my conservative father have switched to women priests."[20] The priestess concerned, Chitra Lela, reported that more than twenty Hindu women from all castes had enrolled in a one-year priesthood course.

The city of Corinth was very advanced, and so were its women. They believed in social, political, and religious equality. In an informative book, Winter discusses the emergence of a "new" kind of women in the Roman Empire who wore provocative dress and sometimes had promiscuous lifestyles.[21] Emperor Augustus legislated against the "new" women, and philosophical schools required their followers to avoid these women's pattern of living. Paul wrote within such a context. Their society plus the

---

20. Sonia Phalnikar, "Female Hindu Priests in India Are Making Strides in a Male-Dominated Profession," *Deutsche Welle* (14 May 2010). A similar story was reported two years earlier by Gangandeep Kaur, "Indian City Opens Doorway to Female Hindu Priests," *We.news* (*womensnews.org*) (26 February 2008).

21. Winter, *Roman Wives, Roman Widows*.

empowerment of the Holy Spirit had liberated some women to speak in the congregation, while others still felt the traditional constraints to remain quiet. Within that context, Paul addressed the church on this very sensitive topic. The next three verses (1 Cor 14:34–36) are some of the most hotly debated of the letter.

Paul gave three commands in this section: "let them be silent" (14:34a), "let them submit" (13:34b), and "let them ask their men at home" (14:35b). Scholars differ in how to understand these commands. Because of the vast research and writing on this section, I have cited just one example per view, and have not given all the arguments and counter arguments.[22] The interpretations can be gathered into four groups.

First, some scholars argue that Paul didn't write these commands but someone else added them to Paul's letter.[23] However, since all the manuscripts of the Greek New Testament have these verses (in some cases placed after v. 40), not many scholars accept this view.

Second, some scholars argue that these are direct universal commands, meaning that Paul prohibited women from speaking in any church and in all eras.[24] Although the plain wording seems to suggest such an interpretation, Paul himself permitted women to pray and prophesy in the congregation (1 Cor 11:5). Therefore, many do not accept this view either.

Third, most contemporary scholars argue that it is a "direct command" but situational, meaning that Paul silenced only some women and only in certain activities. Some argue that the Corinthian women were disruptive in the church, talking aloud and asking questions, so Paul asked such women not to converse.[25] Others argue that the first two verses (1 Cor 14:34–35) were the Corinthians' slogans regarding prohibiting women from speaking and that Paul refuted them by saying, "Did the word of God originate from you?"

---

22. For a summary, see Andrew B. Spurgeon, *1 Corinthians: An Exegetical and Contextual Commentary*, eds. C. Bennema, V. B. Immanuel, and B. C. Wintle, India Commentary on the New Testament (Bangalore, India: Primalogue, 2012), 165–170.

23. William O. Walker Jr., "1 Corinthians 15:29–34 as a Non-Pauline Interpolation," *The Catholic Biblical Quarterly* 69, no. 1 (January 2007): 84–103.

24. George W. Knight, "New Testament Teaching on the Role Relationship of Male and Female with Special Reference to the Teaching/Ruling Function in the Church," *Journal of Psychology & Theology* 3, no. 3 (Summer 1975): 216–229.

25. David S. Dockery, "The Role of Women in Worship and Ministry: Some Hermeneutical Questions," *Criswell Theological Review* 1 (Spring 1987): 370.

(1 Cor 14:36), implying that the women could speak.[26] Others argue that Paul was stopping only uneducated women who were asking inappropriate questions in the church.[27] Some argue that Paul was only prohibiting women from getting involved in the "evaluation" of the prophets.[28] The documents and theories on these verses are extensive and ever growing, and it is impossible to find a consensus.[29]

Fourth, I propose a new interpretation, which is to understand these commands as "permissive commands," meaning that Paul was permitting women who wanted to remain silent to be silent,[30] and not as direct commands prohibiting women from speaking. In a permissive command, the writer *allowed* an action to continue instead of *mandating* it. Earlier, Paul had allowed widowers, widows, and engaged people to marry if they weren't disciplined enough to remain single – all were permissive commands, meaning that Paul wasn't commanding them to marry; he was permitting their marriage (1 Cor 7:9; 7:36). Likewise, he allowed prophets to take turns and speak, and examine one another (1 Cor 14:29). Now, in this context of women speaking, he permitted women who were shy and didn't find the freedom to speak in public to remain silent just as they wished. (It is important to understand the phrases "it is not permissible for them [the women] to speak" [14:34] and "it is a disgrace for women to speak" [14:35] as choices the women made

---

26. Raymond F. Collins, *First Corinthians*, ed. Daniel J. Harrington, Sacra Pagina Series (Collegeville, MN: Liturgical Press, 1999), 514. See Blomberg, *1 Corinthians*, 280, for several objections.

27. Craig S. Keener, *1–2 Corinthians* (Cambridge, UK ; New York: Cambridge University Press, 2005), 70–100.

28. L. Ann Jervis, "1 Corinthians 14.34-35: A Reconsideration of Paul's Limitation of the Free Speech of Some Corinthian Women," *Journal for the Study of the New Testament* 58 (June 1995): 51–74.

29. Some other theories are: (a) Paul was only prohibiting disorderliness (Roger L. Omanson, "The Role of Women in the New Testament Church," *Review & Expositor* 83, no. 1 [Winter 1986]: 21); (b) the message of Gal 3:28 trumps this passage and therefore this passage is to be ignored (Leelamma Athyal, *Man and Woman: Towards a Theology of Partnership* [Tiruvalla, India: Christava Sahitya Samithy, 2005]); (c) these cultural commands do not apply to modern churches (N. J. Hommes, "Let Women Be Silent in Church: A Message Concerning the Worship Service and the Decorum to Be Observed by Women," *Calvin Theological Journal* 4, no. 1 [April 1969]: 5–22); (d) these teachings were only for the married and not for all women (Elizabeth Schüssler Fiorenza, *In Memory of Her: A Feminist Theological Reconstruction of Christian Origins* [New York: Crossroad, 1983], 230–233); and (e) Paul had a change of mind between chapter 11 and chapter 14 (Antoinette Clark Wire, *The Corinthian Women Prophets: A Reconstruction through Paul's Rhetoric* [Minneapolis, MN: Fortress Press, 1990], 59–61).

30. For a detailed study, see Andrew B. Spurgeon, "Pauline Command and Women in 1 Corinthians 14," *Bibliotheca Sacra* 168 (July–September 2011): 317–333.

instead of what Paul imposed upon them. The grammar demands it.)[31] Most likely, some of the women in the Corinthian church were timid and didn't want to speak in public and in front of other men – an attitude similar to that found in Asian cultures today. Receiving the gifts of speaking in tongues and prophesying established a new scenario where everyone thought they should speak in the church. But Paul didn't want anyone to be compelled into speaking. Thus, he gave permission (permissive imperative) to let women who wished to be silent to be silent, and women who wished to learn from their husbands to learn from their own husbands at home. They shouldn't be forced to speak in church or made to learn in church.

Within that context, Paul's instructions may be understood as follows. First, Paul wanted the women to have the freedom to remain silent in church if they themselves did not find the freedom to speak: "Women, let them remain silent, for they do not find it permissible to speak" (1 Cor 14:34a). Second, Paul wanted the women to continue in their submissiveness as they understood it (1 Cor 14:34b). Third, Paul wanted them to have the freedom to learn in their own homes, as they wished: "Just as the law says, 'if anyone wishes to learn,' let them ask their own men in their own homes; because women find it shameful to speak in the church" (14:34c–35). Traditionally, the phrase "as the law says" was added after "submission" (end of the previous statement).[32] But there are no verses in the Old Testament that clearly speak about the submission of wives to their husbands.[33] On the other hand, there are several verses in the Old Testament that speak about women and children learning the law (Deut 31:12; Ezra 10:3). So Paul was saying: if they wished to learn the Scriptures as the law commanded, they didn't have to learn it only in church, they could learn it at home. He argued, "Did the Word of God go out from you or abide only with you?" (1 Cor 14:36). In other words, even non-Christian Jewish husbands knew enough of the Scriptures to answer their wives' questions. The wives didn't have to learn only in church – that is, by violating their personal choices and asking questions of unrelated church leaders who were mostly men.

In conclusion, Paul wanted the Corinthian women to have the freedom to use their gifts in ways they found appropriate, both personally and culturally.

---

31. For arguments, see Ibid., 328–329. Spurgeon, *1 Corinthians*, 168.

32. Madeleine Boucher, "Some Unexplored Parallels to 1 Cor 11, 11–12 and Gal 3, 28: The NT on the Role of Women," *Journal of Biblical Literature* 31, no. 1 (January 1969): 50.

33. Some have suggested Paul was referring to Gen 2:18 (NET Bible footnote) or Gen 3:16 (Morris, *First Epistle of Paul to the Corinthians*, 197).

They could pray and prophesy (1 Cor 11:5), speak in foreign languages or prophecies (1 Cor 14:26–34a), or ask questions in the congregation in order to learn (1 Cor 14:34b–36).[34] On the other hand, if the women were timid and found it culturally inappropriate to speak in public, they could remain silent, honor their understanding of submissiveness, and learn at home from their own husbands. It was up to the women to choose. Spiritual gifts were given for the benefit of the whole church, both men and women (1 Cor 12:7).

India's independence has brought, as Sumithra points out, "the emancipation of Indian women. Traditionally, according to Manusmriti's injunction, an Indian woman is always subjugated to men – as a child under father's custody, in marriage under husband's, in old age under son's and in death under Yama, the god of death. She could not be liberated except by legal measures, such as the abolition of *sati*, compulsory female education, raising of marriage age, anti-divorce acts and social equality of sexes and, most recently, laws concerning sexual harassment on women. All these have made the modern Indian woman a person as never before in Indian History."[35] Yet one place where women do not feel complete freedom and equality is in their own churches. At bare minimum, the women in our churches should be encouraged to exercise all the gifts of the Spirit and also pray. These actions are not in violation of any of God's teachings or commands. In addition, the value of women as co-heirs of God's promises needs to be stressed unashamedly (1 Pet 3:7). When Indian churches join with the nation's interest in exalting women, there will be true revival.

Impermanence (14:37–40)

Buddhism arose in the ancient kingdom of Magadha (now in Bihar, India). A king by the name of Siddhārtha Gautama from central Ganges-plan (now Nepal) was dissatisfied with his life and entered asceticism. Eventually he reached enlightenment (from then on, he was known as Buddha). His teachings became the teachings of Buddhism. Buddhism defines the three "marks of existence" as impermanence (*anicca*), dissatisfaction (*dukkha*) and

---

34. For other gifts that woman have, see Harold W. Hoehner, "Can a Woman Be a Pastor-Teacher?," *Journal of the Evangelical Theological Society* 50, no. 4 (December 2007): 761–771.

35. Sumithra, *Christian Theologies*, 11.

non-self (*anatta*).[36] Impermanence teaches that everything is transient or in a constant state of change.

Everything in the physical world might be subject to constant change, but Paul believed that the Scriptures were stable and inspired by God (cf. 2 Tim 3:16–17). At the end of his teachings on the Spirit's gifts he asserted a similar thought. He said to the Corinthians, "If anyone thinks him- or herself to be a prophet or a spiritual person, let him or her know that what I write to you is the Lord's command" (1 Cor 14:37). His words were from the Lord Jesus Christ. This became of test of validity. If a person was a prophet or a spiritual person, he or she must agree with Paul's teachings because they were truly the Lord's teachings. On the other hand, "If someone doesn't acknowledge the teachings, he or she is not [to be] acknowledged" (1 Cor 14:38).

Having asserted his authority, Paul concluded the section on the Spirit's gifts with one more exhortation: "So, brothers and sisters, be zealous in prophesying and do not forbid anyone from speaking in foreign languages. But do everything in a decent and orderly manner" (1 Cor 14:39–40). Paul didn't want the Corinthians to conclude that Paul opposed exercising spiritual gifts, such as speaking in unknown languages or prophesying. At the same time, though, they needed to exercise orderliness and decency. In other words, they needed to make sure that the Spirit's gifts were used for the benefit of the whole church.

The same principle applies still today. Denominations debate whether a particular gift (such as the gift of tongues) has ceased. In the midst of such debates, they forget the purpose for which the gifts were given in the first place: for unity, edification, and growth. If they forbid the use of some gifts, they should still emphasize the importance and practice of other gifts so that their churches might be healthy. In everything, however, orderliness is very important since God is not a God of chaos but the God of peace and orderliness.

---

36. Tse-fu Kuan, "Rethinking Non-Self: A New Perspective from the Ekottarika-Āgama," *Buddhist Studies Review* 26, no. 2 (2009): 156. Also Kenneth K. Inada, "Amida Buddha, Whitehead's God, and the Temporal Fact," *Pure Land (Berkeley, California)* 0, no. 15 (December 1998): 146–162.

17

1 Corinthians 15

Connections

Paul was still talking about spiritual matters in response to the question that he began to answer in chapter 12. First he explained that spiritual people were those indwelt by the Spirit of God (1 Cor 12:1–3). They alone acknowledged allegiance to the Lord Jesus Christ. Then he talked about the diversity of the Spirit's gifts – how they were meant for the health and proper functioning of the church (1 Cor 12:4–31). Then he talked about love uniting the gifts just as ligaments in a body connect all body parts (1 Cor 13:1–13). He concluded the discussion on the Spirit's gifts by instructing on orderliness, thoughtfulness, and cultural sensitivity in exercising them (1 Cor 14:1–40).

In this final section on spiritual matters, he talked about the reality of resurrection (1 Cor 15:1–58). Perhaps some were curious about the reality and nature of Christian resurrection. So Paul addressed those issues here as part of his discussion on spiritual matters.

Afterlife

Two Hindu scriptures describe the afterlife. According to *Upanishads*, a person's soul discards the body as one discards old clothes to wear new ones. The body is a shell but the soul is immutable and indestructible. In this way the soul migrates from one body to another in a cycle of birth, death, and rebirth. The end of one cycle, birth-death, is *mukti*. When one finally no longer goes through cycles – that is, becomes one with god – that is *moksha* or salvation.

According to another scripture, *Garuda Purana*, the god of death (Yama) sends his representatives to collect the soul of a person from his or her body when that person is due for death. After leaving the body, the soul goes through a long and dark tunnel towards the South. (The dead person's relatives light oil lamps and leave them beside the corpse to guide the soul in the dark tunnel.) The soul is reborn into another form depending on one's deeds: animal form or lower if the person had bad karma, or human form if one had good karma. Yama's assistant, Chitragupta, keeps a person's timing of death and deeds performed in a ledger that determines whether the soul has good or bad karma. Before reincarnations, however, the soul is required to go to *naraka* (hell) as a punishment for bad karma or to *svarga* (heaven) for good deeds.[1] A soul goes through several incarnations until it has satisfied the supreme lord. Then it attains *moksha* or *nirvana* – oneness with the godhead. The soul never dies; only the body – made up of earth, water, fire, air, and sky – dies.[2]

The citizens of Corinth had various religions, each with its own version of the afterlife.[3] One of their religions was the worship of the mother–daughter goddesses, Demeter and Kore. The devotees of Demeter and Kore believed that the afterlife was not painful; instead, it was a "happy status." Alderink writes, "Human life, initially understood as punctuated by death and issuing into a destiny of bad things down in the darkness and gloom, is qualified for initiation by the work of Demeter. The initiate is happy 'on the earth' and has a share of good things in Hades."[4] Jewish converts to Christianity would have been puzzled by the resurrection of Jesus Christ, their Lord – by its impact on

---

1. Hell is different in Hinduism from hell in Christianity. Jacobsen writes, "Hell is not a permanent dwelling place, but a realm from which one returns after the punishments for moral impure deeds have been completed. There are many rebirth realms. Hell is a name for the worst place, a place of punishment for the more impure acts. Hell is like a prison. The prisoner does his time and is thereafter returned to society. Hell functions in binary opposition to heaven, *svarga*, but hell is not in binary opposition to the highest salvific goal, as in Christianity and Islam. Hell is not a contrast to *moksa*, final liberation. Life in this world is the binary opposition to *moksa*" (Jacobsen, "Three Functions of Hell," 386).

2. For a detailed study with diagram, see Reat, "Insiders and Outsiders," 459–476.

3. For a study of Greco-Roman and Jewish views of the afterlife, see Candida R. Moss, "Heavenly Healing: Eschatological Cleansing and the Resurrection of the Dead in the Early Church," *Journal of the American Academy of Religion* 79, no. 4 (2011): 996–1000. For a narrative of mourning and rituals in a Jewish death, see Janet C. Robertson, "Mourning and Ritual: A Death in a Jewish Family," *Reconstructionist* 40, no. 4 (May 1974): 12–17. For Ancient Near Eastern people's belief in life after death, see Adele M. Fiske, "Death: Myth and Ritual," *Journal of the American Academy of Religion* 37, no. 3 (September 1969): 249–265.

4. Larry J. Alderink, "Mythical and Cosmological Structure in the Homeric Hymn to Demeter," *Numen* 29, no. 1 (July 1982): 12.

their understanding of the judgment, the end days, and resurrection. Some started to form their own theories that there was no resurrection as such or that they had missed the resurrection (cf. 1 Thess 4:13–18). So Paul addressed their questions on the resurrection in this section (1 Cor 15:1–58).

First, he assured them of the *certainty* of the resurrection (1 Cor 15:1–34). Resurrection was certain because Jesus' resurrection was attested to by witnesses, a historical fact (1 Cor 15:1–11). His resurrection guaranteed all other people's resurrections (1 Cor 15:12–19). His resurrection initiated the eschatological (last days) events that ultimately would lead everyone to submit to God alone (1 Cor 15:20–28). And this certainty of resurrection enabled Christians to bear suffering (1 Cor 15:29–34).

Second, he explained the *nature* of the resurrection (1 Cor 15:35–58). A seed sown into the ground received a body from God and became a plant; similarly, dead people would receive new bodies after the resurrection (1 Cor 15:35–38). Just as there were differences between celestial bodies like the sun and the moon, so the resurrected body would be different from the earthly body (1 Cor 15:39–50). That transformation into the resurrected body would be instantaneous when the Lord returned (1 Cor 15:51–58).

What is distinctively different about Christianity compared with other religions is the *bodily* resurrection of all people. It was evident in the Lord Jesus Christ's resurrection. He appeared to the disciples in his resurrected body and said, "You see my hands and my feet – I am exactly he whom you knew. Touch me and feel me. Ghosts don't have flesh and bones as I have, as you'll see" (Luke 24:39). The resurrected body would be recognizable, and made of flesh and bone. Yet it would be different from the present physical body, just as the sun is materially different from the moon. All resurrections began with Jesus' resurrection.

Parampara and Kerygma (15:1–11)

Parampara refers to a succession of teachers and students in traditional Vedic culture. It is also known as the *guru-shishya* tradition (*guru*, teacher; *shishya*, student). In the traditional model, the student remained with the *guru* as a family member and learned lessons from the *guru*'s life and teachings. For a Hindu tradition to be authentic, it must have *successive gurus*. Mlecko writes, "For Hindus, religion is manifested or embodied in the continuing, successive presence of the guru. It is the guru who reveals the meaning of life; he is the immediate, incarnate exemplar in life, and as such, the guru is an inspirational source for the Hindu. The basic strengths of the guru's role are such that guruhood is the oldest form of religious education still extant. And understanding of guruhood, therefore, is of paramount importance in any consideration of the Hindu traditions."[5]

Paul's code word for such passing on of tradition from one generation to the next was "*gospelize*" or "to proclaim the good news." He wrote to the Corinthians, "I made known to you, brothers and sisters, the gospel which I *gospelized* [proclaimed] to you – what you have received, in which you stand firm, and through which you are saved (provided you hold on to what you believed)" (1 Cor 15:1–2). Elsewhere, Paul firmly stated that he didn't receive this gospel from anyone other than the Lord Jesus Christ (Gal 1:11–12).[6] As an apostle of Christ Jesus, he received insight into this gospel and he proclaimed it even to the Corinthians. Of course, it wouldn't contradict the gospel of the other apostles (Gal 2:9; also 1 Cor 15:11). The Corinthians gladly accepted that tradition and stood firmly upon it. In the Greek language, writers used tense forms to either highlight or not draw attention to an action. In this sequence of verbs (gospelized, received, believed, stand firm, are saved) the most significant aspect is represented by the verb "you have stood firm" (perfect verb). Since the Corinthians had stood firm in the traditions (i.e. not believed in vain but persevered till the end) their salvation was confirmed. This was an exhortation to perseverance in times of difficulty such as persecution. Although the majority of the Corinthian Christians would have been genuinely holding on (cf. 1 Cor 11:1), some would have been tempted to return to their old ways. If they did that, their belief might seem to be vain. Paul acknowledged that and challenged them. After this brief exhortation, he repeated the tradition – the affirmation of truths – for them.

The tradition – "What I have handed over to you and what you received" – first of all referred to the death of Christ: "Christ died for our sins according to the Scripture" (1 Cor 15:3). Paul was referring not only to the historical death of Jesus Christ but also to the scriptural evidence for the Messiah's substitutionary death for the people (as implied in the phrase "for our sins"). Isaiah, for example, said, "He was pierced because of our transgressions and was crushed on account of our sins" (Isa 53:5a). Caiaphas, the high priest, prophesied, "It is better that one man dies for the whole nation than that the

---

5. Mlecko, "The Guru in Hindu Tradition," 33.
6. Some scholars affirm that Paul did receive this tradition from other apostles (e.g. John Kloppenborg, "An Analysis of the Pre-Pauline Formula 1 Cor 15:3b-5: In Light of Some Recent Literature," *Catholic Biblical Quarterly* 40, no. 3 [July 1978]: 367).

whole nation perishes" (John 11:50). So the first part of the tradition was an affirmation of the substitutionary death of the Messiah. Second, the handed-down tradition confessed the burial of the Messiah – "he was buried" – as evidence of his real death (1 Cor 15:4a; cf. Luke 23:50–53). Wright, after stating the modern objection to Jesus' resurrection ("Jesus did not really die; he somehow survived"), says that such an argument "can be disposed of swiftly because the Romans knew how to kill."[7] The Messiah was not only killed but also buried since he was truly dead.[8] Third, he rose from the dead on the third day according to the Scriptures (1 Cor 15:4b). King David prophesied on behalf of the Messiah, "You will not abandon me to Sheol; you will not allow your faithful one to see the pit" (Ps 16:10). Peter explained David's statement as follows: "David, by foreknowledge, spoke of the resurrection of the Messiah" (Acts 2:31). Just as these prophetic words claimed, the Messiah rose from the dead on the third day.[9] This resurrection was a bodily resurrection (Luke 24:39).[10] Fourth, "He was shown to Cephas and to the Twelve" (1 Cor 15:5). What evidence was there if none witnessed the resurrection? That was not the case with the Messiah; there were many witnesses of his resurrection. Peter and the twelve apostles were the foremost. They plus others (whom Paul would list next) were witnesses to his resurrection. So the basic tradition that the apostles passed on to believers worldwide was this: the Messiah died for the people's sins, was buried, rose from the dead, and was seen by the apostles.

There were more witnesses to the resurrection than Cephas (Peter) and the twelve apostles. Over five hundred Christians saw the resurrected Lord alive, most of whom were still living at the time Paul wrote the letter to the Corinthians, although some had died (1 Cor 15:6). If the Corinthians wanted proof, they could ask each one individually. Afterwards, the Lord appeared

---

7. Wright, "Jesus' Resurrection and Christian Origins," at http://ntwrightpage.com/Wright_Jesus_Resurrection.htm, Originally published in *Gregorianum* 83, no. 4 (2002): 615–635.

8. His burial is conveniently ignored by scholars like Crossan, who argue that dogs ate his body on the cross so that there was nothing substantial to bury (John Dominic Crossan, *Jesus: A Revolutionary Biography* [San Francisco: HarperSanFrancisco, 1994], chapter 6).

9. The three days are counted from the time of his suffering (Thursday night) until his resurrection (Sunday morning, cf. Mark 8:31). For a detailed chronology of the Lord's last days, see Harold W. Hoehner, "Chronological Aspects of the Life of Christ, Part IV: The Day of Christ's Crucifixion," *Bibliotheca Sacra* 131, no. 523 (July 1974): 241–264.

10. For a sound defense of the bodily resurrection of Jesus Christ, see Kirk R. MacGregor, "I Corinthians 15:3b-6a, 7 and the Bodily Resurrection of Jesus," *Journal of the Evangelical Theological Society* 49, no. 2 (July 2006): 225–234. For a history of the various beliefs on the resurrection, see Ronald J. Sider, "St Paul's Understanding of the Nature and Significance of the Resurrection in 1 Corinthians 15:1-19," *Novum Testamentum* 19, no. 2 (April 1977): 124–141.

to James (1 Cor 15:7a). Two of the Lord's disciples had the name "James": James the son of Zebedee and James the son of Alphaeus (Matt 10:3–4). Since they would have been already included in the Twelve (1 Cor 15:5), Paul wasn't talking about them. The Lord's own half-brother James soon became prominent in the church (cf. Mark 6:3; Acts 15:13–29; Gal 1:19; 2:9–12), so it is likely that Paul was affirming that James the Lord's brother also saw the resurrected Lord. In addition, the Lord appeared a second time to all the apostles, possibly including Barsabbas (Justus) and Matthias (1 Cor 15:7b; Acts 1:23). In summary, there were many witnesses to the resurrected Lord.

Paul was an unexpected witness to the resurrected Lord: "last of all he revealed himself to me as to one unexpectedly born" (1 Cor 15:8). Paul used an unusual word, *ektroma*, which could mean "a miscarriage," "an aborted baby," or "an unexpected birth." Aasgaard thinks that the Corinthians rejected Paul as a "miscarriage" and that he quoted it ironically.[11] Fee thinks they might have "dismissed him as a 'dwarf,' a play on Paul's name – *Paulus*, 'the little one.'"[12] Mitchell argues that other apostles rejected Paul as if he was an aborted baby, and Paul cited that ironically.[13] In light of what Paul himself says in the following verses (1 Cor 15:9–11), a better option is to understand *ektroma* as "an unexpected birth."[14] Before ultrasound and other modern technologies, it was not uncommon for a mother to give birth to a baby and think that the labor was over, only to find there was another baby in the womb. Paul was like that second baby. Everyone concluded that the revelation of the Lord was over – apostleship had come to an end. But much later, in an unexpected way, Christ revealed himself to Paul. It was additionally unexpected because Paul was a persecutor: "I am the least of the apostles. I am unworthy to be an apostle for I persecuted the church" (1 Cor 15:9; see Acts 22:4; 22:11; Gal 1:13-15, 23; Phil 3:6–8; 1 Tim 1:13–16 for Paul's frequent references to his persecution of believers). How could a persecutor be a witness? It was through the grace of God: "By the grace of God, I am who

---

11. Reidar Aasgaard, "Paul as a Child: Children and Childhood in the Letters of the Apostle," *Journal of Biblical Literature* 126, no. 1 (2007): 142.

12. Fee, *First Epistle to the Corinthians*, 733.

13. Matthew W. Mitchell, "Reexamining the 'Aborted Apostle': An Exploration of Paul's Self-Description in 1 Corinthians 15.8," *Journal for the Study of the New Testament* 25, no. 4 (2003): 484.

14. Wright has a graphic description of this unexpected birth: "'Last of all, as to one untimely born, he appeared also to me.' This is a violent image, invoking the idea of a Caesarian section, in which a baby is ripped from the womb, born before it is ready, blinking in shock at the sudden light, scarcely able to breathe in this new world" (N. T. Wright, *The Challenge of Easter* [Downers Grove, IL: InterVarsity Press, 2009], 21).

I am" (1 Cor 15:10a). That was the unexpected birth. Paul wasn't a disciple, Paul wasn't a follower, Paul wasn't a believer, Paul wasn't seeking God; instead, he was actively persecuting the church in order to destroy it. But God showed mercy on him and turned him into an apostle, one who witnessed the Lord's resurrection. That was unexpected.

Since God had shown him grace, Paul had been faithful: "His grace in me hasn't been in vain but I labor harder than all [of the apostles], not by my own self but by the grace of God which is with me" (1 Cor 15:10b). Since Paul felt "least" compared with the other apostles (for he had persecuted the church), he worked hard after the grace of God was shown to him and he believed in the Messiah. He wanted to excel above all of the other apostles out of gratitude and indebtedness. In reality, though, it was God's grace that was making him work hard. Nevertheless, the message of all the apostles – of Paul, Cephas, and the Twelve – was the same, the same tradition that the Corinthians believed (1 Cor 15:11). This statement affirms that there were no disagreements between the other apostles and Paul. They were unanimous about the gospel and the tradition: that the Lord Jesus died, was buried, was raised to life, and appeared to many as a proof of his resurrection.

Indian Syllogism (15:12–28)

In an eye-opening essay, Ganeri argues that the accusation that Indian philosophy is speculative, spiritual, and non-rational is conditioned on biases. He writes,

> It is not . . . that India did not have rationalist and scientific traditions, nor that European philosophers in the nineteenth century were unaware of them. Yet, initially favorable responses among European intellectual circles to reports of Indian contribution to logic, and enthusiasm for the idea that logic had its origins as much in India as in Greece, gave way to a more skeptical and dismissive evaluation of the Indian material. This change in attitude had its roots, perhaps, in the passing of Europe's "Oriental Renaissance," and in a harder, utilitarian approach to the government of its Eastern colonies . . . The origins of the myth lie as much in the Indian intellectual quest for an Indian critique of colonial social policies within the framework of an emergent nationalist movement. This movement, searching in India's intellectual past for a native, non-European way of

thinking, saw no reason to promote indigenous traditions of logical or scientific inquiry.[15]

One of the most famous Indian schools of philosophy is the Nyaya school. It primarily tries to prove the existence of God using the teachings of Vedas. A logical theory of the Nyaya school is the Nyaya theory of causation, which simply defines cause as "an unconditional and invariable antecedent of an effect and an effect as an unconditional and invariable consequence of a cause."[16] Of course, this theory has multiple layers and sub-points.

The principle "If one thing is true, then something else is also true" (cause and effect theory) is a Greek concept. Paul employed that principle in this section (1 Cor 15:12–19). In another place where Paul ministered (Thessalonica), the new converts wondered about the resurrection, and to them Paul wrote, "We believe that, *if* Jesus died and rose again, *then* we also believe that God will bring back with him Christians who died" (1 Thess 4:14). Similarly, to those in Corinth who questioned the resurrection, Paul said, "*If* we proclaimed Christ, that he was raised from the dead, *then* why is someone in your midst saying that there is no resurrection?" (1 Cor 15:12). The resurrection of Christ implied the resurrection of the saints. *If* Christ was raised, *then* so would be the Christians. On the other hand, *if* there was no resurrection, *then* Christ wasn't raised (1 Cor 15:13). Either the resurrection was a true event and Christ was resurrected, or the resurrection wasn't true and Christ wasn't resurrected. Further, *if* Christ wasn't resurrected, *then* Paul's proclamation was empty and the Corinthians' faith was without substance (1 Cor 15:14). That would mean there was no salvation, no eternal life, and no redemption. All would be false. Further, *if* there was no salvation, *then* Paul and the other apostles were false witnesses of God since they had proclaimed, as if God had told them, that Christ had risen from the dead when in reality there was no resurrection from the dead (1 Cor 15:16). So a simple denial or questioning of the reality of the resurrection had many consequences. It called into question everything the Christians believed and everything the apostles had proclaimed. The believers' faith would be without substance, the apostles would be false witnesses, and even God would have lied when he told the apostles to proclaim that Christ had risen from the dead!

---

15. Jonardon Ganeri, "The Hindu Syllogism: Nineteenth-Century Perceptions of Indian Logical Thought," *Philosophy East and West* 46, no. 1 (January 1996): 12.

16. Chandradhar Sharma, *A Critical Survey of Indian Philsophy* (Delhi, India: Motilal Banarsidass Publishers, 1987), 209–210.

This syllogism was so important that Paul repeated it again: "*If* Christ is not raised, *then* your faith is useless and you are still in your sins" (1 Cor 15:17). It was Christ's resurrection that guaranteed forgiveness of sins. Elsewhere Paul wrote, "He died for our sins and was resurrected for our righteousness" (Rom 4:25). Therefore, without the resurrection of Christ, there was no forgiveness of sins. Even more absurd: "Those who died believing in Christ are destroyed" (1 Cor 15:18). What a foolish act it was for martyrs to believe in Christ and to give their lives away, if there was no resurrection! Their martyrdom had no meaning at all. In short, "*If* we hoped in Christ for this life alone, *then* we are to be pitied more than anyone else" (1 Cor 15:19). Being beaten, starved, crucified, or burned was the fate of those who believed in Christ. If that was the end and there was no hope of a future resurrection, then they were fools for believing in Christ. But, in reality, there was a resurrection of the dead. Those martyrs would indeed be resurrected and rewarded for their faith. Those who had believed in the resurrected Christ would find resurrection and forgiveness of sins. *Since* Christ was resurrected, all these things were guaranteed.

After stating the "if . . . then" syllogism of the reality of the Lord's resurrection, Paul continued to explain the eschatological (future) events that have been initiated as a result of the Lord's resurrection. The word "eschatology" (study of "future events," *eschaton*) triggers an image of the future from the readers' perspective – that is, Paul was talking about events that would happen ages from now. In the New Testament, however, the *eschaton* ("last days") began with Christ at his first coming and would culminate at his second coming. The foremost event of Paul's eschatology, then, was the resurrection of the Lord: "Now Christ has risen from the dead as the foremost (or firstfruits) of those asleep" (1 Cor 15:20). The term "firstfruits" referred to anything foremost or most significant, rather than simply "the first." When people brought the "firstfruits" as an offering, it was not necessarily the first yield, which was often small; instead, it was the best of the first crops. In the same way, although there were other resurrections (even performed by the Lord himself, such as the resurrection of Lazarus), the Lord's resurrection was the foremost – the one that brought in the *eschaton* (end days) and triggered all other resurrections (cf. John 11:25). Paul stated a theological and anthropological reason for Christ being the trigger of all resurrections: "Just as through one man death came, so through one man comes the resurrection of all the dead" (1 Cor 15:21). In another epistle Paul developed this concept in detail (Rom 5:12–19). When Adam disobeyed God, he brought in death.

Death spread throughout the entire humanity. All died and continue to die. God reversed this in the Lord Jesus Christ. In his resurrection the entire humanity is resurrected and faces judgment (Rom 5:12–19). This, of course, is good news for those who believe in the Messiah, for they will have an abundant life with him. However, it is bad news for those who haven't been reconciled; they need to give an account for their lives. So the resurrection of the Lord Jesus Christ initiated the resurrection of all people: "Just as in Adam all died, thus also in Christ all will be made alive" (1 Cor 15:22).

The Jewish Christians within the Corinthian church would have been very curious as to what the resurrection of Jesus Christ meant for their belief in the *eschaton* ("future events"). They had anticipated the coming of the end days when the Messiah came and the resurrection occurred. So Paul addressed that question next with the conclusion that the resurrection of Jesus Christ had initiated the kingdom of God – it had both present and future aspects. Wright says, "Though the kingdom is still envisaged as future in 1 Corinthians 6:9, it is present in Romans 14:17 (even though Paul has been talking about the future judgment a few verses earlier), and then, in the fullest passage (1 Corinthians 15:25–29), it is both present and future."[17]

So Paul continued to narrate what happened when Christ was resurrected: "Each [was resurrected] in his or her own order: Christ the firstfruits, then those who are of Christ at his coming, then the rest" (1 Cor 1:23–24a). The Lord's resurrection was followed by the resurrection of the believers.[18] The resurrection of the believers was followed by the resurrection of everyone else. These events culminated in the coming of the kingdom of God. Paul had earlier mentioned that the kingdom of God was in the Corinthians' midst in power (1 Cor 4:20) and was actively drawing in members (1 Cor 6:9). The King, Jesus Christ, was ruling and gathering his people. Paul explained what that meant: "Then Christ hands the kingdom of God to God the Father, when he subdues all rulers, all authorities, and powers" (1 Cor 15:24b).[19] The reign of Christ that began at his resurrection continues because "it was necessary for him to continue to reign until 'all enemies have been placed under his feet.' The last enemy he destroyed was death" (1 Cor 15:25–26). Paul quoted

---

17. N. T. Wright, *Paul: Fresh Perspectives* (London: SPCK, 2005), 137.

18. It is possible to understand the phrase "at his coming" as a future event. But most likely Paul was still in the narrative describing the coming of the Lord back from the dead, the resurrection, and implying that his resurrection started the resurrection of Christians. But that is not to deny the future extension of what had begun.

19. The grammar is uncertain as to whether Paul meant "Christ" would subdue or "the Father" would subdue, but, because of the verb's proximity to the Father, the latter is preferable.

a psalm of David that focused on the glory of mankind, whom God created to be over all of creation and under whose care he subjected all things (Ps 8). The last enemy that repeatedly had victory over mankind was death. But the Messiah conquered that last enemy at his resurrection. As a result, everyone's death would be conquered, that is, everyone will be resurrected because Christ reigns.

Christ defeated all things because the Father "placed all things under his feet." The only exception to the Messiah's full authority was the Father: "When he said that all have been subjected to him, it does not include the one who subjected all things to him" (1 Cor 15:27b). When the Father submitted all things to him, the Son in turn submitted all things under the Father's feet, so that God might be all in all (1 Cor 15:28). One must not assume from the phrase "so that God might be all in all" (15:28b) that Christ was ontologically (in his existence) submissive to God. Christ was, is, and will be co-equal with God (John 1:1). Instead, this passage refers to a functional submission of all rule, power, and authority to the Father by the Son. All of these events could happen only if Christ had been raised, just as all the apostles testified and proclaimed.

Just as the Corinthians needed to be affirmed in the truth of the resurrection, so we too need to be firmly convinced of it. Resurrection hope alone enables us to endure the struggles of this present world.

Death Rituals (15:29)

Death is no respecter of persons. Even with their belief of a cyclical reincarnation of souls, Hindus are grieved by death. Since the body that departed was precious to the family, it is treated as sacred. For the Hindus, cremation of the body honors the departed soul the most. Some believe that if the body is not cremated the soul remains nearby for days or months. (The bodies of lower-caste people are not necessarily burned.) The cremation ceremony begins with the ritual cleansing, dressing, and adorning of the body. Then the body is carried to the cremation ground as prayers are chanted to Yama (god of the underworld) to seek his help. The chief mourner (usually the eldest son) takes from the hands of the untouchable people who tend the funeral pyres the twigs of holy kusha grass that has been burning. He circles the pyre anticlockwise, since everything is backwards at the time of death. His sacred thread, which usually hangs on his left shoulder, has been moved to the right. Finally he lights the pyre upon which the dead person is laid. As the corpse is almost burned he performs a rite called *kapālkriyā*, in which he cracks the skull with a long bamboo stick to release the soul from the entrapped body. After cremation, the ashes are thrown in a river (ideally in the Ganges) and the ritual for the body is complete. The soul, however, still needs care. To help the soul in its voyage to the otherworld, an eleven-day ritual (called *shraddha*) is performed. The ritual consists of the daily offering of rice balls (*pindas*) that symbolically give strength to the departed soul in its journey. Also a lamp is lit to help the soul's travel along the dark path. On the twelfth day the soul is understood to have reached its destination and the rituals for the soul are complete.[20]

Apparently the Corinthians had a similar practice that Paul alluded to in 1 Corinthians: "[If there is no resurrection] what are they – 'those who baptize over the dead' – doing? If all the dead people are not raised, why are they baptizing over them?" (1 Cor 15:29). This verse has been so difficult to interpret that scholars have proposed over two hundred views.[21] Some of the most prominent interpretations are as follows. (1) The Corinthians had the practice of being baptized vicariously for their unbelieving relatives or friends who had died.[22] (2) The Corinthians were being baptized for other Christians who had died before being baptized themselves.[23] (3) The new believers in Corinth were being baptized because of the influence of the Christians who were now dead.[24] (4) The Corinthians were being baptized with the hope that they would see their relatives who had died.[25] Whatever the practice was, Paul didn't see it as an issue to argue about. Fee's observation is pertinent: "Paul's apparently noncommittal attitude toward it, while not implying approval, would seem to suggest that he did not consider it to be a serious fault as most interpreters do."[26] Instead, Paul used it as an additional

---

20. Rajat Nayyar, "Antim Samskara (the Final Phase): After Death Rituals in a Hindu Brahmin Family (3 Days Video Documentation)," https://www.academia.edu/2315130/.

21. Conzelmann mentions that there are over two hundred interpretive solutions (Conzelmann, *1 Corinthians*, 276 n. 120). For a survey of several major views on this verse, see John D. Reaume, "Another Look at 1 Corinthians 15:29," *Bibliotheca Sacra* 152 (October-December 1995): 457–475. Also Fee, *First Epistle to the Corinthians*, 764–767.

22. Morris, *First Epistle of Paul to the Corinthians*, 214–215. Richard E. DeMaris, "Corinthian Religion and Baptism for the Dead (1 Corinthians 15:29): Insights from Archeology and Anthropology," *Journal of Biblical Literature* 114, no. 4 (1995): 661–682.

23. Witherington III, *Conflict and Community in Corinth*, 305.

24. John D. Reaume, "Another Look at 1 Corinthians 15:29," *Bibliotheca Sacra* 152, no. 608 (October–December 1995): 475.

25. J. K. Howard, "Baptism for the Dead, a Study of 1 Corinthians 15:29," *Evangelical Quarterly* 37 (1965): 137–141.

26. Fee, *First Epistle to the Corinthians*, 767.

argument to emphasize the assurance of the resurrection of the dead: why would anyone get baptized for those who had died if they didn't believe the dead would be resurrected? They believed in resurrection, and that was why they got baptized.

In fact, the belief in the resurrection strengthened Paul and other Christians to endure persecution. Even at the time of writing the letter Paul was in imminent danger (1 Cor 15:30). Yet Paul could be assured of two things: the Corinthians' faith in Christ Jesus was secure, and he would certainly face further persecution (1 Cor 15:31). He illustrated this with an event that had happened in Ephesus, where he fought wild beasts (1 Cor 15:32a). He might actually have been thrown into an arena with wild beasts, or he might have been referring to a figurative fight he had had with false teachers. But why should he have endured persecutions? Couldn't he have just lived by the motto "let us eat and drink, for tomorrow we die" (1 Cor 15:32b)? He wouldn't live like that because he knew there was a resurrection of the dead; he too would be resurrected. So he challenged the Corinthians again to believe in the certainty of resurrection.

Karma (15:33–34)

Karma is a key doctrine of Hinduism. Often it is misrepresented as "actions and consequences" – that every bad action has a bad consequence, every good action has a good consequence, a bad karma can be reversed by a good action, and so on. But in Hinduism, karma is treated as "character formation," that is, every act – good or bad – impacts one's personality, which in turn impacts one's actions. Rajaram writes, "*Karma* is the fundamental law of the moral world. Every act, good or bad, performed by humans has an impact on their personality. Conscious acts gradually grow into unconscious habits and become part of their character. Character, in its turn, determines action followed by its consequences. This is a vicious circle in which our mind is involved."[27] So a person who does an evil act *bends* his or her personality towards evil, which in turn produces more evil. A beggar's inclination leads him or her to begging, which in turn leads him or her to further begging. A murderer murders, and that in turn leads him or her to further acts of murder.

Paul, in contrast, instructed the Corinthians that the true cause of corruption was the company one kept: "Don't be deceived: 'Bad company

---

27. Rajaram, *Facets of Indian Culture*, 17.

ruins good morals'" (1 Cor 15:33). Paul said this in the context of some questioning the certainty of the resurrection. Keeping company with people who denied the resurrection within the Corinthian congregation could inadvertently corrupt the Corinthians' assurance of the resurrection, so Paul wanted the Corinthians to avoid them. Rather, they were to "Sober up and stop sinning" (1 Cor 15:34a). Those who denied the resurrection, in reality, "have no knowledge of God" and to join them was shameful for the Corinthians (1 Cor 15:34b). The Corinthians should avoid associating with such people and instead believe in the certainty of the resurrection.

Resurrected Body (15:35–50)

The uniqueness of Christianity is the belief in the bodily resurrection of people after their death. Some in the Corinthian congregation had questioned this. So Paul, having asserted the certainty of resurrection, answered two other key questions: "How will the dead be raised?" and "What kind of body will they have?" (1 Cor 15:35).

He first answered the second question: What kind of body will they have? Paul gave one illustration to show the *similarity* of the resurrected body with the present body (1 Cor 15:36–38) and a series of illustrations to show the *difference* between the resurrected body and the present body (1 Cor 15:39–50).

The best illustration of human resurrection was the death-burial-resurrection of a seed. The Corinthians were very familiar with this picture as there were many farmers among them. In addition, their goddesses Demeter and Kore represented this. Paul explained that, when a farmer sowed a seed, it first died under the earth; then God gave it life, and it came up from out of the earth with a body, a plant (1 Cor 15:36–38). This was true of wheat or any other plant. A farmer who sowed a wheat seed expected only a wheat plant; he would be a fool otherwise. Every farmer knew that when the seed of wheat was sown, after a time, a wheat plant would come. God gave it a new body, a plant body. In the same way, God would give *human* bodies to humans who died. The resurrected body would be *human* and *physical*.

Of course, this resurrected body wouldn't be exactly the same as the present body. Paul first asserted this – "All flesh is not the same" (1 Cor 15:39a) – and then he gave a series of illustrations: "People have one kind of flesh, animals have another kind of flesh, birds another kind of flesh, and fish another" (1 Cor 15:39b). Every kind of living creature has a different kind of flesh: birds have feathers, fish have scales, animals have skins, and humans have hair. This was true of the universe, too: "Heavenly bodies and earthly bodies differ: the heavenly glory is a different kind from the earthly glory – the sun has one kind of glory compared with the moon and stars; their glories differ" (1 Cor 15:40–41). Even before the scientific era they knew that the sun was of a different kind than the moon. The sun was fiery, the moon was pleasant, and stars twinkled. Paul said, "Likewise, the resurrected body will be [different from the pre-resurrected body]" (1 Cor 15:42a).

Then Paul explained how they would differ: "What is sown perishable will be raised imperishable, what is sown in dishonor will be raised in glory, what is sown in weakness will be raised in power" (1 Cor 15:42b–43). "Perishable" referred to the fact that the present human body is constantly failing – for example, through kidney failure, heart attacks, and liver damage. All of these would be changed; there would be no more perishing. Our present bodies are dishonorable in that eyes become near-sighted and hearing fails; not so with the resurrected body. Our bodies are weak – unable to run or walk, or easily tired. That too would be changed. There would be a fundamental change in its core: "It is sown as a soul-body but will be raised as a Spirit-body; just as there has been a soul-body, there will be a Spirit-body" (1 Cor 15:44). When Adam was created, he was a "living soul" (Gen 2:7). All humans since then have been living souls. In the resurrection, it would be different: the driving force would be the Spirit and people would therefore be Spirit-body people. Wright articulates it thus: "The present body, Paul is saying, is 'a [physical] body animated by "soul"'; the future body is 'a [transformed physical] body animated by God's Spirit.'"[28] That body would be patterned after the last Adam: "Just as it is written, 'The first man, Adam, became a living soul,' the last Adam would become a life-giving Spirit" (1 Cor 15:45). So the Spirit-body would resemble the last Adam, Jesus Christ, the life-giving Spirit, yet it would be human and bodily. The soul-body came first, then the Spirit-body (1 Cor 15:46). The first man was made up of earthly substance, but the second man would be made of heavenly substance (1 Cor 15:47). Just as humans on earth resembled the man from the dust, so the resurrected ones would resemble the one from heaven and have heavenly bodies (1 Cor 15:48). Just as the whole of humanity bore the image (icon) of the earthly man, so the resurrected ones would bear the image (icon) of the heavenly one (1 Cor 15:49). In other words, although the resurrected bodies would be human and

---

28. Wright, The Challenge of Easter, 26.

bodily, they would be imperishable, honorable, and strong. They would be Spirit-enabled, consisting of Jesus' resurrected and heavenly body materials.

Paul then concluded, "I say this to you, brothers and sisters: flesh and blood are not able to inherit the kingdom of God, nor the perishable inherit the imperishable" (1 Cor 15:50).[29] To be qualified to be a full inheritor of the eternal kingdom of God, one needs to be not in an earthly body but in a heavenly Spirit-resurrected-body. Ordinary flesh and blood cannot inherit it; only a second-born body (resurrected body) can fully inherit it (cf. John 3:3).

Here and Not Yet (15:51–58)

The early Christians lived with the realization that when Christ came, died, buried, and rose again, a new era began. It even affected how eternal life was viewed. Dodd writes, "Eternal life, the 'life of the Age to Come,' is now realized in experience. Christ is risen from the dead, the first-fruits of them that sleep, and we are raised with Him in newness of life. He who believes *has* life eternal."[30] To the Corinthians, Paul first taught the certainty of the resurrection. Then he taught the nature of the resurrection. Now he addressed another question that was raised: "How will the dead be raised?" Although Paul saw that the resurrection had already begun with the resurrection of Jesus Christ, there was a future element too. He explained that in this final section (1 Cor 15:51–58).

Paul began by speaking of a mystery, something previously undisclosed but now disclosed (1 Cor 15:51a). The mystery was: "Not all will sleep, but all will be transformed" (1 Cor 15:51b). He gave similar instructions to the Thessalonians who were worried about Christians who had died. They thought those Christians who had died would miss the resurrection. Paul affirmed that, although not all would die before the coming of Christ, all (alive and dead) would be transformed into the resurrected body. It would happen quickly: "In the flash of a moment, in the blink of an eye, at the trumpet's last call – all the dead will be raised imperishable and we will be transformed" (1 Cor 15:52). In an instant dead Christians would be resurrected in their glorified resurrected bodies and living Christians would be transformed into their glorified resurrected bodies. Such transformation was necessary

---

29. In the New Testament, the phrase "flesh and blood" refers either to humans (Matt 16:17; John 1:13; Gal 1:16; 1 Cor 15:50; Eph 6:12; Heb 2:14) or to Jesus Christ (John 6:53–56) – both being physical and bodily.

30. Dodd, *The Apostolic Preaching*, 86.

since "the perishable must put on the imperishable and the mortal body must wear immortality" (1 Cor 15:53). When this transformation happened, in the twinkling of an eye, then "the death of death" would be final and enduring so that all could say with Isaiah, "Death has been swallowed up in victory. Where, O death, is your victory? Where, O death, is your sting?" (1 Cor 15:54–55; Isa 25:8). The eschatological resurrection would leave death completely defeated. It would no longer have any sting. There would be no more deaths, and no more grief associated with death. Along with death would die two of its accomplices: sin (the guilty accomplice) and the law (the unwilling accomplice, the enabler; cf. Rom 7:13–14) (1 Cor 15:56). Paul wrote to the Romans in very clear terms that the law itself was never sinful. But sin had an agenda: to glorify itself. For that, it used the law and brought about destruction and sin in people's lives. Where there was no law, sin was unable to function. Where there was law, sin was fully functional (Rom 7). To understand this principle all we need to do is image a sign that says, "Wet paint – Don't touch!" The moment a person reads that instruction, sin is triggered so that he or she touches the paint. However, when death is defeated finally and ultimately, then also will the law and sin be defeated.

Only praise will be left: "Praise God who gives us victory through our Lord Jesus Christ" (1 Cor 15:57). When the Lord was resurrected, a series of eschatological events began. The culmination will be the death of sin, law, and death itself. The only voices that will remain will be voices of praise!

With such a hope of resurrection, Paul instructed the Corinthians to stand firm: "Therefore, my brothers and sisters, beloved people, become steadfast and unmovable, always abounding in the work of the Lord, knowing that your labor is not in vain in the Lord" (1 Cor 15:58). Paul's emphasis on their faithfulness in God's work in this concluding verse "could be felt as an anticlimax, but only if we had allowed ourselves to forget the multiple ways in which this extensive discussion of resurrection was linked to the rest of the letter."[31] Wright continues, "The point of it all has been that, despite the discontinuity between the present mode of corruptible physicality and the future world of non-corruptible physicality, there is an underlying continuity between present bodily life and future bodily life, and that gives meaning and direction to present Christian living."[32] It also gives meaning to a life under persecution. Just as the hope of resurrection gave endurance to Paul even to

---

31. Wright, *The Resurrection*, 359.
32. Ibid.

persevere under severe persecution, so he hoped that the Corinthians would be strengthened to work hard for the Lord, even in the midst of persecution, because of their hope of resurrection. He encouraged them by saying that God would honor their hard labor for the expansion of the gospel and the kingdom of God. They were to stand firm, firmly assured of the resurrection that awaited them both now and in the future.

18

1 Corinthians 16

Daan (16:1–4)

The Sanskrit word for charity is *daan*. According to Hindu scriptures, both the giver and the receiver must be of pure heart, otherwise both will go to hell. Helping those in need is the essence of *daan*. Feeding the hungry or teaching Vedas are considered to be the best types of *daan*. According to the Hindu scriptures, a hungry person at one's door is to be treated as a *deva* (a god or a goddess), and there are therefore many stories in the scriptures of how starving families give all they have to others who visit them. One of the scriptures, *Vasistha Samhitha*, sets out guidelines on giving: one who gives water to a stranger obtains all one desires; one who gives food to a stranger will have beautiful eyes and good memories; one who gives gifts for borrowing a cow receives riches equal to bathing in all sacred places; by giving a seat to a guest the giver becomes master of a harem; by giving an umbrella to a stranger the giver obtains a house; by giving a house to a poor person the giver receives a town; and the one who gives a shoe receives a vehicle (ch. 29).

The early Christians also strongly believed in sharing wealth and food with one another. In Jerusalem, for example, the early Christians sold everything they had and placed it at the disciples' feet to be distributed according to need (Acts 4:34–35). Paul was no exception. Wherever he went, he believed in helping the poor in need financially or in other ways (cf. Phil 1:5; 4:8; Gal 2:10). He had a variety of names for such giving: "fellowship" (2 Cor 8:4; 9:13; Rom 15:26), "service" (2 Cor 9:1; Rom 15:31), "grace" (2 Cor 8:6–7, 19), "blessing" (2 Cor 9:5), and "divine service" (2 Cor 9:12; Rom 15:27).[1] Before he concluded his letter to the Corinthians, he exhorted them to continue

---

1. Fee, *First Epistle to the Corinthians*, 812.

their giving to the poor, especially to fellow Christians in Jerusalem. In these eleven verses he addressed three issues: orderliness in collecting the funds (1 Cor 16:1–2), the transportation of the funds to the saints in Jerusalem (1 Cor 16:3–4), and the possibility of Timothy and himself accompanying those who carried the money to Jerusalem (1 Cor 16:5–11). This was Paul's fifth "and concerning . . ." discussion in which he answered questions the Corinthians had raised.

Paul began, "Concerning the collection for the saints, do just as I commanded the churches in Galatia" (1 Cor 16:1). The Galatian churches were more than nine hundred kilometers away from Corinth. It is therefore surprising that he instructed the Corinthians to follow the instructions he had given the Galatians. Contrary to popular belief, however, communications and travel were frequent in those days. Roman roads crisscrossed most of the main cities and people traveled frequently for business, politics, and pleasure. So it would not have been difficult for the Corinthians to get the instructions from the Galatians. In addition, in this way Paul was affirming the principle of the unity of churches worldwide.

Paul then gave specific instructions: "On the first day of the week, each of you should set aside what he or she treasures from his or her abundance so that the collection won't have to be made only when I come" (1 Cor 16:2). In the early Christians' life, a week began on Sunday and ended on the Sabbath (the seventh day, Saturday). Since the Lord was resurrected on the first day of the week (Matt 28:1; Mark 16:2; Luke 24:1; John 20:1), Christians gathered together to celebrate on the first day of the week (Acts 20:7). So Paul wanted the Corinthians to collect the funds every Sunday, the first day of the week, when they gathered together, in order to avoid a hasty collection only when he got there. Paul wanted each person to contribute. This was possible because he wasn't asking for gifts that many might not have had, being slaves. Fee writes, "[Income] is probably a bit too modern, especially for a culture where a number of the community were slaves and had no 'income.'"[2] Rather, Paul wanted them to set aside what they "treasured – out of their abundance." In other words, he wanted their excess, what they had set aside "for a rainy day," what they treasured and hid. He wanted the Corinthians to plan their giving so that it would not be done hastily when he reached Corinth.

When he got there, he would make plans to take the money to the needy: "When I arrive, I will send those whom you deem trustworthy to carry your

---

2. Ibid., 814.

grace to Jerusalem" (1 Cor 16:3). Here Paul referred to their collection of funds as their "grace": something that they provided out of their goodness of heart. He would appoint people whom they trusted to carry the funds to the saints in Jerusalem. But he was willing to do more than that: "If you find it necessary that I also go, then they'll join me" (1 Cor 16:4).[3] If the Corinthians wanted the apostle Paul to carry the funds personally, he would do so.

Travel Plans (16:5–9)

This comment that, if the Corinthians needed him to carry the money to the saints in Jerusalem, he would do so, prompted him to give a quick update on his travel plans. Paul wrote, "I will come to you after I have gone through Macedonia, for I'll be going through Macedonia [first]" (1 Cor 16:5). Corinth was further south than Macedonian cities such as Philippi and Thessalonica, places Paul visited on his second missionary journey. This verse indicates that Paul was most likely in Ephesus, in Asia Minor, and was planning a trip to Corinth via Macedonia, the logical land route (unless one took a ship across the Mediterranean Sea to Corinth from Ephesus). He continued, "Perhaps I will stay with you and even spend the winter with you so that you can send me off leisurely as I plan to leave" (1 Cor 16:6). He was telling them that he would make that stay longer and not hurried before carrying the money to Jerusalem. The phrase "send me off" could imply the Corinthians supporting him financially, but in light of chapter 9, where he vehemently argued that he hadn't exercised that right among them, it would be unlikely that he expected their support. He wanted to postpone his trip to them so that he could "remain longer with you, provided the Lord allows me" (1 Cor 16:7). Although Paul often made plans for his travels, he was always mindful of the fact that God could change them, as he had done before (Acts 16:6). So he made a promise to visit the Corinthians on the condition that his plans were in alignment with the Lord's.

He had another plan too: "I wish to stay in Ephesus until Pentecost" (1 Cor 16:8). This wasn't a selfish desire; it was ministry-oriented: "For a great and effective door has opened for me, although there is opposition" (1 Cor 16:9).

---

3. For some general principles on giving, see Andrew B. Spurgeon, "Paul: Passionate to Help the Poor," *Journal of Asian Mission* 13, no. 2 (October 2012): 15–23. For the problems associated with receiving foreign funds in India, see Frampton F. Fox, "Foreign Money for India: Antidependency and Anticonversion Perspectives," *International Bulletin of Missionary Research* 30, no. 3 (July 2006): 137–142.

Apparently, a new ministry opportunity had opened up for him that kept him in Ephesus. But that ministry wasn't without opposition (cf. Acts 19:22–40). Paul wanted to see the Corinthians, but he would wait until Pentecost was over. Then he would travel through Macedonia and stay with the Corinthians after winter. Then he would carry the funds to the saints in Jerusalem.

Guru-Shishya Relationship (16:10–11)

The religion Sikhism derives its name from the Sanskrit word *shishya*, "disciple."[4] Sikhism is all about the relationship between a teacher and a student. Sikhs are monotheists – that is, they believe in one god. The main source of their knowledge is what the ten *gurus* (teachers) taught, which is written in *Guru Granth Sahib*, the Sikhs' holy book. A *guru* in Sikhism is a teacher-leader (*miri-piri*). He has both spiritual and temporal authority over disciples.

In Judaism there were also teachers and disciples. John the Baptist had disciples, and so did the Lord Jesus. Gamaliel was a famous teacher in Jerusalem and Paul studied under him. When Paul began on his journeys as a teacher, he too took in "disciples" whom he considered as "sons." The best known was Timothy, whose mother was Jewish and his father Greek. Timothy was from Derbe in Asia Minor (modern-day Turkey; Acts 16:1). Paul took him in as his disciple and son, and travelled with him or sent him on his behalf.

The Corinthians first saw Timothy when he came to see Paul in Corinth after spending some time in Macedonia (Acts 18:5). Now Paul was sending him again to Corinth, possibly carrying this letter. He had already told them that Timothy would instruct them about Paul's spiritual lifestyle (1 Cor 4:17). Now he instructed them to show hospitality to Timothy: "When Timothy comes, see to it that he doesn't become afraid of you. That's because he labors hard for the work of God, just as I do" (1 Cor 16:10). Paul might have been sure that the Corinthians, who loved him, would treat Timothy well. But it was a normal custom in those days to add a letter of recommendation for the carrier so that people would accept him or her as trustworthy and also "to protect the people from charlatans"[5] (see Rom 16:1–2). Paul continued, "Let no one treat him with contempt. Send him off in peace. When he comes

---

4. Rajaram, *Facets of Indian Culture*, 29.
5. Stott, *The Message of Romans*, 392.

to me, I am expecting him to come with other brothers or sisters" (1 Cor 16:11). Paul wanted no one to insult Timothy or treat him with contempt, possibly because he was a young man. Instead, he wanted them to send him off happily (in peace), and with other saints who could visit Paul.

Apollos (16:12–14)

Unlike Timothy, Apollos was an equal, a co-worker. Paul referred to him seven times in this epistle (1 Cor 1:12; 3:4, 5, 6, 22; 4:6; 16:12). It may be that some thought that Paul and Apollos were rivals, but Paul harbored no ill-feelings towards Apollos. There was no conflict or disunity between them (1 Cor 3:5, 6; 4:6). They disagreed about their travel plans and Paul wanted the Corinthians to know about that so that they wouldn't think Paul prevented Apollos from visiting them. So he wrote, "Concerning Apollos, brothers and sisters, I encouraged him many times to come to you with his brothers [or Christian friends]." Fee thinks that the "brothers" in question might have been Stephanus, Fortunatus, and Achaicus, who would return to the Corinthians after their visit with Paul (16:17).[6] Whoever was meant, Apollos wasn't able to visit the Corinthians then. But Paul assured them that Apollos would visit them when an opportunity arose (1 Cor 16:12). Something prevented Apollos' visit (perhaps God's will[7]), but it wasn't Paul who stopped him from visiting the Corinthians.

Regardless of whether Apollos or Paul visited them, the Corinthians had a mandate: "Stay alert, stand firm in faith, be courageous, and be strong" (1 Cor 16:13). The call to stay alert might have meant that they should watch out for false teachers. They were able to be alert, stand firm, be courageous and be strong, provided all of them grew in love (1 Cor 16:14), in line with Paul's emphasis on the importance of love in chapter 13. Love never fails.

Stephanus and Family (16:15–18)

Paul then discussed the family of Stephanus. Stephanus, along with others, visited Paul while his family remained back in Corinth. So Paul wanted the Corinthians to care for them, possibly because Stephanus wasn't returning with Timothy, who was carrying the letter to the Corinthians. Paul's

---

6. Fee, *First Epistle to the Corinthians*, 824.
7. Bruce, *1 and 2 Corinthians*, 160.

instructions were: "I ask you, brothers and sisters, you know the household of Stephanus, who were the firstfruits of salvation in Achaia, and how they devoted themselves to serving the Christians. [I am reminding you of this] so that you submit to such people, fellowship with them, and work with them in all things" (1 Cor 16:15–16). They were not only the first converts in Achaia (the region where Corinth was situated) but also some of the few people Paul had baptized (cf. 1 Cor 1:16). It is likely that they hosted the Corinthian church in their house, and that was one reason why Paul spoke highly of them. He wanted the Corinthians to honor them, fellowship with them, and work with them for the gospel.

While the church was taking care of them, Stephanus and others were with Paul. He wrote, "I rejoice at the coming of Stephanus, Fortunatus, and Achaicus, because they have fulfilled what you have lacked in providing" (1 Cor 16:17). Since Paul wasn't expecting any monetary benefits from them, what they provided him with was "fellowship" or "a comforting presence." He affirmed thus: "They refresh my spirit and yours" (1 Cor 16:18a). Fortunatus meant "blessed" or "lucky" and was a common name among slaves and freed slaves.[8] Similarly, Achaicus "belongs to the class of geographical names, which (when not titles of honor bestowed on Roman conquerors) were commonly servile."[9] Interestingly, these men continued their service even after coming to Christian faith, by serving Paul and the Corinthian church. Their work was so valuable that Paul commanded the Corinthians: "Therefore, recognize such people," meaning "honor them with respect" (1 Cor 16:18b).

The Letter's Conclusion (16:19–24)

Indian schools follow different syllabi depending on the board of education, and one dominant board is CBSE (Central Board of Secondary Education). It is a board of education for private and public schools under the Union Government of India and with its headquarters in New Delhi. A standard form of letter-writing is taught in all CBSE schools. A "formal letter" has the following sections, moving from top to bottom: the address of the writer, the date, the designation and address of the recipient, Sir/Madam, a one-sentence subject matter, the body of the letter, "Yours truly/faithfully," and

---

8. Fee, *First Epistle to the Corinthians*, 831.

9. William M. Ramsay, *Historical Commentary on First Corinthians*, ed. Mark Wilson (Grand Rapids: Kregel, 1996), 29.

the sender's full name (handwritten) and designation. An "informal letter" has fewer sections: the address of the writer, the date, salutation, the body, and the subscription.[10]

Letter-writing in the ancient world also followed strict guidelines. It began with a reference to the author, the addressee, and a greeting, and concluded with greetings from the writer's friends, greetings from the writer, and a benediction.

Paul followed a similar pattern when he wrote to the Corinthians, and to conclude the letter he first sent greetings from his friends (1 Cor 16:19–20); second, he sent his own greetings (1 Cor 16:21); and finally, he gave a benediction (16:22–24).

The churches in Asia, where Paul was when he wrote this letter, sent their greetings to the Corinthians (1 Cor 16:19a). It is likely they were churches such as those in Ephesus and Colossae. Also, Aquila and Prisca greeted the Corinthians warmly in the Lord, along with the church that met in their house (1 Cor 16:19b).[11] Aquila and Prisca were the husband and wife whom Paul had met in Corinth when he visited the first time (Acts 18:1). They were originally from Rome and had been expelled under Claudius' edict ejecting all the Jews from Rome (Acts 18:2). They settled in Corinth and worked as tentmakers. They took Paul into their home and employed him, since he knew their trade. Somehow they had relocated to Asia, where Paul was. They might have been wealthy business people, given that they had homes in Rome, Corinth, and Ephesus. They also were generous – they hosted a house church wherever they were (1 Cor 16:19; Rom 16:3–5).

Aquila and Prisca and the church that they hosted in their house sent their greetings to the Corinthian church. They and Paul extended their "holy kiss" to the Corinthians. Blomberg writes, "The 'holy kiss' was probably borrowed from common ancient practice, both sacred and secular, Jewish and Gentile. Customarily, men greeted other men and women other women by embracing each other and kissing one another on the cheek."[12] Interestingly, this command to greet one another with a holy kiss occurs in only four of Paul's letters: Romans, 1 Corinthians, 2 Corinthians, and 1 Thessalonians. Most likely the recipients, being Romans, already had the practice of greeting

---

10. http://sanjukta.org/wp-content/uploads/2013/04/Formal-and-Informal-Letters.pdf

11. Kistemaker writes, "The name *Aquila* is Latin for 'eagle' and Prisca is a diminutive form of Priscilla, which in Latin means 'ancient' or 'elderly'" (Kistemaker, *Exposition of the Acts of the Apostles*, 648).

12. Blomberg, *1 Corinthians*, 339.

each other with a kiss. So Paul, Aquila, Prisca, and the church in their house wished the same for the Corinthians.

Amanuensis (16:21)

It is common in India to see several typists and stenographers around a courthouse. Illiterate people come to them, report their complaints, and the typists and stenographers type those complaints for them in order to submit them in court.

In ancient cultures like the Greco-Roman culture, teachers like Paul used a secretary to write letters. Such a person is known as an amanuensis. The role of an amanuensis ranged from word-for-word dictation to writing the author's thoughts in the amanuensis's language and style. It is probable that Paul's amanuenses took dictations since his message was significant, authoritative, and he was an eloquent, educated person. Because the amanuensis would write most of the letter in his or her own hand, the author would pen his or her own greetings in the concluding paragraphs. This is why Paul attached a note to the Corinthians, saying, "The greeting of Paul in my own hand," meaning that he signed the document at the end so as to authenticate it and to give it authority (1 Cor 16:21).

Benediction (16:22–24)

Most ancient letters ended with just a benediction. But Paul's letter to the Corinthians included a warning, a wish, a benediction, and a personal note. The warning was: "If anyone does not love the Lord, he or she abides accursed" (1 Cor 16:22a). Paul constantly evangelized and wished that all people would come to know Jesus Christ as the Lord. But he also knew that many rejected the gospel, even in Corinth (Acts 18:6) – hence this warning.

His wish was stated in two single Aramaic words: *marana tha* (1 Cor 16:22b) – "Our Lord, come!" Interestingly, it could also be read as *maran atha*, meaning "Our Lord has come!" Both were true in Paul's teaching: the Lord Jesus Christ has come once, and he will come again.

The benediction was "The grace of the Lord Jesus be with you" (1 Cor 16:23). Paul had begun the letter with a reference to the grace of God the Father and the Lord Jesus Christ (1 Cor 1:3); now he concluded the letter with a reference to the grace of the Lord Jesus. Grace summarized how Paul and the Corinthians were included in God's family. That is why he used this phrase as the benediction.

His personal note was "My love is with you all in Christ Jesus" (1 Cor 16:24). Paul never stopped loving the Corinthians. They were people who kept all the traditions Paul had handed to them (1 Cor 11:1). As he reminded them repeatedly, they were his beloved people (1 Cor 4:14; 10:14; 15:58).

Conclusion

The study of Paul's letter to the Corinthians in the context of Indian culture is exhilarating. It is like being on a roller coaster: there are upbeat discussions (e.g. the joy of marriage, the reverence of the Lord's Supper, and the certainty of resurrection) and downbeat ones (e.g. someone living with his father's wife, the Corinthians visiting temple prostitutes, or some abusing the Lord's Supper). Paul not only addressed questions that the Corinthians raised, but he did so with Pauline flair: each topic has so many twists and turns that one is left with the awesome realization of his intelligence and the impact of God's Word. This letter, 1 Corinthians, is truly amazing and we are privileged to have it in our possession so that we can study and apply the principles it contains to our own lives.

Bibliography

Aasgaard, Reidar. "Paul as a Child: Children and Childhood in the Letters of the Apostle." *Journal of Biblical Literature* 126, no. 1 (2007): 129–159.

Abel, M. *The Church of South India after Thirty Years*. Madras (Chennai): Christian Literature Society, 1978.

Abraham, K. C., and Ajit K. Abraham. "Homosexuality: Some Reflections from India." *Ecumenical Review* 50, no. 1 (January 1998): 22–29.

Adesina, Abdur-Razaq B. "Islam and Female Circumcision: A Critical Appraisal." *Hamdard Islamicus* 29, no. 2 (April–June 2006): 59–67.

Adewuya, J. Ayodeji. "Revisited 1 Corinthians 11.27-34: Paul's Discussion of the Lord's Supper and African Meals." *Journal for the Study of the New Testament* 30, no. 1 (2007): 95–112.

Alderink, Larry J. "Mythical and Cosmological Structure in the Homeric Hymn to Demeter." *Numen* 29, no. 1 (July 1982): 1–16.

Alford, Deann. "Tongues Tied: Southern Baptists Bar New Missions Candidates from Glossolalia." *Christianity Today* 50, no. 2 (February 2006): 21.

Allison, Dale C. Jr. "Divorce, Celibacy and Joseph (Matthew 1:18–25 and 19:1–12)." *Journal for the Study of the New Testament*, no. 49 (March 1993): 3–10.

Allocco, Amy Leigh. "Rear, Reverence and Ambivalence: Divine Snakes in Comtemporary South India." *Religions of South Asia* 7 (2013): 230–48.

Andrews, Charles F. *Mahatma Gandhi: His Life & Ideas*. Delhi: Jaico Publishing House, 2005.

Ankara, Anton. "Loving the Lepers: A Murdered Missionary's Widow Carries on Her Husband's Work." *Christianity Today* 44, no. 1 (2000): 32, 34.

Appasamy, A. J. *As Christ in the Indian Church (A. J. Appasamy Speaks to the Indian Church)*. Chennai, India: Christian Literature Society, 1935.

Athyal, Leelamma. *Man and Woman: Towards a Theology of Partnership*. Tiruvalla, India: Christava Sahitya Samithy, 2005.

———. "India: The Joint Council of the Church of North India (CNI), Church of South India (CSI), and the Malankara Mar Thoma Syrian Church (MTC)." *The Ecumenical Review* 52, no. 1 (January 2000): 11–19.

Avalon, Arthur. *Sāradā-Tilaka Tantram*. Delhi, India: Motilal Banarsidass, n.d.

Avery, Peter, and Susan Ehrlich. *Teaching American English Pronounciation*. Oxford: Oxford University Press, 1992.

Bailey, Kenneth E. *Paul through Mediterranean Eyes: Cultural Studies in 1 Corinthians*. Downers Grove, IL: IVP Academic, 2011.

Baird, William. "Among the Mature: The Idea of Wisdom in 1 Corinthians 2:6." *Interpretation* 13, no. 4 (1959): 425–432.

———. "1 Corinthians 10:1–13." *Interpretation* 44, no. 3 (July 1990): 286–290.

Barré, Michael L. "To Marry or to Burn: Pyrousthai in 1 Cor 7:9." *Catholic Biblical Quarterly* 36, no. 2 (April 1974): 193–202.

Barrett, C. K. *A Commentary on the First Epistle to the Corinthians.* Harper's New Testament Commentaries, edited by Henry Chadwick. New York: Harper & Row, 1968.

———. *The First Epistle to the Corinthians.* Vol. 47, Black's New Testament Commentary Series, edited by Henry Chadwick. Peabody, MA: Hendrickson, 1968.

Basu, Asoke. "Advaita Vedanta and Ethics." *Religion East & West* 4 (June 2004): 91–105.

Beard, Mary. *The Roman Triumph.* Cambridge: The Belknap Press of Harvard University Press, 2007.

Bedale, Stephen. "The Meaning of *Kephale* in the Pauline Epistles." *Journal of Theological Studies* 5 (1984): 211–215.

Bedi, Sohindar Singh Wanajara. *Folklore of the Punjab.* Bombay: India Book Trust, 1971.

Bennema, Cornelis. "Early Christian Identity Formation and Its Relevance for Modern India." In *Indian and Christian: Changing Identities in Modern India: Papers from the First SAIACS Annual Consultation 9–12 November 2010*, edited by Cornelis Bennema and Paul Joshua Bhakiaraj, 59–76. Bangalore, India: SAIACS Press.

———. "Mimesis in John 13: Cloning or Creative Articulation?" *Novum Testamentum* 56 (2014): 261–274.

Bergant, Dianne. "The Ousider Becomes an Insider: The New Center Is on the Margin." *Living Pulpit* 13, no. 4 (October–December 2004): 8–9.

Blomberg, Craig L. *1 Corinthians: The NIV Application Commentary, from Biblical Text . . . To Contemporary Life.* The NIV Application Commentary Series, edited by Terry Muck. Grand Rapids: Zondervan, 1995.

Blue, Bradley B. "The House Church at Corinth and the Lord's Supper: Famine, Food Supply, and the Present Distress." *Criswell Theological Review* 5, no. 2 (1991): 221–239.

Borchert, Gerald L. "1 Corinthians 7:15 and the Church's Historic Misunderstanding of Divorce and Remarriage." *Review & Expositor* 96, no. 1 (Winter 1999): 125–129.

Bosch, Lourens P. van den. "A Burning Question: Sati and Sati Temples as the Focus of Political Interest." *Numen* 37, no. 2 (December 1990): 174–194.

Boucher, Madeleine. "Some Unexplored Parallels to 1 Cor 11, 11–12 and Gal 3, 28: The NT on the Role of Women." *Journal of Biblical Literature* 31, no. 1 (January 1969): 50–58.

Broneer, Oscar. "Corinth: Center of St. Paul's Missionary Work in Greece." *Biblical Archaeologist* 14, no. 4 (December 1951): 78–96.

Bruce, F. F. *1 and 2 Corinthians.* New Century Bible Commentary, edited by Ronald E. Clements and Matthew Black. Grand Rapids: Eerdmans, 1971.

Burk, Denny. "Discerning Corinthian Slogans through Paul's Use of the Diatribe in 1 Corinthians 6:12–20." *Bulletin for Biblical Research* 18, no. 1 (2008): 99–121.

Byrne, Brendan. "Sinning against One's Own Body: Paul's Understanding of the Sexual Relationship in 1 Corinthians 6:18." *Catholic Biblical Quarterly* 45, no. 4 (October 1983): 608–616.

Callaway, Joseph A. "Corinth." *Review & Expositor* 57, no. 4 (October 1960): 381–388.

Campbell, Barth Lynn. "Flesh and Spirit in 1 Cor 5:5: An Exercise in Rhetorical Criticism of the NT." *Journal of the Evangelical Theological Society* 36, no. 3 (September 1993): 331–342.

Caragounis, Chrys C. "Opsonion: A Reconsideration of Its Meaning." *Novum Testamentum* 16, no. 1 (1974): 35–57.

———. *The Development of Greek and the New Testament: Morphology, Syntax, Phonology, and Textual Transmission.* Grand Rapids: Baker Academic, 2006.

Cervin, Richard S. "Does *Kaphale* Mean 'Source' or 'Authority over' in Greek Literature?" *Trinity Journal* 10 (1989): 85–112.

Chatterjee, Satischandra. *The Fundamentals of Hinduism.* Calcutta, India: The University of Calcutta, 1970.

Chilton, Bruce. "Churches." *The Living Pulpit* 9, no. 4 (October–December 2000): 18–19.

Chisholm Jr, Robert B. "'To Whom Shall You Compare Me?' Yahweh's Polemic against Baal and the Babylonian Idol-Gods in Prophetic Literature." In *Christianity and the Religions: A Biblical Theology of World Religions*, edited by Edward Rommen and Harold Netland, 56–71. Pasadena, CA: William Carey Library, 1995.

Ciampa, Roy E. "Revisiting the Euphemism in 1 Corinthians 7:1." *Journal for the Study of the New Testament* 31, no. 3 (March 2009): 325–338.

Clarke, Sathianathan. "Dalits Overcoming Violation and Violence: A Contest between Overpowering and Empowering Identities in Changing India." *The Ecumenical Review* 54, no. 3 (July 2002): 278–295.

Collier, Gary D. "'That We Might Not Crave Evil': The Structure and Argument of 1 Corinthians 10.1-13." *Journal for the Study of the New Testament* 55 (1994): 55–75.

Collins, Adela Yarbro. "The Function of 'Excommunication' in Paul." *Harvard Theological Review* 73, no. 1–2 (January–April 1980): 251–263.

Collins, Raymond F. *First Corinthians.* Sacra Pagina Series, edited by Daniel J. Harrington. Collegeville, MN: Liturgical Press, 1999.

Consortium, The Indian Genome Variations, "The Indian Genome Variation Database (Igvdb): A Project Overview", http://www.imtech.res.in/raghava/reprints/IGVdb.pdf.

Conzelmann, Hans. *1 Corinthians: A Commentary on the First Epistle to the Corinthians*. Hermeneia: A Critical & Historical Commentary on the Bible. Philadelphia: Fortress Press, 1975.

Corley, Jeremy. "The Pauline Authorship of 1 Corinthians 13." *Catholic Biblical Quarterly* 66, no. 2 (April 2004): 256–274.

Cosgrove, Charles H. "A Woman's Unbound Hair in the Greco-Roman World, with Special Reference to the Story of the 'Sinful Woman' in Luke 7:36–50." *Journal of Biblical Literature* 124, no. 4 (Winter 2005): 675–692.

Courtright, Paul B. "Book Review: Ashes of Immorality: Widow-Burning in India by Catherine Weinberger-Thomas, Translated by Jeffrey Mehlman and David Gordon White (Chicago: Chicago University Press, 1999)." *Journal of the American Academy of Religion* 69, no. 2 (June 2001): 516–519.

Cox, Steven L. "1 Corinthians 13 – an Antidote to Violence: Love." *Review & Expositor* 93 (1996): 529–536.

Crossan, John Dominic. *Jesus: A Revolutionary Biography*. San Francisco: HarperSanFrancisco, 1994.

Danino, Michel. *Indian Culture and India's Future*. New Delhi, India: D. K. Printworld Limited 2011.

Deadwyler, William H. "The Devotee and the Deity: Living a Personalistic Theology." In *Gods of Flesh, Gods of Stone: The Embodiment of Divinity in India*, edited by Joanne Punzo Waghome, Norman Cutler and Vasudha Narayanan, 69–88. New York: Columbia University Press, 1985.

Debroy, Bibek. *Sarama and Her Children: The Dog in Indian Myth*. New Delhi, India: Penguin Books, 2008.

Deissmann, Adolf. *Light from the Ancient East*. Translated by Lionel R. M. Strachan. New York: George H. Doran, 1927.

Delasanta, Rodney. "Putting Off the Old Man and Putting on the New: Ephesians 4:22–24 in Chaucer, Shakespeare, Swift, and Dostoevsky." *Christianity and Literature* 51, no. 3 (Spring 2002): 339–362.

DeMaris, Richard E. "Corinthian Religion and Baptism for the Dead (1 Corinthians 15:29): Insights from Archeology and Anthropology." *Journal of Biblical Literature* 114, no. 4 (1995): 661–682.

Deming, Will. "The Unity of 1 Corinthians 5–6." *Journal of Biblical Literature* 115, no. 2 (Summer 1996): 289–312.

DeNapoli, Antoinette. "'Real Sadhus Sing to God': The Religious Capital of Devotion and Domesticity in the Leadership of Female Renouncers in Rajasthan." *Journal of Feminist Studies in Religion* 29, no. 1 (Spring 2013): 117–133.

Dharamraj, Havilah, and Angukali V. Rotokha. "History, History Books and the Blue Jackal." In *Indian and Christian: Changing Identities in Modern India (Papers from the First SAIACS Annual Consultation 9–12 November 2010)*, edited by Cornelis Bennema and Paul Joshua Bhakiaraj. Bangalore, India: SAIACS Press, 2011.

Dockery, David S. "The Role of Women in Worship and Ministry: Some Hermeneutical Questions." *Criswell Theological Review* 1 (Spring 1987): 363–386.

Dodd, C. H. *The Apostolic Preaching and Its Developments: Three Lectures with an Appendix on Eschatology and History.* London: Hodder & Stroughton Limited, 1936.

Dugan, John. "Preventing Ciceronianism: C. Lucinius Calvus' Regimen for Sexual and Oratorical Self-Mastery." *Classical Philology* 96, no. 3 (2001): 400–428.

Dunn, James D. G. *Romans 1–8.* Vol. 38 A Word Biblical Commentary, eds David A. Huggard, Glenn W. Barker and Ralph P. Martin. Dallas, TX: Word Publishing, 1988.

———. *The Theology of Paul the Apostle.* Grand Rapids: Eerdmans, 1998.

———. *1 Corinthians.* T&T Clark Study Guides, eds. Michael A. Knibb, A. T. Lincoln and R. N. Whybray. London: T&T Clark International, 1999.

Ekem, John David K. "Does 1 Cor 11:2-16 Legislate for 'Head Covering'?" *Neotestamentica* 35, no. 1–2 (2001): 169–176.

Ellis, E. Earle. "Note on 1 Corinthians 10:4." *Journal of Biblical Literature* 76, no. 1 (March 1957): 53–56.

Ellis, J. Edward. "Controlled Burn: The Romantic Note in 1 Corinthians 7." *Perspectives in Religious Studies* 29, no. 1 (Spring 2002): 89–98.

Engelbrecht, Edward A. "'To Speak in a Tongue': The Old Testament and Early Rabbinic Background of a Pauline Expression." *Concordia Journal* 22, no. 3 (July 1996): 295–302.

Engineer, Asgharali. "Politics of Identity, Caste and Religion in India." *Hamdard Islamicus* 33, no. 3–4 (July–December 2010): 186–190.

Erickson, Millard J. *Christian Theology.* 2nd ed. Grand Rapids: Baker Academic, 1998.

———. *Making Sense of the Trinity: Three Crucial Questions.* Grand Rapids: Baker, 2000.

Evans, Craig A. "How Are the Apostles Judges? A Note on 1 Corinthians 3:10–15." *Journal of the Evangelical Theological Society* 27, no. 2 (June 1984): 149–150.

Evenson, George O. "Force of *Apo* in 1 Corinthians 11:23." *Lutheran Quarterly* 11, no. 3 (1959): 244–246.

Falusi, Gabriel K. "African Levirate and Christianity." *AFER* 24, no. 5 (October 1982): 300–308.

Fantin, Joseph D. *The Lord of the Entire World: Lord Jesus, a Challenge to Lord Caesar?* New Testament Monographs. Sheffield, England: Sheffield Phoenix Press, 2011.

Fee, Gordon D. "Tongues–Least of the Gifts? Some Exegetical Observations on 1 Corinthians 12-14." *PNEUMA: The Journal of the Society for Pentecostal Studies* (1980).

———. "1 Corinthians 7:1 in the NIV." *Journal of the Evangelical Theological Society* 23, no. 4 (December 1980): 307–314.

———. *The First Epistle to the Corinthians.* 1ˢᵗ ed. New International Commentary on the New Testament. Grand Rapids: Eerdmans, 1987.

Fellows, Richard G. "Renaming in Paul's Churches: The Case of Crispus-Sosthenes Revisited." *Tyndale Bulletin* 56, no. 2 (2005): 112–130.

Ferguson, Neil. "Separating Speaking in Tongues from Glossolalia Using a Sacramental View." *Colloquium* 43, no. 1 (May 2011): 39–58.

Fernandes, Walter. "Implications of the Involvement of a Minority Group in People's Struggles: The Case of India." *Mission Studies* 2, no. 1 (1985): 26–31.

Fesko, J. V. "N. T. Wright on Imputation." *Reformed Theological Review* 66, no. 1 (April 2007): 2–22.

Fetherolf, Christina M. "The Body for a Temple, a Temple for a Body: An Examination of Bodily Metaphors in 1 Corinthians." *Proceedings (Grand Rapids, MI)* 30 (2010): 88–106.

Finney, Mark. "Honour, Head-Coverings and Headship: 1 Corinthians 11.2–16 in Its Social Context." *Journal for the Study of the New Testament* 33, no. 1 (September 2010): 31–58.

Fiore, Benjamine. "'Covert Allusion' in 1 Corinthians 1–4." *The Catholic Biblical Quarterly* 47 (1985): 85–102.

Fiorenza, Elizabeth Schüssler. *In Memory of Her: A Feminist Theological Reconstruction of Christian Origins.* New York: Crossroad, 1983.

Fiske, Adele M. "Death: Myth and Ritual." *Journal of the American Academy of Religion* 37, no. 3 (September 1969): 249–265.

Fotopoulos, John. "The Rhetorical Situation, Arrangement, and Argumentation of 1 Corinthians 8:1–13: Insights into Paul's Instructions on Idol-Food in Greco-Roman Context." *Greek Orthodox Theological Review* 47, no. 1–4 (2002): 165–198.

Fox, Frampton F. "Foreign Money for India: Antidependency and Anticonversion Perspectives." *International Bulletin of Missionary Research* 30, no. 3 (July 2006): 137–142.

Furnish, Victor Paul. "Fellow Workers in God's Service." *Journal of Biblical Literature* 80, no. 4 (1961): 364–370.

Gandhi, M. K. *From Yeravda Mandir (Ashram Observances).* Translated by Valji Govindji Desai. Ahmedabad, India: Jitendra T. Desai, 1932.

Ganeri, Jonardon. "The Hindu Syllogism: Nineteenth-Century Perceptions of Indian Logical Thought." *Philosophy East and West* 46, no. 1 (January 1996): 1–16.

Garcia, Mark A. "Imputation and the Christology of Union with Christ: Calvin, Osiander, and the Contemporary Quest for a Reformed Model." *Westminster Theological Journal* 68, no. 2 (Fall 2006): 219–251.

Garg, Chitra. *Indian Champions.* New Delhi: Rajpal & Sons, 2010.

Garland, David E. "The Christian's Posture toward Marriage and Celibacy: 1 Corinthians 7." *Review & Expositor* 80, no. 3 (Summer 1983): 351–362.

———. "The Dispute over Food Sacrificed to Idols (1 Cor 8:1–11:1)." *Perspectives in Religious Studies* 30, no. 2 (Summer 2003): 173–197.

Gaventa, Beverly Roberts. "'You Proclaim the Lord's Death': 1 Corinthians 11:26 and Paul's Understanding of Worship." *Review & Expositor* 80, no. 3 (Summer 1983): 377–387.

Geetz, Armin W. "Religious Narrative: An Introduction." *Bulletin for the Study of Religion* 42, no. 4 (November 2013): 3–9.

Georges, Jayson. "From Shame to Honor: A Theological Reading of Romans for Honor-Shame Contexts." *Missiology* 38, no. 3 (July 2010): 295–307.

Geyer, Alan. "The NCC's Rediscovery of India." *The Christian Century* 100, no. 14 (4 May 1983): 420–421.

Gill, David W. J. "The Importance of Roman Portraiture for Head-Coverings in 1 Corinthians 11:2–16." *Tyndale Bulletin* 41, no. 2 (1990): 245–260.

———. "The Meat-Market at Corinth (1 Corinthians 10:25)." *Tyndale Bulletin* 43, no. 2 (1992): 389–393.

Gillihan, Yonder Moynihan. "Jewish Laws on Illicit Marriage, the Defilement of Offspring, and the Holiness of the Temple: A New Halakic Interpretation of 1 Corinthians 7:14." *Journal of the Biblical Literature* 121, no. 4 (2002): 711–744.

Godet, F. *Commentary on the First Epistle of St. Paul to the Corinthians.* Translated by A. Custin. Grand Rapids: Zondervan, 1957.

Godman, David, ed. *Be as You Are: The Teachings of Sri Ramana Maharshi.* St. Ives, England: Clays Ltd, 1985.

Golden, Mark. *Children and Childhood in Classical Athens.* Baltimore, MD: Johns Hopkins University Press, 1990.

Goodman, Felicitas D. "Phonetic Analysis of Glossolalia in Four Cultural Settings." *Journal for the Scientific Study of Religion* 8, no. 2 (Fall 1969): 227–239.

Gravrock, Mark. "Why Won't Paul Just Say No? Purity and Sex in 1 Corinthians 6." *Word & World* 16, no. 4 (Fall 1996): 444–455.

Green, Donald E. "The Folly of the Cross." *The Master's Seminary Journal* 15, no. 1 (Spring 2004): 59–69.

Grudem, Wayne. "The Meaning of *Kephale* ('Head'): A Response to Recent Studies." In *Recovering Biblical Manhood and Womanhood*, edited by John Piper and Wayne Grudem. Wheaton, IL: Crossway, 1991.

———. "1 Corinthians 14.20-25: Prophecy and Tongues as Signs of God's Attitude." *Westminster Theological Journal* 41, no. 2 (Spring 1979): 381–396.

———. "Does *Kephale* ('Head') Mean 'Source' or 'Authority over' in Greek Literature? A Survey of 2,336 Examples." *Trinity Journal* 6, no. 1 (Spring 1985): 38–59.

Guin, Madhuri. "Brahma the Creator amongst the Hindu Trinity." *DollsofIndia* (2004).

Gupta, Dipankar. "Killing Caste by Conversion." *The Hindu* (13 November 2001).

Hamerton-Kelly, Robert G. "A Girardian Interpretation of Paul: Rivalry, Mimesis and Victimage in the Corinthian Correspondence." *Semeia* 33 (1985): 65–81.

Hanges, James C. "1 Corinthians 4:6 and the Possibility of Written Bylaws in the Corinthian Church." *Journal of Biblical Literature* 117, no. 2 (1998): 275–298.

Hansen, Collin. "The Son and the Crescent." *Christianity Today* 55, no. 2 (Fall 2011): 18–23.

Hays, Richard B. *First Corinthians*. Interpretation: A Bible Commentary for Teaching and Preaching, edited by James Luther Mays, Patrick D. Miller Jr and Paul J. Achtemeier. Louisville, KY: Westminster John Knox Press, 1997.

Hepner, Gershon. "The Morrow of the Sabbath Is the First Day of the Festival of Unleavened Bread (Lev 23, 15–17)." *Zeitschrift für die alttestamentliche Wissenschaft* 118, no. 3 (2006): 389–404.

Ho, Edward. "In the Eyes of the Beholder: Unmarked Attributed Quotations in Job." *Journal of Biblical Literature* 128, no. 4 (Winter 2009): 703–715.

Hodge, Charles. *1 Corinthians*. Crossway Classic Commentaries, edited by Alister McGrath and J. I. Packer. Wheaton, IL: Crossway Books, 1995.

Hoefer, Herbert. "Principles of Cross-Cultural/Ethnic Ministry: The Stories of Barnabas and Paul and the Jerusalem Council." *International Journal of Frontier Missions* 22, no. 1 (Spring 2005): 17–24.

Hoehner, Harold W. *Ephesians: An Exegetical Commentary*. Grand Rapids: Baker Academic, 2002.

———. "Can a Woman Be a Pastor-Teacher?" *Journal of the Evangelical Theological Society* 50, no. 4 (December 2007): 761-771.

———. "Chronological Aspects of the Life of Christ, Part IV: The Day of Christ's Crucifixion." *Bibliotheca Sacra* 131, no. 523 (July 1974): 241–264.

Holmyard, Harold R. III. "Does 1 Corinthians 11:2-16 Refer to Women Praying and Prophesying in Church?" *Bibliotheca Sacra* 154 (October–December 1997): 461–472.

Hommes, N. J. "Let Women Be Silent in Church: A Message Concerning the Worship Service and the Decorum to Be Observed by Women." *Calvin Theological Journal* 4, no. 1 (April 1969): 5–22.

Hooker, Morna D. "Interchange in Christ and Ethics." *Journal for the Study of the New Testament* 25 (1985): 3–17.

Horrell, J. Scott. "Cautions Regarding 'Son of God' in Muslim-Idiom Translations of the Bible: Seeking Sensible Balance." *St Francis Magazine* 6, no. 4 (August 2010): 638–666.

Horsley, G. H. R. "Name Change as an Indication of Religious Conversion in Antiquity." *Numen* 34, no. 1 (June 1987): 1–17.

Horsley, Richard A. *1 Corinthians*. Nashville, TN: Abingdon Press, 1998.

Houghton, Myron J. "A Reexamination of 1 Corinthians 13:8-13." *Bibliotheca Sacra* 153, no. 611 (July–September 1996): 344–356.

House, H. Wayne, ed. *Divorce and Remarriage: Four Christian Views*, Spectrum Multiview Book. Downers Grove, IL: InterVarsity Press, 1990.

Howard, J. K. "Baptism for the Dead, a Study of 1 Corinthians 15:29." *Evangelical Quarterly* 37 (1965): 137–141.

Hurley, Neil P. "The Two Faces of India." *Christian Century* 92, no. 33 (15 October 1975): 905–907.

Hutchinson, Paul. "Christianity in a Free India." *The Christian Century* 63, no. 46 (13 November 1946): 1366–1368.

Igboanyika, Sylbester U. N. "The History of Priestly Celibacy in the Church." *AFER* 45, no. 2 (June 2003): 98–105.

Inada, Kenneth K. "Amida Buddha, Whitehead's God, and the Temporal Fact." *Pure Land (Berkeley, Calif.)* 0, no. 15 (December 1998): 146–162.

Instone-Brewer, David. "1 Corinthians 7 in the Light of the Graeco-Roman Marriage and Divorce Papyri." *Tyndale Bulletin* 52, no. 1 (2001): 101–115.

———. "1 Corinthians 7 in the Light of the Jewish Greek and Aramaic Marriage and Divorce Papyri." *Tyndale Bulletin* 52, no. 2 (2001): 225–243.

———. *Divorce and Remarriage in the Bible: The Social and Literary Context*. Grand Rapids: Eerdmans, 2002.

———. *Divorce and Remarriage in the Church: Biblical Solutions for Pastoral Realities*. Downers Grove, IL: InterVarsity Press, 2006.

Ishida, Hoyu. "Nietzhe and Samsāra: Suffering and Joy in the Eternal Recurrence." *Pure Land (Berkeley, CA)* 15 (December 1998): 122–145.

Jacobsen, Knut A. "Three Functions of Hell in the Hindu Traditions." *Numen* 56, no. 2–3 (2009): 385–400.

Jenett, Dianne. "A Million *Shakti*srising: Pongala, a Women's Festival in Kerala, India." *Journal of Feminist Studies in Religion* 21, no. 1 (Spring 2005): 35–55.

Jenkins, Philip. "Whose Holy Ground?" *Christian Century* 129, no. 6 (March 21, 2012): 45.

Jervis, L. Ann. "1 Corinthians 14.34-35: A Reconsideration of Paul's Limitation of the Free Speech of Some Corinthian Women." *Journal for the Study of the New Testament* 58 (June 1995): 51–74.

Jones, E. Stanley. "Report on the New India." *Christian Century* 64 (1947): 555–556.

Jongkind, Dirk. "Corinth in the First Century AD: The Search for Another Class." *Tyndale Bulletin* 52, no. 1 (2001): 139–148.

Kaimal, Padma. "Learning to See the Goddess Once Again: Male and Female in Balance at Kailāsanāth Temple in Kāncipuram." *Journal of the American Academy of Religion* 73, no. 1 (March 2005): 45–87.

Kaiser Jr., Walter C. "The Current Crisis in Exegesis and the Apostolic Use of Deuteronomy 25:4 in 1 Corinthians 9:8-10." *Journal of the Evangelical Theological Society* 21, no. 1 (March 1978): 3–18.

Kakar, Sudhir. *Intimate Relations: Exploring Indian Sexuality.* New Delhi, India: Penguin Books, 1989.

———. *Indian Identity.* New Delhi: Penguin Books, 1996.

Kakar, Sudhir, and Katharina Kakar. *The Indians: Portrait of People.* New Delhi, India: Viking, 2007.

Katz, Nathan. "Our Hindu-Jewish Romance: A Few of the Reasons Why Jews and Hindus Enjoy a Unique Camaraderie in This Pluralistic World." *Hinduism Today* (April–June 2008): 9.

Kaur, Gangandeep. "Indian City Opens Doorway to Female Hindu Priests." *We.news (womensnews.org)* 26 February 2008.

Keener, Craig S. *1–2 Corinthians.* Cambridge, UK; New York: Cambridge University Press, 2005.

———. "Interethnic Marriages in the New Testament (Matt 1:3–6; Acts 7:29; 16:1–3; Cf. 1 Cor 7:14)." *Criswell Theological Review* 6, no. 2 (Spring 2009): 25–43.

Keown, Damien. "Karma, Character, and Consequentialism." *Journal of Religious Ethics* 24, no. 2 (Fall 1996): 329–350.

Ker, Donald P. "Paul and Apollos: Colleagues or Rivals." *Journal for the Study of the New Testament* 77 (2000): 75–97.

Khan, Saeed. "There's No National Language in India: Gujarat High Court." *The Times of India* (25 January 2010).

Kinman, Brent. "'Appoint the Despised as Judges!' (1 Corinthians 6:4)." *Tyndale Bulletin* 48, no. 2 (1997): 345–354.

Kirk, James A. "Sport of the Gods: Religion and Sexuality in India." *Iliff Review* 35, no. 2 (Spring 1978): 41–53.

Kistemaker, Simon J. *Exposition of the Acts of the Apostles.* New Testament Commentary, edited by William Hendriksen and Simon J. Kistemaker. Grand Rapids: Baker, 1990.

———. "'Deliver This Man to Satan' (1 Cor 5:5): A Case Study in Church Discipline." *Master's Seminary Journal* 3, no. 1 (Spring 1992): 33–46.

————. *Exposition of the First Epistle to the Corinthians.* New Testament Commentary Series, edited by William Hendricksen. Grand Rapids: Baker, 1993.

Klein, W. W. "Noisy Gong or Acoustic Vase? A Note on 1 Corinthians 13:1." *New Testament Studies* 32 (1986): 286–289.

Kloppenborg, John. "An Analysis of the Pre-Pauline Formula 1 Cor 15:3b-5: In Light of Some Recent Literature." *Catholic Biblical Quarterly* 40, no. 3 (July 1978): 351–367.

Knight, George W. "New Testament Teaching on the Role Relationship of Male and Female with Special Reference to the Teaching/Ruling Function in the Church." *Journal of Psychology & Theology* 3, no. 3 (Summer 1975): 216–229.

Korom, Frank J. "Holy Cow! The Apotheosis of Zebu, or Why the Cow Is Sacred in Hinduism." *Asian Folklore Studies* 59, no. 2 (2000): 181–203.

Krauss, Samuel. "The Jewish Rite of Covering the Head." *Hebrew Union College Annual* 19 (1945–1946): 121–168.

Kreitzer, Larry. "1 Corinthians 10:4 and Philo's Flinty Rock." *Communio Viatorum* 35, no. 2 (1993): 109–126.

Krishnan, Murali. "Hindu Priests Cashing in on Ancient Traditions." *Australia Network News* 16 (August 2012).

Kruse, Colin G. "The Offender and the Offence in 2 Corinthians 2:5 and 7:12." *The Evangelical Quarterly* 60, no. 2 (April 1988): 129–139.

Kuan, Tse-fu. "Rethinking Non-Self: A New Perspective from the Ekottarika-Āgama." *Buddhist Studies Review* 26, no. 2 (2009): 155–175.

Kümmel, Werner G. "Verlobung Und Heirat Bei Paulus (1. Cor 7, 36-38)." In *Neutestamentliche Studien Für Rudolf Bultmann Zu Seinem Siebzigsten Gerburtstag Am 20. August 1954*, edited by Walther Eltester, 275–295. Berlin: A. Töpelmann, 1957.

Lanci, John R. *A New Temple for Corinth: Rhetorical and Archaeological Approaches to Pauline Imagery.* Studies in Biblical Literature. New York: Lang, 1997.

Lanier, David E. "With Stammering Lips and Another Tongue: 1 Cor 14:20–22 and Isa 28:11–12." *Criswell Theological Review* 5 (Spring 1991): 259–285.

Lariviere, Richard W. "Justices and Panditas: Some Ironies in Contemporary Readings of the Hindu Legal Past." *Journal of Asian Studies* 48 (1989): 757–769.

Lemuel, R. S. "Salvation According to Hinduism." *Direction* 23, no. 1 (Spring 1994): 22–26.

Lens, Sidney. "A Letter from India." *Christian Century* 98, no. 34 (October 28, 1981): 1085–1087.

LiDonnici, Lynn R. "The Images of Artemis Ephesia and Greco-Roman Worship: A Reconsideration." *Harvard Theological Review* 85, no. 4 (Ocotber 1992): 389–415.

Lintott, Andrew William, and George Ronald Watson. "Crucifixion." In *Oxford Classical Dictionary*. Oxford: Oxford University Press, 1996.

López, René A. "Does the Vice List in 1 Corinthians 6:9-10 Describe Believers or Unbelievers." *Bibliotheca Sacra* 164, no. 653 (January-March 2007): 59–73.

Ludwig, Frieder. "Gandhi's India and Nigeria's Christians: Political and Ecumenical Interactions." *Swedish Missiological Themes* 89, no. 1 (2001): 41–54.

Lugil, Ligela. "Meaning without Words: The Contrast between *Artha* and *Ruta* in the *Mahayana Sutras*." *Buddhist Studies Review* 27, no. 2 (2010): 139–176.

Macchia, Frank D. "'I Belong to Christ': A Pentecostal Reflection on Paul's Passion for Unity." *PNEUMA: The Journal of the Society for Pentecostal Studies* 25, no. 1 (Spring 2003): 1–6.

MacDonald, Margaret Y. "Unclean but Holy Children: Paul's Everyday Quandary in 1 Corinthians 7:14c." *Catholic Biblical Quarterly* 73, no. 3 (July 2011): 526–546.

MacGregor, Kirk R. "1 Corinthians 15:3b-6a, 7 and the Bodily Resurrection of Jesus." *Journal of the Evangelical Theological Society* 49, no. 2 (July 2006): 225–234.

Malina, Bruce. *New Testament World: Insights from Cultural Anthropology*. Atlanta, GA: John Knox Press, 1981.

Malina, Bruce, and Jerome H. Neyrey. "Honor and Shame in Luke-Acts: Pivotal Values of the Mediterranean World." In *The Social World of Luke-Acts: Models for Interpretation*, edited by Jerome H. Neyrey, 25–66. Peabody, MA: Hendrickson, 1991.

Mani, Lata. *Contentious Traditions: The Debate on Sati in Colonial India*. Berkeley, CA: University of California Press, 1998.

Manor, Dale W. "A Brief History of Levirate Marriage as It Relates to the Bible." *Restoration Quarterly* 27, no. 3 (1984): 129–142.

Marcus, Joel. "Idolatry in the New Testament." *Interpretation* 60, no. 2 (April 2006): 152–164.

Margul, Tadeusz. "Present-Day Worship of the Cow in India." *Numen* 15, no. 1 (Fall 1968): 63–80.

Martens, Michael P. "First Corinthians 7:14: 'Sanctified' by the Believing Spouse." *Notes on Translation* 10, no. 3 (1996): 31–35.

Martin, Dale B. "Tongues of Angels and Other Status Indicators." *Journal of the American Academy of Religion* 59, no. 3 (Fall 1991): 547–589.

Martin, Sara Hines. "Shame-Based Families." *Review & Expositor* 91, no. 1 (Winter 1994): 19–30.

Matthews, Ed. "Yahweh among the Gods: A Theology of World Religions from the Penteteuch." In *Christianity and the Religions: A Biblical Theology of World Religions*, edited by Edward Rommen and Harold Netland, 30–44. Pasadena, CA: William Carey Library, 1995.

McDaniel, June. "Sacred Space in the Temples of West Bengal: Folk, Bhakti, and Tantric Origins." *Pacific World* 3, no. 8 (Fall 2006): 73–88.

McElhanon, Kenneth A. "1 Corinthians 13:8–12: Neglected Meanings of *Ek Merous* and *to Telion*." *Notes on Translation* 11, no. 1 (1997): 43–53.

McRae, Rachel M. "Eating with Honor: The Corinthian Lord's Supper in Light of Voluntary Association Meal Practices." *Journal of Biblical Literature* 130, no. 1 (Spring 2011): 165–181.

McRay, John R. "To Teleion in 1 Corinthians 13:10." *Restoration Quarterly* 14, no. 3–4 (1971): 168–183.

Meier, John P. "On the Veiling of Hermeneutics (1 Cor 11:2–16)." *Catholic Biblical Quarterly* 40, no. 2 (April 1978): 212–226.

Metzger, Bruce M. *A Textual Commentary on the Greek New Testament: A Companion Volume to the United Bible Societies' Greek New Testament.* 2nd ed. Stuttgart: Deutsche Bibelgesellschaft; New York: United Bible Societies, 1994.

Miller, Gene. "Apcontwn Tou Aiwnou Toutou: A New Look at 1 Corinthians 2:6–8." *Journal of Biblical Literature* 91, no. 4 (1972): 522–528.

Misra, Babagrahi. "*Sitala*: The Small-Pox Goddess of India." *Asian Folklore Studies* 28, no. 2 (1969): 133–142.

Mitchell, Matthew W. "Reexamining the 'Aborted Apostle': An Exploration of Paul's Self-Description in 1 Corinthians 15.8." *Journal for the Study of the New Testament* 25, no. 4 (2003): 469–485.

Mlecko, Joel D. "The Guru in Hindu Tradition." *Numen* 29, no. 1 (July 1982): 33–61.

Moiser, Jeremy. "A Reassessment of Paul's View of Marriage with Reference to 1 Cor 7." *Journal for the Study of the New Testament* 18 (June 1983): 103–122.

Moll, Rob. "Pension Tension: Lawsuit Questions 'Church Related' Retirement Plans." *Christianity Today* 54, no. 10 (October 2010): 11–12.

Morris, Leon. *The First Epistle of Paul to the Corinthians: An Introduction and Commentary.* The Tyndale New Testament Commentaries, edited by Leon Morris. Leicester, England: IVP, 1985.

Moss, Candida R. "Heavenly Healing: Eschatological Cleansing and the Resurrection of the Dead in the Early Church." *Journal of the American Academy of Religion* 79, no. 4 (2011): 991–1017.

Mount, Christopher. "1 Corinthians 11:3–16: Spirit Possession and Authority in a Non-Pauline Interpolation." *Journal of Biblical Literature* 124, no. 2 (2005): 313–340.

Murphy-O'Connor, Jerome. "Corinthian Slogans in 1 Cor 6:12–20." *Catholic Biblical Quarterly* 40, no. 3 (July 1978): 391–396.

———. "The Corinth That Saint Paul Saw." *Biblical Archaeologist* 47, no. 3 (1984): 147–159.

———. "1 Corinthians 11:2–16 Once Again." *Catholic Biblical Quarterly* 50 (1988): 265–274.

———. *St. Paul's Corinth: Texts and Archaeology.* Good News Studies. Collegeville, MN: Liturgical Press, 1990.

Myrou, Augustine. "Sosthenes: The Former Crispus (?)." *The Greek Orthodox Theological Review* 44, no. 1–4 (1999): 207–212.

N.a., "Hindu Rituals and Routines: Why Do We Follow Those?", http://sanskritdocuments.org/articles/Hindu_Rituals.pdf (accessed 17 July 2014).

N.a. "Imprisoned for Life." *The Hindu* (9 January 2011).

Nair, Sandhya. "Man Held for Raping Mute Niece." *The Times of India* (27 May 2014).

Nanda, Serena. "Arranging a Marriage in India." In *Stumbling toward Truth: Anthropologists at Work*, edited by Philip R. Devita, 196–204. Long Grove, IL: Waveland Press, 2000.

Nayyar, Rajat, "Antim Samskara (the Final Phase): After Death Rituals in a Hindu Brahmin Family (3 Days Video Documentation)", https://www.academia.edu/2315130/.

Nevile, Pran. *Lahore: A Sentimental Journey.* New Delhi, India: Penguin Books, 2006.

Newton, Derek. "Food Offered to Idols in 1 Corinthians 8–10." *Tyndale Bulletin* 49, no. 1 (1998): 179–182.

Neyrey, Jerome H. "Ceremonies in Luke–Acts: The Case of Meals and Table-Fellowship." In *The Social World of Luke–Acts: Models for Interpretation*, edited by Jerome H. Neyrey, 361–387. Peabody, MA: Hendrickson, 1991.

———., ed. *The Social World of Luke-Acts: Models for Interpretation.* Peabody, MA: Hendrickson, 1999.

Nichols, Michael David. "Dialogues with Death: Māra, Yama, and Coming to Terms with Mortality in Classical Hindu and Indian Buddhist Traditions." *Religions of South Asia* 6, no. 1 (June 2012): 13–32.

Nichols, Sue. "Lawsuit in a Richmond Church." *Christian Century* (5 January 1966).

O'Day, Gail R. "Jeremiah 9:22–23 and 1 Corinthians 1:26–31: A Study in Intertextuality." *Journal of Biblical Literature* 109, no. 2 (1990): 259–267.

O'Rourke, John J. "Hypotheses Regarding 1 Corinthians 7:36–38." *Catholic Biblical Quarterly* 20, no. 3 (July 1958): 292–298.

Okita, Kiyokazu. "Quotations in Early Modern Vedānta: An Example from Gaudiya Vaisnavism." *Religions of South Asia* 6, no. 2 (December 2012): 207–224.

Omanson, Roger L. "The Role of Women in the New Testament Church." *Review & Expositor* 83, no. 1 (Winter 1986): 15–25.

Oomman, Philip P. "Adopt Hindi as Indian Language: Constituent Assembly Authorizes Use in Official Matters – Study of English to Be Retained." *Christian Century* 66, no. 43 (26 October 1949): 1271–1272.

Oommen, George. "Challenging Identity and Crossing Borders: Unity in the Church of South India." *Word & World* 25, no. 1 (Winter 2005): 60–67.

Openshaw, Jeanne. "Home or Ashram? The Caste Vaishnavas of Bengal." *Fieldwork in Religion* 2, no. 1 (April 2006): 65–82.

Orr, William F., and James A. Walther. *1 Corinthians: A New Translation with Introduction and Commentary*. Vol. 32 Anchor Bible, eds. William Foxwell Albright and David Noel Freedman. New York: Doubleday, 1976.

Padgett, Alan. "Paul on Woman in the Church: The Contradictions of Coiffure in 1 Cor 11:2–16." *Journal for the Study of the New Testament* 20 (1984): 69–86.

Park, Sangyl. "Outsiders Become Insiders." *Living Pulpit* 13, no. 4 (October–December 2004): 18–19.

Patrick, James. "Insights from Cicero on Paul's Reasoning in 1 Corinthians 12-14: Love Sandwich or Five Course Meal?" *Tyndale Bulletin* 55, no. 1 (2004): 43–64.

Paul, Rajaiah D. *The First Decade: An Account of the Church of South India*. Madras (Chennai), India: Christian Literature Society, 1958.

Peerman, Dean. "The Flesh Trade in India: Paradise for Pedophilies." *Christian Century* (24 July 2007): 10–11.

Phalnikar, Sonia. "Female Hindu Priests in India Are Making Strides in a Male-Dominated Profession." *Deutsche Welle* (14 May 2010).

Philips, Holly. "Glossolalia in the United Pentecostal Church International: Language as a Relationship." *Council of Societies for the Study of Religion Bulletin* 37, no. 3 (Spring 2008): 64–67.

Pisharoty, Sangeeta. "Marriages Are in Trouble." *The Hindu Newspaper* (15 May 2010).

Plummer, Alfred, and Archibald T. Robertson. *1 Corinthians*. International Critical Commentary. Edinburgh: T&T Clark, 1914.

Poirier, John C., and Joseph Frankovic. "Celibacy and Charism in 1 Cor 7:5–7." *Harvard Theological Review* 89, no. 1 (January 1996): 1–18.

Porter, Stantley E. *Idioms of the Greek New Testament*. Vol. 2, Biblical Languages: Greek. Sheffield: Sheffield Academic Press, 1999.

Potter, F. M. "Churches Unite in South India." *The Christian Century* 64, no. 43 (22 October 1947): 1263–1265.

Pritchard, James B., ed. *Ancient Near Eastern Texts Relating to the Old Testament*. Princeton, NJ: Princeton University Press, 1969.

Proctor, John. "Fire in God's House: Influence of Malachi 3 in the NT." *Journal of the Evangelical Theological Society* 36, no. 1 (March 1993): 9–14.

Rajaram, Kalpana, ed. *Facets of Indian Culture*. New Delhi, India: Spectrum Books, 2013.

Rambachan, Anantanand. "Seeing the Divine in All Forms: The Culminatio of Hindu Worship." *Dialogue & Alliance* 4, no. 1 (Spring 1990): 5–12.

Ramelli, Ilaria L. E. "Spiritual Weakness, Illness, and Death in 1 Corinthians 11:30." *Journal of Biblical Literature* 130, no. 1 (Spring 2011): 145–163.

Ramsay, William M. *Historical Commentary on First Corinthians*, edited by Mark Wilson. Grand Rapids: Kregel, 1996.

Ravindra, Geetha, "Impact of Religion and Culture on Divorce in Indian Marriages", http://www.americanbar.org/content/dam/aba/publications (accessed 16 July 2014).

Reat, N. Ross. "Insiders and Outsiders in the Study of Relgious Traditions." *Journal of the American Academy of Religion* 51, no. 3 (September 1983): 459–476.

Reaume, John D. "Another Look at 1 Corinthians 15:29." *Bibliotheca Sacra* 152 (October–December 1995): 457–475.

Reichenbach, Bruce R. "The Gift of Singleness." *Reformed Journal* 32, no. 3 (March 1982): 4–5.

Richard, H. L. "A Survey of Protestant Evangelistic Efforts among High Caste Hindus in the Twentieth Century." *Missiology: An International Review* 25, no. 4 (October 1997): 419–445.

Richardson, Peter. "Judgment in Sexual Matters in 1 Corinthians 6:1–11." *Novum Testamentum* 25, no. 1 (January 1983): 37–58.

Robertson, Janet C. "Mourning and Ritual: A Death in a Jewish Family." *Reconstructionist* 40, no. 4 (May 1974): 12–17.

Rocher, Ludo. "Law Books in an Oral Culture: The Indian Dharmaśāstras." *Proceedings of the American Philosophical Society* 137 (1993): 254–267.

Rosario, Jerry. "Mission from the Perspective of Dalits: Some of Its Concerns and Options." *Mission Studies* 8, no. 1–2 (1996): 281–290.

Rosner, Brian. *Paul, Scripture, Ethics: A Study of 1 Corinthians 5–7*. Biblical Studies Library. Grand Rapids: Baker, 1999.

———. "Temple and Holiness in 1 Corinthians 5." *Tyndale Bulletin* 42, no. 1 (1991): 137–145.

———. "'Stronger Than He?' The Strength of 1 Corinthians 10:22b." *Tyndale Bulletin* 43, no. 1 (1992): 171–179.

———. "Temple Prostitution in 1 Corinthians 6:12–20." *Novum Testamentum* 40, no. 4 (October 1998): 336–351.

Salvesen, Alison. "Keter (Esther 1:11; 2:17; 6:8): 'Something to Do with a Camel?'" *Journal of Semitic Studies* 44, no. 1 (Spring 1999): 35–46.

Samartha, Stanley J. "Vision and Reality: Personal Reflections on the Church of South India, 1947–1997." *The Ecumenical Review* 49, no. 4 (October 1997): 483–493.

Sanghvi, Vir. "Rude Food: The Curious Case of the Indian Curd." *Hindustan Times* (6 October 2012).

Sarma, Deepak. *Epistemologies and the Limitations of Philosophical Inquiry: Doctrine of Mādhva Vedānta*. London and New York: RoutledgeCurzon, 2005.

Schneider, Sebastian. "Glaubensmängel in Korinth. Eine Neue Deutung Der 'Schwachen, Kranken, Schlafenden' in 1 Kor 11:30." *Filología Neotestamentaria* 9 (1996): 3–20.

Schottroff, Luise. "Holiness and Justice: Exegetical Comments on 1 Corinthians 11.17–34." *Journal for the Study of the New Testament* 79 (2000): 51–60.

Schwiebert, Jonathan. "Table Fellowship and the Translation of 1 Corinthians 5:11." *Journal of Biblical Literature* 127, no. 1 (2008): 159–164.

Sebolt, R. H. A. "Spiritual Marriage in the Early Church: A Suggested Interpretation of 1 Cor. 7:36-38." *Concordia Theological Monthly* 30 (1959): 103–189.

Seccombe, David. "The New People of God." In *Witness to the Gospel: The Theology of Acts*, edited by I. Howard Marshall and David Peterson, 349–372. Grand Rapids: Eerdmans, 1998.

Sen, Antara Dev. "The Living Dead." *The Week* (20 April 2008): 44.

Sharma, Arvind. "Dr. B. R. Ambedkar on the Aryan Invasion and the Emergence of the Caste System in India." *Journal of the American Academy of Religion* 73, no. 3 (September 2005): 843–870.

———. "Marriage in the Hindu Religious Tradition." *Journal of Ecumenical Studies* 22, no. 1 (Winter 1985): 69–80.

Sharma, Chandradhar. *A Critical Survey of Indian Philsophy*. Delhi, India: Motilal Banarsidass Publishers, 1987.

Shillington, V. George. "Atonement Texture in 1 Corinthians 5.5." *Journal for the Study of the New Testament* 71 (1998): 29–50.

Sider, Ronald J. "St Paul's Understanding of the Nature and Significance of the Resurrection in 1 Corinthians 15:1-19." *Novum Testamentum* 19, no. 2 (April 1977): 124–141.

Singh, Nikky-Guninder Kaur. "The Sikh Bridal Symbol: An Epiphany of Interconnections." *Journal of Feminist Studies in Religion* 8, no. 2 (Fall 1992): 41–64.

Singh, Nikky-Guninder Kaur. "Why Did I Not Light the Fire? The Refeminization of Ritual in Sikhism." *Journal for Feminist Studies in Religion* 16, no. 1 (Spring 2000): 63–85.

Sivaraman, K. "Meaning of Moksha in Contemporary Hindu Thought and Life." *Ecumenical Review* 25, no. 2 (April 1973): 148–157.

Smit, J. "'Do Not Be Idolaters': Paul's Rhetoric in First Corinthians 10:1-22." *Novum Testamentum* 39, no. 1 (January 1997): 40–53.

Smith, J. "The Genre of 1 Corinthians 13 in the Light of Classical Rhetoric." *Novum Testamentum* 33, no. 3 (1991): 193–216.

Smith, Jay E. "The Roots of a 'Libertine' Slogan in 1 Corinthians 6:18." *Journal of Theological Studies* 59, no. 1 (April 2008): 63–95.

———. "Slogans in 1 Corinthians." *Bibliotheca Sacra* 167, no. 665 (January–March 2010): 68–88.

Snyder, Howard A. "God's Housing Crisis." *Christianity Today* 49, no. 5 (May 2005): 54.

Spurgeon, Andrew B. *1 Corinthians: An Exegetical and Contextual Commentary.* India Commentary on the New Testament Series, edited by Venkataraman B. Immanuel, Brian C. Wintle and C. Bennema. Bangalore, India: Primalogue, 2011.

———. *1 Corinthians: An Exegetical and Contextual Commentary.* India Commentary on the New Testament, edited by C. Bennema, V. B. Immanuel and B. C. Wintle. Bangalore, India: Primalogue, 2012.

———. "Caring for Widows (and Widowers): 1 Timothy 5:3–16." In *Leitourgia – Christian Sevice, Collected Essays: A Festschrift for Joykutty M. George,* edited by Andrew B. Spurgeon, 287–304. Bangalore, India: Primalogue, 2015.

———. "Pauline Command and Women in 1 Corinthians 14." *Bibliotheca Sacra* 168, no. 671 (July–September 2011): 317–333.

———. "Paul: Passionate to Help the Poor." *Journal of Asian Mission* 13, no. 2 (October 2012): 15–23.

Stackhouse, Max L. "Tensions Beset Church of South India." *The Christian Century* 104, no. 25 (9–16 September 1987): 743–744.

Still III, E. Coye. "Paul's Aims Regarding Eidolothuta: A New Proposal for Interpreting 1 Corinthians 8:1–11:1." *Novum Testamentum* 44, no. 4 (2002): 333–343.

Stokes, H. Bruce. "Religion and Sex: A Cultural History." *Kesher: A Journal of Messianic Judaism* 9 (Summer 1999): 65–78.

Stott, John R. W. *The Message of Romans: God's Good News for the World.* The Bible Speaks Today, ed. John R. W. Stott. Downers Grove, IL: InterVarsity Press, 1994.

Sugirtharajah, Sharada. "Courtly Text and Courting Sati." *Journal of Feminist Studies in Religion* 17, no. 1 (Spring 2001): 5–32.

Sumithra, Sunand. *Christian Theologies from an Indian Perspective.* Bangalore, India: Theological Book Trust, 1990.

Sumney, Jerry L. "The Place of 1 Corinthians 9:24–27 in Paul's Argument." *Journal of Biblical Literature* 119, no. 2 (Summer 2000): 329–333.

Sundkler, Bengt. *The Church of South India: The Movement Towards Union 1900-1947.* Edinburgh and Madras (Chennai): United Society for Christian Literature, 1965.

Tatarnic, Martha Smith. "Whoever Comes to Me: Open Table, Missional Church, and the Body of Christ." *Anglican Theological Review* 96, no. 2 (Spring 2014): 287–304.

Teays, Wanda. "The Burning Bride: The Dowry Problem in India." *Journal of Feminist Studies in Religion* 7, no. 2 (Fall 1991): 29–52.

Tennent, Timothy. "Human Identity in Shame-Based Cultures of Asia." *Doon Theological Journal* 4, no. 2 (July 2007): 162–188.

Thiselton, Anthony C. *The First Epistle to the Corinthians*. The New International Greek Testament Commentary, edited by I. Howard Marshall and Donald A. Hagner. Grand Rapids: Eerdmans, 2000.

Thomas, J. D. "Corinth–the City." *Restoration Quarterly* 3, no. 4 (1959): 147–157.

Thomas, Lynn. "The Identity of the Destroyer in the Mahābhārata." *Numen* 41, no. 3 (September 1994): 255–272.

Thomas, Lynn M. "Does the Age Make the King or the King Make the Age? Exploring the Relationship between the King and the Yugas in the Mahābhārata." *Religions of South Asia* 1, no. 2 (December 2007): 183–201.

Thomas, Norman E. "Liberation for Life: A Hindu Liberation Philosophy." *Missiology* 16, no. 2 (April 1988): 149–162.

Thompson, Cynthia L. "Hairstyles, Head-Coverings, and St Paul: Portraits from Roman Corinth." *Biblical Archaeologist* 51, no. 2 (June 1988): 99–115.

Thompson, William G. "1 Corinthians 8:1–13." *Interpretation* 44, no. 4 (October 1990): 406–409.

Thong, Joseph S., and Phanenmo Kath. *Glimpses of Naga Legacy and Culture*. Kottayam, Kerala: Society for Naga Students' Welfare, 2011.

Tobin, Marie. "Working with the Poor and Marginalized in India: The Process and Choices." *International Review of Mission* 76, no. 304 (October 1987): 521–525.

Toussaint, Stanley D. "The Spiritual Man." *Bibliotheca Sacra* 125, no. 498 (April 1968): 139–146.

Trimmer, James Maurice. "Disciple Laymen Meet at Bethany: Five Thousand Attend Two-Day Even on Historic Campus – Church of God Hits Ecclesiastical Lawsuits." *Christian Century* 68, no. 39 (26 September 1951): 1103–1104.

Trudinger, L. Paul. "Shakespeare's 'Ages of Man' and the Development of the Early Church." *Perspectives in Religious Studies* 11, no. 2 (Summer 1984): 133–138.

Tucker, J. Brian. "The Role of Civic Identity on the Pauline Mission in Corinth." *Didaskalia (Otterburne, Man.)* 19, no. 1 (Winter 2008): 71–91.

Tucker, Lee. "Child Slaves in Modern India: The Bonded Labor Problem." *Human Rights Quarterly* 19, no. 3 (August 1997): 572–629.

Tyler, Ronald L. "The History of the Interpretation of to Mh Uper a Gegraptai in 1 Corinthians 4:6." *Restoration Quarterly* 43, no. 4 (2001): 243–252.

Unnik, Willem C. van. "The Meaning of 1 Corinthians 12:31." *Novum Testamentum* 35, no. 2 (1993): 142–159.

Upadhyaya, Krishna Prasad. "Poverty, Discrimination and Slavery: The Reality of Bonded Labor in India, Nepal and Pakistan." *Anti-Slavery International* (2008).

Uprety, Ajay. "Butcher's Bill Goes Up: A Dalit CM Doesn't Mean No Dalits Murdered." *The Week* (25 May 2008): 22.

Vail, Lise F. "'Unlike a Fool, He Is Not Defiled': Ascetic Purity and Ethics in the Samnyasa Upanisads." *Journal of Religious Ethics* 30, no. 3 (Fall 2002): 373–397.

Versnel, H. S. *Triumphus: An Inquiry into the Origin, Development and Meaning of the Roman Triumph.* Leiden: Brill, 1970.

Wagenaar, Jan A. "Passover and the First Day of the Festival of Unleavened Bread in the Priestly Festival Calendar." *Vetus Testamentum* 54, no. 2 (2004): 250–268.

Walker Jr., William O. "1 Corinthians 15:29–34 as a Non-Pauline Interpolation." *The Catholic Biblical Quarterly* 69, no. 1 (January 2007): 84–103.

———. "Is First Corinthians 13 a Non-Pauline Interpolation?" *Catholic Biblical Quarterly* 60, no. 3 (July 1998): 484–499.

Walker, Ken. "Youtube's Blocked Testimony: An Ex-Muslim's Lawsuit Has Implications for Law and Church." *Christianity Today* 57, no. 10 (December 2013): 23.

Wallace, Daniel B. *Greek Grammar Beyond the Basics: An Exegetical Syntax of the New Testament with Scripture, Subject, and Greek Indexes.* Grand Rapids: Zondervan, 1996.

Walvoord, John F. "The Holy Spirit and Spiritual Gifts." *Bibliotheca Sacra* 143, no. 570 (April-June 1986): 109–122.

Ward, Roy Bowen. "Paul and Corinth–His Visits and Letters." *Restoration Quarterly* 3, no. 4 (1959): 158–168.

Watson, Duane F. "1 Corinthians 10:23–11:1 in Light of Greco-Roman Rhetoric: The Role of Rhetorical Questions." *Journal of Biblical Literature* 108, no. 2 (1989): 301–318.

———. *Dictionary of the Later New Testament & Its Developments.* Downers Grove, IL: InterVarsity Press, 1997.

Weber-Han, Cindy. "Sexual Equality According to Paul: An Exegetical Study of 1 Corinthians 11:1–16 and Ephesians 5:21–33." *Brethren Life and Thought* 22, no. 3 (Summer 1977): 167–170.

Webster, John C. B. *The Dalit Christians: A History.* Vol. 4 Contextual Theological Education. Delhi, India: ISPCK, 1992.

———. "The Dalit Situation in India Today." *International Journal of Frontier Missions* 18, no. 1 (Spring 2001): 15–17.

Wenham, David. *Paul: Follower of Jesus or Founder of Christianity.* Grand Rapids: Eerdmans, 1995.

Weisberg, Dvora E. "The Widow of Our Discontent: Levirate Marriage in the Bible and Ancient Israel." *Journal for the Study of the Old Testament* 28, no. 4 (June 2004): 403–429.

Williams, Raymond B. "The Guru as Pastoral Counselor." *Journal of Pastoral Care* 40, no. 4 (December 1986): 331–340.

Wilson, Kenneth T. "Should Women Wear Headcoverings." *Bibliotheca Sacra* 148, no. 592 (October–December 1991): 442–462.

Wilson, Nicole A. "Confrontation and Compromise: Middle-Class Matchmaking in Twenty-First Century South India." *Asian Ethnology* 72, no. 1 (2013): 33–53.

Winter, Bruce W. "Theological and Ethical Responses to Religious Pluralism – 1 Corinthians 8–10." *Tyndale Bulletin* 41 (1990): 209–226.

———. *Seek the Welfare of the City: Christians as Benefactors and Citizens.* Grand Rapids: Eerdmans, 1994.

———. "The Achaean Federal Imperial Cult Ii: The Corinthian Church." *Tyndale Bulletin*, no. 46 (1995): 169–178.

———. "Puberty or Passion? The Referent of Uperakmos in 1 Corinthians 7:36." *Tyndale Bulletin* 49, no. 1 (1998): 71–89.

———. *Roman Wives, Roman Widows: The Appearance of New Women and the Pauline Communities.* Grand Rapids: Eerdmans, 2003.

Wire, Antoinette Clark. *The Corinthian Women Prophets: A Reconstruction through Paul's Rhetoric.* Minneapolis, MN: Fortress Press, 1990.

Witherington III, Ben. *Conflict and Community in Corinth: A Socio-Rhetorical Commentary on 1 and 2 Corinthians.* Grand Rapids: Eerdmans, 1995.

Wong, C. M., C. E. Williams, J. Pittock, U. Collier and P. Schelle. "World's Top 10 Rivers at Risk." Edited by WWF International. Gland, Switzerland, March 2007.

Wright, N. T. *The Resurrection and the Son of God.* Vol. 3 Christian Origins and the Question of God. Minneapolis, MN: Fortress Press, 2003.

———. *Paul: Fresh Perspectives.* London: SPCK, 2005.

———. *The Challenge of Easter.* Downers Grove, IL: InterVarsity Press, 2009.

Wright, N. T., and Marcus Borg. *The Meaning of Jesus.* London: SPCK, 1999.

Wright, Tom. *Romans Part 1: Chapters 1–8.* Paul for Everyone. London: SPCK, 2004.

———. *Romans Part 2: Chapters 9–16.* Paul for Everyone. London: SPCK, 2004.

Yadav, Niyesh and Abha Malik. *History of India's Glorious Traditions: Indian Art and Culture.* New Delhi: Arihant Publications (India) Limited, 2013.

Yamauchi, Edwin M. "Magic in the Biblical World." *Tyndale Bulletin* 34 (1983): 169–200.

Langham Literature and its imprints are a ministry of Langham Partnership.

Langham Partnership is a global fellowship working in pursuit of the vision God entrusted to its founder John Stott –

> *to facilitate the growth of the church in maturity and Christ-likeness through raising the standards of biblical preaching and teaching.*

Our vision is to see churches in the majority world equipped for mission and growing to maturity in Christ through the ministry of pastors and leaders who believe, teach and live by the Word of God.

Our mission is to strengthen the ministry of the Word of God through:
- nurturing national movements for biblical preaching
- fostering the creation and distribution of evangelical literature
- enhancing evangelical theological education

especially in countries where churches are under-resourced.

Our ministry

Langham Preaching partners with national leaders to nurture indigenous biblical preaching movements for pastors and lay preachers all around the world. With the support of a team of trainers from many countries, a multi-level programme of seminars provides practical training, and is followed by a programme for training local facilitators. Local preachers' groups and national and regional networks ensure continuity and ongoing development, seeking to build vigorous movements committed to Bible exposition.

Langham Literature provides majority world preachers, scholars and seminary libraries with evangelical books and electronic resources through publishing and distribution, grants and discounts. The programme also fosters the creation of indigenous evangelical books in many languages, through writer's grants, strengthening local evangelical publishing houses, and investment in major regional literature projects, such as one volume Bible commentaries like *The Africa Bible Commentary* and *The South Asia Bible Commentary*.

Langham Scholars provides financial support for evangelical doctoral students from the majority world so that, when they return home, they may train pastors and other Christian leaders with sound, biblical and theological teaching. This programme equips those who equip others. Langham Scholars also works in partnership with majority world seminaries in strengthening evangelical theological education. A growing number of Langham Scholars study in high quality doctoral programmes in the majority world itself. As well as teaching the next generation of pastors, graduated Langham Scholars exercise significant influence through their writing and leadership.

To learn more about Langham Partnership and the work we do visit **langham.org**

Lightning Source UK Ltd.
Milton Keynes UK
UKHW02f2344200718
326078UK00006B/147/P

9 781783 681181